Quality of Life
Volume II

Application to Persons With Disabilities

Edited by
Robert L. Schalock
Hastings College

Gary N. Siperstein
Editor, Special Publications

AAMR
American Association on Mental Retardation

Published by
American Association on Mental Retardation
444 North Capitol Street, NW, Suite 846
Washington, DC 20001-1512

The points of view herein are those of the authors and do not necessarily represent the official policy or opinion of the American Association on Mental Retardation. Publication does not imply endorsement by the Editor, the Association, or its individual members.

Printed in the United States of America.

Library of Congress Cataloging-in-Publication Data
Quality of life/edited by Robert L. Schalock.
      p.   cm.
    Includes bibliographical references.
    ISBN 0-940898-41-1
    1. Mentally handicapped—Services for—United States. 2. Mental retardation—United States. 3. Quality of Life—United States. 4. Quality of Life—Measurement. I. Schalock, Robert L. II. American Association on Mental Retardation.
HV3006.A4Q34 1995   95-50087
362.3'8'0973 — dc20   CIP

Contents

Contributors

James Bothwell
Rehabilitation Psychology
Department of Educational Psychology
University of Connecticut
62 Washington Street
Middleton, CT 06457-2844

Valerie J. Bradley
Human Services Research Institute
2336 Massachusetts Avenue
Cambridge, MA 02140

Gary L. Brunk
Bureau of Child Research
Beach Center, University of Kansas
4138 Haworth Hall
Lawrence, KS 66045

John Butterworth
Institute for Community Inclusion
Children's Hospital
300 Longwood Avenue
Boston, MA 02115

David Coulter
Associate Professor of Pediatrics and
    Neurology
Boston University School of Medicine
Division of Pediatric Neurology
Talbor Building, Room 210
Boston City Hospital
818 Harrison Avenue
Boston, MA 02118

Joyce Albin Dean
Specialized Training Program
University of Oregon
Eugene, OR 97403-1235

James F. Gardner
Chief Executive Office
The Accreditation Council on Services
    for People with Disabilities
100 West Road, Suite 406
Towson, MD 21204

David Goode
Associate Professor of Sociology
PSA Department
College of Staten Island/CUNY
2800 Victory Boulevard, 4S 236
Staten Island, NY 10314

Rachel M. Gordon
Waisman Center
University of Wisconsin-Madison
1500 Highland Drive
Madison, WI 53705-2280

Barbara A. Hawkins
Associate Professor
School of Health, Physical Education
    and Recreation
Indiana University
HPER Building, Room 133B
Bloomington, IN 47405

Matthew P. Janicki
Director for Aging and Special Populations
New York State Office of Mental Retardation
    and Developmental Disabilities
44 Holland Avenue
Albany, NY 12229-0001

Orv C. Karan
Professor of Education
Department of Educational Psychology
University of Connecticut
249 Glenbrook Road, U-64
Storrs, CT 06269-2064

William E. Kiernan
Institute for Community Inclusion
University Affiliated Program
Children's Hospital
300 Longwood Avenue
Boston, MA 02115

Marty Wyngaarden Krauss
Heller School
Brandeis University
64 Amory Street
Brookline, MA 02146

Judith Leff
Human Services Research Institute
2336 Massachusetts Avenue
Cambridge, MA 02140

Ruth Luckasson
Regents' Professor and Professor of
    Special Education
University of New Mexico
Albuquerque, NM 87131

David M. Mank
Specialized Training Program
University of Oregon
Eugene, OR 97403-1235

Joseph Marrone
Coordinator, Technical Assistance
Institute for Community Inclusion
University Affiliated Program
Children's Hospital
300 Longwood Avenue
Boston, MA 02115

Virginia Mulkern
Human Services Research Institute
2336 Massachusetts Avenue
Cambridge, MA 02140

Sylvia Nudler
Chief Operating Officer
The Accreditation Council on Services
  for People with Disabilities
100 West Road, Suite 406
Towson, MD 21204

Robert L. Schalock
Department of Psychology
Hastings College
Hastings, NE 68901

Marsha Mailick Seltzer
Waisman Center
University of Wisconsin-Madison
1500 Highland Avenue
Madison, WI 53705-2280

Martha E. Snell
Currey School of Education
University of Virginia
Ruffner Hall
405 Emmet Street
Charlottesville, VA 22903-2495

Daniel E. Steere
Special Education and Rehabilitation
  Department
East Stroudsburg University
200 Prospect Street
East Stroudsburg, PA 18301

Marianne Taylor
Human Services Research Institute
2336 Massachusetts Avenue
Cambridge, MA 02140

Jean Whitney-Thomas
Institute for Community Inclusion
Children's Hospital
300 Longwood Avenue
Boston, MA 02115

H. Rutherford Turnbull III
Bureau of Child Research
Beach Center
University of Kansas
4138 Haworth Hall
Lawrence, KS 66045

Laura K. Vogtle
Currey School of Education
University of Virginia
Ruffner Hall
405 Emmet Street
Charlottesville, VA 22903-2495

Foreword

Ruth Luckasson
The University of New Mexico

In 1990, in the predecessor to this volume, I wrote a chapter urging that the phrase "quality of life" be abandoned in discourse and policies about individuals with mental retardation. I concluded that its risks outweighed whatever benefits it might hold. I argued the following:

1. Imposition of a global calculation: "Quality of life" is a conclusory calculation that is almost always based on unspecified criteria by a powerful person or institution on a nonpowerful person's life.

2. History of discrimination: The history of individuals with mental retardation makes clear they frequently find themselves in unbalanced power relations. They have been especially susceptible to harm from discrimination and fears. Vigilance against potential vehicles for harm is warranted. The phrase "quality of life" can too easily disguise unspoken harmful prejudices and stereotypes.

3. Lack of clear definition: The phrase "quality of life" has no commonly agreed upon meaning. Criteria for making the judgment are almost always unspecified. Even when criteria are part of the decision-maker's own internal dialogue, they are almost always idiosyncratic to the particular decision-maker and not necessarily shared by others. There are as many definitions of "quality of life" as there are people who use the phrase. As a result, the phrase rarely communicates more than a speaker's subjective conclusion.

4. Limitation of discussions: The shorthand phrase limits rather than clarifies discussions. Speakers should express clearly any factors contained in their attempted use of a "quality of life" conclusion. What is their purpose for desiring a global conclusion about another? What factors are they valuing and devaluing in making their conclusion about the individual's life? Precisely how have they calculated their conclusion?

Does the speaker mean "We must ration health care resources and this person shall not receive any"? or "This person will be in too much pain if this treatment is administered"? or "These habilitation techniques do not increase work productivity fast enough"? "This school program isolates children"? In each of these examples, the discussion would be advanced by plain language.

The phrase is still widely used. In the intervening years, many of these objections have been addressed as the phrase "quality of life" has been refined. This book and the accompanying Volume I describe the high level of work currently being done incorporating the phrase quality of life. Use of the phrase persists, and I have come to believe that something about the phrase more deeply than previously understood appeals to professionals in the field of mental retardation. While I remain uncomfortable with the phrase, in this foreword I explore its appeal.

Is there a critical concept captured by the phrase quality of life that might account for its heartiness? In my opinion, although the words are different, the phrase is rooted in an earlier time's language of happiness. The simplest meaning of quality of life may be happiness, and the impetus to assure the presence of quality of life in the lives of individuals with mental retardation may be a variation on the theme of "pursuit of happiness" found in early American political documents. In the field of mental retardation, the recent attempts to define, measure, improve, or otherwise experiment with quality of life may be attempts to "scientificize," for our day and for our field, the Enlightenment concept of happiness.

Consider the use of the phrase "pursuit of happiness" in the American experience. Jones (1953), in classic legal lectures on the phrase "pursuit of happiness" found in the Declaration of Independence, concluded that the idea of pursuing happiness "is basic and pervasive in our cultural development" (p. 5). He traced its development to the 18th century, when many Enlightenment philosophers asserted that the only aim of government was to assure the greatest happiness to the greatest number.

The phrase "pursuing and obtaining happiness and safety" appeared in the Virginia Declaration of Rights in 1776, and one month later in the Declaration of Independence: "among these are life, liberty, and the pursuit of happiness." Jefferson later wrote, in 1812, that the only aim of government is "to secure the greatest degree of happiness possible to the general mass of those associated under it" (Jones, 1953).

Like the definition of quality of life, the definition of happiness has always been elusive, which is probably one of the reasons it does not appear in the Constitution. It is also socially constructed, interpreted differently at different times and in different contexts. Earlier it was interpreted as a divine or natural right, then as property, and later as business efficiency. Today, happiness appears in more personal terms as self-fulfillment and personal adjustment. It appears in public discourse, if at all, only in self-help books. Pursuing happiness is regarded, at worst, as a rather weak and immature whine, or, at best, as a naive throwback to the 1950s or 1960s happy faces.

But perhaps the founders were right—it is natural law or an inalienable right to pursue happiness and now we are simply attempting a more sophisticated language, appropriate to our time and society. Happiness is out. Quality of life is in. In our attempt to make the field of mental retardation more a science (is this a remnant of the medical model?), we have put the cloak of quality of life on the right of happiness.

The field has been attempting to address the same problems with quality of life that philosophers faced with happiness: What is it, can it be measured, can anyone really achieve it, whose right is it, is it individually or societally determined? And perhaps we are hitting the same wall, "the ghastly privilege of pursuing a phantom and embracing a delusion" (Jones, 1953, p. 17). But perhaps the concept is so important or so deeply rooted that these obstacles do not matter.

A doubter might assert, as I did in 1990, that the enterprise of quality of life is dangerous (Luckasson, 1990). And that the subject of quality of life only gets raised as an issues when attempts are being made to deny something to people with disabilities: life, medical care, supports, opportunities. That it is indefinable, subjective, and open to manipulation by others. But after observing the development of the work on quality of life over the recent years, I am beginning to change my mind: The phantom of quality of life/happiness, as a guide to good, may be absolutely appropriate, and may even be a right. And perhaps, in the words of the founders, it is inalienable.

References

Jones, H.M. (1953). *The pursuit of happiness.* Cambridge, MA: Harvard University Press.

Luckasson, R. (1990). A lawyer's perspective on quality of life. In R.L. Schalock (Ed.), *Quality of life: Perspectives and issues* (pp. 211–214). Washington, DC: American Association on Mental Retardation.

Preface

This is the third volume on quality of life published by the American Association on Mental Retardation. In the previous two volumes (Schalock, 1990, 1996), considerable discussion was devoted to conceptualizing quality of life and its measurement within the current paradigm with its focus on equity, inclusion, empowerment, and supports. From those discussions, 10 core quality of life principles have emerged that provide the framework for this volume on applications in the lives of people with disabilities:

- Quality of life for persons with disabilities is composed of those same factors and relationships that are important to all persons.

- Quality of life is experienced when a person's basic needs are met and when he or she has the same opportunities as anyone else to pursue and achieve goals in the major life settings of home, community, school, and work.

- Quality of life is a multidimensional concept that can be consensually validated by a wide range of persons representing a variety of viewpoints of consumers and their families, advocates, professionals, and providers.

- Quality of life is enhanced by empowering persons to participate in decisions that affect their lives.

- Quality of life is enhanced by the acceptance and full integration of persons into their local communities.

- Quality of life is an organizing concept that can be used for a number of purposes including evaluating those core dimensions associated with a life of quality, providing direction and reference in approaching customer services, and assessing persons' feelings of satisfaction and well-being.

- The study of quality of life requires an in-depth knowledge of people and their perspectives, and multiple methodologies.

- The measurement of quality of life requires multiple measurement techniques.

- Quality of life variables should occupy a prominent role in program evaluation.

- The application of quality of life data is important in developing resources and supports for persons with disabilities and their families.

The purpose of Volume II is to summarize current policies and programmatic practices that are influencing persons with disabilities. Part I summarizes a number of service delivery applications including those related to person-centered planning, families, education, work life, supported living, health, recreation and leisure, and older persons with mental retardation. Part II focuses on organizational change applications including those related to accreditation, direct care personnel, organizational management changes, and participatory action research. Part III discusses some of the more relevant public policy applications focused on quality of life that need to be considered nationally and internationally. The volume concludes with two chapters that focus on salient issues for the future: the importance of ethnicity in understanding and applying the quality of life concept; and identifying key areas in service delivery, organizational change, and public policy that need to be addressed if the quality of life movement is to improve the lives of people with disabilities. In these chapters, I ask readers to consider culture in the application of quality of life and to think about whether the concept of quality of life can make a difference.

Throughout the volume's 16 chapters, the reader will want to pay close attention to how the core quality of life dimensions discussed in Volume I are applied to persons with disabilities. The eight core dimensions are these:

- Emotional well-being
- Physical well-being
- Interpersonal relations
- Self-determination
- Material well-being
- Social inclusion
- Personal development
- Rights

Like all of us, persons with mental retardation and closely related disabilities increasingly ask questions about their lives, such as, What futures can we look forward to? What roles do we have in the community? What significant relationships are there in my life? What has to change for my life to be improved? Answers to these questions depend in part on how we as a society apply the concept of quality of life to enhance the lives of persons with disabilities. But such enhancement doesn't just happen. It requires informed public policy and appropriate services and supports provided by well-trained, competent staff. How this can be accomplished provides the basis for this volume.

This volume is not the final word in our attempts to understand and apply the concept of quality of life to persons with mental retardation and closely-related disabilities. Quality of life is a social construct and hence has meaning only in its application. Throughout this book, the reader will grapple with some of the same issues and questions asked by all of us: What is quality, and will the application of the concept of quality of life to persons with disabilities make a difference in their lives?

Persons with disabilities have experienced a number of social and political movements over the years, such as normalization, deinstitutionalization, mainstreaming, and community integration. The essential question that lies before us is, Is quality of life merely a current buzzword that, like its predecessors, will pass? Or is it truly a service-delivery principle that has substance and longevity? The chapters of this volume sensitize us to that question, and in addition ask that we seriously resolve the following issues:

- Reach consensus on the core dimensions to a life of quality for all persons, including those with disabilities.

- Align service delivery and supports with predictors of the core quality of life dimensions.

- Continue to embrace total quality management.

- Develop a technology of supports.

- Align public policy with the concept of quality of life.

- Evaluate the outcomes of public policy that is oriented toward quality of life.

I appreciate the hard work and dedication of a number of valued colleagues who have contributed their time and expertise both to this volume and to the ongoing efforts to improve the quality of life of persons with disabilities. To each of them I say, Thank you for a job well done. My appreciation also to Gary Siperstein, AAMR Monograph and Special Publications Editor, and to the external reviewers, who provided excellent suggestions regarding earlier drafts. My thanks also to Ann Podraza for her expert technical assistance in preparing the manuscript.

Robert L. Schalock, Ph.D.

References

Schalock, R.L. (Ed.). (1990). *Quality of life: Perspectives and issues.* Washington, DC: American Association on Mental Retardation.

Schalock, R.L. (Ed.). (1996). *Quality of life: Vol. I. Conceptualization and measurement.* Washington, DC: American Association on Mental Retardation.

Part I

Service Delivery Application

Quality services should begin with the person. Individualization is the core value of human service and education programs and a key principle in the legislation that guides these programs. It is addressed primarily in human service systems through an individual planning process. However, we should not forget that planning is also a common activity throughout our lives, and the ability to plan and organize resources effectively is critical to achieving our goals related to a life of quality. Because of the essential role that individualization plays in (re)habilitation services, we begin this first section with a discussion of person-centered planning, a rapidly emerging approach to addressing the unique priorities and preferences of individuals and realigning both system and community resources to support individual outcomes. In Chapter 1, John Butterworth, Daniel Steere, and Jean Whitney-Thomas summarize the components of this approach and outline the principles on which it is based: primary direction from the individual in both shaping the planning process and formulating plans; emphasis on the involvement of family members and friends in the planning process and reliance on personal social relationships as the primary source of individual support; a focus on preferences, talents, and

dreams of the individual rather than on needs or limitations; a vision of the life-style the individual would like to have and the goals needed to achieve that vision; and a broad implementation approach that employs for the individual resources and supports that are as local, informal, and generic as possible. The authors also review qualitative and quantitative research on person-centered planning, as well as its application in supported employment, curriculum design and review, transition from school to adulthood, positive behavior support, community living, and assistive technology. The chapter concludes with a number of recommendations and challenges regarding the implementation and evaluation of person-centered planning.

Chapter 2 by Rachel Gordon, Marsha Mailick Seltzer, and Marty Wyngaarden Krauss represents a significant contribution for two reasons. First, it encompasses a number of core quality of life dimensions, including emotional well-being, interpersonal relations, personal development, physical well-being, self-determination, and social inclusion. Second, it uses the best of qualitative and quantitative research methods to understand better the contextual nature of quality of life. The authors investigate a topic of

1

considerable importance: the consequences of parental death on the life circumstances and quality of life of adults with mental retardation. Both qualitative and quantitative research methods are used to address this topic in a longitudinal sample of 66 families in which a parent has died and 66 randomly selected comparison families in which both parents are still alive. Three research questions are addressed: What are the living arrangements and levels of family involvement for adults with mental retardation following parental death? What life-style changes occur with respect to day or work programs, social activities, and formal services received? How is the well-being of the adult with mental retardation affected by parental death with respect to activities of daily living skills, health, and behavior problems?

Over the past five years we have seen a significant movement toward inclusiveness and supports in the areas of living, employment, and education. These three areas have tremendous potential to enhance core quality of life dimensions such as emotional well-being, interpersonal relations, material well-being, personal development, self-determination, and social inclusion. We devote three chapters to exciting developments in these three areas. In Chapter 3, Martha Snell and Laura Vogtle focus on the critical importance that early social relationships and interactions play in life, suggesting that social well-being, defined primarily through interpersonal relationships with friends and family, is an essential aspect of quality of life. The authors discuss how social skills and relationships can be facilitated in school-aged individuals with mental retardation. Based on a

thorough review of the literature, they suggest that (a) teachers and peers play a critical role in fostering positive relations between persons with mental retardation and their classmates; (b) specific strategies that facilitate social relationships in school include teaching social skills in context with interaction partners, socially validating skill selection with peers, teaching children to deal with rejection, beginning integration early, and focusing on horizontal (equity) relationships; and (c) inclusive schools that are sensitive to the support needs of students with mental retardation hold the most promise for developing interpersonal relationships, and by inference, for enhancing a student's sense of well-being and perceived quality of life.

In Chapter 4, Bill Kiernan and Joe Marrone suggest that quality of life refers to the degree of an individual's satisfaction with his or her role, relationships, and duties in the workplace. This satisfaction is predicated on a variety of factors affecting the individual including personality variables, family expectations, social-cultural norms, workplace culture, and concrete facets of the job itself. The authors base their discussion on the notion that quality of work life is provided through "a philosophical commitment to the development of an interactive relationship between a worker and an employee." In tracing the development of the concept of quality of work life, the authors suggest that while factors such as compensation, working conditions, growth and advancement opportunities, interpersonal factors, and inclusion in the workplace may be important, the key factor in assessment and measurement of quality of work life is the degree of an individual's satisfaction with his or her role, relationships, and duties in the workplace.

In Chapter 5, Orv Karan and James Bothwell discuss three essential elements of supported living: The location of the consumer's home must be based on that person's informed choice; the individual and not the service provider should either own or rent the property in which the individual lives; and the level and intensity of supports must be flexible enough to vary with the person's changing needs and life circumstances. The authors go on to discuss how the supported living model creates opportunities to choose where one wishes to live, with whom, and how. Poignant examples illustrate how the supported living movement is causing our field to stretch beyond the limits of our conventional thinking and practice, as together we provide opportunities for community living and expression. The authors also discuss the critical area of supporting the service provider, summarizing their qualitative research on support staff concerns about consumer relationships, staff training needs, and personal concerns.

Nowhere do the combined issues of quality of life and available services potentially conflict more than in the areas of health, aging, and leisure and recreation. Thus, we devote three chapters to these emerging critical areas. In Chapter 6, David Coulter discusses a number of health-related quality of life issues. He begins by defining health as "a state of complete physical, mental, and social well-being, not merely the absence of disease or infirmity." The main thrust of the chapter is that the notion of health-related quality of life should not be applied to persons with mental retardation, per se, because having mental retardation is not the same as having a "disease." To approach it from that perspective can result potentially in a number of dangers inherent in applying quality of life in medical contexts. In answering the question, "what makes a good life," Dr. Coulter discusses three broad philosophical approaches, the hedonistic, preference satisfaction, and ideal theories of a good life. He suggests that the contribution of health to the goodness of life may be different in each of these philosophical approaches. The chapter concludes with a discussion of the potential purposes of measuring health-related quality of life that include enhancing the individual's quality of life, informing treatment decisions, and allocating health resources fairly and equitably.

In Chapter 7, Matt Janicki discusses two primary factors contributing to our greater awareness of older adults with mental retardation: their greater longevity and increased numbers residing among the general population. The chapter discusses a number of key policy and service delivery issues regarding transitional challenges facing older persons with mental retardation: forming new social networks, aging families, growing old at home, and retirement. Additionally, Dr. Janicki outlines a number of challenges that face the current service delivery system: societal attitudes that affect the quality of life of older adults with mental retardation; transitional occurrences that affect the life-style of older adults with mental retardation; growing older within an overall system of care that has not previously accommodated older persons; and gaining acceptance into mainstream senior activities. Throughout the chapter, it is suggested that the factors associated with the notion of quality of life for older adults with mental retardation are not necessarily different from those concerning other older adults: an acceptable living environment, cognitive stimulation, freedom to choose activities and friends, social and psychological well-being, financial security, and physical independence through good health.

In Chapter 8, Barbara Hawkins argues that if one's life-style is balanced in quality and quantity across work, leisure, and personal maintenance responsibilities, then there is a greater likelihood of higher satisfaction with life. Dr. Hawkins suggests strongly that in time, leisure and recreation may be recognized as prominent components in the quality of life of persons with disabilities. In preparation for this, the author explores a number of ways to enhance leisure and thus promote high quality life-styles for persons with disabilities. Core areas for leisure education and life-style development include leisure awareness and appreciation; self-awareness and leisure; self-determination, leisure choices, and decision-making skills; knowledge of leisure opportunities and resources; and leisure activity skills.

Throughout Part I, the reader will want to pay close attention to critical service delivery issues regarding the application of quality of life to persons with disabilities. Chief among them are these:

- Providing school and classroom options for students with disabilities

- Developing inclusive special education delivery models

- Enhancing interactive relationships between the worker and the employer

- Balancing self-determination and risks

- Measuring health-related quality of life and determining which aspects of a person's life should be considered and valued

- Responding to the needs of seniors, including the challenges of aging families, growing old in one's home, and retirement

- Promoting leisure choice and decision-making skills

- Lessening and removing social, attitudinal, and physical barriers to recreation and leisure

- Changing policy to recognize leisure as a fundamental domain of daily life.

Using Person-Centered Planning to Address Personal Quality of Life

John Butterworth
Institute for Community Inclusion

Daniel E. Steere
East Straudsburg University

Jean Whitney-Thomas
Institute for Community Inclusion

Quality of life has been described as a uniquely personal construct that is difficult to measure because the standards and criteria vary so widely from person to person. In fact, it has been suggested that quality of life must be understood as a unique personal experience; that individuals will experience the same circumstances differently (Taylor & Bogdan, 1990). Capturing quality of life has been an elusive effort in human service systems, which need to assure quality on a broad scale. Quality assurance commonly requires setting standards that are system-wide, rather than reflecting individual choices. This chapter will address the role of person-centered planning as one approach to addressing the unique priorities and preferences of individuals and to realigning both system and community re-sources to support individual outcomes. Although a new concept and one that needs further validation, person-centered planning represents a promising process for enhancing a person's quality of life.

Individualization is a core value of most human service and educational systems and a key principle in federal legislation that guides these programs. It is primarily addressed in human service systems through an individual planning process. Planning is needed throughout life for each of us, and our ability to plan and organize resources effectively has an impact on our ability to achieve quality of life goals. A variety of generic community resources exist to help with major life decisions such as employment and housing. Some decisions, such as which college to attend or which house to buy, are carefully planned and implemented, while more commonly plans are made informally or coincidentally. Formal planning is a more dominant feature in the lives of individuals with disabilities. Most human service systems require a specific approach to planning including the individual education plan (IEP), individual service plan (ISP), and individual written rehabilitation plan (IWRP). These plans, unlike those of people without disabilities, are carefully regulated and controlled, and represent an agreement or contract between an individual and a governmental agency or program. At the same time, individuals with disabilities often have minimal involvement in forming plans and limited opportunities to modify plans on a day-to-day or even year-to-year basis.

There has been a great deal of criticism of the effectiveness of educational and human service planning approaches. Recent qualitative studies of the transition process support the view that the involvement of families and friends in transition planning is unsatisfactory (Gallivan-Fenlon, 1994; Lichtenstein & Michaelides, 1993). Studies of planning within special education suggest that students are often not present at their IEP meetings, and that students and families contribute little to the discussion. Goals and plans are frequently developed and dictated by professionals with little discussion (Racino, Walker, O'Connor, & Taylor, 1993). Goals may also reflect the availability of services more than individual preferences. Plans also tend to emphasize agency resources rather than friends and community resources.

Operationalizing individual quality of life considerations in the design and delivery of supports for individuals requires that human service professionals accommodate individual perspectives on quality of life more effectively into their work. This requires recognizing that quality of life is a multidimensional construct that involves interaction among a variety of personal and environmental factors (Hughes & Hwang, 1996). Felce and Perry (1996) have suggested that attention be paid to three major dimensions: life conditions, personal satisfactions, and personal values. Stark and Faulkner (1996) suggest that several domains in an individual's life need to be considered including health care, living environment, family, social/emotional relationships, education, work, and leisure. Effective life planning should broadly address these life areas and incorporate both subjective factors, such as satisfaction and values, and concrete factors, such as work and living arrangements.

Effective planning must also incorporate an in-depth knowledge of the person that makes it possible to make inferences about true feeling (Taylor & Bogdan, 1990). Personal empowerment is a critical element of quality of life, and supports must be redesigned to provide for enhanced opportunities for self-advocacy and personal decision-making. There is evidence that strategies to increase individual and family participation and control of a planning process can influence the number and quality of goals developed (Campbell, Strickland, & la Forme, 1992; Van Ruesen & Bos, 1994).

Systemically, emphasizing the individual's unique subjective experience requires that human service systems become more flexible in how supports are designed, delivered, and funded in order to provide opportunities for individuals to pursue their preferences. This fundamental shift from a services paradigm to a supports paradigm is expected to influence public policy in the coming decades (Schalock, 1990).

This chapter addresses the impact that person-centered planning can have on quality of life by first providing an overview of approaches to person-centered planning, common elements that these planning processes share, and ways in which person-centered planning is being used. Current research is reviewed to address some of the personal and organizational issues involved in implementing person-centered planning that is effective in producing true quality of life changes. The final section raises a number of concerns about using person-centered planning and offers recommendations for future practice and research.

Person-Centered Planning

In recent years, a variety of alternatives to systems-level planning have been proposed. These processes have become commonly known as person-centered planning, and include whole life planning (Butterworth et al., 1993), MAPS (Vandercook, York, & Forest, 1989), personal futures planning (Mount & Zwernik, 1988), essential life-style planning (Smull & Harrison, 1992), and outcome-based planning (Steere, Wood, Pancsofar, & Butterworth, 1990). All of these approaches share several common principles:

- Primary direction from the individual both in shaping the planning process and in formulating plans

- Emphasis on the involvement of family members and friends in the planning process and reliance on personal social relationships as the primary source of individual support

- A focus on the preferences, talents, and dreams of the individual rather than on needs or limitations

- A vision of the life-style the individual would like to have, and the goals needed to achieve it, that is unrestricted by current resources or services

- A broad implementation approach that uses resources and supports for the individual that are as local, informal, and generic as possible.

Person-centered planning is designed to lead the individual and participants to an unrestricted vision for a positive future and to develop creative action plans to address personal goals. Planning is conceptualized as a vehicle for including individuals with severe disabilities more centrally in the process of developing goals and plans and for involving family members and other friends and community resources as partners with professionals (Stineman, Morningstar, Bishop, & Turnbull, 1993). It is intended to be a process that creates broad personal and systems change. Mount (1994) noted that "Personal futures planning is much more than a meeting; it is an ongoing process of social change. The effectiveness of a plan depends on a support group of concerned people who make a plan a reality by learning to solve problems, build community, and change organizations over time" (p. 97). Person-centered planning has been described primarily as a process that occurs separate from the formal planning processes required by educational and adult service systems, in order to provide maximum flexibility in planning, resource development, and implementation. It can, however, be used effectively to supplement and inform the service planning process.

Person-centered planning addresses many of the concerns raised regarding the conceptualization and measurement of quality of life. It is inherently a process that is built on the preferences and dreams of an individual, on their subjective view of themselves and their lives. Implemented effectively, it provides a view of possibilities in life that are

7

unrestricted by the structure and availability of services. Implementing these changes implies both personal change for human service professionals in the way that relationships are built with individuals and the members of their support network and systemic change in how resources are organized and funded by human service agencies.

Approaches to Implementing Person-Centered Planning

Implementing a person-centered planning process involves establishing a partnership with an individual and his or her family or significant others, creating a compelling image of a desirable future, and inviting participation to help achieve those goals (O'Brien & Lovett, 1993). It is the personal commitment of each participant that defines a successful process. Typically, a facilitator sets the tone for the dynamic interaction and guides the group through the planning process. Several approaches for person-centered planning have been disseminated widely. Although these approaches share a set of common elements, they also differ in the conceptual basis for the approach and the specific procedures used to accomplish the goals of the process. These approaches may also differ in their intended purpose and in the populations with whom they are commonly used.

Personal Futures Planning

Personal futures planning was one of the first processes to be fully described (Mount & Zwernik, 1988; O'Brien, 1987). It emphasizes outcomes that address individual quality of life including choice, community presence and participation, competence, and respect (O'Brien, 1987). The process empha-

sizes finding capacities in the individual by constructing a personal profile that includes a person's history, relationships, places they are present in, choices, and what works or does not work. This profile forms the basis for developing a vision and specific action planning. Personal futures planning also emphasizes strategies for making the process more accessible to the focus person, such as using graphics to record discussion. Personal futures planning is by design a group process that seeks to engage people across typical organizational and status boundaries (O'Brien & Lovett, 1993).

McGill Action Planning System

The McGill Action Planning System (MAPS) is a more structured process that has been developed in schools to assist in including individuals with disabilities in regular classrooms (Vandercook et al., 1989). The MAPS process is driven by a series of seven questions that guide the planning team in developing strategies to enhance the success of the focus person in inclusive school settings. Emphasis is placed on immediate modifications and supports, and participants typically include nondisabled school peers, along with educators and family members. A strong emphasis is the development of a collaboration between regular and special educators, peers, and family members.

Essential Life-Style Planning

Smull and Harrison (1992) describe a process known as essential life-style planning, which emphasizes supporting individuals with challenging behaviors and planning for systems supports that address an individual's core values and preferences. Like MAPS, it revolves around a core set of questions leading toward specific action plans and supports. It differs from other processes in its emphasis on influencing formal services rather than broadly engaging family and community resources as sources of support, although family and others are involved as sources of information in the planning process.

Whole Life Planning

Whole Life Planning (Butterworth et al., 1993), like personal futures planning, emphasizes an open-ended planning process with several primary steps intended to lead toward an unrestricted vision and specific action plans. Emphasis is also placed on engaging members of a person's social network in planning and support. The process is based on creative problem-solving models and leads participants through developing a personal profile, establishing a clear vision for a quality life, and action planning and resource development. Particular emphasis is placed on organizing the process in a way that meets the preferences of the individual, including choosing and inviting participation, planning for participation of the focus individual, and choosing an appropriate structure, including whether or not a group process will be used in planning. Whole life planning may be used to plan broadly the structure of an individual's life or for a more focused purpose, such as career planning. Used either way, it recognizes the importance of information from various areas of a person's life in understanding any specific goal area.

Common Elements in Approaches

The approaches to person-centered planning described above share common elements that are compatible with implementing planning and supports in ways that respect and address individual quality of life. These defining elements are discussed below, and serve as distin-

guishing features that differentiate person-centered planning from traditional forms of service and educational planning.

Empowerment of the Individual

Person-centered planning emphasizes the central role of the individual with a disability in organizing and implementing a planning process. This is reflected in simple ways by providing the focal individual with the opportunity to choose participants or the format of meetings, including the use of an individual or group process. More critically, planning is intended to strengthen the individual's opportunity to define clearly his or her preferences and desires. Processes address in varying ways the role of the focal individual in planning sessions and strategies for involving them in the process. Much of this responsibility falls on the role of the facilitator who needs to manage participation in planning. The focus in person-centered planning on group participation also makes it difficult to maintain a clear role for individuals who do not communicate effectively in group situations. Typical strategies for involving the focal person include the following (Steere, Gregory, Heiny, & Butterworth, 1995):

1. Using a facilitator to lead the planning process and ensure active involvement of the focus person and other participants. Facilitators are also responsible for establishing a productive atmosphere and for recording the discussion.

2. Giving the focal individual control over who will and will not be invited to planning meetings.

3. Separating problem definition and problem solving from development of a vision. Thus, individuals are supported in stating goals without

9

restriction from the structure and resources of the service system. These planning approaches are unrestricted in content and what is considered relevant or important information.

4. Using a facilitator to help the focal person prepare to participate in meetings.

Involvement of Natural Sources of Support

It is broadly recognized that social relationships play an essential role in the personal and work adjustment of individuals with and without disabilities and contribute to quality of life (House, Landis, & Umberson, 1988; Hughes & Hwang, 1996; Knox & Parmenter, 1993; Lichtenstein & Michaelides, 1993). Involvement of family, friends, and other natural sources of support in both planning and implementation is an explicit goal of most approaches to person-centered planning. The extent to which plans explicitly intend to develop an ongoing circle of support vary. Establishing an atmosphere of creative collaboration without concern for roles or status allows full participation by all group members. Engaging sources of support, including family, friends, coworkers, community members, neighbors, and clergy, in planning ensures that a broad range of opinions and possibilities are included, and that potential sources of support are engaged in the process as early as possible.

Changing Role for Professionals in Service Planning

Person-centered planning approaches implicitly or explicitly include a change in the role of professionals from a dominant role in planning and resource development to a partnership with individuals, families, and communi-

ties (Mount, 1994). This changing role parallels the growing emphasis on the importance of natural supports in people's lives, and the changing paradigm of human service workers from service providers to facilitators and consultants (Bradley, 1994; Rogan, Hagner, & Murphy, 1993). In the area of employment, for example, these changes include employment specialists supporting coworkers as they train a worker with a disability rather than providing training directly, or involving personal and family social networks in the job search.

Use of a Facilitator

The facilitator has been a central element in the development of person-centered planning. As noted by Smull and Harrison (1992), "The facilitator conducts the meeting on behalf of the individual with the disability. In this sense, it is the person with the disability who directs and propels the meeting" (p. 22). The facilitator is intended to be an independent agent who manages the planning process and ensures equitable participation by all involved. The facilitator may be responsible for organizing the planning process, establishing the tone and ground rules for planning sessions, and managing the interaction of the participants by asking questions and keeping discussion on track. A major issue is the objectivity of the facilitator. It is assumed that the facilitator can maintain and support an open and unrestricted discussion that is not affected by individual or systems priorities.

Opportunity for Redefining the Person for All Participants

A common criticism of traditional planning processes is that they focus on an individual's needs or deficits (Mount & Zwernik, 1988; Smull & Harrison, 1992; Steere et al., 1995). Similarly, participants bring to planning views of the focus person based in part on their roles, beliefs, history with the person, or personal values. These views may not be compatible with the focal individual's preferences and goals. One intended outcome of person-centered planning is the development of a shared positive view of the focal person (Mount, 1994). This is achieved differently across processes. Some emphasize understanding the person through his or her history, while others emphasize the present. Whole life planning uses the development of a positive personal profile that catalogs activities and specifies the preferences of the individual across all life areas. Essential life-style planning and MAPS ask participants to answer key questions such as "Describe [the individual's] greatest gifts and abilities" or "People who really know and care about him/her say. . . ." Each participant has the opportunity to contribute unique perspectives on the individual, resulting in a composite image that helps to redefine the individual for the participants. Smull and Harrison (1992) describe this process as going beyond the labels to critical characteristics of the individual.

Clear Unrestricted Vision for the Future

A central assumption of person-centered planning is that discussion and goals will not be restricted by practical issues such as the availability of services, the skills or behaviors of the individual, or the availability of funding. As a creative brainstorming process, these issues are considered problems to be solved. Person-centered planning addresses this principle in a variety of ways. One primary strategy is through the role of the facilitator and the ability of the facilitator to establish ground rules for planning sessions. The discussion of vision and goals is commonly separated

from the discussion of problems or barriers during person-centered planning. A common rule is that discussion cannot include negative information about the person during profile development. In whole life planning, discussion of problems or barriers is deferred to later steps of the planning process after a personal vision has been established (Butterworth et al., 1993). This structure, adapted from creative brainstorming approaches, is designed to prevent barriers (or perceived barriers) from influencing the development of the vision, and establishes them as problems to be solved rather than absolutes. In Whole Life Planning, the facilitator asks participants to merge the information in the profile into key descriptors of a quality life for the person in preparation for defining concrete outcomes. In MAPS, the facilitator asks participants to develop a description of an ideal day at school for the individual. An effective person-centered planning process leads to clear criteria for a quality life. Smull and Harrison (1992) define this by identifying negotiable and nonnegotiable elements in an individual's vision.

Creative Brainstorming

Implementing an unrestricted vision requires that a variety of systemic and attitudinal barriers be addressed. In addition to clearly defining barriers as problems to be solved, this requires that effective creative brainstorming and action planning take place. Personal futures planning (Mount & Zwernik, 1988), for example, explicitly describes both threats and opportunities toward the desirable future and then describes strategies for overcoming the barriers. MAPS incorporates steps that describe the participants' nightmares for the focus individual as a way to put problems on the table (Vandercook et al., 1989). The emphasis on involving a variety of resources in planning helps to provide multiple perspectives on solutions that include both systems and natural community resources as possible solutions to barriers.

Immediate Life-Style Change

Person-centered change can be a slow and frustrating process. Major changes, such as changing a living situation, home ownership, or identifying a job, can take a long time to achieve. However, while you cannot solve all of the problems at once, a defining feature of person-centered planning approaches is that change begins immediately. Plans are not long range (to get a job), but immediate (what are we going to do about that next week).

Research on Person-Centered Planning

While the number of anecdotal descriptions of person-centered planning experiences is growing, there is only limited research addressing the process or outcomes of person-centered planning more critically. Most of the current literature on person-centered planning provides case study description of planning processes and outcomes (Beeman & Ducharme, 1988; Mount, Ducharme, & Beeman, 1991; Smull & Harrison, 1992; Stineman et al., 1993; Vandercook et al., 1989). It is clear that in individual circumstances, extraordinary results have taken place through the work of a committed network of support resources. It is less clear what the specific variables are that influence the success of a person-centered planning process.

Quantitative Research

Mallete et al. (1992) describe the effectiveness of a "life-style development process" used with two children and two adults with developmental disabilities. Participants had been referred for consultative services. The authors describe an approach to defining a vision based on the discrepancy between the life-style of the target individual and a typical peer, assessing and addressing barriers to participation, assembling meaningful routines and schedules, and developing specific intervention strategies. Not clearly a person-centered planning approach, this approach apparently relies on professional information gathering rather than engaging natural supports in planning, and emphasizes a discrepancy approach to goal development and personal vision. Despite these differences, Mallete et al. (1992) report a variety of outcomes, including increases in community involvement, social relationships, and skills.

Mount (1987) field tested personal futures planning for six people transitioning from school to adult life, and the results were compared to the content and results of a comparison group who used the individual program plan (IPP) required by the system. While the IPP did not lead to change in participants' lives, the personal futures planning process did produce positive changes for both the focus person and staff. Mount reports that the personal futures planning process leads to both individual and organizational change, and that there are both planned and unplanned consequences of participating in personal futures planning, suggesting that personal futures planning has an impact beyond the boundaries of the action plans developed during the planning process.

There is growing emphasis on strategies for involving natural support resources in planning and support. Hagner, Butterworth, and Keith (1995) reported the results of a study that addressed the ways in which human service and educational programs in Massachusetts engage natural support resources. Despite a clear recognition of the importance of natural supports and a stated emphasis on facilitating involvement, respondents had difficulty specifying strategies used to facilitate involvement.

Qualitative Research

There is little information available about the actual implementation of person-centered planning and its impact of the planning process. Studies at the Institute for Community Inclusion provide more comprehensive qualitative information about the impact and process of person-centered planning. This research is part of the Massachusetts Natural Supports Project, a demonstration project in 10 communities that is focusing on strategies for increasing in participants' lives the involvement of natural supports, including family, friends, and coworkers. Facilitators receive training in using whole life planning as part of their participation in the project (Butterworth et al., 1993).

As an example, Hagner, Helm, and Butterworth (1996) describe the implementation of whole life planning for six individuals with developmental disabilities from four communities. Participants' ages ranged from 16 to 22. This study illustrates both the benefits and the difficulties in broad-scale implementation of a person-centered planning process. The focal person clearly had more control of the planning process and was involved in choosing the time, place, and guests for the meeting. Facilitators had varying success, however, at supporting participation of the individual in the meeting. There were instances of the individual's views being ignored or reinterpreted by both the facilitator and other participants.

It was clear that the role of the facilitator is a difficult one, and facilitators described the planning process as complex and unpredictable. They led the meeting in a variety of ways, including reminding the group to return to the topic, changing topics, and summarizing comments. Facilitators asked quiet participants for input, asked people to elaborate on input, and offered suggestions to encourage creative thinking. Facilitators tended to be professionals who also had a specific role in the focus person's life, and they often brought their professional roles into their role as a facilitator. This showed in a variety of ways including concerns about working outside of contractual hours, a narrow view of what goals might be feasible, and concern for maintaining relationships with other professionals. Facilitators did not effectively enforce ground rules about negative comments. Some comments from both professionals and, in four of nine meetings, from family members were critical of the focal individual.

More positively, there was evidence of both the mobilization of natural and agency resources to address plans. Participants described themselves as energized as a result of the increased sense of community, shared responsibility, and clearer focus generated by the planning process. There was active participation by family and friends. In particular, family members provided information, gave prompts, or rephrased information to support the focal person's participation, and served as advocates for the focal person. Parents were active in developing plans and committing to action steps. Adult friends also participated actively. Siblings and same-age peers, however, were noticeably quiet at meetings, suggesting that the sessions were not sufficiently comfortable for these participants. A central component of quality of life is an individual's network of interpersonal relationships, and these results suggest that person-centered planning can both strengthen relationships and focus significant others on the process of personal development (Schalock, 1996).

A study of project participants in four new communities, currently in process, has expanded the scope of inquiry to include organizational issues such as staff training and the planning process, as well as the process of organizing planning for an individual focus person. The study includes four schools that entered the Massachusetts Natural Supports Project in the spring of 1995. Each school identified three students with whom they would implement person-centered planning and develop individual jobs with natural supports. Researchers observed all organizational and planning meetings for each student and organizational meetings at the school level, and they interviewed parents, students, and facilitators.

This research is in its initial phases and has observed the first cycle of person-centered planning for three students and the organizational meetings for four more students. Two findings have become the focus of the researchers' attention. First varying levels of student participation have been observed, suggesting that planning needs to be individualized more effectively to accommodate personal needs. Second, a variety of factors influence the way parents participate in the meetings and their impressions of the process as a whole.

The variation in student participation indicates the challenge faced in actualizing the values of individual empowerment and self-determination in both person-centered planning and improving quality of life. Four levels of student participation have been observed.

Participation of some students was limited (characterized by "zoning out," demonstrating escape behaviors, or giving brief and noncommittal responses to questions) or absent (falling asleep or physically leaving a meeting). One example of limited participation was observed in a meeting for a young woman in which she only initiated communication twice. Both times that she independently contributed to the planning she turned to her father or sisters and whispered what she wanted to say rather than speaking to the group. Participation that better exemplifies an emphasis on quality of life includes active participation, characterized by a student talking freely and contributing to the flow of the conversation and the planning, and instances of control, when a student disagrees with what is said and others in the meeting respect that disagreement, corrects others, or asserts a point even when there might be conflict. One young man engaged very actively in his first planning meetings. As his family talked about his likes and dislikes he told stories that illustrated their points, cracked jokes, and shouted out examples of things he wanted added to his profile. Examples of student participation that could be coded as control were fewer than any of the other types. In one instance, however, the mother of one young man was telling the group about how her son and daughter have an arrangement that involves the daughter paying the son a dollar to do her chores around the house. The mother said that she had set down rules that she intended to enforce, and the son interrupted her to say, "Mother, I'm 20 years old!"

The range in the students' levels of participation is interesting and to some extent represents their personalities and characteristics. Nevertheless, planning for the future was going on when each of these behaviors was observed, and the stated goal of person-centered planning is to maximize both participation and control of the process by the focal person regardless of personal style. Clearly more attention is needed to strategies that facilitate participation and control and to structuring the format of the meetings or planning sessions to meet the needs of the focal person.

The participation of family members and others in person-centered planning may support or impede opportunities for personal development and self-determination. Parents' expectations for their child's role in the planning process were influenced by their fears and concerns and by the support they feel. Their concerns were not always expressed explicitly, but were sometimes revealed in how they stated their visions for the future. For example, when talking about the young person moving out of his or her family home, a number of parents said things like, "I'm not ready to be thinking about this" or "I can't ever see him living in his own apartment." Parents' visions can, however, be expanded, and this happened in a number of ways. One parent said she was very encouraged by the active participation of her family and friends who came to her daughter's planning meetings, and that it was extremely helpful for her to hear about the range of options for her daughter. In other instances, when parents did not express such explicit encouragement, their family members and support network provided gentle challenges to their limited visions. In one situation an aunt asked the mother why she always saw her son doing recreational activities with other people with disabilities. Challenged to provide an answer, the mother acknowledged that this limitation might not always be good.

Uses of Person-Centered Planning

In recent years, person-centered planning strategies have been applied to a number of areas of challenge in providing quality services to people with disabilities (Steere et al., 1995). In this section, we review briefly the application of person-centered planning strategies to addressing quality of life outcomes in the following areas: supported employment; curriculum development in education settings; transition from school to adulthood; positive behavioral support; community living/housing and support; enhancing community participation; and selection of assistive technology devices and services. In each of these areas, person-centered planning focuses attention on core quality of life variables including expanding personal relationships; self-determination; social inclusion in schools, workplaces, and community; and personal development.

Supported Employment

Person-centered planning has been suggested as a preferred strategy to guide the supported employment process. Powell et al. (1991) described the use of a career planning process, adapted from O'Brien's (1987) life-style planning process to guide initial job development activities. This process was viewed as integral to the supported employment process and was considered the foundation upon which the subsequent activities of job development, job skills instruction, and ongoing support were based. Murphy and Rogan (1995) describe the use of individualized, person-centered assessments in setting direction for individuals who were leaving a sheltered workshop to enter supported employment as part of an agency-wide conversion effort. Although not specifically described as person-centered planning, the approach to these assessments was consistent with the principles of person-centered planning described earlier in this chapter. In addition to these applications of person-centered planning, Wood and Steere (1992) and Fabian (1991) have suggested that the impact of supported employment is best measured through an analysis of life-style change. Such an analysis is the natural result of using person-centered planning on an ongoing basis.

Curriculum Design and Revision

The relevance of curricular content is a key concern in the education of students with disabilities. Educational services should result not only in skill acquisition but also in meaningful social relationships, increased self-esteem, and an expanded ability to make informed choices. O'Brien's (1987) life-style planning process focused on these broad outcomes as a rationale for selecting annual goals and objectives on service plans for adolescents and adults. The MAPS process has typically been used in schools to clarify curricular activities that enhance inclusion in regular classrooms and throughout the educational process. By reaching out to and involving peers in the process, MAPS also influences quality of life by strengthening the student's network of relationships. As with transition planning, educational planning in general should be grounded in a broad vision of success for students, and person-centered planning is effective in helping to establish such a vision.

Transition from School to Adulthood

Transition planning, as mandated in the Individuals With Disabilities Education Act of 1990 (IDEA, P.L. 101-476), should be a process wherein students clarify personal aspirations that in turn guide their efforts to secure jobs, pursue postsecondary education, and enter community living as adults. Because transition planning is most effective when a personal vision of success is clarified and supported by the transition planning team, person-centered planning strategies are useful in this situation. Stineman et al. (1993) described the use of person-centered planning to clarify desired transition goals and to guide the transition planning process. Similarly, Steere et al. (1990) adapted the career planning approach described above for use in transition planning. This conceptual model incorporated broad quality of life outcomes that were desired by focus students as being the necessary rationale for the selection of transition goals. In addition, annual goals and short-term objectives on student IEPs are selected in light of these broad outcomes.

Positive Behavioral Support

Horner et al. (1990) describe several essential themes in an emerging technology of positive behavioral support for individuals whose behavior creates challenges for community inclusion. A change in life-style for an individual is described as essential to such efforts, and these authors caution against viewing simple behavioral change as equivalent to positive life-style change. The first step in developing a comprehensive plan for positive behavioral support is the implementation of person-centered planning to clarify a desired future life-style. Lucyshyn, Olson, and Horner (1995) provide an excellent case study with a young woman who moved from an institution to community living. The authors report that life-style planning was an initial step in her efforts to reenter community life. In addition, the authors provide a superb example of combining quantitative and qualitative measures of life-style change over a three-year period.

Community Living/Housing and Support

Racino et al. (1993) describe person-centered planning as the most useful approach to assess supported community living. These authors point out that decisions about where people with disabilities should live, fundamentally a quality of life issue, have often been confused with the level of support that they require to be successful. Consequently, as peoples' needs for support change, they have had to move to a more restrictive housing option in the continuum of residential services. The authors argue that members of the general population usually stay in their homes and arrange for increased or decreased support without moving to a more restrictive option. Such an approach calls for effective planning of support in a flexible, fluid, and ongoing manner. Person-centered planning is the most responsive approach that maximizes the person's control of needed supports.

Enhancing Community Connections

Participation in leisure and other activities in one's community is an important aspect of overall community inclusion. As with employment, the selection of activities in which to participate should be individually driven. Pancsofar (1992) recommends the clarification of a positive profile of a focus person as well as their desired quality of life outcomes to guide the process of matching individuals with community experiences that have the highest likelihood of contributing to an improved quality of life. In this regard, person-centered planning is used to enhance the focus person's participation in community experiences that have a high likelihood of enhancing community presence and participation.

Selection of Assistive Technology

Kelker (1994) adapted previously described approaches to person-centered planning in developing the Solution Circle approach to planning assistive technology services. Developed in conjunction with the Alliance for Technology Access, the Solution Circle puts decisions about assistive technology selection, procurement, and use within the broader context of dreams and aspirations. Poor decision-making can lead to wasteful technology abandonment (Phillips & Zhao, 1993). Thus, ensuring that assistive technology is viewed as one source of support among many to assist someone in reaching short- and long-term aspirations can result not only in better decisions, but also in more effective use of finite assistive technology resources.

Recommendations for Practice and Research

Person-centered planning was initiated as a small-scale, grass-roots intervention that has been primarily used outside of formal systems activities. As a technique, person-centered planning is compatible with many of the current trends in service systems, including the increased emphasis on personal quality of life, the shift from a services to a supports paradigm, and increasing individualization and flexibility of fiscal resources. As a result of the increasing visibility of these approaches, there is increasing emphasis on using person-centered planning within formal service systems.

As this growth occurs, there are increasing concerns about maintaining the focus of person-centered planning as the approach is implemented more broadly and, in some cases, attempts are made to incorporate it into the activities of state service systems. This section of the chapter addresses issues in implementation, followed by recommendations for practice at an individual and systems level.

Issues in Person-Centered Planning

The concerns raised in the research summarized above indicate that in wider-scale implementation it is difficult to maintain a clearly person-centered and person-directed emphasis in implementing planning. The skills and values of the facilitator have a strong impact on the planning process, and concerns are sometimes raised about the ability of the facilitator to maintain independence and objectivity, and to manage the participation of the group. Facilitators are not always conscious of decisions they make in directing the conversation, and sometimes they avoid controversial topics or goals.

Despite the broad consensus about core principles and features of person-centered planning approaches, several issues have been identified that represent differences among the approaches discussed. Chief among them are these (O'Brien & Lovett, 1993):

- The extent to which the focus person should control the direction of the process

- Whether assistance should be given to a person who clearly chooses to live in a congregate, disability-segregated setting

- Whether person-centered planning should take place within organized service settings.

- How much a person's family, friends, neighbors, and coworkers can and should be expected to do

- The importance of convening an identified, ongoing support group for the focus person.

A wide range of concerns have also been expressed about the appropriateness of implementing person-centered planning on a systemic level (O'Brien & Lovett, 1993). Mount (1994), for example, cautions that "personal futures planning is least effective when it is used in isolation from other complementary change activities. This fragmentation is most likely to occur if the futures planning process is standardized, implemented on a large scale, or otherwise molded to fit into existing structures of service instead of challenging them" (p. 102).

Considerations for Individuals

The focus individual should retain control over both the process and outcomes of the person-centered planning process. One implication of this is the need for training in self-advocacy skills. Preliminary results from current research by the authors suggest that family members who participate in training for facilitators of whole life planning are more able to maintain the integrity of the process and serve as advocates for their son or daughter. This is consistent with Mount (1994), who suggests that the presence of a strong advocate is one condition for successful life-style change. Investigation of these findings needs to be extended to include better preparation of the focus person. The expectation that this will have a positive effect is supported by research into participation of students in the IEP process that suggests that students who received instruction in participating in the process were more active in providing information and goals at the IEP meeting (Van Ruesen & Bos, 1994). The success of the creative brainstorming process may also inhibit the participation of the focus individual. This apparent paradox is caused by the inability of some focus individuals to keep up with the rapid pace of brainstorming.

Continued analysis of the circumstances and strategies that lead to full control and participation are necessary for person-centered planning to achieve its promise. There is also evidence that the outcomes of person-centered planning are more indirect than those of traditional planning processes. Understanding the impact of planning requires that attention be paid to identifying and assessing the outcomes of planning, including both outcomes that are specifically identified by participants and outcomes that are more serendipitous. Future research should investigate specific strategies.

Considerations for Organizers and Facilitators

Questions about the role of the facilitator relate to selection, strategies for achieving independence from professional roles and relationships, and training and support needs. Facilitators need to become more effective at engaging the focus person at all stages of the planning process. This requires, in addition to improving the skill level of facilitators, more attention to individualizing the structure of the planning process to meet individual preferences, and more attention to preparatory work with the focus person. Preparatory work may include strategies such as preparing alternative forms of communication including videotape or pictures, and gathering "props" that assist the person in organizing and communicating preferences.

One variable that focus individuals need a clear choice in is the selection of facilitators. The ability of the facilitator to influence the process is great, and it is essential that individuals be able to select a facilitator with whom they are comfortable. The results cited above also indicate the need for a more comprehensive approach to training and supporting facilitators. A mentorship experience, in which facilitators receive feedback and guidance from an experienced facilitator, may be an essential part of facilitator training. The use of facilitator support groups has been piloted to assist facilitators in maintaining an objective stance and resolving conflicts in roles and resources.

Mount (1994) suggests that person-centered planning is most useful when there is a clear desire for change and shared values and assumptions among the key participants. Successful implementation of person-centered planning requires that participants engage in an ongoing process of change and resource development. This commitment is a defining feature of person-centered planning, and research suggests that the dynamics of planning and support change over time in important ways.

Considerations for Systems

Person-centered planing is one piece in larger current efforts to redefine the ways that services are provided and to return control of their lives to individuals with disabilities. Efforts to emphasize home ownership and the role of natural supports in employment represent changes in goals and strategies for individual support. The development of person-directed funding options is one way in which systems are beginning to redirect resources in ways that support individual dreams. Although person-centered planning is compatible with these larger systems initiatives, most advocates are cautious about the role of person-centered planning on a systems level.

Most person-centered planning advocates agree that we are not yet able to transfer effectively this technology from an individual level to a larger systems level. Person-centered planning emphasizes grass-roots organizational change that will, over time, influence the opportunities for others (Mount, 1994). O'Brien and Lovett (1993) express concern that systems boundaries may remain intact without clear change in the relationship of professional and community resources, and that planning often occurs separate from changes in service system policies and practices. The scope of change required in a large-scale implementation is too great. Similarly, advocates are cautious about the appropriateness of systems adopting person-centered planning as a planning strategy.

Questions for research revolve around the circumstances in which person-centered planning can be implemented with integrity and success as part of systems change efforts. Clearer knowledge about the circumstances in which different approaches to person-centered planning are most useful may provide guidance about the relationship between the process and individual and systemic circumstances.

Conclusion

The development of a wide array of person-centered planning approaches represent an important part of current efforts to redefine the relationship between individuals with disabilities and the service system. As a group person-centered approaches emphasize quality of life, as defined by each unique individual, as the only justifiable outcome of the supports individuals receive from both systems and community resources, and they advocate for life-style change that is unrestricted by the typical boundaries of human service structures.

Many unanswered questions remain to be addressed if person-centered planning is to continue as a positive force for change and an integral part of the quality revolution. Some of the most important challenges are these:

1. Seeking strategies for ensuring control of both planning and supports for individuals with disabilities

2. Ensuring that adequate time is allocated for planning

3. Increasing the active participation of natural sources of support including families, friends, coworkers, and other community members

4. Ensuring that planning is an ongoing process rather than an annual event that emulates the patterns of the service plan

5. Addressing the role of person-centered planning as a tool within larger systems, maintaining the focus on creativity and personal empowerment.

By definition, quality of life is a subjective concept that has meaning only as experienced and expressed by the individual. The value of person-centered planning is that it ensures that services, supports, and desired outcomes begin with the person. Operationalizing individual quality of life core dimensions in the design and delivery of supports for individuals also requires that human service professionals accommodate to the individual's unique needs and personal goals. This concept is the essence of both the application of the concept of quality of life to persons with disabilities and of person-centered planning.

Author Note

Preparation of this article was supported in part by grant #90DN0013 from the U.S. Department of Health and Human Services, Administration on Developmental Disabilities, and grant #H133A30036 from the U.S. Department of Education, National Institute on Disability and Rehabilitation Research.

References

Beeman, P., & Ducharme, G. (1988). *One candle power: Building bridges into community life for people with disabilities.* North Granby, CT: Northspring Consulting.

Bradley, V.J. (1994). Evolution of a new service paradigm. In V. Bradley, J. Ashbaugh, & B. Blaney (Eds.), *Creating individual supports for people with developmental disabilities* (pp. 3-10). Baltimore: Brookes.

Butterworth, J., Hagner, D., Heikkinen, B., Faris, S., DeMello, S., & McDonough, K. (1993). *Whole life planning: A guide for organizers and facilitators.* Boston: Children's Hospital, Institute for Community Inclusion.

Campbell, P.H., Strickland, B., & la Forme, C. (1992). Enhancing parent participation in the individualized family service plan. *Topics in Early Childhood Special Education, 11*(4), 112-124.

Fabian, E. (1991). Using quality of life indicators in rehabilitation program evaluation. *Rehabilitation Counseling Bulletin, 34,* 344-356.

Felce, D., & Perry, J. (1996). Assessment of quality of life. In R. Schalock (Ed.), *Quality of life: Vol. I. Conceptualization and measurement* (pp. 63-72). Washington, DC: American Association on Mental Retardation.

Gallivan-Fenlon, A. (1994). "Their senior year": Family and service provider perspectives on the transition from school to adult life for young adults with disabilities. *Journal of the Association for Persons with Severe Handicaps, 19,* 11-23.

Hagner, D., Butterworth, J., & Keith, G. (1995). Strategies and barriers in facilitating natural supports for employment of adults with severe disabilities. *Journal of the Association for Persons with Severe Handicaps, 20,* 110-120.

Hagner, J., Helm, D., & Butterworth, J. (1996). "This is your meeting": A qualitative study of person-centered planning. *Mental Retardation, 34,* 159-171.

Horner, R.H., Dunlap, G., Koegel, R., Carr, E., Sailor, W., Anderson, J., Albin, R., & O'Neill, R. (1990). Toward a technology of "nonaversive" positive behavioral support. *Journal of the Association for Persons with Severe Handicaps, 15,* 125-132.

House, J.S., Landis, K.R., & Umberson, D. (1988). Social relationships and health. *Science, 540-545.*

Hughes, C., & Hwang, B. (1996). Attempts to conceptualize and measure quality of life. In R. Schalock (Ed.), *Quality of life: Vol. I. Conceptualization and measurement* (pp. 51-62). Washington, DC: American Association on Mental Retardation.

Individuals with Disabilities Education Act of 1990, Public Law 101-476. (October 30, 1990).

Kelker, K. (1994). *Solution circle.* Billings, MT: Parents, Let's Unite for Kids (PLUK).

Knox, M., & Parmenter, T.R. (1993). Social networks and support mechanisms for people with mild intellectual disability in competitive employment. *International Journal of Rehabilitation, 16,* 1-12.

Lichtenstein, S., & Michaelides, N. (1993). Transition from school to young adulthood: Four case studies of young adults labeled mentally retarded. *Career Development for Exceptional Individuals, 16,* 183-195.

Lucyshyn, J., Olson, D., & Horner, R. (1995). Building an ecology of support: A case study of one young woman with severe problem behaviors living in the community. *Journal of the Association for Persons with Severe Handicaps, 20,* 16-30.

Malette, P., Mirenda, P., Kandborg, T., Jones, P., Bunz, T., & Rogow, S. (1992). Application of a lifestyle development process for persons with severe intellectual disabilities: A case study report. *Journal of the Association for Persons with Severe Handicaps, 17,* 179-191.

Mount, B. (1987). *Personal futures planning: Finding directions for change.* Unpublished doctoral dissertation, University of Georgia, Athens.

Mount, B. (1994). Benefits and limitations of personal futures planning. In V. Bradley, J. Ashbaugh, & B. Blaney (Eds.), *Creating individual supports for people with developmental disabilities: A mandate for change* (pp. 97-108). Baltimore: Brookes.

Mount, B., Ducharme, G., & Beeman, P. (1991). *Person-centered development: A journey in learning to listen to people with disabilities.* Manchester, CT: Communitas, Inc.

Mount, B., & Zwernik, K. (1988). *It's never too early, it's never too late: A booklet about personal futures planning.* Mears Park Centre, MN: Metropolitan Council.

Murphy, S., & Rogan, P. (1995). *Closing the shop.* Baltimore: Brookes.

O'Brien, J. (1987). A guide to lifestyle planning: Using the Activities Catalog to integrate services and natural support systems. In B. Wilcox & G.T. Bellamy (Eds.), *The Activities Catalog: An alternative curriculum design for youth and adults with severe disabilities* (pp. 104-110). Baltimore: Brookes.

O'Brien, J., & Lovett, H. (1993). *Finding a way toward everyday lives: The contribution of person centered planning.* Harrisburg: Pennsylvania Office of Mental Retardation.

Pancsofar, E. (1992). *Community connections.* Manchester, CT: Communitas.

Phillips, B., & Zhao, H. (1993). Predictors of assistive technology abandonment. *Assistive Technology, 5,* 36-45.

Powell, T., Pancsofar, E., Steere, D., Butterworth, J., Itzkowitz, J., & Rainforth, B. (1991). *Supported employment: Developing integrated employment opportunities for people with disabilities.* White Plains, NY: Longman.

Racino, J., Walker, P., O'Connor, S., & Taylor, S. (1993). *Housing, support, and the community.* Baltimore: Brookes.

Rogan, P., Hagner, D., & Murphy, S. (1993). Natural supports: Reconceptualizing job coach roles. *Journal of the Association for Persons with Severe Handicaps, 18,* 275-281.

Schalock, R. (Ed.). (1990). *Quality of life: Perspectives and issues.* Washington, DC: American Association on Mental Retardation.

Schalock, R. (1996). Reconsidering the conceptualization and measurement of quality of life. In R. Schalock (Ed.), *Quality of life: Vol. I. Conceptualization and measurement* (pp. 146-165). Washington, DC: American Association on Mental Retardation.

Smull, M., & Harrison, S.B. (1992). *Supporting people with severe reputations in the community.* Alexandria, VA: National Association of State Mental Retardation Program Directors.

Stark, J., & Faulkner, E. (1996). Quality of life across the life span. In R. Schalock (Ed.), *Quality of life: Vol. I. Conceptualization and measurement* (pp. 23-32). Washington, DC: American Association on Mental Retardation.

Steere, D.E., Gregory, S.P., Heiny, R.W., & Butterworth, J. (1995). Lifestyle planning: Considerations for use with people with disabilities. *Rehabilitation Counseling Bulletin, 38,* 207-223.

Steere, D.E., Wood, R., Pancsofar, E.L., & Butterworth, J. (1990). Outcome-based school-to-work transition planning for students with severe disabilities. *Career Development for Exceptional Individuals, 13*(1), 57-69.

Stineman, R.M., Morningstar, M.E., Bishop, B., & Turnbull, H.R. (1993). Role of families in transition planning for young adults with disabilities: Toward a method of person-centered planning. *Journal of Vocational Rehabilitation, 3*(2), 52–61.

Taylor, S., & Bogdan, R. (1990). Quality of life and the individual's perspective. In R. Schalock (Ed.), *Quality of life: Perspectives and issues* (pp. 27–40). Washington, DC: American Association on Mental Retardation.

Van Ruesen, A.K., & Bos, C.S. (1994). Facilitating student participation in Individualized Education Programs through motivation strategy instruction. *Exceptional Children, 60*, 466–475.

Vandercook, T., York, J., & Forest, M. (1989). The McGill Action Planning System (MAPS): A strategy for building the future. *Journal of the Association for Persons with Severe Handicaps, 14*, 205–215.

Wood, R., & Steere, D. (1992). Evaluating quality in supported employment: The Standards of Excellence for Employment Support Services. *Journal of Vocational Rehabilitation, 2*, 35–45.

The Aftermath of Parental Death: Changes in the Context and Quality of Life

Rachel M. Gordon
Waisman Center
University of Wisconsin-Madison

Marsha Mailick Seltzer
Waisman Center
University of Wisconsin-Madison

Marty Wyngaarden Krauss
Heller School
Brandeis University

This chapter examines the aftermath of parental death for adults with mental retardation who have lived at home throughout their lives. For many parents of persons with mental retardation, the most difficult issue they face is what will happen to their son or daughter when they are no longer alive or able to provide care. Questions that haunt them include, "Where will my daughter live?" "Who will take care of him?" "How can the quality of her life be maintained?" "Will my other children be able to help their brother (or sister) with everyday life?" These persistent and nagging questions affect parents, other children in the family, the family member with mental retardation, and the service systems in every state.

It has not always been so. As recently as 40 years ago, it was common for persons with mental retardation to predecease their parents. The dramatic increase in the expected life span of the current generation of adults with mental retardation is attributed to advances in medical and human service systems that have extended the quality and quantity of life of persons with mental retardation

(Carter & Jancar, 1983; Eyman & Borthwick-Duffy, 1994; Thase, 1982). Consequently, many adults with mental retardation can now anticipate several decades of life after their parents have died. Understanding the consequences of parental death with respect to the life circumstances and quality of life of adults with mental retardation is now a topic of considerable importance from both service systems and family policy perspectives (Edgerton, 1994; Heller & Factor, 1991).

Parental death is not an inconsequential event with respect to the service delivery system for persons with mental retardation. It is increasingly recognized that the most common provider of long-term supports for persons with mental retardation is the family. Estimates, though imprecise, suggest that close to 85% of the population with mental retardation live with or under the supervision of their families throughout their lives (Fujiura & Braddock, 1992). Acceptance into the publicly financed residential service system is, indeed, rare for the majority of persons with mental retardation. The family, particularly mothers and fathers, is the durable and steady support system for most persons with mental retardation. The family creates and sustains the quality of daily life and is responsible for articulating future care arrangements that will play out when the parents are no longer alive or able to manage day-to-day care (Seltzer & Krauss, 1994).

The twin forces of the increased life span of persons with mental retardation and the prevalence of family-based care well into adulthood emphasize the need to understand what happens to adults with mental retardation when one or both parents die. The published literature on this topic is meager. Little is known about how individuals with mental retardation understand and

respond to death, and how best to help them through the bereavement process (Seltzer, 1985). Although it is widely assumed that parental death will be a catalyst for placement into a licensed residential program, there is nothing in the literature that tests the accuracy of that assumption. Indeed, our knowledge of how persons with mental retardation cope emotionally and psychologically with parental death, and how parental death alters their residential, social, legal, and service profile is woefully inadequate.

For adults with mental retardation, the experience of parental death and subsequent grieving is complicated by their particular life experiences, cognitive and verbal skills, and the ability of surviving family members and friends to recognize and attend to their possibly atypical manifestations of grief (Kloeppel & Hollins, 1989; Lipe-Goodson & Goebel, 1983; Mansdorf & Ben-David, 1986; Wadsworth & Harper, 1991). Adults with retardation who live at home with their parents are generally much more emotionally and instrumentally dependent on their parents than their nondisabled siblings and peers are. The death of a parent can be profoundly disturbing to all aspects of their lives. If parental death results in a residential relocation for the surviving adult child, it may also trigger a change in day or work programs, disrupt access to familiar friends and family members, and result in service changes (Wadsworth & Harper, 1991). Those with mental retardation are at greater risk for mental health problems due to the lack of support they receive in the grieving process (Wadsworth & Harper, 1991). One study reported that 50% of the clients with mental retardation with sudden emotional or behavioral changes had recently experienced a death or loss (Emerson, 1977).

Thus, parental death is a major life event, often unleashing a host of emotional reactions that are conditioned, in part, by the quality and intensity of the relationship between parent and child. For persons with mental retardation, particularly those who were residing with their parent(s) prior to the mother's or father's death, the loss of a parent may also set in motion major alterations in the fundamental structures that determine the adult's quality of life—where he or she lives, works, or spends the days, and who provides or supervises his or her daily care.

This chapter explores these issues in detail. Since 1988, we have followed 461 families in which the mother was at least 55 years of age and had a son or daughter with mental retardation living at home with her when the study began. Over the past eight years, a parental death has occurred (of either the mother, the father, or both parents) in 66 of these families. The design of our study has permitted us to collect information on the aftermath of parental death and to address a number of research questions. First, what are the living arrangements and levels of family involvement for adults with mental retardation following parental death? Second, what life-style changes occur with respect to day or work program, social activities, and formal services? And third, how is the well-being of the adult with mental retardation affected by parental death with respect to activities of daily living skills, health, and behavior problems?

The next section presents a description of the study and discusses some of the methodological challenges and constraints that affect our research and findings. We then present descriptive data profiling the quality of life of adults who have experienced the loss of a mother, a father, or both. Next we report the results of analyses designed to answer three major questions. We conclude with implications for practice suggested by our results.

Methods

All of the 461 families in our study met two criteria when the research began in 1988: The mother was between the ages of 55 and 85 and an adult son or daughter with mental retardation lived at home with her. Our purposes are to examine the later stage of the family life course in families who have atypical caregiving challenges and to describe the natural history of the transition from parental to nonparental care.

We collect data from each family every 18 months. At each point of data collection, the mother is interviewed and completes a set of self-administered measures. We have collected supplemental data from the father at each of the points of data collection. We also have collected data at different times from adult siblings in these families and from the adult with retardation. In some cases, the adult with retardation has moved to a residential placement during the course of the study. In these instances, we collect data from the primary care provider in the residential setting, as well as continuing to interview family members. We treat the family as the unit of analysis for data collection purposes.

In cases in which a mother has died, we turn to the "successor caregiver" and conduct a special interview with him or her. This interview contains all of the questions we ordinarily ask about the son or daughter (e.g., questions about his or her functional abilities, health, behavioral problems, social activities, services, etc.) and questions about the family (e.g., changes in family composition, sources of care for the adult with mental retardation, etc.), as well as special questions about the circumstances of the mother's death, the reaction of the adult to this loss, sources of support to the family and the adult during their time of grief, and changes in living arrangement or services that have resulted from the inevitable reorganization of the family following the mother's death. If there is a surviving father, he is the respondent for these interviews. In instances in which the father has died during the course of the study and the mother is still alive, we conduct a parallel interview with the mother about the father's death. In cases in which the mother and father have both died, a sibling is interviewed. When there is no surviving family we have turned to a service provider or a friend, who becomes the primary respondent. Thus, for all 66 adults who have lost either a mother or a father (or both) since our study began, we have a description of their reactions to this loss and their current quality of life. We also have longitudinal data on their functional abilities, health, and behavior problems so we are able to construct comparisons between their situations prior to and after the death of the parent.

An obvious consequence of the data collection strategy of interviewing the primary caregiver is that in some cases, the respondent changes over time. A change in respondent occurs in two types of instances: 1) when the mother has died and the father, sibling, or other care provider becomes the primary respondent, and 2) when the adult with retardation has moved to a nonfamily residential setting and a care provider becomes a respondent in addition to a surviving family member. Our strategy is to interview the persons with the most up-to-date information about the individual with retardation. Although we believe this is the best approach (and it is the *only* approach when the mother has died), it has the limitation of introducing yet another source of variance

into an already complicated situation. In the analyses presented in this chapter, which are based on a sample of 132 families (66 families in which a parent has died and 66 randomly selected comparison families in which both parents are still alive), a change in reporter occurred in 52 families, either as a result of placement (11 families), death of a parent (15 families), or both (26 families).

In 11 families, the mother in fact is not deceased, but rather has become totally incapacitated, generally as a result of dementia. In these families, the responsibility for caregiving is no longer the mother's and has clearly shifted to another family member. For the present analysis, we included these families in the same group as those in which a death has occurred because there are minimal differences in the family caregiving arrangements between families in which the mother is deceased and families in which the mother is no longer in the caregiving role (and often in a nursing home) due to dementia.

For this analysis, we are contrasting four subgroups of our sample. Group 1 consists of 33 families in which the father died at some time after Time 1 date collection, but the mother is still alive. Group 2 consists of 12 families in which the father has survived but the mother died (in 9 of the 12 families) or became totally incapacitated (in 3 families) at some point after Time 1. Group 3 consists of 21 families in which both mother and father are deceased (in 13 of the 21 families) or the father is deceased and the mother became incapacitated (in 8 of the families). In all of the Group 3 families, the mother died or became incapacitated after the Time 1 point of data collection. In 7 of these families the father also died during the study period, but in the remaining 14 families in Group 3, the father died before the study began. Group 4 is a comparison group of families in which both mother and father were still alive at Time 5 data collection. Of the 208 families in our sample who met the criterion for inclusion in Group 4, we randomly selected 66 families—the same number as the families in which a parental death or incapacitation occurred (Groups 1, 2, and 3 combined)—to include in this analysis. The characteristics of the adults with retardation in the four groups, and the characteristics of their mothers and fathers at Time 1, are described below. In some instances, the groups and subgroups are quite small. We report the data nonetheless, with the awareness that these are necessarily preliminary estimates that warrant confirmation in larger-scale studies. Note that in the tables in this chapter, only the *F*-ratios that were significant are reported.

The timing of the parental death or incapacitation varied considerably (23 at Time 2, 15 at Time 3, 14 at Time 4, and 14 at Time 5). Our purpose in this chapter is to describe the *initial reactions* of the adult with retardation following the death of his or her parent(s) and the changes in his or her quality of life in response to this loss. Our primary strategy is to use data from the first point of data collection *after* the death or incapacitation occurred (which, in this chapter, we term "Wave 2"). For many of our analyses, we compare the situation as it was at the beginning of our study (which we term "Wave 1") with the first point of data collection after the death or incapacitation of the parent (i.e., Wave 2). In other analyses, we compare the four groups at Wave 2[1].

Qualitative Findings

Profiles of Subgroups

Group 1: Father deceased and mother alive. Group 1 consists of 33 families in which the father died after the study began and the mother is alive. The sons (55%) and daughters (45%) in this group were between 21 and 58 years of age when the study began (mean = 33). At that time, they were in excellent or good health (94%); only 6% were considered to be in fair or poor health. Most have moderate (42%) or mild (40%) retardation, 18% are classified as having severe retardation, and no one is classified as having profound retardation in this group. Most of these adults (76%) continued to live at home with their mother at the Wave 2 point of data collection.

When the study began (prior to the death of the father), the mothers of adults in Group 1 averaged 66 years of age (range 55-83). Most were in excellent or good health (82%), although 18% were in fair or poor health. At Wave 1, their husbands were somewhat older (mean = 71 years) and were in poorer health than the wives—only 68% were in excellent or good health and 32% were in fair or poor health.

Although there was considerable variability in this group, a dominant theme was the need for both the adult with retardation and the mother to adapt to the loss of the father. We have found in our past research that the mother is clearly the primary caregiver for the adult with retardation. However, the

---

[1] It is important to note that the amount of time that elapsed between Wave 1 and Wave 2 in this analysis is not constant across all cases. To investigate the possible confounding effects introduced by having Wave 2 be at varying lengths of time after Wave 1, we conducted a series of preliminary analyses in which we controlled for the amount of time between Wave 1 and the death (or incapacitation) and Wave 2. In none of these analyses was either of these covariates significant, suggesting that the point in time and the duration between Wave 1 and Wave 2 when the death (or incapacitation) occurred was not related to patterns of short-term adaptation and quality of life. Although these preliminary analyses suggest that there is no systematic bias introduced by allowing for variation in the length of time between Wave 1 and Wave 2, it remains a potential limitation in our study. Note that for Group 4, Wave 2 was the fifth point of data collection in all instances.

father plays an important secondary role, providing emotional and instrumental help to the mother (Essex, Seltzer, & Krauss, 1993) that is related to maternal well-being. Thus, even though the primary caregiver remains constant in this group, the family is in flux after the death of the father.

Group 2: Mother deceased and father alive.
Group 2 consists of 12 families in which the mother died or became incapacitated after the study began and the father is alive. Of these 12 adults, 10 continued to live at home with the father; the other two had moved to a nonfamily living arrangement. The sons (58%) and daughters with retardation (42%) averaged 34 years of age when the study began in 1988 (range 18-51). At that time most were in excellent or good health (83%), but 17% were in fair or poor health. Most were classified as having mild (36%) or moderate (27%) retardation, and the others as having either severe (18%) or profound (18%) retardation.

When the study began, their mothers averaged 67 years of age (range 55-79). Their health status was classified as either excellent or good (67%) or fair or poor (33%). In contrast, their husbands who survived them averaged 68 years of age at the beginning of the study and were in better health—82% in excellent or good health and only 18% in fair health (none classified as poor health). Although this group of families was highly variable, one notable feature was the reciprocity of care exchanged between the adults with retardation and their fathers, who are now in a new role of primary caregiver.

Group 3: Both parents deceased.
Group 3 consists of 21 families in which the father is deceased and the mother is deceased or totally incapacitated. In all of these families, the death or incapacitation of the mother occurred after the study began. As noted earlier, in 7 of these families, the father also died during the study period, while in the other 14 families in Group 3 the father's death preceded the beginning of the study. The adults with retardation in these families were nearly evenly split between sons (52%) and daughters (48%). Most were in excellent or good health (91%) when the study began, with the remaining 9% in poor or fair health. The majority were classified as having mild (53%) or moderate (37%) retardation, with fewer classified as having severe or profound retardation (5% each).

When the study began, their mothers averaged 70 years of age (range 57-82), the oldest group of mothers in this study. Most were in excellent or good health (62%), but fully 38% were in fair or poor health when the study began. Their husbands averaged 73 years of age (range 67-82), again the oldest group in this study. Their health was similar to their wives at Wave 1—60% in excellent or good health and 40% in fair or poor health. Forecasting their future mortality, the health of these parents at Wave 1 was the most impaired of all parents in the study.

The adults who have lost both parents experienced significant changes in their quality of life, often resulting in a placement in a nonfamily setting (76%). Some of them experienced multiple placements before a satisfactory arrangement was found. In 17 of the 21 families in Group 3, a sibling (8 brothers and 9 sisters) is now responsible for either overseeing the care provided to the brother or sister (in 12 of the families) or providing the direct care (in the 5 cases in which they live together in the same household). In 1 family, a cousin is now the primary person responsible for overseeing the care of the adult, while in another 3 families, this role is filled by a nonfamily guardian.

Group 4: Both parents alive. For contrast purposes, we also include in this analysis a group of 66 families who were randomly selected to represent the families in our study in which both mother and father are still alive at the fifth point of data collection. The sons (58%) and daughters (42%) in these families mainly continued to live with their parents (83%), although 17% have moved to a nonfamily residential setting.

At the beginning of the study, these adults were in excellent or good health (92%), with only 8% in fair or poor health. Like the other groups of adults, they tend to have mild (29%) or moderate (42%) retardation. This group has the highest percentage of those classified as having severe retardation (23%) and another 7% are classified as having profound retardation. At the beginning of the study they averaged 32 years of age (range 15 to 47).

Their mothers averaged 63 years of age (range 55-77) when the study began, the youngest mothers in this study. They were in excellent or good health for the most part (83%), with only 17% in fair or poor health. Their husbands also were young relative to the other groups in the study, averaging 64 years of age when the study began (range 55-77). Their health was also excellent or good (81%) much more often than fair or poor (19%).

Reactions of Adults with Mental Retardation to Parental Death

In our interviews with primary respondents following the death or incapacitation of a parent, we asked them to characterize how the adult with retardation coped with his or her loss. These qualitative data offer insight into the range of reactions of adults with retardation to this life transition.

Although the details of each person's reaction to the death of the mother were highly individualized, several broad patterns were suggested. Some adults were described as able to talk about the mother's death and to express emotion along with other family members. A sister told us, "She did fantastic. She took cues from us. If we cried, she cried. But she bounced back from it."

Others were described as coping well because they relied on their religious beliefs, permitting the use of prayer and attendance at religious services to calm themselves, and adopting explanations of death, such as their mother went to live with the angels or was reunited with other deceased family members. Many were described as having participated in the rituals of death—going to the hospital towards the end of the mother's life, being part of wakes and funeral services, and visiting the cemetery.

Other adults were described as not fully understanding the reality of parental death or as not seeming to comprehend that the mother had died. In several situations, surviving siblings confessed that they were unsure what impact their mother's death has had on their brother or sister with retardation or how aware of the death he or she was.

Only a few were described as being (and remaining) agitated, nervous, and depressed over the death. Several received psychiatric counseling or relied heavily on the outpouring of support from day program staff and family members.

In instances of paternal death, we obtained descriptions of how adults with mental retardation coped with the death of their father. In general, the adults were described as muted in their response—being quiet or sad and keeping feelings internalized. Some benefited from counseling provided by surviving family, clergy, or service providers who offered explanations of what death means. Many were described as having delayed reactions, such as erupting into tears for the first time months after the father's death. Others were described as keeping their father's memory alive by continuing to look at family photographs, reminiscing about pleasurable events, and expressing warm feelings and longing for their deceased father.

Quantitative Findings

Impact of Parental Death on Quality of Life

We turn now to our quantitative analyses, which address our three research questions. (a) What are the living arrangements and levels of family involvement for adults with mental retardation following parental death? (b) What life-style changes occur after parental death with respect to day or work program, social activities, and formal services? (c) How is the well-being of the adult with mental retardation affected by parental death, with respect to health status, activities of daily living (ADL)/instrumental activities of daily living (IADL) skills, and behavior problems?

Current Living Arrangements

We found that there was an elevated likelihood of out-of-home placement following the death or incapacitation of both parents ($F = 12.21, p < .001$). The highest rate of placement is in Group 3, when both parents have died, in which 76% of the adults have moved to a residential placement. Residential placement is considerably less likely when at least one parent is alive. Interestingly, maternal death with a surviving father (Group 2) is *less likely* to precipitate a placement than paternal death with a surviving mother (Group 1). Specifically, 24% of the adults who experienced the

death of their father have been placed even though their mother is still alive. The rate of placement in adults whose mother has died and who have a surviving father is only 17%, which is equivalent to the placement rate in Group 4, the contrast group. Overall, it appears that the death or incapacitation of both parents sharply increases the likelihood of residential placement in comparison to the death of one parent.

Of the 66 adults who experienced the death or incapacitation of a parent, 26 have moved to a nonfamily living arrangement. These adults now live in a variety of settings. Half (13) live in community residences, including group homes, community-based ICFs-MR, and fully staffed apartments. Another 3 adults live in foster homes and one lives in a semiindependent apartment (with less than full staff coverage). Two of the adults live in nursing homes, while another 7 living in institutional settings. Of those living in institutions, 5 live in private institutions, 1 lives in a county home, and 1 lives in an institution for persons with mental illness.

In the other 40 families in which there has been a parental death or incapacitation, the adult with retardation still lives with family. In Group 1, all 25 adults who still live with family live with their mother. In Group 2, all 10 adults who still live with family live with their fathers. In Group 3, all 5 adults who live with family live with their siblings.

Although the majority of adults who have experienced parental death continue to live with their families, the durability of this arrangement is unknown, and the possibility of future residential placement remains. In some instances, the adult's name has been added to a waiting list for residential placement. However, we found no increased likelihood of being on a waiting list among adults who had experienced the death or incapacitation of a parent as compared with the contrast group in which both parents were still alive. Overall, less than one-third of the adults who still lived with family were on a waiting list for residential placement, suggesting the presumption of continued family-based care or, alternatively, the reluctance of surviving family members to address future care planning.

Although there was great variability in the sample with respect to their living arrangements following parental death, these placements were generally guided by the mother's preferences. At the beginning of the study, when all mothers were alive and functioning as the primary caregiver for their adult son or daughter with mental retardation, we asked each mother to indicate her preferences regarding where her adult child would live after she and her husband are no longer able to provide care. Focusing only on the 33 families in which the mother subsequently died or became incapacitated (Groups 2 and 3), we found that in 11 families, the mother's plan was implemented. For example, one mother both named a "successor caregiver" (her daughter) and indicated that she hoped her son with retardation would eventually move to a group home. Following the mother's death, the sister took over responsibility for overseeing her brother's care as planned, and the brother moved to a placement fitting the mother's description. In another 5 of the 33 cases, the mother's plan was partially implemented. For example, a mother named a "successor caregiver" (again, a daughter) and hoped for placement of her child with retardation into an apartment. After the mother's death, the sister did assume responsibility but the adult moved in with the sister, representing a partially implemented plan.

In only 2 of the 33 families was the mother's preference not implemented at all. For example, a mother named her son to be the successor caregiver for her daughter with retardation, and added her daughter's name to a waiting list for a group home. Following the mother's death, the son refused to take responsibility for his sister and cut off all contact with her. A different sibling assumed responsibility for her care and arranged for her to move into an apartment. Thus, neither part of the mother's plan was implemented.

In another 5 families, there was no plan articulated by the mother prior to her death. Finally, in the remaining 10 cases, the father is still alive and residing with the son or daughter, so it is premature to assess whether the plan has been implemented. Thus, in 16 of the 18 families in which a plan for the future care of the adult with retardation could have been implemented, the living arrangement of the adult at Wave 2 is either fully or partially consistent with the mother's prior plan.

To summarize, there is an elevated likelihood of residential placement following the death of both parents. In nearly one-quarter (23.8%) of these families, the adult moved in with his or her sibling. When one parent survives, there is an impressive amount of continuing family involvement with the adult with retardation.

Continued Family Involvement in Caregiving

Table 2.1 portrays the sources of direct care provided to the adult with retardation. The entries in the table indicate the average number of tasks (maximum = 27) for which the mother, father, sibling/other relative, or paid helper provided care to the adult with retardation. For any of the 27 tasks (e.g.,

Table 2.1
Sources and Extent of Assistance for Adults at Wave 1 and Wave 2

	Mother		Father		Sibling/Other Relative		Paid Help	
	With family	Placed[a]	With family	Placed[a]	With family	Placed[a]	With family	Placed[a]
Wave 1								
Group 1[b]	10.36	12.75	2.76	3.88	0.36	0.00	0.32	0.13
Group 2[c]	8.78	14.00	5.33	7.50	0.20	0.00	0.33	0.00
Group 3[d]	7.80	9.25	0.80	0.56	0.00	0.13	0.20	0.31
Group 4[e]	12.27	12.46	4.87	3.64	0.35	0.27	0.36	0.18
Wave 2								
Group 1[b]	9.40	1.75	0.00	0.00	0.64	0.25	0.56	5.50
Group 2[c]	0.00	0.00	10.78	1.00	1.70	0.00	1.68	9.50
Group 3[d]	0.00	0.00	0.00	0.00	12.40	0.75	0.80	5.25
Group 4[e]	9.20	0.82	2.22	0.36	0.09	0.00	1.04	7.09

Note. The entries reflect the number of tasks for which help is provided.

[a] Data for column at Wave 1 represent scores of people later placed. Data for column at Wave 2 represent scores of people in their placement. [b] Group 1 = Father only deceased. [c] Group 2 = Mother only deceased. [d] Group 3 = Both parents deceased/incapacitated. [e] Group 4 = Both parents alive.

dressing, setting the table, shopping), multiple sources of help could be counted. For example, if the adult received help in dressing from both the mother and the father, both were "credited" with providing help.

As shown in Table 2.1, at Wave 1 the mother was the primary caregiver in all groups. The highest rate of direct care from the mother was in Group 4, in which both mother and father were alive. The father was in a secondary caregiving role at Wave 1, while the siblings and paid helpers played an incidental role. At Wave 2, the supportive "cast" changed. In the case of Group 1 (in which the father had died between Wave 1 and Wave 2), there was an increase in care provided by siblings and

paid helpers, although the absolute magnitude of their help remained very low. In the case of Group 2 (in which the mother had died or became incapacitated between Wave 1 and Wave 2 and the father was still alive), the role of the father increased dramatically (assisting with 5 tasks at Wave 1 and nearly 11 tasks at Wave 2, on average). Also, the contributions of siblings and paid helpers increased, although again the absolute level of their assistance was small. In the case of Group 3 (in which both parents had died or became incapacitated before Wave 2), the siblings' assistance became prominent (increasing from virtually zero contribution to helping with 12 tasks), primarily as a result of co-residence with the adult with mental retardation. Finally, Group 4 provides an estimate of the distribution of caregiving when both parents are alive. Here we see that the number of tasks for which help was given by both mother and father declined, possibly reflecting their aging and increasing frailty. Although siblings did not emerge as important sources of assistance when both parents were still alive, paid helpers made an increasingly large contribution.

Table 2.1 also portrays similar data with respect to adults who were placed in a residential setting between Wave 1 and Wave 2, and we see both similar and distinct patterns. The primary difference concerns the role of paid helpers. Not surprisingly, following the placement, paid helpers were the primary source of direct care assistance to adults with mental retardation, and the role of surviving mothers and fathers, and of siblings diminished considerably.

These data suggest that there is a substitution process governing which family members will provide care to an adult with retardation and when they will be called on to do so. That is, when the mother is alive, she is the primary caregiver. If the mother dies or becomes incapacitated and the adult continues to live in the parental home, the contribution previously made by the mother is taken on by the father. It is only when both parents are deceased that the sibling becomes an important source of direct care, and only in those instances in which the adult lives with a sibling. However, this pattern is markedly different following a placement. At that point, direct care from relatives becomes minimal, and paid staff provide the care. Note, however, that the level of care provided by paid staff at Wave 2 is considerably lower than the level provided by the mother at Wave 1, prior to placement.

Life-Style Changes Following Parental Death

Adults with mental retardation are at risk for many changes following parental death. In addition to change in their living arrangements, there is an increased risk of change in their day programs, as shown in Table 2.2. Among adults with both parents alive, few changed day program or work placement between Wave 1 and 2 (4% if still living with parents and 11% if placed). The risk is considerably higher following the death of one or both parents. The probability of change in day program or work placement tends to be even higher following a residential placement, possibly attributable to geographic shifts and the need for proximity between the residential site and the day program.

Adults also tend to experience a change in social activities following the death of their parent. Table 2.2 also presents data about the frequency with which adults with retardation participate in three types of recreational and social activities at Wave 2. Adults who have been placed show less frequent contact with family, more frequent contact with friends from work, and more frequent participation in group recreational activities than adults who continue to live with family members. Also, adults who live with recently widowed mothers (Group 1) show the most frequent contact with relatives and co-workers. These data suggest the importance of parental mortality and placement status for the social activities of adults with retardation.

An additional indicator of the quality of life of adults following the death or incapacitation of a parent concerns the services they receive. As shown in Table 2.3, we found that adults who live in a nonfamily setting receive more services than adults who live with family. This

Table 2.2
**Changes in Day Program and Social Activity Frequency[a]
at Wave 2 by Residential Status**

	Group 1[b]		Group 2[c]		Group 3[d]		Group 4[e]	
	With family	Placed[f]	With family	Placed[f]	With family	Placed[f]	With family	Placed[f]
% change in day program between Wave 1 and 2[g]	7%	40%	30%	50%	75%	25%	4%	11%
Frequency of time spent with relatives[h]	3.04	1.57	2.30	1.00	2.00	1.75	1.98	1.00
Frequency of time spent with co-workers[i]	1.57	1.43	0.10	2.00	0.00	1.44	0.42	0.60
Frequency of participation in group recreational activities[j]	2.04	2.86	1.50	3.50	2.00	2.88	1.07	2.80

[a] 0 = never; 1 = several times a year; 2 = once a month; 3 = once a week; 4 = several times a week. [b] Group 1 = Father only deceased. [c] Group 2 = Mother only deceased. [d] Group 3 = Both parents deceased. [e] Group 4 = Both parents alive. [f] Data for column at Wave 1 represent scores of people later placed. Data for column at Wave 2 represent scores of people in their placement. [g] F (residential status x group) = 3.69, p = .015. [h] F (residential status) = 15.64, $p < .001$; F (group) = 5.00, p = .003. [i] F (residential status) = 5.29, $p < .001$; F (group) = 5.37, p = .002. [j] F (residential status) = 17.26, $p < .001$.

probably reflects the fact that some services provided by parents (e.g., transportation, social activities) are not "counted" as discrete services, whereas comparable supports provided in residential programs are viewed as discrete and "countable" services. Interestingly, at Wave 2, among all those who were placed in a nonfamily living arrangement, adults whose mother and father were both deceased (Group 3) received the *fewest* services. In contrast, among all those who continued to live with family, adults in Group 3 received the *largest* number of services.

The Well-Being of Adults with Retardation

Adults with retardation who experience the death of their parent may be at increased risk for poor health, decline in ADL/IADL skills, and increased levels of behavior problems. We examined the extent to which each of these indicators of poor quality of life was evident in our sample. As shown in Table 2.4, there was a general decline in the health of the adults in our study, regardless of parental mortality or changes in residential arrangement. These changes may reflect age-related health problems. Note that

Table 2.3
Number of Services Received by Adults with Retardation

	Group 1[a]	Group 2[b]	Group 3[c]	Group 4[d]
Wave 1				
With family	3.81	2.40	2.00	3.71
Later placed	3.25	1.50	3.50	3.82
Wave 2				
With family	3.19	2.80	4.20	3.40
Placed	5.88	5.50	4.06	5.91

[a] Group 1 = Father only deceased. [b] Group 2 = Mother only deceased. [c] Group 3 = Both parents deceased/incapacitated. [d] Group 4 = Both parents alive.

F (residential status) = 4.58, $p < .05$. F (wave) = 24.92, $p < .001$. F (wave x residential status) = 12.03, $p < .001$. F (wave x residential status x group) = 5.16, $p = .002$.

adults whose parents were alive (Group 4) showed virtually the same pattern of declining health status as adults whose father had died (Group 1), whose mother had died (Group 2), or those who had lost both parents (Group 3).

The pattern with respect to ADL/IADL skills is quite different. In this case, we see evidence that adults whose parents were both alive (Group 4) acquired new skills between Wave 1 and Wave 2, a pattern not evident in any of the other groups. This increase parallels the finding reported earlier that Group 4 adults received less help from parents, siblings, or paid helpers at Wave 2 than at Wave 1. Thus, there was an increase in independence in the adults in Group 4 that might have been prompted by the parents' age-related declining abilities and decreasing caregiving assistance. Adults in Group 4 who were placed between Wave 1 and Wave 2 showed a particularly marked increase in skills. This increase may be the result of new opportunities for independence provided by the residential setting, coupled with the support of their parents as these adults made the transition from home to a residence. In contrast, adults who had lost a parent showed a pattern of either declining skills or no change between Wave 1 and Wave 2.

Finally, we analyzed data regarding the behavior problems of adults with retardation at Wave 2. Those adults who continued to live with family at Wave 2 had significantly fewer behavior problems than adults who had moved to a nonfamily residential placement ($F = 6.13, p = .015$). There is no difference, however, in the number of behavior problems manifested by those who experienced the death or incapacitation of a parent as compared to those for whom both parents survived. It is possible that a high level of behavior problems is a precipitant rather than a consequence of placement. As no data on behavior problems were available in the Wave 1 data set, it is not possible to fully describe the change process.

Implications for Practice

To conclude, the quality of life of adults with retardation following parental death is dominated by an extraordi-

Table 2.4
Health Status[a] and ADL/IADL Skills[b] of Adults at Wave 1 and 2 by Residential Status

	Group 1[c]	Group 2[d]	Group 3[e]	Group 4[f]
Health at Wave 1				
With family[g]	2.44	2.20	2.20	2.50
Later placed	2.50	2.50	2.40	2.46
Health at Wave 2				
With family	2.20	1.80	2.00	2.26
Placed	2.25	2.50	1.87	2.18
ADL/IADL at Wave 1				
With family[h]	61.48	63.30	67.75	59.78
Later placed	64.60	52.25	65.00	56.07
ADL/IADL at Wave 2				
With family	62.98	61.15	64.75	61.23
Placed	65.80	55.75	64.70	63.74

[a] 0 = very poor; 1 = poor; 2 = fair; 3 = good; 4 = excellent. [b] For each of 27 tasks, 0 = totally dependent; 1 = can do but doesn't; 2 = with help; 3 = independent. Scores are summed and range from 0 to 81. [c] Group 1 = Father only deceased. [d] Group 2 = Mother only deceased. [e] Group 3 = Both parents deceased/incapacitated. [f] Group 4 = Both parents alive. [g] F (wave 1) = 5.47, p = .022. [h] F (group x wave) = 3.76, p = .01.

nary amount of change. The sadness and loss that is a universal reaction to parental death is magnified in this instance because of the prior dependence of adults with retardation on their parents, for care, for emotional support, and for a shared social world. Little is known about the long-range pattern of adaptation by these adults to the loss of their parents, but in the short term their quality of life is altered pervasively. In addition to these general conclusions, our study points to a number of implications for practice.

From what we have observed to date, living with family over the long term is not the norm once both parents are deceased. Fully three-fourths of the adults who have lost both parents live in a nonfamily residential setting. In contrast, those families in which only one parent has passed away (Groups 1 and 2)

have a relatively low rate of residential placement, at least in the immediate or short-term period following parental death.

When the adult continues to live with family, there is a hierarchy of care provision. Responsibility shifts from the mother, who is generally the primary caregiver or overseer for these adults as long as she is able to provide this care, to a surviving father following her death. It is only when neither parent remains alive that this responsibility is taken over by siblings or, if there are no surviving siblings, by a friend or nonrelative. Indeed, it is rare for there to be no family involvement, and it is only in those cases in which both parents have passed away and there are no surviving siblings that this occurs—in our study, in only 3 instances. Even when the siblings are not geographically in close proximity, they generally still assume and carry through on this responsibility from afar.

This convoy of caregiving (from mother to father to sibling) is governed by gender and generational patterns. Although fathers are not in the role of primary caregiver to the adult with retardation while their wives are alive, fathers play an important supportive role that sets the stage for their new responsibilities after the death of their wife. Fathers have long shared their living space with their son or daughter. The low rate of placement of adults who have a surviving father may suggest that it is easier for fathers to move into the role of primary caregiver than to adjust to the empty nest resulting from placement. Placement may also be a reminder of the father's own mortality and the reality that the adult child will eventually be parentless. Regardless of what causes this pattern, it is clear that fathers are flexible in taking on new caregiving roles.

In those families in which there are no surviving parents, siblings also exhibit great flexibility in taking over responsibility. In five families, a sibling has invited the brother or sister with retardation to live with him or her, while in the other families with no surviving parents, the siblings have taken on the roles of guardian and advocate, and include the brother or sister in outings and family gatherings. In some cases, the siblings said they felt obligated to take on this responsibility, while others reported that they did so willingly. In every family with nondisabled siblings, there is some sibling involvement, and for families with multiple siblings, there generally is regular contact with more than one of them.

A second implication for practice concerns life-style changes that follow the death of a parent. We found that life for those adults who are living with at least one parent is fairly stable. However,

for those who have experienced the loss of their last surviving parent, which generally leads to a move outside of the parental home and inevitably to a change in caregiver, and for those who have lost one parent and subsequently moved to a residential placement, the world these adults have known all of their lives is turned upside down. For most, there is a change in residence, day or work program, and social life.

Social activities also undergo profound changes associated with parental death. Interestingly, the most frequent contact with relatives occurs in those families in which the father has died and the adult is still living with the mother, even more frequent than in families in which there are two surviving parents. It may be that widowed mothers act as kin-keepers and encourage family involvement by creating occasions for their son or daughter to be with relatives. It also may be that widowed mothers are seen by family members as particularly vulnerable and they rally around her, with consequent increased contact with her son or daughter.

Participation in group recreational activities increases following residential placement. As parents age, arranging for their son or daughter to attend nonfamily social activities may become increasingly difficult and less a priority. Providing transportation to these social activities, particularly those that take place in the evening or during inclement weather, may be difficult for older parents. It may also be that adults who live with family are content to spend time at home and are less interested in participating in group recreational activities than those who live in residential placements (Krauss, Seltzer, & Goodman, 1992). At times, participation in group recreational activities may reflect plans made by the residential setting staff and may not be indicative of the preferences of an individual. Thus, a lower rate of participation in group recreational activities by adults who continue to live with family should not necessarily be interpreted as social isolation.

The number of services received by these adults is affected by the loss of the parent as well as placement in a nonfamily setting. For those who continue to live with family, it is only those adults who have a change in primary caregiver who experience an increase in the number of services following parental death. The largest increase comes when the adult moves in with a sibling. It may be that these siblings perceive that their brother or sister with retardation needs more services than he or she received when the parents were alive. It may also be that competing commitments do not allow these siblings to provide the same level of care to their brother or sister that their parents did; consequently, these siblings may be relying on the service system to make up the difference.

All in all, we see evidence of a ripple effect of life-style changes occurring after parental death, particularly when there is also a placement. Little in the adult's life remains the same. There is an increased risk of change in where he or she lives, where he or she works or spends the daytime hours, the pattern of contact with friends and family, the context in which social activities take place, and the services that he or she receives. It is difficult to separate out the effect of parental death from the effect of placement here. However, it is noteworthy that the least amount of disruption in life-style following placement is found in families in which both parents are still alive but no longer living with their son or daughter. The comparative stability of the lives of these adults following placement as contrasted with the lives of adults who have lost a parent suggests the desirability of advance planning on the part of families and the benefits of placement prior to parental death.

The difficulty of the transition to nonparental care is also evident in the well-being of adults after the death of a parent. We found that health declined in all four groups over time, but was not related to either placement or parental death. Although the adults we studied are in their mid-thirties, on average, there is evidence of declining health even at this stage of life. This pattern of decline is the backdrop for all other changes in personal well-being that may be associated with parental death.

In contrast to the pattern of declining health evident for all groups regardless of parental death or change in residential arrangements, there is a more varied pattern of change over time in ADL/IADL skills. For adults who have not experienced parental death, there is evidence of skill acquisition from Wave 1 to Wave 2. Although the increase in skills is marginal when the adult continues to live with parents, it is quite substantial following placement into a residential setting.

The pattern is sharply different when the adult has lost one or both parents. For adults who have a surviving mother, we found a very modest increase in ADL/IADL skills over time regardless of residential status. For adults who do not have a surviving mother, however, there is a decline in skills over time, again regardless of residential status. When an adult has experienced the death of either parent, he or she tends not to gain new skills after placement, as is generally the case when both parents were alive and available to smooth the transition and continue to provide support.

There is no doubt that these adults experience grief at the loss of their parents and find the transition to nonparental care to be a rocky road. Many respondents expressed great admiration for the way in which the adult with retardation in their family had handled all of these changes and losses. It is not without assistance that this pattern of individual and family adaptation occurs. Supportive extended family members and a variety of professionals, including clergy, social workers, service providers, and psychologists, have all been identified as assisting these adults in understanding what has happened and adjusting to their new lives. Whereas for adults in the general population the death of a parent is softened by the existence of spouse, children, and a lifestyle independent of their parents, for adults with retardation the centrality of their parents does not diminish until parental death. It is only then that they are put in a position of adapting to their lives as separate from their parents and are exposed to aspects of life from which they were previously shielded.

Author Note

Support for this chapter was provided by the National Institute on Aging (R01 AG08768), the Rehabilitation Research and Training Center on Aging and Developmental Disabilities of the University of Illinois at Chicago, the Waisman Center on Mental Retardation of the University of Wisconsin-Madison, and the Starr Center on Mental Retardation at the Heller School of Brandeis University. The authors are grateful to Barbara Larson, Renee Lewandowski, and Dotty Robison for coordination of the data collection and to Seung Chol Choi for the conduct of the data analysis.

References

Carter, G., & Jancar, J. (1983). Mortality in the mentally handicapped: A 50 year survey at the Stoke Park group of hospitals (1930-1980). *Journal of Mental Deficiency Research, 27,* 143-156.

Edgerton, R. (1994). Quality of life issues: Some people know how to be old. In M.M. Seltzer, M.W. Krauss, & M.P. Janicki (Eds.), *Life course perspectives on adulthood and old age* (pp. 53-66). Washington, DC: American Association on Mental Retardation.

Emerson, P. (1977). Covert grief reaction in mentally retarded clients. *Mental Retardation, 15,* 46-47.

Essex, E.A., Seltzer, M.M., & Krauss, M.W. (1993). Aging fathers as caregivers for adult children with developmental disabilities. Paper presented at the National Institute on Aging Symposium on "Men's Caregiving Roles in an Aging Society." Rockville, MD.

Eyman, R.K., & Borthwick-Duffy, S. (1994). Trends in mortality and predictors of mortality. In M.M. Seltzer, M.W. Krauss, & M.P. Janicki (Eds.), *Life course perspectives on adulthood and old age* (pp. 93-105). Washington, DC: American Association on Mental Retardation.

Fujiura, G.T., & Braddock, D. (1992). Fiscal and demographic trends in mental retardation services: The emergence of the family. In L. Rowitz (Ed.), *Mental retardation in the year 2000* (pp. 316-338). New York: Springer.

Heller, T., & Factor, A. (1991). Permanency planning for adults with mental retardation living with family members. *American Journal on Mental Retardation, 96,* 163-176.

Kloeppel, D., & Hollins, S. (1989). Double handicap: Mental retardation and death in the family. *Death studies, 13,* 31-38.

Krauss, M.W., Seltzer, M.M., & Goodman, S. (1992). Social support networks of adults with mental retardation at home. *American Journal on Mental Retardation, 96,* 432-441.

Lipe-Goodson, P., & Goebel, B. (1983). Perception of age and death in mentally retarded adults. *Mental Retardation, 21,* 68-75.

Mansdorf, I., & Ben-David, N. (1986). Operant and cognitive intervention to restore effective functioning following a death in a family. *Journal of Behavioral Therapy and Experimental Psychiatry, 17,* 193-196.

Seltzer, G. (1985). Selected psychological processes and aging among older developmental disabled persons. In M.P. Janicki & H.M. Wisniewski (Eds.) *Aging and developmental disabilities: Issues and approaches.* (pp. 211-227). Baltimore: Brookes.

Seltzer, M.M., & Krauss, M.W. (1994). Aging parents with coresident adult children: The impact of lifelong caregiving. In M.M. Seltzer, M.W. Krauss, & M.P. Janicki (Eds.), *Life course perspectives on adulthood and old age* (pp. 3-18). Washington, DC: American Association on Mental Retardation.

Thase, M.E. (1982). Longevity and mortality in Down's syndrome. *Journal of Mental Deficiency Research, 26,* 177-192.

Wadsworth, J., & Harper, D. (1991). Grief and bereavement in mental retardation: A need for a new understanding. *Death Studies, 15,* 281-292.

Facilitating Relationships of Children with Mental Retardation in Schools

Martha E. Snell and Laura K. Vogtle
University of Virginia and University of Alabama at Birmingham

Although quality of life definitions appear to vary widely, Felce and Perry (1995) describe substantial agreement in researchers' identification of its relevant domains. Many recent views of quality of life regard interpersonal relationships as a main component of social well-being, with friends and social life constituting a primary source of such relationships. When you ask children about the best part of their life at school, most mention times when they can choose their activity and companions: during freetime, recess, lunchtime, while "hangin' out" in the halls, and in extra-curricular activities after school. Although researchers may argue over the definition of friendships and at what age they are formed, they agree upon the importance of friendships. Children learn skills applicable to their later adult relationships through the friendships they have at younger ages. Competence in conflict negotiation, intimacy, trust, and responding to others' needs appear

to be some of the critical skills involved in forming close associations (Furman & Robbins, 1985).

Social relationships are a valuable part of going to school and a rich medium for learning for students, including students with mental retardation, yet their experiences with social relations have been reported to be qualitatively different and less successful. Given the diversity of their support needs, the social relationships of children and adolescents with mental retardation cannot be summarized in simple terms.

According to an extensive review by Parker and Asher (1987), there appears to be general support for the hypothesis that young children and adolescents who have poor relationships with their peers are more likely to experience difficulties later in life. Individuals with mental retardation are not an exception to this hypothesis. Thus, it is appropriate to seek answers about how the complex array of responsible factors contributes to an adult's social outcomes. How social skills and relationships are facilitated in school-aged individuals with mental retardation is the main focus of this chapter.

The chapter reviews the procedures that seem to promote learning and the environments where that learning is fostered. In this review, the reader will note some similarities and differences between research dealing with preschoolers and that dealing with elementary school students. The research strategies used with different age groups are not widely disparate, but instead represent the gradual developmental changes and logical differences one would expect with increasing age. Both similarities and differences can be noted. Chief among the similarities are the use of peer intervention, the centering of research on play behaviors or language during play, and the location of research in groups organized for research or in play or free-time groups. Several differences can be noted: research in elementary-aged children takes place more often in the classroom and broadens from simply play behavior to include on-task behavior and classroom performance; the study of attitude change in children without disabilities towards children with disabilities occurs more frequently in elementary groups up through high school ages, less so in preschool, for developmental reasons (language and stability of attitude); the research with elementary-aged children tends to be more experimental, while preschool studies are more descriptive (e.g., Guralnick & Paul-Brown, 1984); and the interventions with elementary-aged children are much more varied, including the use of peer tutoring and social scripts. Throughout this chapter, we will make a case for the value of teaching social skills and focusing on

quality of life oriented outcomes in the context of school settings that are conducive to this learning.

Social Relationships

Factors That Impact on Making Friends

For children, social relationships provide a way to learn about cultural and group norms, an arena in which to realize and understand their own feelings about themselves, and a vehicle to learn about intimacy between people. They also provide opportunities for cognitive development. Acquaintances and friends contribute an array of qualities that enhance life for both adults and children, such as instrumental aid, affection, companionship, intimacy, nurturance, reliable alliance, enhancement of worth, and a sense of inclusion (Furman & Robbins, 1985). Each kind of relationship may enhance different qualities: friends facilitate intimacy, while siblings promote companionship. Because partners in a friendship differ, the relationship often involves some balancing of traits and abilities between the partners; this balance fluctuates over time and may influence the mutuality of the relationship (Raup, 1985).

Influences on Social Relationships

Many of the social tasks that provide a medium for developing social relationships with peers happen first during parent-child interactions and sibling interactions. How parents relate to their young children with mental retardation may directly and indirectly affect this development (Beckman & Lieber, 1992). Attachment and emotional security, maternal perception of the child's competence, and dysfunction in the family have been connected with the presence of competent and incompetent social behaviors towards peers (Odom, McConnell, & McEvoy, 1992).

In an attempt to understand why persons with developmental disabilities have difficulty establishing social relationships with their peers, several lines of investigation have evolved. The notion of social competence and the part it plays in peer acceptance have been investigated in some depth. Other issues that may relate to the limited social interactions of persons with disabilities include rejection of children with different appearances and attribution theory.

1. **Social competence.** Social competence has been defined from both cognitive and behavioral perspectives. The cognitive definition of social competence focuses on a child's knowledge of social relationships and awareness of his or her own goals in interpersonal interactions (Shure, 1981). In contrast, a behavioral approach to social competence evaluates a child's actions in a social context, rather than the child's knowledge of what those actions should be (Putellaz & Gottman, 1982; Strain, Odom, & McConnell, 1984). Various methods have been used to evaluate social competence. Perhaps the most comprehensive method, performance evaluation, is based on the concept that interpersonal competence is best identified by a summary of judgments made by those having the opportunity to engage socially with the individual (Odom & McConnell, 1985). By incorporating the judgment of people who interact with the child in a variety of settings, a broader scope of social competence is elicited that allows for more exact remedial strategies.

2. **Social interaction.** Studying relationships through a focus on the social competence of children with disabilities tends to ignore the interactional nature of relationships. Research on friendships in children indicates that children seek out as friends peers who look like themselves (Corsaro, 1985; Raup, 1985; Strain, 1984). Strain (1985) studied the presence of social and nonsocial behaviors in high and low rated preschool children with disabilities. He found that several nonsocial variables, including physical attractiveness and athletic skill, accounted for as much variance in sociometric ratings as did several social behaviors, such as the frequency of negative initiations and the probability that participants would respond positively to positive social initiations. Strain concluded that variation in sociometric ratings could not be attributed to social behavior alone, but depended equally upon ability and appearance variables.

Hubbard and Coie (1994) discussed the role of emotion in peer relationships and its contribution to children's popularity. Based on research bridging children's popularity with the ability to read emotions, the authors suggest that regulation of emotions, emotional display rules, and sympathetic responding are relevant emotional factors in children's social relationships. The capability of children with developmental disabilities, particularly autism, to understand facial expressions and emotions in others, has had limited study (Baron-Cohen, 1988; Loveland & Tunali, 1991; Prior, Dahlstrom, & Squires, 1990).

3. **The impact of labels.** The effect of labels on the perception children without disabilities have toward their

45

peers with disabilities has been studied (Bromfield, Weisz, & Messer, 1986; Elam & Sigelman, 1983; Graffi & Minnes, 1988), as have the attitudes of persons with disabilities toward peers with similar disabilities (Gibbons, 1985; Gibbons & Kassin, 1982). Although outcomes are not totally consistent across investigations, some commonalities exist. Younger children (kindergarten through fourth grade) showed a progressive tendency for negative bias toward children with mental retardation labels. The association of mental retardation with such diagnoses as Down syndrome was not seen in kindergarten children, but did appear in third-graders (Graffi & Minnes, 1988). When asked to contrast their perceptions of a low-achieving child who was not mentally retarded with a low achieving child who was, older students (6th–12th grade) were more biased by the label and saw individual effort as less of a performance factor. The term "special dispensation" has been used to describe the belief that children with retardation are destined to low achievement because of their mental retardation. The work of Gibbons (1985) and Gibbons and Kassin (1982) demonstrates that persons who were themselves developmentally disabled had a similar disapproving bias toward other persons who were developmentally disabled, preferring friends who were not disabled.

4. **Reputational bias.** Hymel, Wagner, & Butler (1990) discuss preestablished reputational expectations within the peer group and how they can serve to maintain the rejected status of certain members. For example, Siperstein and Bak (1989) found status hierarchies in seven self-contained classes, indicating that persons with mental retardation in segregated groups also demonstrate potential reputational bias.

Social Interactions of Persons With Developmental Disabilities

In a series of studies investigating linguistic interactions between children without disabilities and their peers with mild, moderate, and severe disabilities, several characteristics of sociolinguistic behavior were detailed (Guralnick & Paul-Brown, 1977; 1980; 1984). Children without disabilities and children with mild disabilities adjusted their mean length of utterance and sentence complexity to the developmental level of children with moderate and severe disabilities in a comparable fashion. More adaptive strategies were demonstrated by children without disabilities when communicating with children having more extensive disabilities. The recent findings of Roberts, Burchinal, and Bailey (1994) were similar when they compared same age and mixed age preschool play groups including children with mild and moderate developmental delay. They found that mixed age groups resulted in better communicative interaction between children with disabilities and those without: Typical preschoolers in mixed age groups appeared better able to adjust their communication complexity and play with those who had disabilities.

Guralnick and Groom (1987) documented social interaction differences in preschool children with and without developmental disabilities. They found that children with mild disabilities engaged in more solitary play, received a declining level of positive responses to their social bids from peers, and appeared less interested in their peers than younger children without disabilities.

Cole (1986) aggregated data from two separate investigations involving social interactions between children with and without severe disabilities and found that children who had physical disabilities, in addition to severe cognitive delays, seemed to provide less reinforcement and elicit fewer social interactions from children without disabilities in research settings. These studies have served as stimuli for some of the intervention research we will review later.

Overall this research tells us that children with disabilities act differently in group settings than their peers without disabilities, but it does not tell us why. However, these descriptive studies of social interactions and relationships do provide a baseline of information against which to compare the effects of intervention. In the next section, we summarize research directed toward improving social relations between children with disabilities and their nondisabled peers.

Social Skills Intervention

One approach many researchers have taken to address concerns about social competence and relationships in children with disabilities is to teach social skills. Researchers tend not to debate the benefits of learning social skills, but the relationship between social skills and the ability to make friends has not been clearly established (Evans, Salisbury, Palombaro, Berryman, & Hollowood, 1992). Building a repertoire of social engagement skills, such as making eye contact, responding to and initiating interactions, or taking turns, is valuable to a child's social life. Whether or not competency in these skills or others furthers the capacity to make and keep friends remains to be demonstrated.

Segregated Versus Integrated Environments

A number of researchers have compared the types of social, play, and cognitive behaviors seen in children who attend segregated and integrated classrooms, primarily without specific intervention except setting (Beckman & Kohl, 1987; Cole & Meyer, 1991), while others have assessed the effects of intervention plus setting (Jenkins, Odom, & Speltz, 1989; Kennedy & Itkonen, 1994). With the shift to schools practicing inclusion, a brief overview of these studies is important.

For example, Gottlieb, Gampel, and Budoff (1975), Brinker (1985), and Beckman and Kohl (1987) compared differences in social behaviors in students with disabilities who were placed in either segregated or integrated settings. All researchers found increases in the prosocial behavior of students placed in the integrated settings, though only Beckman and Kohl examined the effects longitudinally. Similarly, Cole and Meyer (1991) and Evans et al. (1992) conducted longitudinal analyses of children with severe disabilities in inclusive classrooms. Cole and Meyer found no difference in academic achievement between segregated and integrated classrooms; but those who were integrated progressed in social skills, while those who were segregated appeared to regress. Evans et al. found that social interactions of the included children became more typical of that between most classmates. Finally, Buysse and Bailey (1993) reviewed 22 studies comparing integrated and segregated settings. The combined findings suggested that integrated settings facilitate social interactions in children with disabilities, but that more detailed analyses are necessary in order to understand how children contribute to each other's total development.

Peer Mediation

Some researchers have involved peers without disabilities in order to facilitate social learning by children with disabilities (e.g. Goldstein, Wickstrom, Hoyson, Jamieson, & Odom, 1988; Lefebvre & Strain, 1989; Sisson, Van Hasselt, Hersen, & Strain, 1985). Although designed to benefit children with disabilities, peer-mediated interventions also allow peers without disabilities to learn how to relate to children who are different from themselves. The work of Kohler and Fowler (1985) suggests that certain behaviors, such as invitations, are more likely to yield reinforcing materials and situations and the return of invitations later than are other behaviors, like amenities. The children without disabilities in their study were taught to reciprocate invitations as a reinforcement for the children with disabilities. Other examples can be found in the work of Chin-Perez et al. (1986), Haring and Lovinger (1989), and Wolfberg and Schuler (1993).

If social skills are to be maintained, they must be used and reinforced during daily routines. Brown and Odom (1994) discuss the value of teaching children with disabilities to access their natural and socially responsive community and of teaching all children that peer social exchanges are reinforcing. These salient points could be addressed by incorporating a child's natural environment as part of the intervention instead of attempting to transpose to it later. Goldstein and Ferrell (1987) and Goldstein and Wickstrom (1986) used a peer mediation strategy that incorporated actual classmates without disabilities in an integrated preschool. In their first study, only selected classmates without disabilities were involved. The second study expanded training to all classmates without disabilities, so that the group of students who were peer mediators were also

classroom peers. Rewards for the number of successful engagements were given to both the peer mediators and the children with disabilities. By incorporating the natural environment (setting and peers) of the children with social limitations, it would seem logical that the potential for greater social gains over the long run could be improved, since the context in which social skills were developed was natural and would continue as a responsive environment.

Activity Mediums

While peer mediation alone has been the focus of many investigations, a number of researchers have combined this tool with a range of other activities and contingencies to enable or motivate the interaction of children with disabilities and their peers. Some examples of the modalities tapped include the following: group contingencies (Lefebvre & Strain, 1989; McConnell, Sisson, Cort, & Strain, 1991); activities specifically structured to increase group interaction (DeKleyn & Odom, 1989; Eichinger, 1990); cooperative learning class activities (Hunt, Staub, Alwell, & Goetz, 1994); communication via badges to indicate play activity choices (Jolly, Test, & Spooner, 1993); drama and social scripts (Goldstein et al., 1988; Loveland & Tunali, 1991; Miller, Rynders, & Schelein, 1993); different types of group interactions such as leisure activities, Circle of Friends, and peer tutoring (Cole, Vandercook, & Rynders, 1988; Kishi & Meyer, 1994; Murray-Seegart, 1989; Peck, Donaldson, & Pezzoli, 1990; Voeltz, 1980, 1982); and camp integration (Rynders, Schelein, & Mustonen, 1990). All of these studies report some level of success in changing the level of interaction between children with disabilities and their peers, and many report positive attitude changes by the typical peers.

Teacher Roles in Social Skills Training

In several qualitative studies of classrooms that included children with severe disabilities, teachers reported that part of their role was to foster positive social interactions between peers and the students with disabilities (Giangreco, Dennis, Cloninger, Edelman, & Schattman, 1993; Janney, Snell, Beers, & Raynes, 1995b; Kozleski & Jackson, 1993; York, Vandercook, MacDonald, Neise-Neff, & Caughey, 1992). Qualitative analyses of interviews with 53 teachers and administrators in integrated schools by Janney and her colleagues (1995b) revealed that general education teachers viewed themselves as helping the integrated student feel they belonged to the school community. Teachers intentionally nurtured positive relationships among students through their own modeling: "By my accepting them and... talking to them just like the other students, and not making them different, the other kids will accept them like I did" (p. 436).

Maintenance and Generalization of Social Skills Training Benefits

Researchers, teachers, and parents have expressed concern about the carryover of learned social behaviors from the research setting to real life situations. More studies have attempted to see if the skills being developed generalize to other settings or classmates *during* the investigation rather than *after* the intervention has ceased. However, both lines of information are needed to help evaluate the effectiveness of social skills training and modify programs as necessary.

Brown and Odom (1994) describe several tactics of training that promote generalization and maintenance of social skill outcomes, including the use of many peers to mediate, intervention methods that are not obvious (intermittent or delayed reinforcement, reinforcement of spontaneous skill use, etc.), and "loose" or natural training conditions (teaching in the actual play settings, among classmates, during routine activities). There is ample confirmation that if little attention is given to the advancement of social skill retention and transfer in children with disabilities, it will not occur.

In one of the few long-term efforts at evaluating maintenance of social skills intervention, Storey, Danko, Strain, and Smith (1992) assessed changes in preschoolers' social interactions a year after intervention. They discussed several methodological issues that come into play when attempting to measure treatment maintenance, among them continuity of context and ecology factors, maturation, and the need for comprehensive dependent variables to measure complex issues like social change. Chandler, Lubeck, and Fowler (1992) reviewed 45 studies where preschool social skills training was the focus and found that only 14 studies (31%) achieved generalization of the target skills to settings outside the experimental setting, while 8 studies (17%) reported some generalization (some target skills in some children to some test settings). The ability to sustain and develop a broader repertoire of social skills and social interactions hinges on a number of factors, including the child's ability to use the information learned, opportunities to practice skills learned, and environmental responsiveness to the child over time.

The Relationship Between Social Skills Interventions and Quality of Life

Several social skills intervention studies describe the establishment of friendships as a result of the intervention; these descriptions occur in the discussion and are not presented as measured findings (Cole, 1986; Cole & Meyer, 1991; Evans et al., 1992; Miller et al., 1993; Rynders et al., 1990; Wolfberg & Schuler, 1993). Friendship typically is not assessed as an dependent variable. An underlying assumption of the work we have reviewed appears to be that friendships will result when children with disabilities achieve certain levels of social interactions, yet our understanding of what variables contribute to such relationships is incomplete at best. Quality of life entails many issues, as the chapters in this volume indicate. If social acceptance and friendship are to be part of the life we visualize for persons with disabilities in our society, do not our research efforts need to reflect this goal? While social skills logically may seem part of building relationships, efforts to date have revealed that children with mental retardation have not been able to generalize well the skills they have been taught. Yet from anecdotal evidence in some investigations, a few friendships on some level seem to have evolved in spite of barriers to their generalization. According to Furman and Robbins (1985), it is pointless to argue which positive social relationships are more important, friendships or general relationships, of which many types exist. All have value and contribute to one's quality of life. The point is that research addressing some types of relationships (e.g., instances of reciprocal social interactions, entry into ongoing play groups) does not automatically contribute to what we know about friendship. Perhaps it is time to rethink the approach to social skills research. Much has been learned in the process of such work, but has thinking been so focused on certain types of social interactions that others, specifically friendship, have not been addressed in detail?

We have learned much from the social skills research that can be transposed to the classroom. Table 3.1 sets forth seven recommendations for facilitating social relationships in schools. Each recommendation is expanded upon next.

1. **Teach social skills in context.** Most important in our understanding of the literature is that teaching social skills through the medium of peers has become accepted practice and has benefits for both groups. The expectation that reciprocal relationships can be taught in isolation or through adults is no longer viable. Teaching social skills in context promotes learning under realistic conditions, which in turn enables retention and advances generalization.

2. **Teach interaction partners.** Interactions are bidirectional; just as children with mental retardation need an array of social skills, children without disabilities need to be prepared for engagements with

---

Table 3.1
Strategies for Facilitating Social Relationships in Schools

1. Teach social skills in context, through the medium of peers.

2. Teach interaction partners.

3. Socially validate skill selection with peers.

4. Teach children to deal with rejection.

5. Begin integration early.

6. Interventions that promote horizontal (equity) rather than vertical (authoritarian) relationships facilitate "friendlier" interactions.

7. Intervention strategies need to be mutually enjoyable.

children having special challenges. To only teach children with disabilities negates the role of nondisabled peers and ignores their concerns and their contributions. Nondisabled peers appear to benefit from ongoing "peer support" discussions regarding their peers with disabilities; such discussions tap their ideas on ways to support their peers with disabilities whose behavior may differ markedly from their own and also involve them in providing that support (Van Dyke, Stallings, & Colley, 1995). The variation among children who do not have disabilities has been touched upon in the literature as well. Not all children are successful in dealing with peers who have disabilities. Finding this in research settings reminds us that this will also be true in school environments.

3. **Socially validate skill selection with peers.** The procedures of Chin-Perez et al. (1986) queried the peers of those with disabilities as to what social skills would be important to them. Adult decisions regarding peer group norms are likely to be less accurate. Ensuring acceptance of children with special needs into the lives of their peers necessitates understanding what is important to this group socially and planning interventions accordingly.

4. **Teach children to deal with rejection.** Children with disabilities need to be prepared for real world responses to their social efforts. (Haring & Lovinger, 1989). For example, more than 50% of the attempts of nondisabled preschoolers to enter ongoing peer activities were unsuccessful (Corsato, 1981). If this is typical of children without disabilities, children with disabilities also must learn how to deal with rejection of their bids to

join peer groups. Salisbury et al. (1989) describe behaviors observed in children with disabilities as efforts at communication, noting that the teachers and students around them see such attempts as aggressive acts. While a certain level of behavioral disparity can be explained and excused, children with disabilities often need to learn alternative behaviors that are acceptable by peer standards.

5. **Begin integration early.** Starting integration in the preschool years when children are most adaptable makes acceptance of individual differences easier. Building a concept of community, an important step in facilitating acceptance of peers with atypical behaviors, is easier when the differences do not appear so great. The idea that each person has strengths to offer the school community and benefits by being appreciated for these aspects of self is important when attempting to build relationships.

6. **Promote horizontal relationships.** Interventions that promote horizontal rather than vertical relationships seem to facilitate "friendlier" interactions. The comparison of peer tutoring and Circle of Friends programs (Cole et al., 1988) demonstrated some of these differences. When children without disabilities were put in a teaching position, they tended to assume a more authoritative role. By contrast, the Circle of Friends intervention focused on sharing, enjoying play activities, and reciprocity, and, as a result, produced more parallel interactions between children. Such outcomes suggest that the nature of the intervention will predict to some degree the type of social relationship that will evolve. Both kinds of

programs facilitate interactions, but choices about kinds of intervention need to be structured to the outcome desired: teaching/helping, social skill, or friendship.

7. **Use mutually enjoyable intervention strategies.** Researchers have put considerable thought into the medium they use to promote interactions. No one type of activity seems to offer benefit over others, but variety appears to be key for eliciting participation and promoting generalization. Another consideration is the carry-over of games and play strategies to actual peer cultures. Children with disabilities need to learn the games and know the interests of their peers without disabilities. Incorporating peer preferences into interventions may help with generalization and affect mutual enjoyment of interaction.

Rynders et al. (1990) suggest reevaluating our notion of friendship from one that transcends all parts of both partners' lives to a less lofty plane. They propose that the abilities of persons without disabilities to enjoy those who are very different from themselves and to display feelings of respect for small accomplishments are valuable attainments. As Evans and his colleagues (1992) demonstrated, interactions of peers with children in their classes who had more extensive support needs were "invariably positive," but were often not traditionally reciprocal because of the many differences partners had in communication, thinking ability, and movement (p. 211). Rather than expecting in-depth, long-term friendships to come from all intervention efforts, a more appropriate goal might be mutual enjoyment between partners in regular engagements.

Schools as a Supportive Environment for Social Relations

Attending schools with peers who display appropriate social abilities can have a positive influence on children with disabilities (Buysse & Bailey, 1993; Cole & Meyer, 1991); but whether or not such children get into schools and classrooms with their nondisabled peers depends on a myriad of factors. Part-time membership in a general education classroom, particularly for younger children, may not have the benefits that full-time membership has (Schnorr, 1990). Mere placement in general education classes without needed individualized supports also may be nonbeneficial (Gottlieb, 1981). The quality of the opportunities for social interaction (as well as for academic learning) is influenced by numerous factors related to the presence of individualized and appropriate special education supports that enable success in the integrated setting.

Therefore, the last section of this chapter discusses factors that affect whether schools become supportive environments for the development of social skills and relationships between children with disabilities and their peers. First, we will address the ways in which special education services are delivered to children and the related barriers these service delivery models impose. Second, we will touch upon inclusive schools, their characteristics and staff roles, and how they differ from schools where special education is primarily offered as pull-out services.

Placement: School and Classroom Options

According to the Individuals with Disabilities Education Act (IDEA), placement issues should be decided in logical sequence after a child is determined eligible for special education, and after an individualized educational plan (IEP) has been designed by the student's educational team. Also, according to the mainstreaming requirement of IDEA, schools are prohibited from placing students with disabilities "outside the regular classroom if educating the child in the regular classroom with supplementary aids and support services can be achieved satisfactorily" (Oberti v. Board of Education of Clementon School District, p. 3).

For students with disabilities, the child's special education label, IEP, and placement choice impact directly upon the opportunity to be around nondisabled peers, a context essential to learning relevant social skills and developing supportive social relationships. Specifically, these decisions determine the school and classroom to which students are assigned, the amount of time they spend in school around peers, the means by which special education services are delivered to students in that school, and the amounts and types of support services.

Placement decisions concerning both the school and the classroom(s) a student will attend are often intertwined. Several placement options currently exist. Students may attend their *neighborhood or "home" school* and be members of general education classrooms with nondisabled peers on a part- or full-time basis. The neighborhood school is defined as the school they would have attended had they not been diagnosed as having a disability. Placement also may be in an *integrated school,* attended by both typical students and students with mental retardation, but which may not be the student's neighborhood school. Integrated placements typically involve clustering students by disability categories to receive

special education services in a *resource room* on a part-time basis or in a *self-contained classroom* on a full-time basis. Integrated placements require students with disabilities to travel away from their siblings and neighborhood peers, a practice that can make the development of relationships and peer support networks very difficult. A third school option is the *separate school,* public or private, where individuals with disabilities are the only students.

Analyses of federal 1989-90 school placement data indicate that persons with mental retardation are more frequently placed in restrictive separate classrooms (61%) than in regular classrooms (7%) or resource rooms (20%) (U.S. Department of Education, 1991). Approximately 12% of students with mental retardation were placed in separate schools, public or private, a figure that is more than double that for all other students with disabilities. The practice of placing students in separate classes and separate schools is highly inconsistent from state to state for students with mental retardation. For example, only 3 states placed more than 50% of their students in resource rooms, enabling them to spend part of their day in the regular classroom; yet, in 31 states, the resource placement was used with less than 25% of students with the same classification, with most students with mental retardation attending self-contained classes. The proportion of more restrictive placements being recommended for persons with labels of mental retardation is higher than for children with labels of learning disabilities, speech impairments, and emotional disturbance.

Service-Delivery Models and Their Characteristics

How children with special education needs obtain these services is highly dependent upon placement, though the quality of the service may be more related to the school district and its socioeconomic status (Alabama Coalition for Equity, Inc., v. Hunt, 1993). Service delivery therefore affects the capability of an educational setting for fostering positive social interactions and academic gains. Self-contained classrooms cannot provide regular opportunity for social interactions, while inclusive and integrated models can.

1. **Inclusive option.** In the inclusive service delivery option, students with disabilities are members of general education classes and the needed special education supports are delivered there. The special education teacher fills more of a consulting teacher role: visiting the classroom, often team-teaching or teaching a group or child alongside the classroom teacher, planning and problem-solving with the general education teacher, and designing and implementing accommodations and curriculum adaptations so the student will benefit from classroom activities, while also achieving his or her IEP objectives (Janney, Snell, Beers, & Raynes, 1995a; Snell & Eichner, 1989).

2. *Pull-out option.* "Pull-out" options refer to the delivery of special education services outside of the general education classroom either in a resource setting or a self-contained class, or pulling the child from a classroom placement to an isolated setting for various special education therapies. The majority of pull-out special education programs involve speech services; a far smaller number of students receive services from other therapists (occupational, physical, and vision therapy). The resource room also provides special education services away from the general education classroom. In this option, the special education teacher's role may be traditional and noncollaborative, particularly since it becomes difficult to operate both as a special classroom teacher and as a consulting teacher. However, this option has numerous variations on how much time is spent in each setting, on whether the special education teacher facilitates the student's accommodation in the regular classroom, and on whether the special education teacher serves more than a single category of students (cross-categorical programs). Research on the efficacy of the resource room appears inconclusive due to methodological difficulties and the broad nature of the term (Wiederholt & Chamberlain, 1989).

3. **Self-contained option.** A final service delivery option is that the student's placement is primarily or totally in a self-contained class where classmates also have the same disability label. Students may be integrated either for less academic classes (physical education, music, etc.), for school activities (lunch, recess, assemblies), for neither, or for both. The special education teacher's role is highly influenced by the type of service delivery system used in the school: integrated, pull-out, or self-contained.

Many schools currently try to offer a *continuum of services* or placements, which means that parents may select the service delivery model they want for their child. But in reality this practice of offering all models to all age and disability groups is practically and economically difficult. It is difficult to have the special education staff both clustered for categorical programs and distributed for providing services in every neighborhood school. Inclusive programs require that special education teachers fill consultative and team-teaching roles with adequate time to collaborate with each teacher having a student on his or her caseload and assist in the provision of needed special education supports. Typically, such teachers will have training across several categories with an emphasis on mild disabilities (learning disabilities, behavior disorders, and mental retardation with intermittent or limited support needs) or on more severe disabilities (mental retardation with extensive or pervasive support needs, multiple handicaps). Teachers with training in sensory disabilities often fill itinerant roles and work with both the students who need them and their teachers. Both school and transportation schedules need to be matched to the service model for special education, thus making change more difficult. Special education teachers who try to operate a resource or self-contained room all day and also support students who are mainstreamed part- or full-time do not have time to meet all the demands of their job; relying on paraprofessionals to provide most of the mainstreamed support with minimal special education teacher collaboration undermines the quality of the services.

Factors Influencing Integrated Programs

The options for special education placement and service delivery used by schools are highly influenced by sociopolitical factors both internal and external to the school system (Peck, Furman, & Helmstetter, 1992). In the last decade many schools have been focused on "restructuring" and "school reform," despite the often ambiguous meaning of the terms.

1. **Initiating school change.**
   Involved in all reform efforts have been concerns about the quality of education and its learning outcomes, often measured as scores on standardized achievement tests. For some systems, reform has meant meeting the needs of a more diverse group of students; for other schools, the main issue has been distributing decision-making away from a central office focus and more evenly across the system. In many cases, these two issues—diversity and the locus of decision-making—go hand in hand. Diversity has often encompassed multicultural groups, nontraditional family structures, increases in students from families below the poverty line, and disability. In agreement with courts, many schools have decided that diverse student groups need to be integrated, not separated for their education. Laws like IDEA and the Americans with Disabilities Act (ADA) have supported this interpretation, though not without controversy. Change in education not only is rarely welcomed by educators, it appears to require more effort than maintaining the status quo.

   Reforming the ways in which schools provide special education is very complex (Peck et al., 1992). Several external factors at the state level influence these changes. These factors include the state's regulations on least restrictive environment, the special education funding formula used to reimburse school systems for part of their special education costs, and the state's capability to monitor schools' special education programs and provide them with technical assistance. Funding formulas have been cited as significant barriers to the placement of students with disabilities in general education because schools often receive more funds for restrictive placements than for inclusive placements (Parrish, 1994).

As we noted earlier, neighboring school systems operating under the same state regulations can have vastly different records on the restrictive versus inclusive nature of their special education programs. Perhaps this is another way of saying that factors internal to the school system impact heavily on change in special education. Internal factors include the school's resources, its philosophy on serving students with disabilities, and its history with special education. Decentralizing school decision-making appears to be more conducive to a change to inclusive practices, although having a superintendent or central office administrator who understands the benefits of integrated special education may be an essential positive spark to initiating such change (Fullan, 1991). Schools need financing policies that do not act as incentives to restrictive placements, but that guarantee accessible services, ensure accountability, and allow the flexibility needed to serve children in the least restrictive environment (McLaughlin & Warren, 1992).

2. **Sustaining integrated programs.** Just as there is evidence indicating that added effort is required to implement integrated special education programs, it also appears that effort is required to sustain them (Peck et al., 1992). Surviving programs more often are planned with input from all stakeholders and with compatibility between the design of special education instruction and the routines and practices of the child development setting in which they are implemented. Peck and his colleagues also

noted differences in the outcomes of programs that lasted versus those that were discontinued. In surviving programs, child improvements were consistently described and adult relationships were primarily positive. In nonsurviving programs, conflict and dissatisfaction between adults was common, with differences occurring between special educators and child development professionals around philosophy, time, activities, and programs for the children with special needs. Peck et al. (1992) identified a major difference in the ideological perspective of integrated preschools that survived:

The value of integration did not depend on peer modeling processes alone, but also on the social benefits of inclusion, and on the positive value of accepting and supporting diversity in all the children involved.

(p. 198)

Future research will need to determine whether these characteristics, which Peck and his colleagues found in preschool programs, are the same as those found in schools.

Summary

Social well-being, defined primarily through one's interpersonal relationships with friends and relatives, is often regarded as an essential aspect of quality of life. The social relationships of children and adults with mental retardation appear to be less successful than those of their nondisabled peers. However, attending schools with peers who display appropriate social abilities can have a positive influence on children with mental retardation. Although mere presence may not be adequate for mastery of social skills by these students, social skills cannot be learned in segregated settings. Along with peers, teachers have been shown to play critical roles in fostering positive relationships between persons with mental retardation and their classmates. The literature reviewed in this chapter is rich with findings pertinent to this teaching-learning process. Overarching the use of social interventions, however, is the sociopolitical reality of the school system and the practices used to place students with disabilities, to deliver special education services to them, and to support their individualized needs in school. Schools need to examine and change the separate nature of special education services in light of the least restrictive environment doctrine of IDEA and ADA's focus on equity for persons with disabilities. Factors at the state level that consistently act as barriers to change are funding formulas, eligibility and placement regulations, and categorical teacher certification requirements. At the local level, the absence of inclusive school models and incentives for change often means that things tend to remain the same.

References

Alabama Coalition for Equity, Inc. v. Hunt, CVNO. 90-883-R, CVNO. 91-0117-R, March 31, 1993.

Baron-Cohen, S. (1988). Social and pragmatic deficits in autism: Cognitive or affective? *Journal of Autism and Developmental Disorders, 18,* 379–402.

Beckman, P.J., & Kohl, F.L. (1987). Interactions of preschoolers with and without handicaps in integrated and segregated settings: A longitudinal study. *Mental Retardation, 25,* 5–11.

Beckman, P.J., & Lieber, J. (1992). Parent-child social relationships and peer social competence of preschool children with disabilities. In S. L. Odom, S. R. McConnell, & M. A. McEvoy (Eds.), *Social competence of young children with disabilities* (pp. 65–92). Baltimore: Brookes.

Brinker, R.P. (1985). Interactions between severely mentally retarded students and other students in integrated and segregated public school settings. *American Journal of Mental Deficiency, 89,* 587–597.

Bromfield, R., Weisz, J.R., & Messer, T. (1986). Children's judgment and attributions in response to the "mentally retarded" label: A developmental approach. *Journal of Abnormal Psychology, 95,* 81–87.

Brown, W.H., & Odom, S.L. (1994). Strategies and tactics for promoting generalization and maintenance of young children's social behavior. *Research in Developmental Disabilities, 15,* 99–118.

Buysse, V., & Bailey, D.B., Jr. (1993). Behavioral and developmental outcomes in young children with disabilities in integrated and segregated settings: A review of comparative studies. *Journal of Special Education, 26,* 434–461.

Chandler, L.K., Lubeck, R.C., & Fowler, S.A. (1992). Generalization and maintenance of preschool children's social skills: A critical review and analysis. *Journal of Applied Behavior Analysis, 25,* 415–428.

Chin-Perez, G., Hartman, D., Sook-Park, H., Sacks, S., Wershing, A., & Gaylord-Ross, R. (1986). Maximizing social contact for secondary students with severe handicaps. *Journal of the Association for Persons with Severe Handicaps, 11,* 118–124.

Cole, D. A. (1986). Facilitating play in children's peer relationships: Are we having fun yet? *American Educational Research Journal, 23,* 201–215.

Cole, D.A., & Meyer, L.H. (1991). Social integration and severe disabilities: A longitudinal analysis of child outcome. *Journal of Special Education, 25,* 340–351.

Cole, D.A., Vandercook, T., & Rynders, J. (1988). Comparison of two peer interaction programs: Children with and without severe disabilities. *American Educational Research Journal, 25,* 415–439.

Corsaro, W.A. (1981). Friendships in nursery school. In S. Asher & J. Gottman (Eds.), *The development of children's friendships* (pp. 207–241). New York: Cambridge University Press.

Corsaro, W.A. (1985). *Friendship and peer culture in the early years.* Norwood, NJ: Ablex Publishing Corp.

DeKleyn, M., & Odom, S.L. (1989). Activity structure and social interactions with peers in developmentally integrated play groups. *Journal of Early Intervention, 13,* 342–352.

Eichinger, J. (1990). Goal structure efforts on social interaction: Nondisabled and disabled elementary students. *Exceptional Children, 56,* 408–416.

Elam, J.J., & Sigelman, C.K. (1983). Developmental difference in reactions to children labeled mentally retarded. *Journal of Applied Developmental Psychology, 4,* 303–315.

Evans, I.M., Salisbury, C.L., Palombaro, M.M., Berryman, J., & Hollowood, T.M. (1992). Peer interactions and social acceptance of elementary-age children with severe disabilities in an inclusive school. *Journal of the Association for Persons with Severe Handicaps, 17,* 205–212.

Felce, D., & Perry J. (1995). Quality of life: Its definition and measurement. *Research in Developmental Disabilities, 16,* 51–74.

Fullan, M.G. (1991). *The new meaning of educational change* (2nd ed.). New York: Teachers College Press.

Furman, W., & Robbins, R. (1985). What's the point: Issues in the selection of treatment objectives. In B.H. Schneider, K.H. Rubin, & J.E. Ledingham (Eds.), *Children's peer relations: Issues in assessment and intervention* (pp. 41–56). New York: Springer-Verlag.

Giangreco, M.F., Dennis, R., Cloninger, C., Edelman, S., & Schattman, R. (1993). "I've counted Jon": Transformational experiences of teachers educating students with disabilities. *Exceptional Children, 59,* 359–372.

Gibbons, F.X. (1985). A socio-psychological perspective on developmental disabilities. *Journal of Social and Clinical Psychology, 3,* 391–404.

Gibbons, F.X., & Kassin, S.M. (1982). Children's behavioral expectations of their retarded peers. *Journal of Applied Developmental Psychology, 3,* 85–104.

Goldstein, H., & Ferrell, D. (1987). Augmenting communicative interaction between handicapped and nonhandicapped preschool children. *Journal of Speech and Hearing Disorders, 52,* 200–211.

Goldstein, H., & Wickstrom, S. (1986). Peer intervention effects on communicative interaction among handicapped and nonhandicapped preschoolers. *Journal of Applied Behavior Analysis, 19,* 209–214.

Goldstein, H., Wickstrom, S., Hoyson, M., Jamieson, B., & Odom, S.L. (1988). Effects of sociodramatic script training on social and communicative interaction. *Education and Treatment of Children, 11,* 97–117.

Gottlieb, J. (1981). Mainstreaming: Fulfilling the promise? *American Journal of Mental Deficiency, 87,* 115–126.

Gottlieb, J., Gampel, D.H., & Budoff, M. (1975). Classroom behavior of retarded children before and after integration into regular class. *Journal of Special Education, 9,* 307–315.

Graffi, S., & Minnes, P.M. (1988). Attitudes of primary school children toward the physical appearance and labels associated with Down syndrome. *American Journal of Mental Deficiency, 93,* 28–35.

Guralnick, M.J., & Groom, J.M. (1987). The peer relations of mildly delayed and nonhandicapped preschool children in mainstreamed play groups. *Child Development, 58,* 1556-1572.

Guralnick, M.J., & Paul-Brown, D. (1977). The nature of verbal interaction among handicapped and nonhandicapped preschool children. *Child Development, 48,* 254-260.

Guralnick, M.J., & Paul-Brown, D. (1980). Functional and discourse analyses of nonhandicapped preschool children's speech to handicapped children. *American Journal of Mental Deficiency, 84,* 444-454.

Guralnick, M.J., & Paul-Brown, D. (1984). Communicative adjustment during behavior-request episodes among children at different developmental levels. *Child Development, 55,* 911-919.

Haring, T.G., & Lovinger, L. (1989). Promoting social interaction through teaching generalized play initiation responses to preschool children with autism. *Journal of the Association for Persons with Severe Handicaps, 14,* 58-67.

Hubbard, J.A., & Coie, J.D. (1994). Emotional correlates of social competence in children's peer relationships. *Merrill-Palmer Quarterly, 40,* 1-20.

Hunt, P., Staub, D., Alwell, M., & Goetz, L. (1994). Achievement by all students within the context of cooperative learning groups. *Journal of the Association for Persons with Severe Handicaps, 19,* 290-301.

Hymel, S., Wagner, E., & Butler, E.J. (1990). Reputational bias: View from the peer group. In S.R. Asher & J.D. Coie (Eds.), *Peer rejection in childhood* (pp. 156-186). Cambridge, England: Cambridge University Press.

Janney, R.E., Snell, M.E., Beers, M.K., & Raynes, M. (1995a). Integrating students with moderate and severe disabilities into general education classes: Advice from teachers and administrators. *Exceptional Children, 61,* 425-439.

Janney, R.E., Snell, M.E., Beers, M.K., & Raynes, M. (1995b). Integrating students with moderate and severe disabilities: Classroom teachers' beliefs and attitudes about implementing educational change. *Educational Administration Quarterly, 31,* 86-114.

Jenkins, J.R., Odom, S.L., & Speltz, M.L. (1989). Effects of social integration on preschool children with handicaps. *Exceptional Children, 55,* 420-428.

Jolly, A.C., Test, D.W., & Spooner, F. (1993). Using badges to increase initiations of children with severe disabilities in a play setting. *Journal of the Association for Persons with Severe Handicaps, 18,* 46-51.

Kennedy, C.H., & Itkonen, T. (1994). Some effects of regular class participation on the social contacts and social networks of high school students with severe disabilities. *Journal of the Association for Persons with Severe Handicaps, 19,* 1-10.

Kishi, G.S., & Meyer, L.H. (1994). What children report and remember: A six-year follow-up of the effects of social contact between peers with and without severe disabilities. *Journal of the Association for Persons with Severe Handicaps, 19,* 277-289.

Kohler, F.W., & Fowler, S.A. (1985). Training prosocial behaviors to young children: An analysis of reciprocity with untrained peers. *Journal of Applied Behavior Analysis, 18,* 187-200.

Kozleski, E.B., & Jackson, L. (1993). Taylor's story: Full inclusion in her neighborhood elementary school. *Exceptionality, 4,* 153-175.

Lefebvre, D., & Strain, P.S. (1989). Effects of a group contingency on the frequency of social interactions among autistic and nonhandicapped preschool children: Making LRE efficacious. *Journal of Early Intervention, 13,* 329-341.

Loveland, K.A., & Tunali, B. (1991). Social scripts for conversational interactions in autism and Down syndrome. *Journal of Autism and Developmental Disorders, 21,* 177-186.

McConnell, S.R., Sisson, L.A., Cort, C. A., & Strain, P.S. (1991). Effects of social skill training and contingency management on reciprocal interaction of preschool children with behavioral handicaps. *Journal of Special Education, 24,* 473-495.

McLaughlin, M.J., & Warren, S.H. (1992). *Issues and options in restructuring schools and special education programs.* College Park: University of Maryland and Westat, Inc.

Miller, H., Rynders, J.E., & Schelein, S.J. (1993). Drama: A medium to enhance social interaction between students with and without mental retardation. *Mental Retardation, 31,* 228-233.

Murray-Seegart, C. (1989). *Nasty girls, thugs, and humans like us: Social relations between severely disabled and nondisabled students in high school.* Baltimore: Brookes.

Oberti v. Board of Education of the Borough of Clementon School District, 995 F.2d 1204 83 Ed.Law Rep. 1009 (3rd Cir. 1993).

Odom, S.L., & McConnell, S.R. (1985). A performance-based conceptualization of social competence of handicapped preschool children: Implications for assessment. *Topics in Early Childhood Special Education, 4,* 1-19.

Odom, S. L., McConnell, S. R., & McEvoy, M. A. (1992). Peer-related social competence and its significance for young children with disabilities. In S. L. Odom, S. R. McConnell, & M. A. McEvoy (Eds.), *Social competence of young children with disabilities* (pp. 1-35). Baltimore: Brookes.

Parker, J. G., & Asher, S. R. (1987). Peer relations and later personal adjustment: Are low-accepted children at risk? *Psychological Bulletin, 102,* 357-389.

Parrish, T. B. (1994, October). *Removing incentives for restrictive placements.* Policy paper #4. Palo Alto, CA: Center for Special Education Finance.

Peck, C., Donaldson, J., & Pezzoli, M. (1990). Some benefits nonhandicapped adolescents perceive for themselves with peers who have severe handicaps. *Journal of the Association for Persons with Severe Handicaps, 15,* 241-249.

Peck, C. A., Furman, G. C., & Helmstetter, H. (1992). Integrated early childhood programs: Research on the implementation of change in organizational contexts. In C. A. Peck, S. L. Odom & D. D. Bricker (Eds.), *Integrating young children with disabilities into community programs* (pp. 180-209). Baltimore: Brookes.

Prior, M., Dahlstrom, B., & Squires, T. L. (1990). Autistic children's knowledge of thinking and feeling states in other people. *Journal of Child Psychology and Psychiatry, 31,* 587-601.

Putellaz, M., & Gottman, J. (1982). Conceptualizing social competence in children. In P. Karoly & J. Steffin (Eds.), *Improving children's competence: Advances in child behavioral analysis and therapy, Vol. 1* (pp. 1-37). Lexington, MA: D.C. Heath.

Raup, C. (1985). Approaching special needs children's social competence from the perspective of early friendships. *Topics in Early Childhood Special Education, 4,* 32-46.

Roberts, J. E., Burchinal, M. R., & Bailey, D. B. (1994). Communication among preschoolers with and without disabilities in same-age and mixed-age classes. *American Journal on Mental Retardation, 99,* 231-249.

Rynders, J.E., Schelein, S.J., & Mustonen, T. (1990). Integrating children with severe disabilities for intensified outdoor education: Focus on feasibility. *Mental Retardation, 28,* 7-14.

Salisbury, C., Britzman, D., & Kahn, J. (1989). Using qualitative methods to assess the social-communicative competence of young handicapped children. *Journal of Early Intervention, 13,* 153-164.

Schnorr, R.F. (1990). "Peter? He comes and goes . . .": First graders' perspectives on a part-time mainstream student. *Journal of the Association for Persons with Severe Handicaps, 15,* 231-240.

Shure, M.B. (1981). Social competence as a problem-solving skill. In J. Wine & M. Syme (Eds.), *Social competence* (pp. 158-185). New York: Guilford Press.

Siperstein, G.N., & Bak, J.J. (1989). Social relationships of adolescents with moderate mental retardation. *Mental Retardation, 27,* 5-10.

Sisson, L.A., Van Hasselt, V.B., Hersen, M., & Strain, P.S. (1985). Peer interventions: Increasing social behaviors in multihandicapped children. *Behavior Modification, 9,* 293-321.

Snell, M.E., & Eichner, S.J. (1989). Integration for students with profound disabilities. In F. Brown & D.H. Lehr (Eds.), *Persons with profound disabilities: Issues and practices* (pp. 109-138). Baltimore: Brookes.

Storey, K., Danko, C., Strain, P.S., & Smith, D. J. (1992). A follow-up of social skills instruction for preschoolers with developmental delays. *Education and Treatment of Children, 15,* 125-139.

Strain, P.S. (1984). Social behavior patterns of nonhandicapped and developmentally disabled friend pairs in mainstream schools. *Analysis and Intervention in Developmental Disabilities, 4,* 15-28.

Strain, P.S. (1985). Social and nonsocial determinants of acceptability in handicapped preschool children. *Topics in Early Childhood Special Education, 4,* 47-58.

Strain, P.S., Odom, S.L., & McConnell, S. (1984). Promoting social reciprocity of exceptional children: Identification, target behavior, selection, and intervention. *Remedial and Special Education, 5,* 21-28.

U.S. Department of Education. (1991). *To assure the free appropriate public education of all handicapped children: Thirteenth annual report of Congress on the implementation of the Education of the Handicapped Act.* Washington, DC: U.S. Department of Education, Office of Special Education and Rehabilitative Services.

Van Dyke, R., Stallings, M.A., & Colley, K. (1995). How to build an inclusive school community. *Phi Delta Kappan, 76,* 475-479.

Voeltz, L.M. (1980). Children's attitudes toward handicapped peers. *American Journal of Mental Deficiency, 84,* 455-464.

Voeltz, L.M. (1982). Effects of structured interactions with severely handicapped peers on children's attitudes. *American Journal of Mental Deficiency, 86,* 380-390.

Wiederholt, J.L., & Chamberlain, S.P. (1989). A critical analysis of resource programs. *Remedial and Special Education, 10*(6), 15-27.

Wolfberg, P J., & Schuler, A.L. (1993). Integrated play groups: A model for promoting the social and cognitive dimensions of play in children with autism. *Journal of Autism and Developmental Disorders, 23,* 467-489.

York, J., Vandercook, T., MacDonald, C., Neise-Neff, C., & Caughey, E. (1992). Feedback about integrating middle-school students with severe disabilities in general education classes. *Exceptional Children, 58,* 244-258.

Quality of Work Life for Persons with Disabilities: Emphasis on the Employee

William E. Kiernan and Joseph Marrone

Institute for Community Inclusion
Boston Children's Hospital

During the last decade there has been a growing awareness of the need to examine the impact that supports and services have upon the quality of life of persons with disabilities (Accreditation Council, 1992; Bradley, Ashbaugh, & Harder, 1984; Committee on Accreditation of Rehabilitation Facilities [CARF], 1994; Goode, 1989; Schalock, 1990). Addressing the needs of the employee and assuring that they are met not only through employee compensation plans but design of supportive work settings and development of a positive work culture have been areas of investigation and consideration by industry for more than two decades (Kahnweiler & Kahnweiler, 1992; Kiernan & Knutson, 1990; Loscocco & Roschelle, 1991; Shellenbarger, 1993). Service industries, recognizing the need to satisfy their customers, have developed many strategies to assess the level of satisfaction the customer has with the services provided.

This recognition of customer and employee needs has become a core issue for human service agencies and pro-grams supporting persons with disabilities over the past decade (Accreditation Council, 1992; CARF, 1994; Kiernan, Schalock, McGaughey, Lynch, & McNally, 1991). It is no longer sufficient to deliver a service and assume that the recipient's needs will be met simply by providing the service; there must also be ways of gauging the consumer's satisfaction. The passage of the Americans with Disabilities Act, the 1992 Rehabilitation Act Amendments, and the Individuals with Disabilities Education Act (IDEA) all have placed the issue of quality on the front burner (Boone & Stevens, 1991; Champney & Dzurec, 1992; Fabian, 1991; Flanagan, 1982; Kibele, 1988; Kiernan & Mank, 1994; Kozleski & Sands, 1992). Unfortunately, there is little data to date regarding the quality of work life for persons with disability (Kiernan & Schalock, in press).

This chapter reviews the concept of quality of work life (QWL) from both an industry and a disability perspective. The final section discusses policy and research implications of an enhanced quality of work life for persons with disabilities.

Overview of Quality of Work Life

The Concept of Quality of Work Life

Quality of work life is a concept and practical tool that has been discussed, examined, and debated by social scientists, psychologists, and the business world for more than 30 years (Beer & Walton, 1987; Braus, 1992; Faucheux, Amado, & Laurent, 1982; Loscocco & Roschelle, 1991; Nadler & Lawler, 1983; Sashkin & Burke, 1987; Seashore, 1975). Significant discussions continue as to what factors constitute quality of work life and how setting and personal attributes impact perceptions of QWL. Despite the attention QWL has received over the years, a divergent set of definitions and perspectives surrounding this phenomenon remains:

- Focusing on a person's job satisfaction as the key determinant (Flanagan, 1982; Loscocco & Roschelle, 1991; Zeffane, 1994).

- Increasing worker participation and control of the work environment (Havlovic, 1991; Stepp, 1985).

- Incorporating workers' personal needs with company role expectations (Kiernan & Knutson, 1990).

- Stressing the interaction of individual needs with the organizational and social dynamics of the workplace (Bowditch & Bouno, 1982; Sashkin & Burke, 1987).

A number of researchers have identified key variables that enhance QWL (Davis & Cherns, 1975; Gadon,

1984; Seashore, 1975; Taylor, 1987; Walton, 1975). For example, Walton (1975) identified eight key variables associated with a high quality of work life. It is clear from the variables summarized in Table 4.1 that QWL pertains not just to earnings and work space, but to a number of factors that impact on work directly and indirectly. Thus QWL is a complex set of factors that contribute to workers' sense that their contributions and involvement make a difference in the production of goods or delivery of services that are valued by society.

QWL is frequently viewed as a subset of quality of life (QOL). Most writers postulate connections between a person's overall life quality and characteristics of their working situation (Barnett, Marshall, & Singer, 1992; Bromet, Dew, & Parkinson, 1990; Galvin, 1986; George & Brief, 1990; Steiner & Truxillo, 1989), but some discount this connection, noting no clear relationship in the empirical literature (Loscocco & Roschelle, 1991). Nor, for that matter, have those who have asserted the connection been congruent as to the degree, intensity, or direction of such a relationship, should it exist. Debate as to a relationship between quality of life and QWL will continue into the next decade. However, for purposes of this chapter, the authors feel that there is a need to consider quality of life and QWL as separate issues and that a high level of quality in one area should not be taken as an indication of a high degree of quality in the other. Thus, this chapter's primary focus is on issues relating to QWL.

The authors' definition of QWL is an update on one developed earlier (Kiernan & Knutson, 1990).

QWL refers to the degree of an individual's satisfaction with his/her role, relationships, and

Table 4.1
Quality of Work Life Variables

Adequate and fair compensation

Safe and healthy working conditions
- reasonable hours
- minimized risk of injury or illness

Immediate opportunity to use and develop human capacities
- autonomy or self control in job
- range of skills and abilities used or learned
- knowledge of results of actions on job
- knowledge of entire task and meaningfulness of tasks
- is there opportunity to get involved in planning

Opportunity for continued growth and security
- development of one's capabilities
- possibility of using skills in the future
- advancement opportunities
- job or income level security

Social integration in the work organization
- freedom from prejudice
- equal opportunities
- rate of job mobility
- supportive primary work group
- sense of community beyond work group
- interpersonal openness

Constitutionalism in the work organization
- privacy
- free speech
- equity
- due process

Work and the total life space
- balanced role of work

Social relevance of work life
- social responsibility of the work organization

duties in the workplace. This satisfaction is predicated on a variety of factors affecting the individual including, but not limited to, personality variables, family expectations, social cultural norms, workplace culture, and concrete facets of the job within the setting where the duties are performed.

Job Satisfaction and Quality of Work Life

The quality of a person's work life is individually evaluated and subject to external influences. Some factors have been positively correlated with the job satisfaction component of QWL. These factors can be categorized as job characteristics, worker characteristics, and social context.

Some of the specific job characteristics include intrinsically interesting work (Braus, 1992), work congruent with actualization of professional goals, task variety (Zeffane, 1994), participation in decision-making (Fields & Thacker, 1992; Havlovic, 1991; Rossmiller, 1992), and autonomy on the job. Some of the characteristics of the workers studied included job tenure and age (Zeffane, 1994), past work experiences, ability to envision having a better job, and individual proclivities and dispositions. Social context factors reported include parental status (Barnett et al., 1992; Shellenbarger, 1993), marital status (Barnett et al., 1992), spouse's occupation, and networks in which the person participates. But, similar to the connection between quality of life and QWL, no consensus currently exists as to what critically influences or best enhances the quality of an individual's working life.

Quality of Work Life From the Industry Perspective

1. **Historical precedents.** Over the past 30 years, QWL has evolved through various definitional stages, each having contributed to the current conceptualization of the term (Bowditch & Bouno, 1982; Davis & Cherns, 1975; Sashkin & Burke, 1987). Academia and the business world have long been concerned with the psychology of the workplace, particularly focusing on worker attitudes and behaviors as they affect individual productivity and, correspondingly, the company's bottom line (Goode, 1989). Such issues have been addressed histori-cally under the concept of organiza-tional development (OD). The more recent focus on quality is an attempt to resolve the conflict between bottom-line and humanistic values in OD (Gadon, 1984; Kanter, Summers, & Stein, 1986; Sashkin & Burke, 1987). In response to this and other changes, QWL has evolved into an expansion of the business world's OD programs.

2. **Origin and development of QWL.** The term QWL was first used in the late 1960s, originating with General Motors and the United Auto Workers to describe workers' levels of job satisfaction. Irving Bluestone coined the term Quality of Work Life, which began as a variable expressing the level of worker satisfaction and developed into an approach and series of programs designed ulti-mately to increase worker productiv-ity (Goode, 1989). Labor-manage-ment cooperation guided the devel-opment and implementation of these early QWL efforts, resulting in workplaces where employees partici-pated in problem-solving and decision-making efforts to improve their work lives. In addition, manage-ment became more concerned with the individual's welfare, stressing positive interpersonal relations and overall improved working conditions (Bowditch & Bouno, 1982; Goode, 1989).

In the mid 1970s, the concept of QWL was instituted in companies not only to enhance bottom line productivity, but also to increase employees' identification, sense of belonging, and pride in their work (Davis & Cherns, 1975; Sashkin & Burke, 1987). Examples of these approaches include work teams, autonomous groups, job enrichment, and sociotechnical change (Charland, 1986; Gadon, 1984). These types of programs reflect the interaction of the bottom line, the employee, and society (Kanter et al., 1986; Modic, 1987; Sashkin & Burke, 1987; Taylor, 1987).

3. **Key concepts in QWL.** Three key concepts are manifest in QWL attitudes and approaches from the industry perspective: productivity and job satisfaction, participative management style, and flexibility in meeting individuals' needs (Sashkin & Burke, 1987).

Although the research is inconclu-sive, there is a prevailing belief within organizations that individuals who are highly satisfied with their jobs are more productive (Bowditch & Bouno, 1982; Loscocco & Roschelle, 1991). This is the funda-mental reason why management invests time, money, and energy towards improving the QWL of their employees. Productivity and job performance are often not presented as QWL aims, in order to prevent workers from perceiving that man-agement is merely trying to get more productivity out of them at no cost

(Sashkin & Burke, 1987). There has been some evidence showing that QWL efforts produce benefits including higher product quality, lower absenteeism, lower employee sabotage, fewer grievances, and good publicity (Goode, 1989).

Participative management style has been almost universally accepted as a significant QWL concept (Bowditch & Bouno, 1982; Davis & Cherns, 1975; Kolodny & van Beinum, 1983). The core of QWL is the opportunity for employees at all levels in the organization to have an impact on the work environment by participating in decision-making processes regarding the job, thereby enhancing their self-esteem and satisfaction (Bowditch & Bouno, 1982; Davis & Cherns, 1975). Development of decision-making mechanisms, such as work-management problem-solving committees or task forces, has been a common strategy to enhance QWL.

Flexibility is the benchmark in enhancing QWL for individual workers. Flexibility allows workers to customize their work spaces while respecting industry expectations. Additionally, it allows employees to balance their personal, family, and social responsibilities more effectively for improved overall quality of life (Gadon, 1984; Kanter et al., 1986; Sashkin & Burke, 1987). Because quality of work life means different things to different people, organizations increasingly are offering more individualized benefits packages, work schedules, and task and work space design to meet employees' varied needs. The relationship of this tendency toward flexibility with the changing role of work in our society is addressed further in the next section.

Factors Influencing Quality of Work Life

We consider QWL a social movement that is interdependent with other aspects of life. QWL is not simply a series of services or programs or a menu of fringe benefits or perks offered to an employee by an employer, as in earlier conceptions. Rather, it is a philosophical commitment to developing an interactive relationship between the worker and the employer. Each of the three key concepts of QWL—productivity and job satisfaction, participative management, and flexibility—produces a whole set of challenges to individuals, organizations, and society. The question is, what must we do to meet the needs and expectations of all involved, so that people in organizations will have healthy working relationships?

1. **QWL is interactive.** In order to better understand the interdependent nature of QWL, we must consider it as part of a larger social system. QWL is not just what the worker needs; it is also the interaction between workplace expectations and individual needs. It is when industry expectations and employee needs match that greater satisfaction is realized (Getzel & Guba, 1957). This social system model notes that the individual's needs reflect the individual's personality, while industry's expectations reflect the role that the worker should and must play in that industry. When there is congruence between expectations and needs, satisfaction is high. When there is dissonance, as when the worker fails to meet industry expectations or vice versa, job satisfaction and corresponding QWL for the individual are lower. Ultimately, resolution of this dissonance depends on a change in industry expectations or provisions, a change in the individual's needs or performance,

or dissolution of the employment relationship. The social system model of Getzel and Guba (1957) reflects the interdependence of the individual and the employer or, more specifically, how the needs of the worker and the expectations of the workplace impact on the individual employee's QWL.

2. **QWL is responsive to the environment.** QWL does not exist in a vacuum. Changes in demand for business services, in labor supply, and in societal expectations have led to major shifts in the workplace (Bogue, 1985; Harris, 1987). Chief among these shifts are the following (Cornish, 1993):

   • Movement from manufacturing to service industries

   • Fewer younger workers entering the labor force, with an estimated 27% reduction in 19-year-olds entering the work force in 1995 compared to 1985

   • More persons over the age of 65, increasing demand for services such as shopping, transportation, health care, and home services

   • More women entering the work force, with more than one-half of the work force in 1995 female.

Changes in demand and an associated decline in supply have stimulated industry to pay more attention to the needs of workers as well as the interests of customers (Bluestone, 1989). The growing motivation to respond to employee needs has furthered the development and adoption of practices that increase productivity, decrease absenteeism, and improve employee morale and commitment to the company.

3. **QWL is work-stage related.** The changes noted above have led to a greater awareness of worker needs. As noted by Yankelovich (1988), jobs are critical to identity and general happiness for workers both on and off the job. Work has been a form of self-expression in many ways. The more educated work force of the baby boom generation is looking to the job not only as a means of economic independence, but also as a mechanism for social and interpersonal support (Bogue, 1985; Harris, 1987).

The role of work is not constant, but rather evolving. People's needs change over time, with work taking on more or less significance depending on age and other factors such as family demands, personal goals, and income expectations. This variability contributes to the interactive nature of QWL. When considering an individual's QWL, it is important to pay attention to where he or she is in terms of job or career development. For example, in the early career years many people are more concerned about experience than money, whereas later, issues of salary, success, and security appear stronger. Thus, it is important in assessing QWL to consider the employee's work stage.

Quality of Work Life From the Disability Perspective

For persons with disabilities, the work environment as a focus for identifying and examining quality issues is now emerging, joining the residential, social, and personal spheres as an area of interest (Charland, 1986; Goode, 1989; Kolodny & van Beinum, 1983). There are numerous reasons for this new vision of work, not the least of which is the growing recognition that a real job for a person with disabilities is a viable option, given the many accomplishments of supported employment programs nationally over the past 15 years (McGaughey, Kiernan, Lynch, Schalock, & Morganstern, 1991; McGaughey, Kiernan, McNally, Gilmore, & Keith, 1993; Wehman, Kregel, & Shafer, 1989). Work is becoming increasingly important not only because of the increasing amount of time that people spend on the job, but also because work is assuming a larger, more meaningful role in most people's lives (Taylor, 1987). Work is often a vehicle through which we establish our identity and place in society, our peer groups, and our level of economic independence (Holland, 1983; Super, Starishevski, Matlin, & Jordaan, 1963).

The authors contend that QWL should be understood as an individual phenomenon in a helping context, focusing on a specific person's quality of working life. However, global activities such as systems design, political advocacy, program evaluation, and quality assurance must be considered in the discussion of QWL. As was presented earlier, certain factors can be correlated with individual satisfaction. In this section of the chapter, these are grouped into three broad QWL-related categories: specific job characteristics, worker characteristics, and social context. The following section examines these broad categories and presents some of the dilemmas found when considering QWL for individuals with disabilities.

Specific Job Characteristics

Job factors integral to QWL that have been identified in the literature—interesting work, important work, task variety, opportunities for advancement, autonomy, and participation in decision-making—traditionally have not been available to people with significant developmental disabilities. Over the last 10 years, the number of people with developmental disabilities who have entered the work force has increased dramatically due to increased attention, resources, and legislative changes such as the Americans with Disabilities Act (Kiernan et al., 1991; McGaughey et al., 1994; West, Revell, & Wehman, 1992). Despite this progress, the overwhelming majority of jobs held have been in precisely the sorts of employment situations where job factors important to QWL are most difficult to find—food service, cleaning, hospitality, light manufacturing, assembly, and contract labor (Mank, 1994).

Questions abound when this dilemma is examined more closely. Some of the most salient issues in studying policy implications of QWL for people with developmental disabilities are these:

- The United States is apparently undergoing an economic restructuring away from long-term employment with one company, which provides benefits, career advancement, and job security, toward a mix of contract, short-term project labor with few benefits and a radically downsized permanent labor force. The challenge of finding work situations conducive to QWL is therefore increasing.

- Given the unique skills and specific support requirements of people with severe disabilities, job restructuring and job creation have been stressed as options to help people formerly excluded from the work force. These generated niche opportunities are often difficult to fill, unappealing to other workers, or add-on, rather than integral, job duties.

- The rehabilitation field has managed

to dispel the myth that people with developmental disabilities cannot work in the community. What remains open to debate and verification is whether we have the capacity to obtain employment that transcends entry-level, high-turnover occupations, which do not usually contain elements associated with increased QWL. It is unclear whether this lack of career growth options is a reflection of worker skill levels or of the limited resources and expectations of the employment helpers.

Characteristics of Workers

The QWL of workers with disabilities poses special challenges due to some of the characteristics of the worker. To some extent, these characteristics are individual in nature and thus cannot be analyzed by group variables. Workers with developmental disabilities display the same variations in personality across the group as any other group of workers (Kiernan & Knutson, 1990). Distinctive characteristics can be inferred for them as a group based on the way they have been engaged by others in our society due to that label. Characteristics such as past work experiences, ability to envision a better job for oneself, and job tenure might reasonably be considered as challenges for the worker with a disability.

A thorough analysis of worker characteristics in relation to quality of work life also requires a brief discussion of the concept of "individual satisfaction" as the crucial indicator of QWL. As we have noted above, the quality of a person's work life is individually evaluated, and subject to external influences. It is incumbent on those who aid people in improving their quality of work life and on those who assess the success of these efforts to understand that decisions about satisfaction are influenced by

experience and that restricted experience and limited choices may reduce the worker's potential for satisfaction. QWL judgments of people with developmental disabilities that are determined in whole or in part by worker characteristics that reflect the more circumscribed employment history of workers with disabilities must be viewed with a jaundiced eye. Until fairly recently, it was quite uncommon for students with developmental disabilities to be treated as potential workers in the community, thus limiting their exposure to vocational discussions, career counseling, work-study programs, vocational education curricula, and after school jobs. Once leaving school, they often were tracked into either nonwork day habilitation or day activity programs or, if job options were considered, into segregated settings (Wehman et al., 1989). Consequently, it can hardly be considered surprising if individuals with such histories report satisfaction in types of work, job tasks, working conditions, and salary levels that their nondisabled peers shun or strongly dislike. Furthermore, the capacity to foresee a better work opportunity is sorely inhibited by a dearth of employment experience or exposure.

Social Context

Social context factors, such as parental status, marital status, spouse's occupation, and social networks, pose a different set of challenges to the person with a developmental disability. The most salient factor is that people with significant disabilities are generally much more likely to be socially isolated—to lack a spouse or intimate life partner, not be a parent, and have a smaller number of friends and acquaintances—than are people without disabilities. Social isolation may place limits on the levels of QWL realized by an individual with a developmental disability. Historically, isolation and segregation have lowered expectations and limited opportunities in many instances. These factors are a reflection of a history in the U.S. And Western Europe of institutionalization, segregated schooling, and stigmatization, all of which are being addressed, but hardly overcome, through contemporary U.S. And European public policy.

Expansion of opportunity may, as a by-product, reduce involvement with those a person has come to rely on as primary social supports. An obvious employment example is leaving a segregated work environment where a person has developed close friendships over the years. This issue arises for anyone, of course, who leaves a job after a long time; but it is compounded for people with developmental disabilities because they usually have fewer people within their social networks and fewer opportunities to augment them.

Additionally, in our society, the freedoms of choice, movement, and association are offset by personal risks. However, in the case of people perceived as more vulnerable, whether this perception is based on fact or stereotype, the concept of risk raises ethical, legal, attitudinal, and emotional concerns. Parents are rightly concerned about safety issues; program staff have legal responsibilities to safeguard people whom they are serving; the general public's stereotype of dependence and need for care remains widely held for certain persons with significant disabilities; protection from harm and injury is a clear issue, but when issues of choice in sexual activity arise, the dilemma is much less clear. Most real choices involve risk.

Some of the policy implications of social context as it affects the quality of work life of people with developmental disabilities are influenced by the issues presented below.

1. **Discriminatory practices.** U.S. society is much more susceptible to changing deep-seated discriminatory behavior against stigmatized minorities in practices subject to public policy legislation (e.g., hiring decisions, real estate sales decisions) than it is to affecting positive behavior patterns such as voluntary residential housing choices or personal friendship affiliations. What strategies can be used by persons interested in creating increased friendship and social networks to overcome stigma, discrimination, and social isolation for people with developmental disabilities? More simply, how can we help people with significant challenges imposed on them by the consequences of disability be more welcome in our work communities?

2. **Risk factors.** Individuals with significant disabilities face many risks as they participate more fully within our society. The authors support the concept of allowing people the "dignity of risk" and believe that people with disabilities are capable of exercising the benefits and uncertainties of free choice that other citizens exercise. This belief does not absolve its supporters of responsibility for helping people learn to use reasonable prudence and caution in their choices. Most importantly, risk has dignity in our society because many rewards (monetary, social, personal satisfaction) flow from risk. What strategies can enhance informed choice-making so that the risks associated with such choices are reasonable and self-defined goals are likely to be realized?

3. **Overprotectiveness.** Overprotectiveness of family members and caregivers toward the person with a disability has often been a conse-

71

quence of underappreciation of the person's capacities to learn, grow, and adapt to changing life circumstances in an integrated society. But people with physical or cognitive limitations can be especially vulnerable, and family members will be naturally cautious about exposing their relative to risk. What strategies will enhance the capability of the person with a disability to self-advocate more effectively?

4. **Inclusion.** It is clear from both the popular and scientific literature that belonging, being part of a social network, is a major positive factor in work environment quality. Thus, the rehabilitation field can be secure in the knowledge that increasing the opportunities for integrated employment for a person with a developmental disability will improve, at least in part, that individual's QWL. But knowing this does not remove the issue that helpers face—what right do they have to intervene in a person's voluntary habits of association (whether those of the person with a disability or of other nondisabled individuals), even if a change in those behavior patterns would produce life-enhancing results for the person with the disability?

Assessment and Measurement Implications

The concept of QWL is a reflection of those factors that create a level of satisfaction for the individual. These factors vary among individuals and over time for the same individual. They also reflect the interaction of individual needs and workplace expectations. Despite the individual nature of the factors determining QWL, a number of assessment and measurement implications are considered in this final section.

Quality of Work Life Assessment

The evaluation of QWL, for persons with disabilities, begins with an examination of the job selection process. Frequently, development of employment opportunities is done by a helper or agency that seeks job openings, places the individual in employment, and perhaps assumes the person should be satisfied with the position not only in the initial stages but for many years to come. Overall, QWL for individuals with disabilities is considerably compromised in many instances because they are not included in the decision-making process for identifying, obtaining, and maintaining employment. It is critical that they participate in the decision-making process and have full involvement in selecting their jobs. The right to choose is an important right for all persons, particularly those with disabilities. We need to provide persons with disabilities the opportunity to know about their options and support them in making choices. They must be given sufficient experience and opportunity to develop preferences, so that they can make effective choices when given the opportunity to do so. This preparation must be incorporated into their daily activities early in life, so that when the time comes for adult decision-making, they are ready.

If the individual with disabilities is involved in the job selection process, it is appropriate to examine the more traditional concepts of QWL. Because work is a dynamic experience, one must frequently make choices based on changing expectations (e.g., new job demands, different co-workers/supervisors, etc.). Any measurement scale for evaluating QWL for an individual with a disability must be flexible enough to reflect the changing needs of the individual and the evolving expectations of the job. The key variables constituting QWL identified by Walton (1975) as shown in Table 4.1 can serve as a basis for evaluating the QWL for persons with disabilities.

Any assessment of QWL must consider the issues of presence, opportunity, and access. The work environment must make available those factors that constitute QWL. When some or all of the key variables are not present, as in those instances where the work space is hazardous, the wages are inadequate, worker need and employer expectation are incompatible, or the options for growth limited, the chances of achieving a high QWL are poor. In other instances, when key variables are present but the individual is not given the opportunity to participate, again the level of QWL will be reduced. In these instances, the issue is a deficiency in the workplace. There are occasions when the key factors are present and opportunity is available, yet the worker will not access them. The reasons for lack of access can be many, such as lack of skill, willingness, intent, or interest on the part of the worker.

Quality of Work Life Measurement

The measurement of QWL is a complex process that reflects numerous variables and the interaction of the individual worker with these variables in a specific environment. What is quality for one individual in one situation may not be for someone else. Additionally, as noted earlier, QWL may change as job expectations or individual needs change. Assessment of QWL must take into consideration a set of key variables while acknowledging that they may fluctuate in importance for the individual over time. Furthermore, the perception of the individual regarding his or her specific environment at a point in time is what will ultimately constitute the individual's sense of QWL. A thoughtful measurement procedure for documenting QWL should include these elements:

- Identification of key variables constituting QWL

- Clear strategies to assess these variables in reference to

  - their presence on the job.

  - the opportunity for the individual to interact with these variables.

  - the level of access the individual exercises.

  - the level of satisfaction expressed by the worker with each variable at a specific point in time.

- A procedure to evaluate (quantitatively and qualitatively) the match of the individual's needs to the job expectations (goodness-of-fit measures using the key variables constituting QWL).

Persons without disabilities, like others, are interested in assuring that their work is valued, that they have a say in the decision-making process, and that they are appropriately reinforced economically, socially, and emotionally for their work. How employees feel about their involvement and about how significant their input is perceived to be is critical. For persons with disabilities, it is often assumed that by virtue of their having jobs, all their needs are met. But, in fact, asking persons with disabilities, or observing how they feel, about their level of autonomy, decision-making opportunities, and ability to influence the work setting is important. Unobtrusive measures such as frequency of interaction with co-workers, whether structured or spontaneous, will give some measurement of the opportunities for social integration and enhanced QWL possible for individuals in the work setting.

Measurement of QWL, just as measurement of success in employment, is not based solely on earnings, but on a combination of factors both actual and in the form of workers' perceptions, including roles in the decision-making process, level of control of the work space, options for growth, level of significance of the worker's contribution to the goods or services provided, impact of work on other life areas, and level of economic independence realized through work.

Conclusion

Obviously, a number of policy implications emerge as a result of looking at the QWL for persons with and without disabilities. For persons with disabilities, frequently the opportunity to decide what types of work to enter is compromised. Thus, the QWL for persons with disabilities may include some measure of independence, decision-making, and opportunities for job selection. Additionally, as in the case of all employees, it is important to ascertain the level of satisfaction regarding tasks performed, level of integration, level of autonomy, level of opportunity for independent decision-making, and ultimately the acceptance and satisfaction derived through employment.

It is clear from the above discussion that QWL is a complicated phenomenon. It reflects a philosophical commitment by employers and employees to work constructively to establish an interactive communication system that allows each an opportunity to influence the levels of satisfaction and self-esteem realized through employment. QWL changes over time and must reflect differences for individuals over their work years. In examining QWL it is clear that the variables which are important for persons without disabilities are the same variables that are important for individuals with disabilities. Thus, the authors have not made a distinction between persons with and without disabilities in looking at the variables which contribute to QWL. However, to achieve an increased QWL for persons with disabilities, additional efforts are necessary to include them in decision-making processes, not only in the work environment but also in selecting the types of work undertaken. It is this level of involvement by employees that will lead to an increased sense of QWL, increased satisfaction, and reduced turnover. By attending to those areas that enhance QWL, employees, industry, and society win.

References

The Accreditation Council. (1992). *Outcome based performance measures: Field review edition.* Landover, MD: Author.

Barnett, R.C., Marshall, N.L., & Singer, J.D. (1992). Job experiences over time, multiple roles, and women's mental health: A longitudinal study. *Journal of Personality and Social Psychology, 62,* 634-644.

Beer, N., & Walton, A.E. (1987). Organizational development. In M.R. Rosenzweig & R.W. Porter (Eds.), *Annual review of psychology* (pp. 339-367). Palo Alto, CA: Annual Reviews.

Bluestone, B. (1989). Employment prospects for persons with disabilities. In W. Kiernan & R.L. Schalock (Eds.) *Economics, industry and disability: A look ahead* (pp. 17-26). Baltimore: Brookes.

Bogue, D.J. (1985). *The population of the United States: Historical trends and future projections.* New York: Free Press.

Boone, H.A., & Stevens, E. (1991). Towards an enhanced family and child QOL. In M. Krajicek & R. Tompkins (Eds.), *The medically fragile infant.* Austin, TX: Pro-Ed.

Bowditch, J.R., & Bouno, A.F. (1982). *Quality of work life assessment: A survey-based approach.* Boston: Auburn House.

Bradley, V.J., Ashbaugh, J.W., & Harder, P. (1984). *Assessing and enhancing the quality of services: A guide for the human service field.* Boston: Human Services Research Institute.

Braus, P. (1992). What workers want. *American Demographics, 14*(8), 30-37.

Bromet, E.J., Dew, A., & Parkinson, D.K. (1990). Spillover between work and family: A study of blue collar working wives. In J. Eckenrode & S. Gore (Eds.), *Stress between work and family* (pp. 102-121). New York: Plenum.

Champney, T.F., & Dzurec, L.C. (1992). Involvement in productive activities and satisfaction with living situation among severely mentally disabled adults. *Hospital and Community Psychiatry, 43,* 899-903.

Charland, W.A. (1986). *Life work: Meaningful employment in an age of limits.* New York: The Continuum Publishing Co.

Committee on Accreditation of Rehabilitation Facilities. (1994). *1995 CARF standard manual and interpretive guidelines for employment and community support.* Tucson, AZ: Author.

Cornish, E. (1993). Outlook '93. *The Futurist, 26*(6), 29-36.

Davis, L.E., & Cherns, A.B. (Eds.). (1975). *Quality of working life: Volume 2.* New York: Free Press.

Fabian, E. (1991). Using quality of life indicators in rehabilitation program evaluation. *Rehabilitation Counseling Bulletin, 34,* 344-356.

Faucheux, C., Amado, G., & Laurent, A. (1982). Organizational development. In M.R. Rosenzweig & L.W. Porter (Eds.), *Annual review of psychology* (pp. 343-370). Palo Alto, CA: Annual Reviews.

Fields, M.W., & Thacker, J.W. (1992). Influence of quality of work life on company and union commitment. *Academy of Management Journal, 35,* 439-450.

Flanagan, J.C. (1982). Measurement of quality of life. *Archives of Physical Medicine and Rehabilitation, 53,* 56-59.

Gadon, H. (1984). Making sense of quality of working life programs. *Business Horizons, 27,* 42-46.

Galvin, D.E. (1986). Health promotion, disability management, and rehabilitation in the workplace. *Rehabilitation Literature, 47,* 9-10.

George, J.M., & Brief, A.P. (1990). The economic instrumentality of work: An examination of the moderating effects of financial requirements and sex on the pay-life satisfaction relationship. *Journal of Vocational Behavior, 37,* 357-368.

Getzel, J.W., & Guba, E.G. (1957). Social behavior in the administrative process. *School Review, 65,* 423-441.

Goode, D.A. (1989). Quality of life, quality of work life. In W.E. Kiernan & R.L. Schalock (Eds.), *Economics, industry and disability: A look ahead* (pp. 337-349). Baltimore: Brookes.

Harris, L. (1987). *Inside America.* New York: Heritage Books.

Havlovic, S.J. (1991). Quality of work life and human resource outcomes. *Industrial Relations, 30,* 469-479.

Holland, J.R. (1983). Vocational preference. In M. Dunnette (Ed.), *Handbook of industrial and organizational psychology* (pp. 521-571). New York: John Wiley.

Kahnweiler, W.M., & Kahnweiler, J.B. (1992). The work/family challenge: A key career development issue. *Journal of Career Development, 18,* 251-257.

Kanter, R.M., Summers, D.V., & Stein, B. (1986). The future workplace alternatives. *Management Review, 75,* 30-34.

Kibele, A. (1988). Occupational therapy's role in improving the quality of life for persons with cerebral palsy. *American Journal of Occupational Therapy, 43,* 371–377.

Kiernan, W.E., & Knutson, K. (1990). Quality of work life. In R. Schalock (Ed.) *Quality of life: Perspectives and issues* (pp. 101–114). Washington, DC: American Association on Mental Retardation.

Kiernan, W.E., & Mank, D. (1994). *Employment/financing reform. Presidents Committee on Mental Retardation.* Boston: Children's Hospital, Institute for Community Inclusion.

Kiernan, W.E., & Schalock, R.L. (in press). *Integrated employment: Today and tomorrow.* Washington, DC: American Association on Mental Retardation.

Kiernan, W.E., Schalock, R.L., McGaughey, M.J., Lynch, S.A., & McNally, L.C. (1991). *National survey of state information systems related to day and employment programs.* Boston: Children's Hospital, Institute for Community Inclusion.

Kolodny, H., & van Beinum, H. (1983). *Quality of work life in the 1980s.* New York: Praeger Publications.

Kozleski, E.B., & Sands, D.J. (1992, June). The yardstick of social validity: Evaluating quality of life as perceived by adults without disabilities. *Education and Training in Mental Retardation, 23,* 119–131.

Loscocco, K., & Roschelle, A. (1991). Influences on the quality of work and nonwork life: Two decades in review. *Journal of Vocational Behavior, 39,* 182–225.

Mank, D. (1994). *The underachievement of supported employment: A call for reinvestment.* Eugene: University of Oregon.

McGaughey M.J., Kiernan W.E., Lynch, S.A., Schalock, R.L., & Morganstern, D.R. (1991). *National survey of day and employment programs for persons with developmental disabilities: Results from state MR/DD agencies.* Boston: Institute for Community Inclusion (UAP), Children's Hospital.

McGaughey M.J., Kiernan W.E., McNally, L.C., Gilmore, D.S., & Keith, R.B. (1994). *National perspectives on integrated employment: State MR/DD agency trends.* Boston, MA: Children's Hospital, Institute for Community Inclusion.

Modic, S.J. (1987, June 15). Higher quality of work (editorial). *Industrial Week,* 9–12.

Nadler, D.A., & Lawler, E.E., III. (1983). Quality of work life: Perceptions and direction. *Organizational Dynamics, 11*(3), 20–30.

Rossmiller, R.A. (1992). The secondary school principal and teachers' quality of work life. *Educational Management and Administration, 20*(3), 132–146.

Sashkin, M., & Burke, W.W. (1987). Quality of work life. *Journal of Management, 13,* 393–418.

Schalock, R.L. (Ed.). (1990). *Quality of life: Perspectives and issues.* Washington, DC: American Association on Mental Retardation.

Seashore, S.E. (1975). Defining and measuring the quality of work life. In L.E. Davis & A.B. Cherns (Eds.), *Quality of working life: Volume 1* (pp. 93–110). New York: Free Press.

Shellenbarger, S. (1993). Lessons from the workplace: How corporate policies and attitudes lag behind worker's changing needs. *Human Resource Management, 31,* 157–169.

Steiner, D.D., & Truxillo, D.M. (1989). An improved test of the disaggregation hypothesis of job and life satisfaction. *Journal of Occupational Psychology, 62,* 33–39.

Stepp, J. (1985, September). Promoting productivity. *Monthly Labor Review, 108,* 54–55.

Super, D.E., Starishevski, R., Matlin, V., & Jordaan, J.T. (1963). *Career development: Concept theory*. New York: College Examination Board.

Taylor, H. (1987). Evaluating our quality of life. *Industrial Development,* 156, 1-4.

Walton, R.D. (1975). Quality of work life: What is it? *Sloan Management Review, 15*(1), 11-21.

Wehman, P., Kregel, J., & Shafer, M.S. (1989). *Emerging trends in the national supported employment initiative: A preliminary analysis of twenty-seven states.* Richmond: Virginia Commonwealth University, Rehabilitation Research and Training Center on Supported Employment.

West, M., Revell, W.G., & Wehman, P. (1992). Achievements and challenges: A five year report on consumers and system outcomes from the supported employment initiative. *Journal of the Association for Persons with Severe Handicaps, 17,* 227-235.

Yankelovich, D. (1988). Our turn. *American Health, 7*(7), 56-60.

Zeffane, R.M. (1994). Correlates of job satisfaction and their implications for work redesign: A focus on the Australian telecommunications industry. *Public Personnel Management, 23*(1), 61-76.

CHAPTER 5

Supported Living: Beyond Conventional Thinking and Practice

Orv C. Karan

A.J. Pappanikou Center on Special Education and Rehabilitation
University of Connecticut

James D. Bothwell

Department of Educational Psychology
University of Connecticut

Over the years, many innovative concepts have been introduced that were intended to improve the quality of life of individuals with disabilities. Too often, however, they ended as empty slogans or, worse, just new names for old practices (Smull & Smith, 1994). Indeed, the field of disability has shown a remarkable ability to adopt new language and techniques without changing its basic underlying values (Racino, 1992).

Today, another new concept has emerged that holds great promise for improving the quality of lives of individuals with disabilities. The concept is supported living. Its promise lies in the fact that the supported living movement reflects the transformed vision of what constitutes a life of quality for persons with mental retardation: an emphasis on self-determination, strengths and capabilities, the importance of normalized

and typical environments, the provision of individualized support systems, and enhanced adaptive behavior.

In this chapter, we discuss how supported living can potentially enhance a person's perceived quality of life. Major sections of the chapter include conventional residential services versus supported living; the definition of supported living; supported living's influence on quality of life; critical issues in self-determination; ethical concerns; and supporting the providers of support.

Conventional Residential Services versus Supported Living

Most conventional residential service programs are based on the premise that they are appropriate and good for the individuals who live there. Our laws, policies, missions, and values even tend to place a premium on the individualized nature of such services. Yet in practice, there are only a limited number of options, and individualized at best means fitting one of these options or getting to choose from among a limited number of options. What is often so easily lost in our conventional approaches is the individual and what is best for that person and his or her family (Greenspan & Love, 1995). Truly individualized services and supports are built around the person and are based on his or her unique needs and choices.

Unfortunately, most of us are limited by the paradigm that guides our disciplines, by funding structures, and by the limits of our own knowledge and experiences. Thus we need to work actively to overcome deeply-ingrained biases and world views (Racino, 1992). To develop individualized services requires new skills, including those of systems change, leveraging resources, collaborating with and empowering others, being a resource to the consumer, and generally becoming a "jack of all trades" (Kiernan & Hagner, 1995). Because the new skills are outside the conventional service paradigms with which most of us are familiar, we offer conventional services within existing structures, requiring individuals to change, rather than changing structures or creating new options to accommodate individual preferences and choices. In such a framework, even when we think we are doing the right thing, we can be making critical errors if we do not incorporate the person's preferences and choices, as described in the following illustration.

"It Must Be Right"

Charles is a 25-year-old man who experienced a traumatic brain injury about six years ago in an automobile accident. The injury caused irritability, short-term memory difficulties, impulsivity, and disorientation, which led to family problems and the loss of his job. After several years of conflict within his family, an opening occurred in a group home for men with traumatic brain injuries. This was a structured setting with three other men and live-in staff. His family, his physician, and his psychologist all supported the move to the setting even though Charles himself was very reluctant.

During Charles' first ten months in the group home, his physician continually adjusted his medication. His psychologist counseled with him and suggested to staff ways to structure the environment and program for him. This was a time of constant battles, and Charles was very unhappy. He felt like he was in jail and being treated like a child. His comings and goings were constantly monitored; he had to earn privileges usually taken for granted by most adults; he had to go to bed, eat, get up, and do chores around the house on a routine basis; and he could not spend time with his girlfriend when he wanted.

From the perspective of the professionals involved, Charles was not adjusting to the group home. His staff and his family were frustrated and angry with him. Countless medication adjustments were made and various behavioral programs were tried to no avail.

One could look at this situation as a potential crisis. Possible outcomes for Charles included hospitalization, loss of the opening, movement to a more restrictive setting, or a return to his family (assuming they would take him back). Whether this was the right place for Charles was not questioned, the presumption being that since this was a group home for men with traumatic brain injuries it must, therefore, be right for Charles. All services were focused on trying to help Charles fit the rules, structure, and culture of the home.

An alternative to more restrictiveness was to reexamine Charles' residential possibilities from the perspective of his preferences. He really wanted to live in his own apartment. He also realized that he had limitations resulting from his injury and was willing to receive some support. Conventional clinical wisdom would say "no"; but an individualized services focus would say, "What would that mean, how can it be created, and what level of support does he need?" Living on his own meant assistance with budgeting and paying bills; cooking and turning off his stove; knowing when to smoke and taking proper precautions; learning how to use public transportation; and planning for taking medications. It also meant opportunities to be with people and have visitors.

A supported living arrangement was created. Charles selected his own apartment. He started with a supported living coordinator spending an average of 20 hours per week with him, a few hours each weekday, and more on the weekends. Occasionally the number of hours increased when he was having difficulty, but then dropped again as he stabilized. Both he and his girlfriend obtained temporary part-time employment, but he had to be careful about his income or risk losing some of his Social Security benefits.

The role of his psychologist also shifted toward supporting the support personnel. The psychologist met with them regularly and helped them deal with their frustrations and learn how to recognize when some of their own values and standards were interfering with trying to provide support for Charles. In essence, the psychologist attempted to help support staff differentiate between situations in which they should simply support Charles' choices, those in which they should try teaching him alternatives, and finally, those in which Charles was clearly making high-risk, potentially dangerous choices over which they must take control. The overall focus of this approach shifted from fitting Charles into an available structure to that of helping him realize his preferences and supporting the staff who support him.

As was true with Charles, most of us are much more committed to obtaining our own goals than those decided on by other people (Racino & Williams, 1994). Even individuals with severe disabilities are capable of a surprising degree of self-determinism when given appropriate supports (O'Brien, 1987).

In our field, we have become good at justifying and rationalizing many of our conventional practices in the name of their alleged benefits for the people we serve. We often truly believe that our services are appropriate even when the person does not like them or want to participate in them, or even does not appear to be benefitting from them. At such times we often compare our practices to those of taking bitter medications; they may not taste good but they're good for you. On the other hand, perhaps we too often justify inappropriate practices because we see no alternatives. This locks us into archaic practices in which the person with a disability ultimately pays the price. A good example of this is represented in the second illustration.

"Someday She May Need It"

Pam is a 42-year-old woman with cerebral palsy. She has quadriplegia, mild mental retardation, and a great deal of difficulty expressing herself.

A number of years ago she was living in a nursing home. Then, an opportunity arose for her to move into a group home, and she readily accepted, although she had no say in where she would be located and the other group home residents were all strangers who themselves had disabilities. Yet she felt that being in a group home with a few others near her own age was preferable to being in a nursing home with many others who were much older. Once in the group home, she learned she had to get a job or participate in some kind of day program. She was enrolled in a work activity center where her job was folding papers. To fold the papers, she had a rubber-tipped pointer attached to her forehead and a specially-made jig was created to hold the papers in place.

At top speed Pam could fold up to six sheets per hour. Her job usually began daily at 9:00 in the morning and ended between 2:30 and 3:00 in the afternoon. She was earning between 10 and 15 cents per week. She was very unhappy, and serious consideration was given to starting her on antidepressants. One might ask whether the skills she was learning were relevant and whether her job was increasing her community participation. When these questions were asked, the answers were that this was the only job the work activity center had for her to do; and it was justified on the basis of increasing her frustration tolerance in preparation for the day she might have a real job where such tolerance would be needed!

Thanks to her advocate, when Pam was finally given the opportunity to express her desires several years later, the focus shifted from fitting her into an available slot to developing supports around her based on her choices and preferences. A new and entirely different set of circumstances was created.

What Pam wanted was her own apartment and an opportunity to work with children. Today she lives in her own apartment with a personal care attendant. She works as a teacher's aide in a preschool. Since she has a large electric wheelchair she is very popular with the children, who like to sit on her lap and steer the wheelchair using the control stick. She also has a computerized augmentative communication device attached to her wheelchair, which is controlled by a laser beam device she wears like a pencil in her ear. Recently, while all the children were sitting in a big circle as one of the teachers was reading a story, one of the little boys got up and began to run around the circle. Pam struggled with her laser beam until it triggered her computer to express what she wanted. Suddenly, an electronic voice said "Branden, sit down!" He did, and the teacher's story continued without further interruption.

As these two illustrations show, through supported living our field is stretching beyond the limits of our conventional thinking and practices. We are now in an era in which the emphasis is on supporting individual choices. As professionals, we are attempting to deal creatively with the complexities arising from the lives of many different individuals (O'Brien, 1993).

Supported Living Defined

Supported living is a process that creates opportunities for individuals with disabilities to choose where they live, with whom they live, and how they lead their lives (Smull, 1994). Supports go to and with the person rather than the other way around; and ultimately, the essential support services are the enduring relationships established within one's

community. Thus, three elements are essential to the definition of supported living (Karan, Furey, & Granfield, 1991):

1. The location of the individual's home must be based on his or her informed choice.

2. The individual and not the service provider either owns or rents the property in which the individual lives.

3. The level and intensity of supports must be flexible enough to vary with the changing needs and life circumstances of the individual.

As O'Brien (1993) has noted, supported living "needs slack to develop and can never be uniform and predictable" (p. 4). Clearly, supported living is not a model in which there is a single, uniform approach, but rather a concept and a process that varies considerably both from person to person and over time for any individual (Klein, 1994). It is, however, driven by a strong value base that puts a premium on choice. Karan, Granfield, and Suiter (1989) identified 15 guiding principles that provide the foundation for supported living. These are summarized in Table 5.1.

Just as the popularization of supported employment changed our conventional ways of vocational programming, the popularization of supported living should change our approach to residential services. The difference between these two concepts, however, is that supported employment was driven by federal monies that were invested in funding demonstration projects and served as incentives for each state. Supported living, on the other hand, is growing from the ground up and coincides with the growing movement of consumer empowerment (Karan et al., 1991).

Table 5.1
Principles of Supported Living

- Supported living must focus exclusively on the individual within and across any chosen community environment.

- Decisions about where and how to live are based on the individual's personal values and preferences, not on his or her functioning level.

- Support services are determined by the individual, and if necessary, with advice and suggestions from a network of chosen friends, acquaintances, and advocates for individual support as well as individual family members.

- A person can live in a variety of housing options and still receive support.

- Individuals will be supported, if necessary, in deciding how and where they will live.

- A person can live alone or with others and can have a choice of roommates.

- The individual's home belongs to the individual, his or her family, or to a landlord to whom rent is paid. Supported living does not involve living arrangements owned or leased by a service provider.

- Supports must be broad enough to incorporate all facets of community living and can be provided in or out of the home.

- Supports must be flexible enough to respond to the individual's needs and desires.

- The amount, frequency, and duration of support depends on the needs of the individual.

- Staffing and coordinated support must include a variety of generic options such as the use of home health aides, homemaker services, (occasional) live-in staff, community counselors, paid neighbors and companions, family and friends.

- Supports provided must enable individuals to strive for autonomy and independence to the maximum extent possible.

- Supports must be provided in the community, thus allowing the individual to experience firsthand the values, process, and outcomes of community involvement.

- Contracts for services must be renegotiated with the funding agency as needs change.

- Cost formulas that determine support are individually-based on real need; service contracts are completed for each person.

Supported Living's Influence on Quality of Life

Because supported living is still a relatively new concept, and because it is now being driven more by values than by research, it is still too early to state emphatically that supported living improves the quality of life of those participating in it. There have been, however, numerous anecdotal reports that strongly imply such relationship (Marone, 1992; O'Brien, 1991; Taylor, Bogdan, & Racino, 1991). In our own work in this area, we have repeatedly found that when consumers are asked how their supported living arrangements compare to their previous living arrangements, most individuals do not want to go back to their previous living arrangements even if they cannot articulate why.

Although measuring another's quality of life is a challenge because it is such a subjective construct, evidence is accumulating that quality of life improves as the residential environment becomes more normalized. For example, Schalock and his colleagues (Schalock & Keith, 1993; Schalock, Keith, Hoffman, & Karan, 1989) have demonstrated higher levels of satisfaction, empowerment, and social belonging for individuals living in supported living arrangements than in supervised ones.

Providers of support must be able to distinguish a consumer's emotional needs from their needs for skills. It is one thing for a person to learn how to cook, for example, but still another to be able to participate in reciprocal relationships. As supported living continues to evolve, we must be careful not to overlook the importance of mutual interdependence as people with disabilities exercise their preferences.

In implementing supported living it is also easy to forget that many consumers, even those who have lived in community settings for years, have had limited opportunities to choose. Thus, even when opportunities are available, consumers may not have the experiences, desire, or judgment to accompany their freedom of choice. And in no way can it be assumed that supported living is always going to be fun or easy for consumers who choose this option. There are, for example, usually more responsibilities and problem-solving experiences for the person in supported living than typically occur in conventional residential options.

In some of our own qualitative studies, we have found that many consumer difficulties have little to do with a lack of skills, but instead are related more to their anxieties, fears, and reluctance to enter new situations. There is also considerable variation in how consumers spend their free time. Some are active and involved in a variety of community activities and have many friends. For such individuals it appears that their satisfaction with their living situation is positively influenced by their involvement in meaningful activities (Champney & Dzurec, 1992). Others are isolated and, in the absence of their paid supports, remain alone. This, however, is not necessarily bad if it is what they prefer doing.

Supported living enables individuals to exercise their choices not just in major life areas, such as where to live, but in daily routines as well. As such, supports have to be flexible to respond to changing needs. Unfortunately, even though it is still a new concept, if we are not careful there may be a tendency to institutionalize supported living. For example, in a recent study of consumers who were receiving supported living services in Connecticut (Dunaway, Granfield, Norton, & Greenspan, 1991), 42% of those surveyed were generally satisfied with the support services they received. Nonetheless, they also indicated that some reallocation of services might be useful. They felt they were receiving too much practical in-home support (e.g., learning how to cook, clean, and budget), and not enough support in using their community. And, instead of support providers being available on the schedules and time preferences of the consumers, all too many consumers were adapting to providers' classic 8 to 5 work schedules.

Critical Issues in Self-Determinism

With the increasing emphasis on self-determinism and the new direction of services and supports being built around the person, the new era we are in is

85

forcing us to confront many critical issues, such as these:

1. Building services around the needs of the individual is inconsistent with the way typical bureaucratic organizations operate.

2. A multicultural perspective and mutual understanding between service provider and consumer need to be incorporated into support services.

3. What a person wants may not be what either the family or the service provider wants or thinks is best.

Building services around the needs of the individual is inconsistent with the way typical bureaucratic organizations operate. Bureaucratic systems function to meet internal needs, such as efficiency, internal power relations, and following the "book of regulations," rather than to benefit the individual. There are literally thousands of pages of statutory and regulatory policies and procedures that control the nature and type of services offered and inhibit the motivation and incentive for taking risks and pursuing new directions.

For example, in a series of focus groups convened by the first author to identify reasons for not shifting to supported living, agency heads representing conventional residential services identified board reluctance; limited financial incentives or financial burdens; increases in administrative costs; fear of decentralizing their programs; concerns over quality assurance; and worries about additional expenses. Staff representatives of these agencies expressed fear of change and loss of their jobs; concerns over the lack of structure; skepticism over whether people with severe disabilities were capable of even making decisions; fear of isolation and lack of support; and reluctance to shift

from the role of decision-maker to one of facilitator. Finally, families of residents served within conventional residential services expressed reluctance to shift from safe environments; fear of losing life-long services and permanent placement; fear that their family member would lose benefits; fear of the choices that their family member would make; and skepticism about the capabilities of the service providers to provide sufficient support. Although more research is needed, the implications of these focus groups point to strong systemic and personal factors that can inhibit movement towards supported living.

Second, multicultural perspectives and mutual understanding between service providers and consumers need to be incorporated into support services. Providing effective services to individuals with disabilities in a pluralistic society implies a consideration of the person's culture. This may include race, ethnicity, life-style, life stages, gender, and one's institutional versus community history. Yet the need to incorporate multicultural perspectives is a recent phenomenon. To facilitate a multicultural perspective requires clarity on several variables that involve cultural identity, beliefs, values, and assumptions of the service provider, consumer, and the consumer's family, which is often extended beyond the immediate family (Ibrahim, 1995). The implications of the gender of the parties involved, their social classes, education levels, and life-styles, and of the impact of these variables, are all important.

To provide meaningful support to diverse individuals with disabilities, the provider must understand his or her own world view, cultural identity, and philosophical and psychological assumptions, as well as have knowledge of both the primary and secondary cultural environments from which he or she comes (Ibrahim & Arredondo, 1986, 1990). For too long there has been a tendency to overemphasize the consumer's behavior or disabilities without understanding the impact of cultural characteristics. Effective support demands mutual understanding between support providers and the consumer.

Third, what a person wants may not be what either the family or the service provider wants or thinks is best. The question that many of us now struggle with is, whose wants take priority? Nowhere in the history of our field has this become more of an issue than in supported living. Certainly, the role and importance of parents and other family members in making decisions on behalf of a person with a disability seems clear when the person is a child. Where this becomes less clear is when the person with a disability becomes an adult. As O'Brien (1993) has noted in identifying the role of friends and family in relation to the individual who is being supported within a supported living framework, "We will maintain respectful contact with all parties but honor the choice of the person we assist" (p. 20).

Ethical Concerns

As our field shifts to fitting supports around people rather than fitting people to services, we must begin to consider new ethical concerns and issues. Most literature on ethics and disability emphasizes biomedical issues; much less attention is paid to ethical aspects of everyday life and services to people with disabilities (Greenspan & Love, 1995).

With empowerment comes the privilege of making decisions and making mistakes. At one time, this was referred to as "the dignity of risk" (Perske, 1972). Inherent in this concept was an underlying belief that individuals with disabilities could not and should not always be protected; that one's life

could have more meaning if one took some risks or chances. As individuals exercise their choices, the rest of us must learn to listen and appreciate differences. This is not easy, particularly when the choices being made are incompatible with our values, inconsistent with our beliefs, do not promote our standards, or, in some cases, are even dangerous. Within conventional residential programs there are usually other staff or supervisors available as well as some fairly clear policy boundaries. Within supported living, support providers are usually on their own making decisions on the spot without the benefit of immediate support or consultation from co-workers or supervisors. Often they must act first and reflect later.

Individuals have different standards relative to what they will willingly support versus what conflicts with their own personal, moral, cultural, ethical, professional, and/or religious codes of conduct (Racino, 1992). There is always a fine line between enabling others to make their own choices and giving people the help they need and depend on to function effectively. Support providers must become adept at walking these lines, and at all times they must guard against abusing their power. Many questions now surfacing within the arena of supported living do not have clear answers because there are no absolute right or wrong decisions.

Within supported living we are struggling with difficult questions and new challenges that conventional residential service providers for the most part have not had to worry much about. As examples, consider some of the following: If a person has a history of diabetes and heart disease and is overweight but chooses to eat high calorie, high cholesterol foods, what do you do? If the person spends money impulsively and does not budget for basic living expenses, what do you do? If a person smokes or drinks excessively, what do you do? If a person engages in unprotected sexual behavior, what do you do? If a person spends most free time watching X-rated videos or calling "900" numbers, what do you do? If a person hangs around with friends who are of questionable character, what do you do? It is challenging to deal with these and myriad similar issues, but the realities of life in the community dictate that whether we choose them or not, these dilemmas will occur. In fact, some of the people now in supported living will lose their places in the community if we exercise poor choices of support (O'Brien, 1993).

Providers of support need to be able to discriminate among situations of personal choice; situations in which they need to share information, but ultimately let the individual make the choice; and situations in which they must take control. To assist in making these decisions, we offer the decision tree presented in Figure 5.1 (Dillman, Karan, & Granfield, 1994). Because supported living is based on the assumption that people have choices regardless of the level of their disability, use of the decision tree may help ensure that people are allowed to make choices. In using the decision tree, it must be remembered that even in situations where the provider of support takes control, it is assumed that the control is temporary or is specific to the particular situation in which the person's actions or choices are potentially or actually dangerous.

Supporting the Providers of Support

We now recognize the importance of supporting consumers, advocating on their behalf, and empowering them to self-advocate. We are considerably less

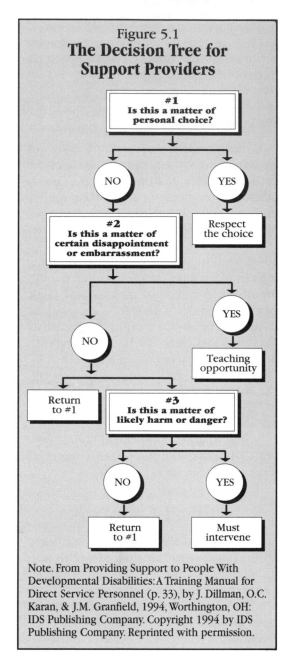

Figure 5.1
The Decision Tree for Support Providers

Note. From Providing Support to People With Developmental Disabilities: A Training Manual for Direct Service Personnel (p. 33), by J. Dillman, O.C. Karan, & J.M. Granfield, 1994, Worthington, OH: IDS Publishing Company. Copyright 1994 by IDS Publishing Company. Reprinted with permission.

skilled, however, at addressing these concerns for those who provide support. Providers are heavily responsible for contributing to healthy psychosocial climates in which consumers are secure enough to exercise choices and take risks. We believe that the ultimate success of supported living for each participant depends on the quality of the relationships between the consumer and his or her support providers. Providers are at the heart of each supported living situation and play numerous important roles (Dillman et al., 1994). It is therefore important that support providers receive support themselves.

There is no question that the job description for a paid support provider is a tall order. It is essential that they have their basic employment needs met and feel respected, valued, and validated. It must be remembered that the paid provider of support is simultaneously in two sometimes conflicting roles: one as an employee and the other as the provider of support to someone else. In our opinion, the quality of the working life of the support provider is closely linked to the quality of life of the consumer who is being supported.

In supported living, perhaps moreso than in any other residential situation, support coordinators operate with a high degree of autonomy, making on-the-spot decisions and either rightly or wrongly, acting first and asking questions later. They face challenges for which they may not have been adequately trained and are susceptible to varying forms of stress. High among these challenges is the continuing need to balance their own values and standards with those of the consumer. Certainly, those who are being supported will have life-style preferences, values, and standards that are different from those of providers. Such differences can cause conflicts that may lead to decisions that are more responsive to the needs of support providers than to those of support recipients. These are subtle yet critical training and technical assistance issues not usually covered in formal training. Providers of support themselves need support in problem-solving, in reframing their negative perceptions, and sometimes even in removing themselves from

---

Table 5.2
Critical Concerns and Needs of Support Providers

Staff/Consumer Relationships

- Values clashes

- Difficulty understanding reasons for consumer's behavior

- Balance between doing too much versus too little

- Power struggle

- Lack of reciprocity

- Friends versus staff

- Consumers' unreasonable expectations

Staff Training Needs/ Staff Development

- Dealing with other agencies

- Handling value clashes; e.g., staff control versus staff support

- Refining role of support coordinator

- Prioritizing and being creative

- Differing standards between support coordinators and families

- On their own making critical decisions

- Changes always occurring/can't depend on specific routines

Staff Personal Concerns

- Desire to punish

- Hurt by consumer accusations and criticisms

- Upset with families

- Frustrated, angered by consumer's actions

- Feeling used/abused by consumer

- Embarrassed by consumer's lack of social skills

- Upset with accusations/criticisms by other providers

situations that are so conflictual as to interfere with their ability to support another person.

Recently, both authors participated in a year-long qualitative research study exploring the critical issues related to the concerns and needs that providers of support identified in their relationships with the consumers they were supporting. These data are summarized in Table 5.2, presented in descending order of priority and representing the top seven themes for each category.

The top section of Table 5.2 presents findings from comments the support providers made regarding their relationships with consumers whom they were supporting. As can be seen, the first theme involved value clashes. These related to any and all situations in which the consumer's choices were inconsistent with the support provider's values and choices. Secondly, providers of support often expressed confusion about why consumers behaved in ways they did. Further, these support providers had difficulty balancing their roles and consistently struggled with whether they were doing too much for the person or not enough.

Interestingly, in spite of constant reminders from supervisors and trainers that their job was to support and facilitate individual choices, they nevertheless found themselves in constant power struggles. They also reported that they often felt they were doing most of the giving in their relationships with consumers and receiving little in return, and that they had difficulty establishing boundaries between themselves and the consumers. Some of their difficulties in this area revolved around trying to distinguish between whether they were consumers' friends or staff. In supported living, these boundaries can blur. Finally, an ongoing concern experienced by

many providers of support was consumers' unreasonable expectations. For many consumers in this study, paid providers of support represented their primary social relationships. As such, it was not unusual for providers of support to be called upon by some consumers even during their time off, even after spending many hours with the consumer all day.

The middle section of Table 5.2 identifies themes pertaining to perceived training needs and areas in which the support providers felt the need for new skills, attitudes, or beliefs. The predominant concern was that of dealing with other agencies. Many consumers in this study were simultaneously clients of programs representing more conventional approaches and philosophies than those of supported living. For example, an individual might be living in his or her own apartment with support and also attending a sheltered workshop or work activity center. Tensions arose when representatives of these other programs criticized support providers about their lack of control, implying that support providers were letting consumers "get away with" too much.

The second major theme had to do with having no real guidelines for deciding when to assume control and when to simply support the individual. Each support provider brings his or her values, beliefs, and standards to the job. What is a perfectly acceptable and reasonable risk in the eyes of one support provider can be viewed as dangerous in the eyes of another. This is a very complicated issue and, as with so many things in supported living, there are no right or wrong answers. Instead, these types of concerns will continually surface, and at a very minimum, providers of support need opportunities to talk about these issues and receive feedback from their peers and others so as to minimize their conflicts and preserve healthy relationships with the consumers they support.

Individuals who prefer clear job descriptions and duties will probably find the role of support coordinator ambiguous at best, since it is so intimately tied to the life-style choices and idiosyncrasies of the individual being supported. At any given moment, the support provider may be serving as a teacher, companion, advocate, counselor, mediator, broker, buffer, ally, bridge builder, confidant, advisor, plumber, auto repair person, etc. (Dillman et al., 1994). Further, these roles are constantly changing as needs and situations change. In many respects, the provider of support must fill a multitude of gaps that have been left unfilled through the history of the consumer's involvement with the fragmented services that continue to exist in the adult services systems of our country (Schalock, 1983).

Knowing when and how to prioritize their time and services while being creative is an ongoing training need for providers of support. Knowing how to support someone whose choices and decisions are different from your own is a challenge under most circumstances.

A somewhat surprising concern was how often support providers felt that supporting the choices of the individual placed them in conflict with the standards and expectations of the family. Many family members saw the role of the support provider as enforcer of the family's values. When this was not the case, and in fact, when the consumer's actions and choices were discrepant from those of the family, it was not unusual for family members to be quite critical of the support provider.

Finally, support providers had difficulty adapting to frequent changes and not being on a specific routine. Their jobs often became consuming and interfered with their personal lives. Without accommodations for personal flexibility that could be exercised at their discretion, the unpredictability of their work hours and intrusions into their personal lives often built resentment and animosity toward the consumers they were supporting.

The bottom section of Table 5.2 summarizes staff personal concerns. The leading theme was a desire to punish, which has many implications for supported living, where checks and balances are less prevalent than in more traditional community living arrangements such as group homes (Furey, Granfield, & Karan, 1994). The common features behind this theme were feelings of being taken advantage of by the consumer and a desire for retribution, reflecting a "just wait until the next time, and I'll show them what it's like" attitude.

The remaining concerns reflect feelings of unhappiness and frustration due to negative interactions and experiences with the consumer, family members, or persons representing other programs who have different perspectives and philosophies.

Clearly, the issues represented in Table 5.2 are critical ones that must be addressed as our field moves forward in supported living. Although it is too early to ascertain job turnover rates for support providers, it is not too early to know that these issues, if left unattended, will not only affect support providers' morale and job satisfaction, but will also spill over and influence the quality of support they provide to individuals (Oberlander, 1990).

Conclusions

Supported living offers considerable potential for reshaping our conventional ways of doing business and enhancing the quality of lives of many persons. Certainly, with its emphasis on personal choice, it is reasonable to expect that those who select supported living arrangements should experience a higher quality of life than those "placed" into typical residential programs. Although more research examining supported living's relationships to quality of life is needed, particularly studies that examine the more subtle features pertaining to daily choices, preliminary indications are that such relationships tend to be positive (Abrams, 1994).

Yet, in spite of such encouraging possibilities, paradigms change slowly, and change is disruptive. Hopefully, those of us involved in the supported living movement will keep moving forward and refuse to be sidetracked by all the typical reasons that might compromise it. In concluding this chapter, we offer our list of features in Table 5.3 of those who "get it," as gathered from our experiences among those we have known who have been able to both "talk the talk" and "walk the walk" of supported living.

Table 5.3
Those Who "Get It"

- Accord others dignity of risk.

- Structure supports around the individual.

- Emphasize a person's strengths.

- Use support model language and practices.

- Don't use services just because they're available.

- Deliver services based on individual needs rather than upon agency needs.

- Spend time with the person.

- Understand that a person-centered approach is more than techniques.

- Listen to the person.

- Do not restrict opportunities.

- Do not solicit superficial choices.

- Do not use excuses for poor judgment.

- Do not distort process by maintaining all the power.

- Support changes at the individual's pace.

References

Abrams, K.R. (1994). *Consumer choice as a predictor of job satisfaction and supervisor rating for people with disabilities.* Unpublished doctoral dissertation. University of Connecticut.

Champney, T.F., & Dzurec, L.C. (1992). Involvement in productive activities and satisfaction with living situation among severely mentally disabled adults. *Hospital and Community Psychiatry, 43,* 899–903.

Dillman, J., Karan, O.C., & Granfield, J.M. (1994). *Providing support to people with developmental disabilities: A training manual for direct service personnel.* Worthington, OH: IDS Publishing Company.

Dunaway, J., Granfield, J., Norton, K., & Greenspan, S. (1991). *Costs and benefits of residential services for persons with mental retardation in Connecticut.* Storrs, CT: Pappanikou Center of the University of Connecticut.

Furey, E.M., Granfield, J.M., & Karan, O.C. (1994). Sexual abuse and neglect of adults with mental retardation: A comparison of victims' characteristics. *Behavioral Interventions: Theory and Practice in Residential and Community-Based Clinical Programs, 9,* 75–86.

Greenspan, S., & Love, P. (1995). Elements for a code of everyday ethics in disability services. In O.C. Karan & S.L. Greenspan (Eds.), *Community rehabilitation services for people with disabilities.* Newton, MA: Butterworth-Heinemann.

Ibrahim, F.A. (1995). Multicultural influences on rehabilitation training and services: The shift to valuing nondominant cultures. In O.C. Karan & S.L. Greenspan (Eds.), *Community rehabilitation services for people with disabilities.* Newton, MA: Butterworth-Heinemann.

Ibrahim, F.A., & Arredondo, P.M. (1986). Ethical standards for cross-cultural counseling: Preparation, practice, assessment, and research. *Journal of Counseling and Development, 64,* 349–351.

Ibrahim, F.A., & Arredondo, P.M. (1990). Essay on law and ethics: Multicultural counseling. In B. Herlihy & L. Golden (Eds.), *Ethics casebook* (4th ed.). Alexandria, VA: American Association for Counseling and Development Press.

Karan, O.C., Furey, E.M., & Granfield, J. (1991). How university affiliated programs can contribute to supported living: The Connecticut experience. *Supported living monograph* (p. 13). Annandale, VA: National Association of Private Residential Resources.

Karan, O.C., Granfield, J.M., & Suiter, D. (1989). Supported living. *Kaleidoscope, 2*(1), 1–6.

Kiernan, W., & Hagner, D. (1995). Rehabilitation counseling and the community paradigm. In O.C. Karan & S.L. Greenspan (Eds.), *Community rehabilitation services for people with disabilities.* Newton, MA: Butterworth-Heinemann.

Klein, J. (1994). Supported living: Not just another "rung" on the continuum. *Living,* 16–18.

Marone, F.J. (1992, November). Truly individualized supported living: Utilizing currently available resources to facilitate community living for persons with challenging behavior. Paper presented at the Annual Conference of the Association for Persons with Severe Handicaps, San Francisco, CA.

Oberlander, L.B. (1990). Work satisfaction among community-based mental health service providers: The association between work environment and work satisfaction. *Community Mental Health Journal, 26,* 517–532.

O'Brien, J. (1987). A guide to life-style planning: Using the activities catalog to integrate services and natural support systems. In G.T. Bellamy & B. Wilcox (Eds.), *A comprehensive guide to the activities catalog: An alternative curriculum for youth and adults with severe disabilities* (pp. 175–189). Baltimore: Brookes.

O'Brien, J. (1991). Down stairs that are never your own. In *Supported living monograph* (pp. 1–12). Annandale, VA: National Association of Private Residential Resources.

O'Brien, J. (1993). *Supported living: What's the difference?* Syracuse, NY: Syracuse University, Research and Training Center on Community Living.

Perske, R. (1972). The dignity of risk and the mentally retarded. *Mental Retardation, 10,* 24–27.

Racino, J. (1992). Living in the community: Independence, support, and transition. In F.R. Rusch, L. Destefano, J. Chadsey-Rusch, L. Phelps, & E. Szymanski (Eds.), *Transition from school to adult life* (pp. 131–145). Pacific Grove, CA: Brooks/Cole.

Racino, J. (1992). *People want the same things we all do: The story of the area agency in Dover, New Hampshire.* Syracuse, NY: Syracuse University, New York Center on Human Policy.

Racino, J.A., & Williams, J.M. (1994). Living in the community: An examination of the philosophical and practical aspects. *Journal of Head Trauma Rehabilitation,* 9(2), 35–48.

Schalock, R.L. (1983). *Services for developmentally disabled adults.* Baltimore: University Park Press.

Schalock, R.L., & Keith, K.D. (1993). *Quality of life questionnaire and standardization manual.* Worthington, OH: IDS Publishers.

Schalock, R.L., Keith, K.D., Hoffman, K., & Karan, O.C. (1989). Quality of life: Its measurement and use. *Mental Retardation, 27,* 25–31.

Smull, M. (1994). Moving toward a system of support. *News and Notes,* 7(5), 3–4.

Smull, M.W., & Smith, G. (1994). Moving to a system of support: Using support brokerage. *News and Notes,* 7(4), 4–6.

Taylor, S.J., Bogdan, R., & Racino, J.A. (1991). *Life in the community: Case studies of organizations supporting people with disabilities.* Baltimore: Brookes.

C H A P T E R   6

Health-Related Application
of Quality of Life

David L. Coulter
Boston University School of Medicine and Boston City Hospital

This chapter reviews first some of the philosophical issues involved in quality of life as it relates to health and points out some of the limitations and misuses of this concept. Practical issues involved in studying health-related quality of life (HRQOL) are then discussed. The section on measurement issues considers how HRQOL has been assessed in the literature and indicates some problems with interpreting results and generalizing. The final section relates these issues to public policy and the lives of people with mental retardation.

Philosophical Issues

A balanced understanding of the idea of HRQOL requires that each of its component be examined carefully. What do we mean by health? What do we mean by quality? What do we mean by life? It seems we need to explore each of these components separately before we can appreciate how they all come together. This exploration will also demonstrate why those who study or discuss HRQOL should answer these questions in their work so that we all know exactly what they are talking about.

Health

Most writers on the subject of HRQOL specify that they are using the definition of health established by the World Health Organization (WHO). This definition states that health is "a state of complete physical, mental and social well-being, not merely the absence of disease or infirmity" (Breslow, 1972). This is an important distinction that deserves elaboration.

If health were "merely the absence of disease or infirmity," then the presence of disease or infirmity would be sufficient to define a lack of health. Furthermore, if this were the meaning of "health" used in a concept of HRQOL, then a lack of health would be associated with impaired quality of life. The presence of a disease or infirmity, by itself, would be sufficient to define a lack of health and therefore to specify an impaired quality of life. According to this logic, HRQOL could thus be considered solely in relation to a specific disease or infirmity.

Consider the following example. Mental retardation could be considered to be an infirmity that would result in a lack of health, according to this view.

Then everyone with mental retardation could be considered to have a diminished HRQOL, No other factor would have to be considered. The level of an individual's HRQOL would be determined by the severity of the individual's infirmity (mental retardation).

What is wrong with this example? Common sense tells us that persons with the same disease or degree of infirmity may have a wide variation in HRQOL. Thus, we can easily imagine a group of individuals who have the same IQ but whose overall functioning varies tremendously and (in common sense terms) whose HRQOL also varies tremendously. One could reconstruct this example using different diseases, such as coronary artery disease or diabetes, and come to the same conclusion: The concept of a disease-specific quality of life is a logical and empirical fallacy.

The WHO's definition of health emphasizes a state of well-being in multiple dimensions, specifically physical, mental, and social well-being. In this sense, well-being should be distinguished from welfare. A person's welfare can be considered to be the combination of things in the person's external and internal environment that, together with the person's activities, contributes to the person's well-being. The elements that constitute a person's welfare (such as socioeconomic status or internal resources) form a foundation for well-being but are not identical with it. Just because a person is poor or disabled (elements of the person's welfare) does not necessarily mean that the person is unhappy or perceives a diminished sense of well-being. Importantly, in this formulation, quality of life resides in a person's sense of well-being, not in the facts or elements of the person's welfare (Nordenfelt, 1994b).

The WHO specifies that health is a state of *complete* physical, mental, and social well-being. This means that health is a global, all-encompassing condition and is not linked to just one aspect of well-being (such as the presence of mental retardation). Indeed, we can rephrase this to say that *health reflects a person's experience of wellness* in the most global sense. The contributions to wellness are many and include physical, mental, and social dimensions. To this should also be added the spiritual dimension, since spiritual wellness is an important element of well-being for many people. Assessment of health in HRQOL must include consideration of all of these dimensions that contribute to a person's well-being.

It should be apparent that the elements that constitute a person's welfare are necessarily different for different people and therefore lead to different understandings of individual well-being. We may be able to assess these elements of human welfare objectively, but our assessment will not necessarily provide an understanding of the person's well-being. Additional subjective information will be needed to fully characterize a person's well-being. Furthermore, if quality of life resides in a person's well-being, then we also need additional information to understand the person's quality of life. The concept of health (or well-being) is necessary but not sufficient to understand HRQOL; thus, we must also consider the impact of notions of quality and of life.

Quality

What makes a life good? The answer to this question can provide some understanding of the meaning of quality in HRQOL. Brock distinguishes three broad philosophical approaches to answering this question that he calls the hedonist, preference satisfaction, and ideal theories of a good life (Brock, 1993). Hedonist theories interpret the ultimate good in terms of conscious experiences such as pleasure or happiness (Nordenfelt, 1994b). Preference satisfaction theories interpret the ultimate good in terms of the satisfaction of individual desires or preferences or the achievement of basic needs (Aggernase, 1994; Liss, 1994). Both hedonist and preference satisfaction theories are fairly subjective, since the determination of what conscious experiences are good or what preferences are desired is left to the individual. Ideal theories interpret the good life in terms of the realization of specific, normative ideals. The ideals may vary, and indeed may include aspects of the other theories, depending on the construct utilized. These ideal theories tend to be more objective, since the specific construct can be stated in ideal terms apart from the viewpoint of the individual.

A more pluralistic approach to the good life considers that multiple components may be present (including components from the other types of theories). Each component can be thought of as an independent vector, each of which contributes to an understanding of how good a person's life is (Sen, 1980). These components may be broadly comparable between individuals (in an objective sense), even though the resulting aggregate understanding of the goodness of a person's life may be mostly subjective.

The contribution of health to the goodness of life may be different in each of these broad philosophical approaches. Health could be thought of as a conscious experience, a preference or need, an ideal to be achieved, or a component vector of a pluralistic theory. What is important here is that there are different ways to answer the question of what makes a life good, and that the answer provided will likely determine what one means by "quality" in discussing HRQOL. The fact that very few discussions of

HRQOL specify what philosophical approach is being used undoubtedly accounts for much of the confusion about HRQOL in the literature.

Life

Nordenfelt observed that, "Notwithstanding the increasingly rich literature on quality of life, the basic notion of life has been almost completely neglected in this context" (Nordenfelt, 1994a). He then discussed life in terms of certain aspects such as the experiences, activities, achievements, events, and circumstances in a person's life. As with quality, those who discuss HRQOL may choose to emphasize one or more of these aspects of life without always being clear about which aspect is being emphasized or why.

Nordenfelt did not include in this list the spiritual aspect of life, but it may also be relevant to a broad understanding of life (Coulter, 1992). Gaventa (1994) considered the spiritual contribution to quality of life in terms of three questions that he related to personal values and to the conventional descriptors of goals of quality of life. "Who am I?" relates to one's sense of personal identity and to the goal of independence. "Whose am I?" relates to one's sense of belonging and to the goal of inclusion or social integration. "Why am I?" relates to one's sense of vocation or purpose and to the goal of productivity. This awareness of the spiritual aspect of life is important because it raises the issue of individual values that must be considered in assessing HRQOL. Our understanding of these values is linked to our answers to Gaventa's questions and is intensely personal. Thus when we talk about HRQOL, we must pause to ask what values a person has and how this affects the person's sense of what life is and means.

In summary, the philosophical basis of HRQOL is extremely rich and important but often overlooked. Those who comment on HRQOL should be more specific in this regard. We have seen that HRQOL is a reflection of global well-being, not linked to a specific disease or infirmity, and is conditioned by individual answers to questions about what life is and what makes life good. Although some aspects of HRQOL may be fairly objective, others are primarily subjective and can only be considered from the viewpoint of the individual. The importance of this philosophical understanding of HRQOL will be apparent when we consider measurement issues: Most instruments for measuring HRQOL only measure well-being and do not consider the goodness (quality) or meaning (value) of a person's life. Well-being might be substantially impaired, but the person may believe that life is very good and precious for reasons that have little to do with health.

Practical Issues

The key issues to consider in discussing HRQOL can be grouped into four categories or questions (Nordenfelt, 1994a), each of which will be considered separately. First, *what is the purpose of measuring HRQOL?* A number of answers are possible. The particular purpose chosen will likely be based on either or both of the ethical principles of beneficence or justice. At least the following purposes can be identified in the literature (Musschenga, 1994):

a. To enhance individual quality of life (a reflection of beneficence). Studies may evaluate the results of treatment, for example (Gill & Feinstein, 1994).

b. To inform treatment decisions (primarily a reflection of beneficence). Studies may evaluate the process of decision-making and consent or refusal for treatment (Brock, 1993; Cohen, 1990).

c. To allocate health resources fairly and equitably (a reflection of justice). Studies may evaluate the societal impact of alternative approaches to treatment (Veatch, 1986).

Other purposes are possible as well. The purpose of a study should be fairly explicit, and comparisons across studies should take the studies' purposes into account.

Second, *what aspects of a person's life should be considered?* This relates to the idea that life can be considered in a variety of aspects that include the experiences, activities, achievements, events, and circumstances in a person's life (Nordenfelt, 1994a). HRQOL studies will normally focus on aspects of life related to health, but this may be too narrow. Other aspects (such as spirituality) might need to be considered as well. As with the purpose of the study, whatever aspect of life is studied should be stated explicitly.

Third, *what dimension of value is appropriate,* and should this be decided by the subject or the evaluator? Possible values to be considered might include intelligence, morality, or dignity, for example. In most studies, the evaluative dimension is chosen by the evaluator. It is not clear whether an objective choice or ranking is possible among multiple possible dimensions of value. Indeed, this is probably the source of many conflicts between providers and consumers of health care, each of whom has different ideas about which dimensions of value are most important (Gill & Feinstein, 1994). Thus, studies need to consider whose values are being considered in measuring HRQOL and indicate how this is determined.

Fourth, *what procedure should be used to determine the approach to measurement?* The procedure may be either paternalistic or individualistic, for example. Paternalistic procedures include authoritative strategies (based on a general concept of what is important), empirical strategies (based on what previous studies have found to be important), and consensus strategies (based on what a group of people agree is important). Individualistic procedures include personal strategies (based on what a person actually says) and inferred strategies (based on what can be inferred about the person's values from observation and interaction). Studies of HRQOL may need to employ multiple approaches to measurement in order to derive a balanced understanding of what it means to the individual, to significant others, and to society.

Measurement Issues

HRQOL is a frequent topic of discussion that cannot be avoided. Advocates may wish it were not so and may argue that quality of life should not be discussed (Luckasson, 1990). But the plain fact is that it is discussed (often badly) and in some form or other is included in many health care encounters. Rather than rely on impressionistic or poorly-articulated ideas of HRQOL (such as those used by many health care providers in making decisions about what treatments to offer), providers and consumers should work together to develop a reliable and valid system for measuring HRQOL that would be acceptable to all.

Measurement of HRQOL can be as naive as the formula proposed by Shaw (1988), in which quality of life was envisioned as the product of the person's natural environment (NE) and the contributions of home (H) and society (S): Quality of life = $NE \times (H + S)$. Although these factors are undoubtedly important, no data exist to support the reliability or validity of this equation as an instrument for measurement and quantification of HRQOL.

Development of an instrument for measuring HRQOL is likely to be linked to the intended application of the instrument. Rather than imagining that a single instrument would be applicable to all situations, good scientific methodology requires that the hypothesis be specified first and the instrument then tailored to answer the question posed. Several possible applications for HRQOL instruments can be recognized in the literature (Fitzpatrick & Albrecht, 1994):

1. Health needs assessment (generally using population survey methodologies)

2. Clinical trials (generally using instruments that measure variables specific to the disorder being treated in the clinical trial; Spilker, 1990)

3. Evaluation research (generally using observational methodologies to assess health services outcomes)

4. Clinical care (generally using patient questionnaires to provide topics for discussion between provider and consumer in making treatment decisions; Cramer, 1994)

5. Resource allocation (generally using variations on cost-benefit analysis methodologies).

The validity of these methodologies varies and is probably greatest for clinical trials and health needs assessments. Evaluation research can also provide valid methodologies. The purpose of clinical care instruments is simply to facilitate discussion, so scientific validity is not really relevant for this application. The greatest controversy is with cost-benefit analyses intended to determine resource allocation, such as the Oregon plan to allocate public health care funds according to such an analysis.

An extremely important point that emerges from this listing of different applications of HRQOL is that the utilization of HRQOL instruments may be valid in some instances and not valid in others (Fitzpatrick & Albrecht, 1994). One need not condemn all applications of HRQOL, when it is really just one application (such as resource allocation) that is being questioned.

An illustration of this point is provided by the effort to assess HRQOL in patients with epilepsy (Cramer, 1994). A consortium of epilepsy and health service researchers developed three instruments for measuring HRQOL in epilepsy, collectively called "Quality of Life in Epilepsy" (or QOLIE). Two instruments (QOLIE-31 and QOLIE-89) were intended for use in research on health needs assessment, clinical trials, and evaluation of treatment outcomes. Both of these instruments were validated using appropriate scientific methodologies. The third instrument (QOLIE-10) was developed for use in clinical care to facilitate discussion between providers and people with epilepsy. QOLIE-10 was derived from the other two instruments but was not validated scientifically and is not intended for use in research. The QOLIE instruments are new and have not been used extensively yet, but they represent a promising approach to solving some of the methodological issues in measuring HRQOL.

The importance of the need for further development of valid measures of HRQOL is indicated by the effort of the World Health Organization to develop an instrument for this purpose. Preliminary results of this effort (Orley, 1994) suggest that at least five domains will need to be considered:

1. Physical health (including health, comfort, energy, rest, and sexuality)

2. Psychological health (including cognition, sensory function, mood, affect, self-esteem, and body image)

3. Independence (including mobility, communication, work, activities of daily living, and medication needs)

4. Social relationship (including social supports, intimacy, and ability to provide for others)

5. Environment (including home, work, finances, safety and security, transportation, health care, and leisure).

This is certainly a more comprehensive list, but may still be incomplete. Furthermore, the WHO needs to consider how these domains should be assessed, how the relative importance of these domains for the individual can be ordered, and how these measurement issues should be adapted to the particular application intended.

Current Status

An indication of the current status of the use of HRQOL measurement was provided by a meta-analytic study published in the *Journal of the American Medical Association* in August 1994. In this study, Gill and Feinstein (1994) reviewed the literature and selected articles that contained the term "quality of life" in the title and used at least one instrument or questionnaire. Twenty-five articles were randomly selected from a HRQOL bibliography that included 579 titles, 25 articles were randomly selected from a computerized search (MEDLINE) that included 434 titles, and 25 articles were randomly selected from 96 titles published in 13 "prominent" medical journals. The authors analyzed the selected articles for "face" validity using two sets of criteria, one directed at the investigators' tactics and one directed at the instruments utilized. With respect to the investigator-specific criteria, they found that 15% conceptually defined quality of life, 47% identified the targeted domains, and 36% gave reasons for choosing the instrument used in the study. With respect to instrument-specific criteria, they found that 17% incorporated a subjective patient rating of quality of life, 13% allowed patients to supplement the measured data with their own responses, and 8.5% asked patients to rate the importance of individual items being measured. The authors' hypothesis was supported: Most HRQOL studies use poorly specified "objective" criteria and do not incorporate a "subjective" patient perspective.

An accompanying editorial was somewhat critical of Gill and Feinstein's methodological approach, which was felt to be too stringent and based on the authors' philosophical belief that only the individual can rate HRQOL. The editorialists listed five different criteria (all generated from a patient-oriented perspective) and applied them to 15 studies randomly selected from the Gill and Feinstein review. They found that 67% used items valued by patients and also used instruments that demonstrated reasonable scientific validity (Guyatt & Cook, 1994).

Both the study authors (Gill & Feinstein, 1994) and the editorialists (Guyatt & Cook, 1994) agreed that the ultimate value of HRQOL studies is how they impact on patient care. Furthermore, they agreed that when making treatment recommendations, clinicians must consider the individual patient's values. Clearly, many current HRQOL studies are considerably less than perfect and provide only incomplete and sometimes invalid answers to the important questions raised. Nonetheless, they agreed that the effort should go forward

to investigate HRQOL in order to progress further toward the humane practice of medicine.

HRQOL and Mental Retardation

Mental retardation is not a disease. It is a state of impaired functioning, first manifest in childhood, in which specific intellectual and adaptive limitations interfere with optimal performance of social roles in the community (Luckasson et al., 1992). Because the idea of a disease-specific HRQOL is a fallacy, we cannot expect to identify a type of HRQOL that is specific for people with mental retardation. Rather, we should apply the general principles outlined in this chapter to evaluating HRQOL for all people, including those who happen to have mental retardation.

The principal problem for the evaluation of HRQOL in people with mental retardation is that it is more difficult to determine the individual's perspective and values. Notwithstanding the difficulty of doing this, we must keep the person's perspectives and values clearly in mind.

Philosophically, a reasonable starting point for public policy would be acceptance of the following assumptions:

1. Every person has a point of view about what life means and what makes lifes good.

2. Every person possesses a unique internal and external environment that defines his or her personal welfare and leads to an individual sense of well-being and a personal experience of wellness.

These assumptions exist independently of any cognitive limitation and are true for individuals with even the most profound degree of disability. We have seen that the elements of HRQOL are contained in these assumptions; thus, these elements are relevant for all people including individuals with mental retardation. From this starting point, we can then ask the practical and methodological questions about how to assess and enhance the HRQOL of people with mental retardation.

By starting from this philosophical perspective, we can properly ask the question, "What does HRQOL mean to this particular individual, who happens to have mental retardation?" It should be apparent that the answer must be provided by the individual and may not be the same as that which would be predicted by health care professionals, parents, or society. Yet it is precisely this answer, provided by the individual with mental retardation, that is most important and must take precedence. We must ascertain this answer before we can apply it to the purposes for which HRQOL is appropriate. This point cannot be emphasized enough: Until we can do this, we have no business applying HRQOL concepts to people with mental retardation. Learning the answer to this question will require all the sensitivity, creativity, and humanity that we can muster for the task. Indeed, we will likely discover that the process of finding this answer will also help us develop policies that will improve HRQOL for everyone.

References

Aggernase, A. (1994). On general and need-related quality of life: A psychological theory for use in medical rehabilitation and psychiatry. In L. Nordenfelt (Ed.), *Concepts and measurement of quality of life in health care* (pp. 241–255). Boston: Kluwer Academic Publishers.

Breslow, L. (1972). A quantitative approach to the World Health Organization definition of health: Physical, mental and social well-being. *International Journal of Epidemiology, 1,* 347–355.

Brock, D. (1993). Quality of life measures in health care and medical ethics. In M.C. Nussbaum & A. Sen (Eds.), *The quality of life* (pp. 95–132). Oxford, England: Claredon Press.

Cohen, L.G. (1990). *Before their time: Fetuses and infants at risk.* Washington: American Association on Mental Retardation.

Coulter, D.L. (1992, May). *The nature of personhood and the value of people with disabilities.* Paper presented at the 104th annual meeting of the American Association on Mental Retardation, New Orleans.

Cramer, J.A. (1994). Quality of life for people with epilepsy. *Neurologic Clinics, 12,* 1–14.

Fitzpatrick, R., & Albrecht, G. (1994). The plausibility of quality of life measures in different domains of health care. In L. Nordenfelt (Ed.), *Concepts and measurement of quality of life in health care* (pp. 201–227). Boston: Kluwer Academic Publishers.

Gaventa, W. (1994, May). *Spirituality and wellness.* Paper presented at the 106th annual meeting of the American Association on Mental Retardation, Boston.

Gill, T.M., & Feinstein, A.R. (1994). A critical appraisal of the quality of quality of life measurements. *Journal of the American Medical Association, 272,* 619–626.

Guyatt, G.H., & Cook, D.J. (1994). Commentary: Health status, quality of life and the individual. *Journal of the American Medical Association, 272,* 630–631.

Liss, P.E. (1994). On need and quality of life. In L. Nordenfelt (Ed.), *Concepts and measurement of quality of life in health care* (pp. 63–78). Boston: Kluwer Academic Publishers.

Luckasson, R. (1990). A lawyer's perspective on quality of life. In R.L. Schalock (Ed.), *Quality of life: Perspectives and issues* (pp. 211-214). Washington: American Association on Mental Retardation.

Luckasson, R., Coulter, D.L., Polloway, E.A., Reiss, S., Schalock, R.L., Snell, M.E., Spitalnik, D.M., & Stark, J.A. (1992). *Mental retardation: Definition, classification and systems of supports.* Washington, DC: American Association on Mental Retardation.

Musschenga, A.W. (1994). Quality of life and handicapped people. In L. Nordenfelt (Ed.), *Concepts and measurement of quality of life in health care* (pp. 181-198). Boston: Kluwer Academic Publishers.

Nordenfelt, L. (1994a). Introduction. In L. Nordenfelt (Ed.), *Concepts and measurement of quality of life in health care* (pp. 1-15). Boston: Kluwer Academic Publishers.

Nordenfelt, L. (1994b). Toward a theory of happiness: A subjectivist notion of quality of life. In L. Nordenfelt (Ed.), *Concepts and measurement of quality of life in health care* (pp. 35-57). Boston: Kluwer Academic Publishers.

Orley, J. (1994). Development of the World Health Organization quality of life instrument. In W.E. Dodson & M.R. Trimble (Eds.), *Quality of life in epilepsy* (pp. 54-69). New York: Raven Press.

Sen, A. (1980). Plural utility. *Proceedings of the Aristotelian Society, 81,* 193-218.

Shaw, A. (1988). Quality of life revisited. *Hastings Center Report, 18,* 10-12.

Spilker, B. (Ed.) (1990). *Quality of life assessments in clinical trials.* New York: Raven Press.

Veatch, R.M. (1986). *The foundations of justice: Why the retarded and the rest of us have claims to equality.* New York: Oxford University Press.

C H A P T E R   7

Quality of Life for Older Persons With Mental Retardation

Matthew P. Janicki

New York State Office of Mental Retardation and Developmental Disabilities

The difficulties inherent in defining the factors associated with quality of life for elderly persons with mental retardation are analogous to difficulties in defining factors for others who are just elderly or who are living their lives with a disability. The key difference between daily life for an independent older person in the general population and one who may be dependent due to his or her disability is that the independent individual may have more options to define what his or her day will be like. Dependency often denies an individual freedom of choice and requires that others provide. The interaction between two individuals with conflicting needs is what tests quality of life—for the provider must "care," and the recipient of the "care" must be provided for. Who defines what is to be done is the essential question, for freedom to make choices is the root of the quality of life concept. Thus is the dilemma of defining quality of life for older persons with mental retardation. Despite this dilemma, I argue throughout this chapter that life factors related to elderly persons with mental retardation are not necessarily different from those affecting other older adults.

Two factors stand out that have contributed to the lack of awareness or concern about the aging of older adults with mental retardation in the past: Persons with severe mental retardation had a relatively short life span, and many adults with mental retardation spent much of their lives in public institutions. However, more readily available medical services and improved overall health status have contributed to increased longevity (Day & Jancar, 1994). Further, with the nation's deinstitutionalization efforts over the past 20 years and increased emphasis on the availability of community living and support programs, many more older adults with mental retardation are present and visible in the community. Consequently, the combination of greater longevity as well as an increase in the number of known individuals with mental retardation residing among the general population have contributed to the greater awareness of aging among this population.

Factors Contributing to a Life of Quality

In our culture we value highly the ability to define our lives and make independent decisions about what we do, where we live, how we spend our time, what we eat, whom we socialize with, and so on. Of course, realism tempers these freedoms. Our income level defines our options for where we live, our experiences and opportunities define what we can do, and our networks define our social life. Persons with lifelong disabilities who are elderly may have limited social or financial options that impinge on how they exercise these decisions. Then the individuals themselves may have limitations that further constrict their choices.

Gerontologists have long debated the qualitative aspects of old age (Achenbaum, 1986; Neugarten & Neugarten, 1986). However, there is general recognition that with social and financial supports (e.g., the benefits of the Social Security Act, reasonable pensions, seniors discounts, housing assistance) old age for contemporary Americans is easier than it was for older persons several generations ago. In many instances this is also the case for adults with mental retardation. However, generational differences in life-style and service availability do exist. The question can be posed: Is life better now for older Americans with a lifelong disability than it was in previous generations?

What factors contribute to what we consider quality of life? Lawton (1983) characterizes "the good life" for older persons as composed of four sectors: behavioral competence, psychological well-being, perceived quality of life, and objective environment. Within the sector of behavioral competence, he proposed a hierarchy that includes health, functional health, cognition, time use, and social behavior. He posited an interrelation among these sectors that influences the self, which in turn reenergizes the sectors. Blunden (1988) offers several dimensions that he considers integral to a life of quality: physical well-being, material well-being, social well-being, and cognitive well-being. Clark (1988) notes that personal dignity, freedom of choice, and self-determination are important contributors to quality of life among elderly persons in long-term care settings. However, Clark notes further that institutional and familial forces are among the threats to these autonomy and personal empowerment factors that contribute to an enhanced quality of life.

Certainly, health or *physical well-being* (the ability to use one's body as effectively as possible) are fundamental to other aspects of quality of life. Freedom from the debilitating effects of illness or disability is an important consideration to older individiuals with mental retardation. The limitations of old age or lifelong physical disability can reduce the individual's independence and lead to profound impediments in life-style. Indeed, some workers have noted that self-rated health and social activity are associated with higher levels of life satisfaction.

Material well-being is the ability to gain and use at one's discretion disposable income, to live in quarters of acceptable physical quality, and to have material possessions of a desirable quantity and quality. Such environmental factors (what Lawton terms the objective environment) have a relationship to perceived quality of life (Lawton, 1983). The implication is that where and under what conditions one lives has a significant effect on one's level of satisfaction.

Blunden (1988) notes that the dimension of *social well-being* offers a vital element to most people's lives. Being part of the greater community, having relationships, being able to make choices, exercising competence (in communication, mobility, self-help, and social and leisure skills), and being the object of respect, are all important ingredients of social well-being. Indeed, class differences can affect social involvement and consequently subjective well-being (Kearney, Plax, & Lentz, 1985). Although choice is a factor in life satisfaction, to exercise choice one must have the social and economic status that affords one the options to choose from (Brown, 1993). Further, being able to express one's membership in society with the same entitlements and rights as others have is an important facet of social well-being (Cotten & Spirrison, 1986).

According to the gerontological literature, *cognitive well-being* is particularly important to a life of quality. This dimension involves one's own perception of quality of life and life satisfaction. Most research has shown that self-perceptions of well-being are strongly related to socioeconomic factors, degree of social interaction, and aspects of living situations (Larson, 1978). Again, the notion of being in a position to exercise choice apparently is tied to greater cognitive well-being and life satisfaction. Further, societal referents are important contributors to self-perception. Clark (1988) makes the point that pejorative labeling (advertent or inadvertent) of older persons can lead to diminished self-esteem. He notes that such labelling can restrict autonomy, life chances, and opportunities.

How do these conceptional notions translate into defining life-styles or services for older adults? A primary consideration is the recognition that senior services are intrinsically different from services for younger adults. Because continued training, vocational preparation, and work productivity are no longer programmatic goals or priorities, senior services can be directed toward higher ends—such as exploring artistic and expressive self-potential, participating in one's community life, engaging in new experiences, learning to make choices, socializing and reminiscing, maintaining wellness and fitness regimens, enjoying leisure experiences, and doing things that are simply fun (Browder & Cooper, 1994; Brown, 1993; Hawkins, 1993).

A second consideration is the confluence of age and disability and its relation to a number of contextual variables. The balance of this chapter addresses three of these contextual variables in reference to which I make the following three assumptions:

- Societal attitudes affect the quality of life for older adults with mental retardation.

- Quality of life factors for older adults with mental retardation are qualitatively similar to those for other older adults.

- Transitional occurrences present challenges that affect the life-styles of older adults with mental retardation.

Societal Attitudes Toward the Elderly

Societal attitudes are often framed by what a majority of the population thinks about minorities within that population. Minorities are characterized as a group of people who, because of their age, racial, physical, cultural, or other characteristics, are singled out from others in the society in which they live for differential and unequal treatment and who therefore regard themselves as objects of collective discrimination (Wirth, 1945). Historically, elderly persons in our nation have been viewed as a minority group and have been stereotyped and discriminated against by virtue of their age. Such discrimination occurs when the minority is ascribed a devalued status.

Some minority populations also can have valued status. Valued status can come from numbers, power, or wealth. Although the population of the United States will never be totally elderly, the character of the population is changing dramatically, and what many have viewed as a passive minority may not remain so for long. Indeed, economists are predicting that our nation's senior citizens will control a significant and increasing share of the disposable income in the nation. This trend will continue well into the 21st century. Such economic wealth should translate into considerable economic power, enhanced valued status, and a changed perception of what it means to be elderly.

Expectations are that the nation's population of older persons with mental retardation will also double over the next 25 years because of parallel population characteristics, that is, the "baby boomers" growing older and increased longevity among individuals with mental retardation (National Institute on Aging, 1987). What of the current older population of adults with mental retardation or developmental disabilities? Some estimates put the contemporary population of elderly persons with mental retardation or other developmental disability at between 200,000 and 500,000 (Seltzer & Krauss, 1994). A conservative estimate is that of every 1,000 older persons, 4 are expected to have mental retardation (Janicki, 1993). Age trends show that women generally outnumber men among persons with mental retardation over the age of 50 and, while the life expectancy of men is increasing, the predominance of older women will continue. Anecdotal information indicates that many older adults with mental retardation live with their families and continue to work well beyond the typical retirement age of the mid-sixties. How this will look in the future remains open to speculation.

Qualitatively Similar Quality of Life Factors

These demographics indicate that we must consider old age an important aspect of the life span. One of the underlying facets of the definition of quality of life for older adults is how society defines this population and what status it ascribes to it. What is important to consider is that older adults with mental retardation must contend with the dual problem of how society views being old and being disabled. Indeed, our society has had a built-in negative bias toward old age. Further, our society still exhibits negative bias toward being disabled.

Consequently, one factor to consider is how cultural factors shape our attitudes toward older persons with mental retardation. We recognize that societal attitudes toward aging and toward mental retardation interact to affect the nature of the integration of older adults with mental retardation into the fabric of society.

Our society ascribes positive value to youth and negative value to age. Butler (1975), who coined the term "ageism," noted that ageism is manifested in a wide range of phenomena such as stereotypes and myths; outright disdain and dislike or simply subtle avoidance of contact; discriminatory practices in housing, employment, and services of all kinds; as well as epithets, cartoons, and jokes. Ageism represents a negative societal attitude. Blatant prejudice against people who are old is demonstrated by emphasis on youth and wellness—the antithesis of our stereotypic perception of the elderly.

Some gerontologists, however, believe that the notion that older people are a devalued minority group is a "social myth" that has been perpetuated without cause. While some might view old age as a social problem because of visible age-associated problems such as frailty, cognitive decline or dementia, and physical illness, these are symptoms of pathological aging, not normal aging. The strides taken to overcome such perceptions by focusing on more normal aging and related well-elderly lifestyles have done much to overcome negative stereotypes of old age. Unfortunately, there are writers in the mental retardation field who continue to expound on the myth of the devalued status of the elderly and, by extension, to promote the notion that for older persons with mental retardation to associate with other older persons devalues their own status (e.g., Blaney, 1992; Steer, 1994).

A parallel negative attitude exists in terms of how some members of our society manifest attitudes toward persons with handicapping conditions. The term *handicapism* has been coined to characterize this attitude. Handicapism is also culture and generation bound; while many younger persons are constantly exposed to persons with mental retardation and physical handicaps, many older persons have not been so for the better part of their lives. Many negative attitudes toward handicap among elderly persons stem from a fear that they themselves can or will become infirm or disabled. Further, different facets of American society show different levels of acceptance of differentness. People also tend to view disabilities along a basic value continuum in relation to notions such as "normalcy," looking at others in terms of their ability to conform to majority standards for work productivity and other prevailing values.

Because of the polycultural nature of American society, each subculture and class within it brings its own attitudes and perceptions toward disablement and age. Some cultural groups are family and kin oriented and perceive disabled members as no different from any other member. Others see disability as a stigma, and the disabled individual becomes an outcast. Between these two extremes are many variations (Janicki, 1987; McCallion, Janicki, & Grant-Griffin, 1996).

Research has shown that in the greater scheme of society persons with a disability, such as mental retardation, are socially devalued (Roberto & Nelson, 1988). Devaluation makes it difficult for those individuals to be accepted and to move freely within society. Further, how a person is perceived affects how that person is treated. If one of the tenets of community integration is to use generic or mainstream services to expand options and choices, then what are the implications of how people with disabilities are perceived by other users of mainstream services? With regard to older adults with mental retardation, the issue is, how do other users of senior services react to seniors with disabilities who want to use the same services (Brown, 1993; LePore & Janicki, 1990).

I have been told by a number of senior program administrators that the individuals using their programs have very set ideas about the senior center and what it should be used for. These set ideas affect how they react to "outsiders," whether or not they are disabled. Also, many older adults in the United States come from ethnic groups that have their own stereotypes and attitudes toward disabled peers (Grant-Griffin, 1994). Consequently, one major consideration with regard to quality of life is how community attitudes of generational as well as cultural groups (and the class differences within those cultures) impinge on the choices that older adults with mental retardation can make. Certainly, their options will be affected by how a select group of elderly persons accommodates newcomers, particularly newcomers who have a lifelong disability.

Our society is changing; it is growing progressively older and as such it should become more accepting of old age. However, we are not yet free from ageism in all its forms. Our society has also made more accommodations for its citizens with handicapping conditions, but has yet to become fully accessible. We have a growing population of older people with life-long disabilities such as mental retardation. We have mixed notions of how best to provide services for this growing population of elders with mental retardation, and we are torn between doing it ourselves and using the generic elder care system (Ansello & Rose, 1989; Janicki, 1993). We understand that it does not make sense to continually offer only segregated programs; yet we fear that what others have to offer will not measure up to our standards. What we do, in light of these attitudes, will be a measure of the quality of life experiences in the future for seniors with mental retardation.

The Challenges of Transition

Qualitative factors affecting the ability of older adults with a disability to define their own life-style interact with what can be best characterized as "problems of transition." These problems of transition pose a number of challenges to maintaining life-style and addressing quality of life concerns for older adults with mental retardation (Janicki, 1994).

The Challenge of Responding to the Needs of Seniors

The increased number of older adults with mental retardation has posed a number of problems that can affect life satisfaction and life-style (Brown, 1993). First, in many states increased longevity has created a demand for services and programs that public authorities may yet be unprepared to provide. Over the years, agencies in these states have developed child-oriented developmental and remedial educational services as well as adult-oriented vocational and social development services. The transition to senior-oriented retardation services (and the divergence from child or work-age adult program practices that these demand) has been slow in coming. Further, many agencies are still facing the challenge of a reactive response to the numbers of unserved older persons seeking supports and aging-related services, and have not been able additionally to focus on a proactive response of enabling adults in their middle age to plan, construct, and realize life goals.

Probably more importantly, disagreement continues among mental retardation policymakers and administrators as to the auspice and nature of these senior services. Whether to create parallel senior programs within the mental retardation service system or to collaborate with the aging network in the use of its existing or augmented senior services has not been resolved (Clark, 1988; Gettings, 1988). This lack of consistency in policy has significant implications for how services are defined and developed, and the manner in which the age-defined needs of seniors can be met. If service providers build from younger adult work or habilitative models for programs and extend these models to senior services, they will create different challenges than if they adapt models of senior services from the aging network (Janicki, 1992, 1993). Further, senior services models must recognize a different set of personal development goals and in fact may need to consider lifetime planning affecting adults in mid-life. These goals, in turn, will significantly affect the quality of life in the latter years.

The Challenge of Aging Families

Another type of challenge is related to the increasing number of adults with mental retardation remaining at home throughout their lives (Seltzer & Krauss, 1994; Smith, Fullmer, & Tobin, 1994). Living with one's family may very well facilite opportunities for an enriched life-style. In some instances, however, living with one's parents can be restrictive and can adversely affect quality of life.

Unlike other elderly persons, older adults with mental retardation generally do not have children or a spouse on whom they can depend for aid and support. In some instances, they live with very old parents who still provide for their day-to-day supports; thus, the notion of the "two-generation-elderly family." In other instances, siblings or the children of siblings provide care. However, because of advancing age, a deteriorating situation can lead to serious concerns about well-being, particularly when an elderly parent (or parents) retains the responsibility for the care of an aging adult son or daughter with mental retardation (Janicki, 1996; Roberto & Nelson, 1988). Yet, there may be still another situation in which an older son or daughter with mental retardation is the sole source of support for an elderly parent and as such is faced with being in a caregiver role. Thus the dilemma: Does the adult subjugate his or her responsibility as a caregiver to a need to be independent and, perhaps, to actualize a different life-style? And if so, does that devalue familial responsibility (a prominent culture-linked value)?

The Challenge of Growing Old in One's Home

Gerontologists refer to the phenomenon of "aging in place," which means growing older while remaining in the same setting. The aging in place of older adults with mental retardation currently living in a variety of residential situations (such as foster family care homes, group homes, board and care homes, apartments, their own homes, and the like) also poses a challenge to maintenance or enhancement of life-style. Generally, this notion refers to the problem of dealing with the growing frailty of older individuals already living in a setting of their choice and the changing demands that growing frailty makes upon the supports in that setting (whether staff, spouse, companions, family, or friends).

Many older adults with mental retardation living in group homes and other similar settings began to reside in the settings as young or middle-aged adults. With the passage of time, they have aged and their abilities and needs have changed. Some are experiencing medical complications or increased frailty that accompany the normal aging process (such as difficulties in ambulation, sensitivity to temperature changes, diminished vision and hearing, and impairments in fine motor dexterity) or the insidious problems associated with pathological aging (such as dementia).

Changes in quality of life may result from situations where movement and participation in loved activities become restricted and labored due to the physical changes associated with aging or disease. In such situations, agencies face problems, including identifying the appropriate supports for residential and day activities and attempting to keep intact friendship networks that the individual has developed and upon which he or she relies. For individuals living on their own, these problems may become critical determinants of how long they can remain fully independent. They may need to draw on all their resources to deal with feelings and aftereffects of the death or serious illness of friends or family members. How these problems are handled will be defined by some of the features of life noted earlier.

The Challenge of Retirement

Of all the transition issues related to aging, the most challenging is retirement (Laughlin & Cotten, 1994). Retirement is a particularly vexing issue because of its impact on all facets of life. Minimally it presents an immediate change in life-style; maximally it may threaten one's living situation, health, social and financial supports, and friendship network. This is why retirement should be seen as "retirement to" and not "retirement from." Among nondisabled persons, the material benefit associated with work is usually substituted by Social Security benefits or a pension. Further, most pensioners, when considering what to do upon leaving the work force, also think in terms of what will replace work and the social and psychological benefits associated with the workplace, such as friendships, a place to go, and the personal identity that is defined by one's job. This is not always the case with older adults with mental retardation.

The challenge to life-style in these situations is closely associated with the lack of appropriate alternatives associated with later life. For example, the available alternatives may not compensate for the loss of the social and financial benefits associated with continued involvement in work. Further, social and personal changes that are associated with retirement can be traumatic when bridging does not occur as part of the transition process. The loss or change of friends when taking on new daily activities (or perhaps lacking them) can pose significant difficulties to the overall well-being of the individual.

Certainly, one of the challenges of enhancing life-style is looking to a

blending of supports and services available within the community with those necessarily provided by the mental retardation system. For example, for older adults who are relatively independent and capable, daily activities can include informal involvement in local clubs, visits with friends, employment, and participation in a host of other ordinary activities. Daily activities may also be more formal, such as joining a local senior center or attending a congregate meal site. For older adults who are more severely mentally impaired, enrolling in adult day services or attending a specialty senior program may be preferred. In all of these situations, one key feature is how the individual manages to be accepted by peers or others in the environment. With age, people tend to become much more codependent and reliant upon social networks.

Yet, each of these involvements may also be either an opportunity or a threat depending on how the person copes with life's changes and integrates new experiences. Early commitment to a particular life-style may affect the quality of life more positively than later commitment. However, the defining factor may be how the transition to retirement activities or the lifelong participation in a range of life-style experiences ultimately affects one's ability to survive.

Conclusion

All of these transitions pose certain challenges, some easily overcome, others much more complex. The notions explored earlier, as posed by Lawton, Blunden, and others, bear heavily on the dignity of old age of older adults with mental retardation. A key question is how these challenges can be used to improve life-style constructively and minimize the restrictions posed by growing old.

Overall, quality of life factors related to elderly persons with mental retardation are not necessarily different from those affecting other older adults. There is a need for an acceptable living environment, freedom to choose activities and friends, social and psychological well-being, financial security, and physical independence through good health. It was proposed that external influences may impinge upon these factors. Such factors include cultural and societal perceptions and attitudes toward the elderly and persons with disabilities, and may also include familial and institutional factors related to living and care arrangements.

In addition, it was noted that points of transition in the lives of older persons with mental retardation will offer challenges that may enhance or diminish factors contributing to quality of life. These transitions include growing older within an overall system of care that has not previously accommodated older persons, living within a two-generation elderly family, aging in place within one's home, facing the transitions and challenges of retirement, and gaining acceptance into mainstream senior activities.

Each successive generation of persons with mental retardation will hold a collective set of experiences that will be its own. Contemporary adults with mental retardation are living longer, in better health, enjoying a broader range of experiences, and growing older with greater dignity than previous generations. This will be doubly true for future generations of seniors. No two generations will be the same. Our current expectations of the potential limits of a valued life-style will be redefined over the years to come. This is healthy, as it shows that life is a valued commodity and that we are constantly stretching the limits of what we, as a society, can offer to persons who increasingly define their needs as similar to ours.

References

Achenbaum, W.A. (1986). America as an aging society: Myths and images. *Daedalus, 115*(1), 13–30.

Ansello, E.F., & Rose, T. (1989). *Aging and lifelong disabilities: Partnership for the twenty-first century.* College Park: University of Maryland Center on Aging.

Blaney, B.C. (1992). The search for a conceptual framework. In S. Moss (Ed.), *Aging and developmental disabilities: Perspectives from nine countries* (Monograph #52). Durham, NH: World Rehabilitation Fund/University of New Hampshire.

Blunden, R. (1988). Programmatic features of quality settings. In M.P. Janicki, M.W. Krauss, & M.M. Seltzer (Eds.), *Community residences for persons with developmental disabilities: Here to stay* (pp. 117–122). Baltimore: Brookes.

Browder, D.M., & Cooper, K.J. (1994). Inclusion of older adults with mental retardation in leisure opportunities. *Mental Retardation, 32,* 91–99.

Brown, R.I. (1993). Quality of life issues in aging and intellectual disability. *Australia and New Zealand Journal of Developmental Disabilities, 18,* 219–227.

Butler, R. (1975). *Why survive? Being old in America.* New York: Harper & Row.

Clark, P.G. (1988). Autonomy, personal empowerment, and quality of life in long-term care. *Journal of Applied Gerontology, 7,* 279–297.

Clark, S. (1988). Room in the aging network? A view from the aging system. *Perspectives on Aging, 17*(5), 13, 22.

Cotten, P.D., & Spirrison, C.L. (1986). The elderly mentally retarded (developmentally disabled) population: A challenge for the service delivery system. In S.J. Brody & G.E. Ruff (Eds.), *Aging and rehabilitation: Advances in the state of the art.* New York: Springer.

Day, K., & Jancar, J. (1994). Mental and physical health and aging in mental handicap: A review. *Journal of Intellectual Disability Research, 38,* 241–256.

Gettings, R. (1988). Barriers to and opportunities for cooperation between the aging and developmental services. *Educational Gerontology, 14,* 419–429.

Grant-Griffin, L. (1994, November). *Demonstration projects that focus on aiding persons from multicultural communities.* Paper presented at the 1994 annual meeting of the Gerontological Society of America, Atlanta, Georgia.

Hawkins, B. (1993). Leisure participation and life satisfaction of older adults with mental retardation and Down syndrome. In E. Sutton, A.R. Factor, B. Hawkins, T. Heller, & G. Seltzer (Eds.), *Older adults with developmental disabilities: Optimizing choices and change.* Baltimore: Brookes.

Janicki, M.P. (1987, May). Cultural attitude perspectives toward elderly persons with mental retardation. In *Cultural factors in mental retardation.* Symposium conducted at the annual meeting of the American Association on Mental Retardation, Los Angeles, CA.

Janicki, M.P. (1992). *Integration experiences casebook: Program ideas in aging and developmental disabilities.* Albany, NY: Office of Mental Retardation and Developmental Disabilities, Community Integration Project in Aging and Developmental Disabilities.

Janicki, M.P. (1993). *Building the future: Planning and community development in aging and developmental disabilities.* Albany, NY: Office of Mental Retardation and Developmental Disabilities, Community Integration Project in Aging and Developmental Disabilities.

Janicki, M.P. (1994). Policies and supports for older persons with mental retardation. In M. Seltzer, M. Krauss, & M. Janicki (Eds.), *Life course perspectives on adulthood and old age* (pp. 143–166). Washington, DC: American Association on Mental Retardation.

Janicki, M.P. (1996). *Help for caring for older people caring for an adult with a developmental disability.* Albany: New York State Developmental Disabilities Planning Council.

Kearney, P., Plax, T.G., & Lentz, P.S. (1985). Participation in community organizations and socioeconomic status as determinants of seniors' life satisfaction. *Activities, Adaptation & Aging, 6*(4), 31–37.

Larson, R. (1978). Thirty years of research on the subjective well-being of older Americans. *Journal of Gerontology, 33,* 109–125.

Laughlin, C., & Cotten, P.D. (1994). Efficacy of a pre-retirement planning intervention for aging individuals with mental retardation. *Journal of Intellectual Disability Research, 38,* 317–328.

Lawton, M.P. (1983). Environment and other determinants of well-being in older people. *The Gerontologist, 23,* 349–357.

LePore, P., & Janicki, M.P. (1990). *The wit to win: How to integrate older persons with developmental disabilities into community aging programs.* Albany, NY: State Office for the Aging.

McCallion, P., Janicki, M.P., & Grant-Griffin, L. (1996, June). *Exploring the impact of culture and acculturation on family caregiving for persons with developmental disabilities.* Paper presented at the Invitational Roundtable on Research Advances in Later Life Family Caregiving of Adults with Disabilities, Chicago, IL.

National Institute on Aging. (1987). *Personnel for health needs of the elderly.* Washington, DC: U.S. Department of Health and Human Services, National Institute on Aging.

Neugarten, B.L., & Neugarten, D.A. (1986). Age in the aging society. *Daedalus, 115*(1) 31–49.

Roberto, K.A., & Nelson, R.E. (1988). The developmentally disabled elderly: Concerns of service providers. *Journal of Applied Gerontology, 8,* 175–182.

Seltzer, M.M., & Krauss, M.W. (1994). Aging parents with coresident adult children: The impact of lifelong caregiving. In M.M. Seltzer, M. Krauss, & M.P. Janicki (Eds.), *Lifespan development and mental retardation: Implications for individuals, their families, and the human services system* (pp. 3–18). Washington, DC: American Association on Mental Retardation.

Smith, G.S., Fullmer, E.M., & Tobin, S.S. (1994). Living outside the system: An exploration of older families who do not use day programs. In M.M. Seltzer, M. Krauss, & M.P. Janicki (Eds.), *Lifespan development and mental retardation: Implications for individuals, their families, and the human services system* (pp. 19–38). Washington, DC: American Association on Mental Retardation.

Steer, M. (1994). Review of "Aging and developmental disabilities: Perspectives from nine countries." *American Journal of Mental Retardation, 99,* 322–324.

Wirth, L. (1945). The problem of minority groups. In R. Linton (Ed.), *The science of man in the world crisis.* New York: Columbia University Press.

Promoting Quality of Life Through Leisure and Recreation

Barbara A. Hawkins
Indiana University

One important aspect of the growing national interest in the quality of American life is related clearly to the life-style that each American citizen creates for him or herself. Professional interest in life-style and quality of life is also apparent in the disabilities field, as well as in the recreation, parks, and leisure services field. Furthermore, as professionals across a number of human service fields struggle to maintain solid funding for services to persons with and without disabilities, the focus on life-style and quality of life can be expected to sharpen. Thus, the relationship between quality of life and leisure and recreation as elements of a personal life-style is relevant to the application of the concept of quality of life for persons with disabilities. This chapter also discusses the need to develop consistent meaning and application of the concept, as well as operational tools with which to evaluate quality of life in service provision and professional practice (Goode, 1994; Schalock, 1990; Wolfensberger, 1994).

Quality of Life, Life-Style, and Leisure

Most readers would agree that leisure is an important aspect of their own life-styles and thus, their quality of life. Leisure time, adequate recreational opportunities, and a strong social relationship network are of vital importance to most people. These are central ingredients in the many descriptions that we use to characterize our individual life-styles. For example, we are active bikers or avid movie-goers or, perhaps, we spend countless hours pursuing a hobby, like antiquing. These examples illustrate the importance that is placed on leisure and recreation activities as primary elements of life-style and, ultimately, main contributors to our subjective view of the quality of our lives. Many Americans tenaciously guard the hours in a day that they have available for their leisure. These simple truths hardly need stating except for the persistent challenges that impact the lives of people with disabilities. Research results underscore the reality that leisure and recreation remain problematic for people with mental retardation. All too often, leisure and recreation are constrained, unfulfilled, incomplete, contrived, or inadequate (Hawkins, 1991, 1993a, 1993b; Hawkins & Freeman, 1993a, 1993b; Hawkins, Freeman, & Mash, 1991).

This chapter is based on the assumption that leisure and recreation are fundamental shapers of a personal life-style. Furthermore, it is personal life-style that instrumentally influences the subjective perception of a satisfying life. If one's life-style is balanced in quality and quantity across work, leisure, and personal maintenance responsibilities, there is a greater likelihood of a perceived higher satisfaction with life. This line of reasoning also suggests that if daily life activity is absent or diminished in any of these major spheres (i.e., work, leisure, and personal responsibilities), then it may be more likely that lower life satisfaction is subjectively perceived and lower quality of life objectively evident. In this simple, straightforward way of describing a high-quality life-style as a balance across the major life spheres of work, leisure, and personal responsibilities), the centrality of leisure to the concept of quality of life is distinct.

The remaining sections of this chapter further clarify the meaning of leisure and recreation, thus firmly binding them to our understanding of life-style. Personal life-style fundamentally influences subjective perceptions of satisfaction with life, and life satisfaction is a commonly used measure of quality of life. Included in this chapter is a brief discussion of the promotion of satisfying life-styles through leisure education and service network supports. The chapter concludes with a short list of suggestions for the future.

Leisure and Recreation Defined

Brightbill and Mobley (1977) noted that leisure is "that part of life that comes nearest to allowing us to be free in a regimented and conforming world, which enables us to pursue self-expression, intellectual and spiritual development, and beauty in their endless forms" (p. 7). Real leisure is not enforced free time; rather, it is the opportunity to choose freely those activities of greatest preference and interest from a variety of options. The choices made reflect self-expression and also may promote self-development—intellectually, socially, physically, and spiritually (Brightbill & Mobley, 1977).

The concept of leisure has been studied systematically by sociologists and psychologists. Over the years, leisure has come to be defined as having the following key elements: freedom (that is, free time as well as freedom of choice), activity (including recreational pursuits as well as self-development interests), and a specific state of mind or affective state, often characterized as pleasurable, joyful, happy, creative, spontaneous, and absorbed (Kelly, 1990; Murphy, 1975; Neulinger, 1974). Common among the array of definitions in the literature is the ideal of *freedom*: freedom to choose what one wants to do, freedom to act on one's choice, and freedom from other obligatory responsibilities (e.g., self-care, work, home, etc.). Freedom is one of the hallmark characteristics of leisure that distinguishes it from work and other obligatory activities of life. It may be this attribute of leisure that makes it so problematic in the lives of people with disabilities. Recent studies have shown that a major barrier to leisure for adults with mental retardation is the role that caregivers and professionals assume in deciding what activities will be pursued during free time (Hawkins, 1993a, 1993b).

Participation in leisure and the experience of leisure are also associated with feelings of pleasure, fulfillment, satisfaction, creativity, joy/happiness, and self-actualization. Leisure is personally directed activity that is motivating in and of itself, and not associated with external rewards or social control. The affective benefits of leisure are as instrumental to the experience as are perceived freedom and the time in which to pursue leisure. Significant associations between leisure and perceived life satisfaction have been found with adults who have mental retardation, thus confirming the instrumental role that leisure plays in subjective perceptions of quality of life (Hawkins, 1993a, 1993b).

Across the years, however, leisure has been most frequently identified with time, personal choice time, discretionary time, time not devoted to work or other personal responsibilities. Leisure time is those free hours in which to enjoy the full range of possibilities offered by the surrounding culture, time that is distinctly directed by personal interest. Recent explorations of constraints on leisure for people with mental retardation have confirmed a lack of personal choice time or perceived free time (Hawkins et al., 1991).

An enduring view of leisure is illustrated in the following definition by Carlson, MacLean, Deppe, & Peterson (1979):

> *Leisure is that portion of time not obligated by subsistence or existence demands. It represents discretionary or free time, time in which one may make voluntary choices of experience.*
>
> **(p. 8)**

What remains central to our conception of leisure is *freedom*. Free time and freely chosen preferred activities may be rare commodities in the lives of persons with disabilities, according to studies by Hawkins and her associates (Hawkins, 1991, 1993a, 1993b; Hawkins & Freeman, 1993a; Hawkins, Freeman, & Mash, 1991). Therefore, opportunities to experience pleasure, joy, and other affective states that are characteristic of leisure seem to be diminished for many persons with disabilities.

Recreation, on the other hand, is but one of many possible ways in which we use or fulfill our leisure. Recreational activities may be active or passive, solitary or social. Recreation also is typically thought of as voluntary. It is important to recognize that experiences other than typical recreational activities may also be pursued as leisure. For example, going to church or synagogue or taking a nap in a hammock on the porch probably are not typically thought of as recreation but may be pursued during leisure. Most individuals conceive their recreation to be characterized by more organized activities such as games and sports, hobbies, arts and crafts, and outdoor pursuits. Important aspects associated with recreation activity include these (Carlson et al., 1979):

- Recreational activities are participation oriented as opposed to nonparticipatory.

- Recreation typically occurs during leisure.

- We expect to feel satisfied and happy with our recreation.

- Recreational activity often provides a change in pace or respite from work.

- Recreation often means more to the individual than just a diversion or time filler.

There is little doubt that leisure is a primary means for experiencing personal freedom. Currently, however, work and personal responsibilities appear to be of main concern to the inclusion of individuals with disabilities into the mainstream fabric of society. It may be that in the future recreation and leisure will take on increasing value as a counterbalance to emphasis on work activity and personal maintenance responsibilities. In this manner, leisure may increase in its importance in describing a high-quality life-style.

In time, leisure may be recognized as a more prominent component in the quality of life of people with mental retardation and closely related disabilities. Because personal freedom is of growing importance to people with disabilities, and leisure embodies personal freedom as a primary characteristic, it is apparent that leisure can be instrumental to perceived satisfaction with the quality of one's life. The freedom to choose leisure activity, some of which may be recreational in nature, has been found to be significantly associated with the perception of a high quality of life across the adult life span in the general population (Mobily, 1987). The same association also has been confirmed in adults with mental retardation (Hawkins, 1993a). Using this rationale for the centrality of leisure and recreation in quality of life, we can now explore ways to enhance leisure and thus promote high-quality life-styles for persons with disabilities.

Education for Leisure-Centered Living

A great deal of attention in recent years has been given to improving the quality of life for persons with disabilities by enhancing their life choices. Enhancements have included providing community-based work/job opportunities, expanding residential alternatives and choices, and most recently, promoting personal empowerment. Each of these advancements has, in some ways, been a revolution. In other ways, we as a society have evolved to a level of understanding that embraces people with disabilities as people first and as individuals with special challenges second. What has not fully occurred yet in these (r)evolutionary processes is the cultivation of life-style development as a primary focus of adult activity.

Among the many challenges that people with disabilities face is the need to discover and nurture their self-identity. This challenge is also shared with adults who do not have disabilities. In most situations, identity is closely tied to work and family roles, and to the leisure repertoire that develops across the life course. Leisure falls naturally into a personally defined life-style. Further, leisure serves to help each of us find out who we are and what brings us the greatest pleasure, fulfillment, and satisfaction throughout life.

Those adults who find themselves experiencing adjustment difficulties often have not allowed adequate time for leisure. They may have permitted work or personal responsibilities to dominate their life-style. Often, these are the people who need leisure counseling or leisure education to rebalance their lives, especially when major events, such as catastrophic illness or retirement, catch them off guard. They need the support of a skill-building, educational process to help them infuse leisure into their lives and thus improve the quality of their life-style.

Unfortunately, a parallel situation characterizes and pervades the adult life course for many people with disabilities. A great deal of attention is paid to developing work attitudes, values, and skills, as well as home personal maintenance skills. However, leisure is leftover time and is assumed to fall into place as what is scheduled by caregivers after work and home obligations are completed. Although some structured activities are available to persons with disabilities who live in supervised living arrangements, leisure resources and opportunities vary greatly from one residence to the next. Often, recreation and leisure are predetermined by caregivers. Leisure pursuits may or may not reflect the personal interests, desires, and choices of the individual with a disability.Learning independent leisure skills and building an independent leisure repertoire are appropriate life-style development goals for people with disabilities. In the leisure services field, it is recognized that leisure education is instrumental in developing a healthy, high-quality life-style. Education for the promotion of an independent leisure repertoire is one avenue for promoting a higher quality of life for persons with disabilities.

Leisure education is intended to assist individuals in developing the knowledge, attitudes, values, and beliefs necessary for the wise use of leisure (Brightbill & Mobley, 1977). Leisure education focuses on learning what leisure is and how it is instrumental in living a high-quality life-style. Leisure education assists individuals in identifying and overcoming barriers to the pursuit of leisure.

Several definitions effectively convey the key ideas behind leisure education as instrumental to life-style development (Bender, Brannan, & Verhoven, 1984; Hawkins, May, & Rogers, 1996; Mundy & Odum, 1979):

- Enhancing the use of free time to improve one's quality of life

- Using learning processes and content to develop the knowledge, attitudes, values, beliefs, and skills necessary to promote the constructive use of leisure

- Learning to use leisure to promote self-development and self-actualization

- Learning to accept, appreciate, and enjoy leisure, as well as achieve a sense of personal freedom to pursue leisure

- Recognizing that personal needs and abilities can be satisfied through leisure

- Assisting persons to establish leisure goals and to develop a leisure repertoire

- Empowering individuals to develop their own life-styles.

In summary, leisure education is a process by which adults discover the benefits of leisure and develop the necessary skills for pursuing a life-style that embraces leisure. Leisure education is appropriate in a wide range of human service settings including community recreation centers, supervised living arrangements, adult day programs, rehabilitation centers, and long-term-care facilities. In these contexts, it is assumed that the individual who is receiving services also needs some assistance in facilitating an independent life-style. Therefore, leisure, life-style, and quality of life are intimately interdependent within the context of the leisure education process. As a fully independent leisure repertoire is developed, the role of the leisure education process fades and community supports increase. In the next section of this chapter the content and processes that form leisure education are described.

Leisure Education and Life-Style Development

A careful consideration of both content and learning processes is used in developing a leisure education program, along with a recognition of learner characteristics (e.g., age, gender, sociocultural background, learning skills, needed supports). Core areas for leisure content include (a) leisure awareness and appreciation; (b) self-awareness and leisure; (c) self-determination, leisure choices, and decision-making skills; (d) knowledge of leisure opportunities and resources; and (e) leisure activity skills (Bender et al., 1984; Dattilo & Murphy, 1991; Hawkins et al., 1996; Howe-Murphy & Charboneau, 1987; Joswiak, 1989; Mundy & Odum, 1979; Schleien, Meyer, Heyne, & Brandt, 1995). The learning processes used in leisure education guide the participant through each of these knowledge areas toward the end goal of an independent, satisfying leisure repertoire. Dattilo and Murphy (1991) provide an excellent resource for selecting learning activities for the different leisure education content areas.

Leisure Awareness and Appreciation

Leisure awareness and appreciation begin the learning process. Participants learn the meaning of leisure and distinguish leisure from other domains of life activity such as work and home responsibilities. Preferences for one kind of leisure activity over another help the individual to identify a range of possible leisure pursuits. This phase assists participants in classifying activities into different life domains and learning to recognize the benefits derived from leisure activity involvement. Barriers to leisure involvement are often identified at this point. An exploration of the meaning of leisure is essential to positioning oneself in a life-style that includes leisure.

Self-Awareness and Self-Determination

The next content area in the leisure education process promotes an understanding of freedom and self-awareness.

This understanding is instrumental for exercising self-determination in leisure. The importance of one's preferences, interests, and specific needs enables the learner to then explore how leisure can be an area of life for self-expression. Self-awareness in leisure is necessary in order to reach the final goal of a personal leisure repertoire.

Opportunities and Resources

In order to act upon leisure opportunities, people need to know about the resources and supports that are available for use in fulfilling their preferred leisure. Typical settings, places, program resources, program leaders, and supports that connect the individual to selected leisure choices need to be taught. Learning to recognize home leisure and community-based opportunities is fostered in order to promote leisure engagement on a natural and daily basis.

In most communities, there are many leisure resources to use in the pursuit of one's leisure preferences. These should be learned by all citizens in the community in order to generate an individual leisure repertoire. Knowledge of social supports and relationship networks is also a critical component in the resource content area.

Leisure Activity Skills

The final content area in leisure education is the development of leisure activity and decision-making skills (Dattilo, 1994). Learners are coached to recognize what resources are needed in order to act upon a leisure interest, the consequences associated with making one choice over another, and how to proceed to engage in an activity once it is selected. Inherent in the leisure education process is the continual exploration of new activities and the development of the participation skills necessary to pursue the chosen activities.

Successful leisure education programs consider several factors about the learner: age, needs, community context, sociocultural heritage, and any other factors that may influence the process of leisure life-style development. In general, the leisure education program development process includes the following steps: delineating the overall purpose of the program, specifying the program goals and objectives, identifying specific content with implementation procedures and performance goals, and documenting and evaluating program outcomes. Several good resources exist for developing program goals and identifying learning exercises (Dattilo & Murphy, 1991; Joswiak, 1989). Learners tend to appreciate and be motivated by learning experiences that use their life experiences and personal abilities. Above all else, leisure education should be fun, exciting, interesting, and motivating for the participants.

As an independent leisure repertoire is learned and reinforced, a personal life-style may evolve. Then, leisure will only need to be facilitated, supported, or enhanced across the adult life course. Supports in the community may include friendships and peer tutors to facilitate the pursuit of leisure preferences. Agencies may need to be educated on the need for facility or program enhancements in order to provide access and involvement by persons with disabilities. Education for leisure-centered living is one strategy for promoting a quality life-style through leisure. The following case example demonstrates such a strategy.

Case Example

Glen is a 43-year-old man with Down syndrome. He lived at home most of his life until about two years ago, when his widowed mother had a stroke that resulted in her permanent placement in a skilled nursing facility. Glen's mother had begun to make plans for his placement in a group home prior to her illness but his move was hastened due to the severity of her stroke. Therefore, when Glen moved in he was already familiar with his new roommates and caregivers at the group home. In his new home, several of the other residents were in the process of retiring from full-time work.

Glen had good work skills but was noticeably declining in his physical reserves and work productivity. His mother had noted to his work supervisors that Glen was really slowing down. He had expressed to his mother and work supervisors that he was interested in spending more time at home. His mood and behavior were somewhat problematic following his mother's illness and for some time after he was moved to the group home. Group-home and work-site support staff agreed that Glen could benefit from programming to prepare him for a life-style more compatible with retired status.

Because other residents at the group home were involved in a leisure education program that was helping them to redesign their life-styles for retired living, Glen entered the home and began to participate on a part-time basis in the leisure education program. Some days he would stay at home from work in the morning or come home early in the afternoon to participate in the program. The goal was to have work time fade,

123

replacing it gradually with a retirement-oriented life-style. Now, two years later, Glen is working about half-time and participating in a retirement program the rest of the time. His life is full of activities—some active and some passive—but definitely full of friends and things to do that maintain his health and well-being. He visits his mother regularly and enjoys showing her pictures of the activities he does.

Five core areas are addressed in most leisure education programs: leisure awareness and appreciation; self-awareness and leisure; self-determination, leisure choices, decision-making skills; knowledge of leisure opportunities and resources; and leisure activity skills. The leisure education program used at Glen's group home engaged the residents in learning activities that helped them to move through each of these areas toward the goal of developing a satisfying and active retirement life-style. Of particular interest to staff at Glen's home was health promotion with an emphasis on a healthy balance between activity involvement and television viewing. Staff were interested in helping Glen seek leisure activities that maintained his involvement outside of the home in the community, as well as developing home-based activities that met his personal needs and interests.

The first step for Glen was to make sure that he understood the meaning of leisure and how it can be as important as work. To reach this awareness, Glen and his coresidents spent time looking at photos and magazine pictures, and telling stories about the leisure activities that they had participated in over their lives. This *autobiographical sketch* helped them to distinguish leisure as different from work, to recognize how important it had been to them over their lives, and to discover which activities were the most meaningful (and perhaps identifiable as peak experiences) to them. Instrumental in raising leisure awareness for persons with cognitive disabilities is to use as many strategies as possible to help develop a recognition of leisure, as well as placing it into context across the life course. Pictures, visits from family members to talk about past events, visits to places where leisure was enjoyed in the past, and other visual and sensory strategies are helpful tools in this process.

In the process of discovering what leisure is, it is not unusual for individuals to also find out how important it is to them, or that leisure activities often can be used in describing one's perception of oneself. While it seems fairly abstract to have insight into who we are as defined by our leisure activities, building a self-identity through leisure can be made more concrete to persons with cognitive disabilities via leisure education process strategies.

For example, Glen and his housemates played a game in which they described themselves in terms of favorite leisure activities. In a discussion group format, each participant was asked to complete the sentence, "My favorite free-time activity is _____." Then each participant was asked to talk about the reasons why it was a favorite activity. The group leader assisted each person in recognizing how their reasons actually described characteristics about themselves. When one resident said she liked an activity "because it was fun," the facilitator processed the response by asking, "Do you like having fun?" This probe and response process helped the resident discover that being a fun-loving person was one of her basic character traits. In this way, leisure activity recollection was used to discover the residents' personal identities. Glen found out through his love of indoor and outdoor gardening that he loves nature and relates well to the natural environment.

As the leisure education process progressed, later phases of the program helped the residents to identify pre-ferred leisure activities and to develop the skills needed to pursue them. Strategies to develop self-determination assisted the participants in learning to make independent decisions. Decision-making in leisure involved several steps, all of which were learned and prac-ticed: (a) to recognize preferred alterna-tives; (b) to understand the conse-quences associated with selecting a choice (e.g., will need money, transpor-tation, someone to do the activity with, etc.); (c) to make the necessary plans to deal with consequences; and finally, (d) to make choices and engage in the selected activities. Group teaching and practice used visual cues and staff support to teach these four steps (see Mahon & Bullock, 1992).

The last two phases of the leisure education program focused on (a) developing the awareness of all the leisure opportunities and resources that were available to the residents at home and in the community, and (b) ensuring that specific activity skills were present. An excellent activity for Glen and his coresidents along with the assistance of group home staff was the development of a picture scrap book of all the places, opportunities, resources, and activities that are available in their local commu-nity, as well as in their home. This inventory process was a fun activity for the group as a whole. Field trips were used to take photos and meet people at local facilities and programs. During times at home, a game was played of trying to think of all the things that they could do at home for fun in their kitchen and other rooms.

Good leadership of this process helped to ensure that the final product remained an easily and often used resource in making decisions about what the home residents wanted to do on a daily, weekly, and monthly basis. For activities that residents wanted to learn but had minimal experience with, the home staff began to help them to de-velop the skills necessary for pursuing these activities.

For Glen and his housemates, leisure education offered multiple opportunities and met varying needs. Leisure educa-tion helped Glen through several major life changes. It facilitated his efforts to redefine and reorganize his life-style and time use patterns. It served as a bridge to retirement as his involvement in full time work was beginning to fade. Further-more, leisure education helped him to discover new meaning in his life by helping him to recognize the talents, interests, and activities that meant the most to him. In Glen's case, the leisure education program at the group home helped him through a complex transition by empowering him with a new, self-developed life-style.

Leisure Repertoire and Perceived Satisfaction with Life

Research confirms that persons with mental retardation tend to show a general passivity and overreliance on caregivers and others for their leisure activity involvement (Birenbaum & Re, 1979; Crapps, Langone, & Swaim, 1985; Voeltz, Wuerch, & Wilcox, 1982). The inability to make choices about leisure and recreation activity involvement is recognized as an isolating and limiting barrier (Ashman, Suttie, & Bramley, 1993; Dattilo, 1995). Several positive findings have been reported as well, however:

- Opportunities to express personal preferences, make independent choices, and pursue individual interests are evident with recent efforts to improve the quality of life for people with disabilities (Abbotts, 1991; Brannerman, Sheldon, Sherman, & Harchik, 1990; Landesman, 1986; Lockwood, Lockwood, & O'Meara, 1991; Newton, Horner, & Lund, 1991).

- Personal autonomy improves perceptions of self-worth and satisfaction with life (Hawkins, 1993a; Houghton, Bronicki, & Guess, 1987).

- Awareness of, exposure to, and experience with leisure skills as developed through leisure education promote a sense of autonomy and thus improve overall life-style (Abbotts, 1991; Certo, Schleien, & Hunter, 1983; Schleien et al., 1995; Schleien & Ray, 1988).

Leisure repertoire may be thought of as the values, attitudes, knowledge, and skills necessary for the independent engagement of one's leisure. Included in the concept of leisure repertoire is the expression of personal preferences and interests, personal choices, and decision-making skills. A mistaken impression is that people with mental retardation are incapable of indicating personal preferences or making informed choices about daily activities (Bercovici, 1983; Guess, Benson, Siegel-Causey, 1985; Kishi, Tellucksingh, Zollers, Park-Lee, & Meyer, 1988; Mahon & Bullock, 1992). However, through carefully constructed instruction and a supportive environment, even persons with significant limitations can be taught leisure activity choice-making skills (Dattilo, 1995; Lovett & Harris, 1987). Personal preferences and interests become evident when a range of leisure pursuits have been experienced (Hawkins, 1991, 1993a, 1993b; Lovett & Harris, 1987).

When combined with other critical social factors such as friendships and opportunities for community inclusion, leisure activity choices will contribute to perceived life satisfaction and the overall well-being of individuals with mental retardation (Hawkins, 1993a; Hutchison & Lord, 1979; Schalock, Keith, Hoffman, & Karan, 1989).

The Outlook for Leisure and Quality of Life

As efforts continue to mount in the empowerment of people with mental retardation, it can be expected that personal autonomy will remain of central interest in conversations about quality of life. In leisure, personal autonomy is a primary characteristic as expressed through freedom of choice. Given this view, several initiatives can be pursued in order to enhance a more normative leisure repertoire and higher quality of life for persons with mental retardation.

- Leisure choice and decision-making skills can be taught in leisure education programs.

- Leisure activity repertoire can be expanded through concerted efforts to remove inappropriate and inaccurate social, attitudinal, and physical barriers.

- People with mental retardation can be allowed to pursue and experience freedom of personal preferences, interests, and choices during their leisure.

- Friendships and natural supports can be provided in an effort to enhance leisure opportunities and involvement.

- Social policies can be formulated and adopted that recognize leisure as a fundamental domain in daily life that needs to be promoted and honored much the same as are work and home life.

- Human service administrators and professionals can increasingly recognize and act in an "enabler" role to promote leisure as a fundamental component in quality of life.

With these goals for the future, readers of this chapter are entrusted to work for a higher quality of life through leisure for all persons. It is also hoped that special efforts will be expended on behalf of persons with disabilities, for they have most likely been impoverished in this area of life-style.

References

Abbotts, P. (1991). Specialist to generic: The path for disability services. *Leisure Options: Australian Journal of Leisure and Recreation, 1*(4), 14-17, 38.

Ashman, A.F., Suttie, J., & Bramley, J. (1993). *Older adults with an intellectual disability*. St. Lucia, Queensland, Australia: Fred and Eleanor Schonell Education Research Centre.

Bender, M., Brannan, S.A., & Verhoven, P.J. (1984). *Leisure education for the handicapped: Curriculum goals, activities, and resources*. San Diego, CA: College-Hill Press.

Bercovici, S. (1983). *Barriers to normalization: The restrictive management of retarded persons*. Baltimore: University Park Press.

Birenbaum, A., & Re, M.A. (1979). Resettling mentally retarded adults in the community almost four years later. *American Journal of Mental Deficiency, 83*, 323-329.

Brannerman, D.J., Sheldon, J.B., Sherman, J.A., & Harchik, A.E. (1990). Balancing the right to habilitation with the right to personal liberties: The rights of people with developmental disabilities to eat too many jelly doughnuts and take a nap. *Journal of Applied Behavior Analysis, 23*, 79-89.

Brightbill, C.K., & Mobley, T.A. (1977). *Educating for leisure-centered living* (2nd ed.). New York: Wiley.

Carlson, R.E., MacLean, J.R., Deppe, T.R., & Peterson, J.A. (1979). *Recreation and leisure: The changing scene* (3rd ed.). Belmont, CA: Wadsworth.

Certo, N.J., Schleien, S.J., & Hunter, D. (1983). An ecological assessment inventory to facilitate community recreation participation by severely disabled individuals. *Therapeutic Recreation Journal, 83*(3), 29-38.

Crapps, J.M., Langone, J., & Swaim, S. (1985). Quantity and quality of participation in community environments by mentally retarded adults. *Education and Training of the Mentally Retarded, 20*, 123-129.

Dattilo, J. (1994). *Inclusive leisure services: Responding to the rights of people with disabilities*. State College, PA: Venture.

Dattilo, J. (1995). Instruction for preference and generalization. In S.J. Schleien, L.H. Meyer, L.A. Heyne, & B.B. Brandt, *Lifelong leisure skills and lifestyles for persons with developmental disabilities* (pp. 133-145). Baltimore: Brookes.

Dattilo, J., & Murphy, W.D. (1991) *Leisure education program planning: A systematic approach*. State College, PA: Venture.

Goode, D. (Ed.). (1994). *Quality of life for persons with disabilities: International perspectives and issues*. Cambridge, MA: Brookline Books.

Guess, D., Benson, H.A., & Siegel-Causey, E. (1985). Concepts and issues related to choice-making and autonomy among persons with severe disabilities. *Journal of the Association for Persons with Severe Handicaps, 10*(2), 79–86.

Hawkins, B.A. (1991). An exploration of adaptive skills and leisure activity of older adults with mental retardation. *Therapeutic Recreation Journal, 25*(4), 9–28.

Hawkins, B.A. (1993a). An exploratory analysis of leisure and life satisfaction in aging adults with mental retardation. *Therapeutic Recreation Journal, 27*(2), 98–109.

Hawkins, B.A. (1993b). Leisure participation and life satisfaction of older adults with mental retardation and Down syndrome. In E. Sutton, A.R. Factor, B.A. Hawkins, T. Heller, & G.B. Seltzer (Eds.), *Older adults with developmental disabilities: Optimizing choice and change* (pp.141–155). Baltimore: Brookes.

Hawkins, B.A., & Freeman, P.A. (1993a). Correlates of self-reported leisure among adults with mental retardation. *Leisure Sciences, 15,* 131–147.

Hawkins, B.A., & Freeman, P.A. (1993b). Factor analysis of leisure constraints for aging adults with mental retardation. *Abstracts from the 1993 Symposium on Leisure Research* (p. 7). Arlington, VA: National Recreation and Park Association.

Hawkins, B.A., Freeman, P.A., & Mash, C. (1991). Leisure interests and preferences of aging adults with mental retardation: An exploration of choice-making determinants. *Abstracts from the 1991 Symposium on Leisure Research* (p. 30). Arlington, VA: National Recreation and Park Association.

Hawkins, B.A., May, M.E., & Rogers, N.B. (1996). *Therapeutic activity intervention with the elderly: Foundations and practices.* State College, PA: Venture.

Houghton, J., Bronicki, G., & Guess, D. (1987). Opportunities to express preferences and make choices among students with severe disabilities in classroom settings. *Journal of the Association for Persons with Severe Handicaps, 12,* 18–27.

Howe-Murphy, R., & Charboneau, B.G. (1987). *Therapeutic recreation intervention: An ecological perspective.* Englewood Cliffs, NJ: Prentice-Hall.

Hutchison, P., & Lord, J. (1979). *Recreation integration: Issues and alternatives in leisure services and community involvement.* Ottawa, Ontario: Leisurability Publications, Inc.

Joswiak, K. (1989). *Leisure education: Program materials for persons with mental retardation.* State College, PA: Venture.

Kelly, J.R. (1990). *Leisure* (2nd ed.). Englewood Cliffs, NJ: Prentice Hall.

Kishi, G., Teelucksingh, B., Zollers, N., Park-Lee, S., & Meyer, L. (1988). Daily decision-making in community residences: A social comparison of adults with and without mental retardation. *American Journal on Mental Retardation, 92,* 430–435.

Landesman, S. (1986). Quality of life and personal satisfaction: Definition and measurement issues. *Mental Retardation, 24,* 141–143.

Lockwood, R.J., Lockwood, A.D., & O'Meara, W. (1991). Focus of change in leisure for people with disabilities. *Leisure Options: Australian Journal of Leisure and Recreation, 1*(1), 15–18.

Lovett, D.L., & Harris, M.D. (1987). Important skills for adults with mental retardation: The client's point of view. *Mental Retardation, 25,* 351–356.

Mahon, M.J., & Bullock, C.C. (1992). Teaching adolescents with mild mental retardation to make decisions in leisure through use of self-control techniques. *Therapeutic Recreation Journal, 26*(1), 9–26.

Mobily, K.E. (1987). Leisure, lifestyle, and life span. In R.D. MacNeil & M.L. Teague, *Aging and leisure:Vitality in later life* (pp. 155-180). Englewood Cliffs, NJ: Prentice-Hall.

Mundy, J., & Odum, L. (1979). *Leisure education: Theory and practice*. New York: Wiley.

Murphy, J.F. (1975). *Recreation and leisure service:A humanistic perspective*. Dubuque, IA: W.C. Brown.

Neulinger, J. (1974). *The psychology of leisure: Research approaches to the study of leisure*. Springfield, IL: Charles C. Thomas.

Newton, J.S., Horner, R.H., & Lund, L. (1991). Honoring activity preferences in individualized plan development:A descriptive analysis. *Journal of the Association of Persons with Severe Handicaps, 16*(4), 207-212.

Schalock, R.L. (Ed.). (1990). *Quality of life: Perspectives and issues*.Washington, DC:American Association on Mental Retardation.

Schalock, R.L., Keith, D.D., Hoffman, K., & Karan, O.C. (1989). Quality of life: Its measurement and use. *Mental Retardation, 27,* 25-31.

Schleien, S.J., Meyer, L.H., Heyne, L.A., & Brandt, B.B. (1995). *Lifelong leisure skills and lifestyles for persons with developmental disabilities*. Baltimore: Brookes.

Schleien, S.J., & Ray, M.T. (1988). *Community recreation and persons with disabilities: Strategies for integration*. Baltimore: Brookes.

Voeltz, L.M., Wuerch, B.B., & Wilcox, B. (1982). Leisure and recreation: Preparation for independence, integration, and self-fulfillment. In B.Wilcox & G.T. Bellamy, *Design of high school programs for severely handicapped students* (pp. 175-209). Baltimore: Brookes.

Wolfensberger, W. (1994). Let's hang up 'quality of life' as a hopeless term. In D. Goode (Ed.). *Quality of life for persons with disabilities: International perspectives and issues* (pp. 285-321). Cambridge, MA: Brookline Books.

Part II

Organizational Change Application

Organizations are struggling to respond effectively to the current quality revolution, which is focused on quality of life, quality enhancement techniques, quality management, and quality assurance. This revolution, evident in both industry and human services, stresses that quality is integral to both the processes we use in service delivery and the outcomes from those services. The four chapters in this section discuss the challenges that the quality revolution brings to human service organizations as they strive for inclusion, equity, quality services, and quality outcomes.

The section begins with a chapter by Jim Gardner and Sylvia Nudler that reflects how we are experiencing a redefinition of quality in terms of outcomes—not program compliance. It is apparent to most of us that human services organizations are currently doing two things: reorganizing resources around individuals rather than rearranging people in program slots and shifting the focus of evaluation to the measurement of person-referenced outcomes. Accreditation efforts are also changing consistent with this redefinition of quality and the changing service paradigm. It is refreshing to read in chapter 9 about current transitions in the definition of quality from compliance to responsiveness; from a product to a

market focus; from procedures to outcomes; and from behavior to performance. In the approach to accreditation discussed in this chapter, 30 measures are grouped into 10 domains, which load on six empirically-derived factors: health and wealth, autonomy and freedom, respect for rights, social relationships, community participation, and satisfaction/security. The emphasis in applying these measures is to focus less on organizational input and process variables (such as written policies and procedures) and more on attaining meaningful outcomes suggestive of agency flexibility, creativity, and responsiveness to consumers' individual needs and goals. The authors also describe how agencies can use valued, person-referenced quality outcomes for formative feedback for educational, self-assessment, and accreditation purposes.

Quality services require competent, well-trained support staff. In chapter 10, Val Bradley, Marianne Taylor, Virginia Mulkern, and Judith Leff update the reader on significant and exciting changes in the workplace. Chief among these changes include the primacy of the community, an emphasis on human relations, person-centered planning, choices, and control. Despite these exciting changes, the authors begin their chapter with a discussion of a number of current trends in community services that should alarm us: a projected declining work force; continued problems in recruitment, compensation, and retention; and a significantly altered workplace. The project described in the remainder of the chapter is an effort to develop competent community support workers. The authors identify key concepts to pay close attention to and think differently about: (a) a "training occupation," which is defined as a composite of several related occupations that require a similar core of skills and knowledge; (b) a "community support worker" who provides direct help within a community to individuals, families, or groups with extraordinary support needs in the areas of service brokerage, social/interpersonal/behavioral areas, residential and employment environments, and personal care and assistance; and (c) "skill standards," which are criteria required to qualify for work in particular occupations or occupational clusters.

Programmatic outcomes reflecting an enhanced quality of life for persons with disabilities result in large part from the organizational management methods employed. Organizational management provides the foundation for all services and supports provided to persons with disabilities as well as the strategy for improving those services. One of the most evident trends in human services today is the effort of education and (re)habilitation programs to respond effectively to the current quality revolution that focuses on quality of life, quality enhancement techniques, quality management, and quality assurance. The major purpose of chapter 11 is to discuss how current human services and mental retardation/developmental disabilities programs can apply the principles and methods of new approaches to organizational management and continuous improvement to the issue of quality of life. In this chapter, Joyce Albin Dean and David Mank outline common features of continuous improvement management: a customer focus, relationships based on mutual trust and respect, staff ownership to improve quality, and systematic strategies for analyzing performance and achieving improvement. The authors conclude by discussing six next steps for organizations who wish to embrace the concepts of continuous improvement and quality of life: (a) take every opportunity to learn more about the philosophy and methods of quality improvement; (b) develop and communicate a vision of the organization as a quality organization, and its relationship to supporting quality of life of its service customers; (c) encourage all personnel inside the organization to discuss quality, improvement, and ideas for change; (d) become a role model of the new way of management; (e) stop defending the status quo, the current methods, or the existing vision; and (f) develop new and more frequent ways of listening to customers.

In recent years human services have seen a paradigm shift in the way research is designed and implemented. Questions under study today emerge frequently not from the researcher alone, but out of collaborative efforts with consumers and practitioners. This new approach is referred to as participatory action research (PAR), which is an approach to identifying research questions, implementing investigations, and insuring that connections between findings and practice are strong. PAR relies on the involvement of stakeholders who can identify elements of their own lives that warrant change and can best understand the social contexts in which changes are to occur. Inherent in the PAR process is the use of research not merely as a tool to document and explain phenomena, but also as a mechanism for action and social change. In chapter 12, Jean Whitney-Thomas discusses how this shift in the design and implementation of research moves us away from the notion of the researcher as a technician who drives the investigation toward a model in which groups of people can organize the conditions under which they learn from their own experiences and make these experiences accessible to others. After reviewing specific techniques used in PAR, the chapter concludes with discussion of three critical points that can contribute to the success of a PAR approach to an action agenda to enhance quality of life outcomes: insuring ongoing, genuine, and negotiated participation in all phases of the process; acknowledging and building upon the diversity of opinions, values, and experiences within the working group; and

considering mutual ownership and benefit as the best compensation for participation.

In these four chapters a number of organizational change issues are identified that will impact the application of the concept of quality of life to persons with disabilities. Among the more important to attend to are these:

• Accrediting and certifying based on quality outcomes

• Improving program quality through outcomes

• Demonstrating the impact of the use of outcomes and outcome measures

• Determining the individual and organizational variables that influence outcome attainment

• Recognizing that the structure of the service system is changing

• Accommodating to new service models

• Upgrading community support workers' skills and compensation

• Embedding the substance of skill standards into high school and community college curricula.

Beyond Compliance to Responsiveness: Accreditation Reconsidered

James F. Gardner and Sylvia Nudler
The Accreditation Council

We are experiencing a redefinition of quality in terms of outcomes for people rather than compliance with program process. This redefinition reflects changes in the field of disabilities and in the larger trends of an increasingly service-driven economy and culture. In the field of disability, professionals, service providers, and the public sector are paying increasing recognition to outcomes. The focus on outcomes in the field of human services is a reflection of the change in the economy and culture as the United States moves toward a knowledge-based, postindustrial society (Bell, 1973).

In the service sector, the definition of quality begins with the perception of the recipient of services rather than with the provider or the content of the service alone. Successful service organizations are moving from a product focus (where they produce a service and then search for customers) to a market focus (where they identify what the customer wants and then customize the service).

The quality of the service is determined by the recipient, not the provider. Albrecht notes that "In the customer value paradigm, the primary focus of measurement is on outcomes" (1992, p. 41). In challenging the mass marketing of the industrial era, Peppers and Rogers (1993) stress dialogue with, and feedback from, the customer. The critical question is "What does *this* customer really want?" (p. 16).

This changing paradigm is also evident in services for people with disabilities (Bradley, Ashbaugh, & Blaney, 1994). Human service organizations are reorganizing resources around individuals rather than rearranging people in program slots (Dillon, 1993). The focus on program evaluation is shifting to the measurement of outcomes for people (McLoughlin, Garner, & Callahan, 1987; Schalock, 1995; Walls & Tseng, 1987). The purpose of this chapter is to review the changes that have occurred in accreditation efforts consistent with the redefinition of quality and the changing service paradigm. The chapter's five sections discuss early efforts at accreditation, transitions in the definition of quality, outcome based accreditation, uses of outcomes and initial results, and future directions.

Early Efforts at Accreditation

The Accreditation Council on Services for People with Disabilities evolved from the work of the American Association on Mental Deficiency (AAMD) in publishing *Standards for State Residential Institutions for the Mentally Retarded* (AAMD, 1964). In 1966, AAMD, the National Association for Retarded Citizens (ARC), the Council for Exceptional Children (CEC), and United Cerebral Palsy Associations, Inc. (UCPA) formed the National Planning Committee on Accreditation of Residential Centers for the Retarded. In 1969, the Joint Commission on Accreditation of Hospitals (JCAH) invited the National Planning Committee to establish an accreditation council within the JCAH. As a component of the JCAH, The Accreditation Council for Facilities for the Mentally Retarded (ACFMR) developed accreditation standards and conducted accreditation reviews of facilities serving people with mental retardation. In 1979, the JCAH reorganized and terminated its agreements with its various accreditation councils. The ACFMR reorganized as an independent, not-for-profit organization, The Accreditation Council on Services for Mentally Retarded and Other Developmentally Disabled Persons. Over the ensuing years the name of the organization has evolved to The Accreditation Council on Services for People With Disabilities.

During the 1980s, The Accreditation Council published standards (1984, 1987) and conducted a national accreditation program for organizations that provided services to people with developmental disabilities. The Council performed a national leadership role in the design and dissemination of habilitation standards that emphasized the interdisciplinary process, individualized program planning, behavior intervention and the promotion of legal rights. During the 1980s, The Accreditation Council's focus on habilitation planning, team process, legal rights, and behavioral intervention defined contemporary practice.

The Standards of The Accreditation Council influenced federal certification requirements for the Intermediate Care Facility for the Mentally Retarded (ICF/MR) Program. The 1973 ICF/MR standards were based on the 1971 standards of The Accreditation Council (U.S. Government Printing Office, 1988). The Health Care Financing Administration acknowledged that its 1988 Intermediate Care Facility for the Mentally Retarded (ICF/MR) Regulation was based on the 1983 draft standards of The Accreditation Council (U.S. Government Printing Office, 1988).

By the 1990s, however, the focus of quality began to move beyond habilitation planning and measures of organizational process. Outcome measures associated with independence, productivity, and integration led to a focus on individual satisfaction and a search for quality of life measures. This evolution in the conceptualization of quality in services and supports for people with disabilities, which coincided with global economic, social, and technological changes, is summarized in Figure 9.1 (adapted from Jaskulski, 1991).

After revising the 1987 *Standards for Services* with the publication of the 1990 *Standards and Interpretation Guidelines for Services for People with Developmental Disabilities,* the Board of

Figure 9.1
The Evolution of Quality Measures

ERA	FOCUS	MEASURE
1970s Institutional reforms	Protection, health, safety	Environmental inputs
Early 1980s Deinstitutionalization	Habilitation planning	Organizational process
Late 1980s Community options	Independence, productivity, integration	Outcomes for people
1990s Non-facility-based services	Empowerment, inclusiveness, quality of life	Satisfaction Well-being

Note. From *Affecting the Quality of Services: Perspectives on Quality and Home and Community Based Services for People with Disabilities* (p. 15), by T. Jaskulkski, 1991, Landover, MD: Jaskulski & Associates. Copyright 1991 by Jaskulski & Associates. Adapted by permission.

Directors of The Accreditation Council decided against continued incremental change through further revision of the 1984-1987-1990 sequence of standards. Instead, the Council embarked on a new course, deciding in 1991 to redefine quality in services in terms of an organization's capability to facilitate outcomes for people. The Board of Directors adopted four design criteria for a new set of quality measures: outcome based, concise, applicable to people with different disabilities, and applicable to a wide range of services and supports.

With grant funding from the Illinois Department of Mental Health and Developmental Disabilities and the Illinois Planning Council on Developmental Disabilities, The Accreditation Council conducted individual and focus group interviews with people with disabilities in the summer of 1992. People with disabilities were interviewed to determine the outcomes they wanted from services and supports they received.

The responses were formulated as preliminary *Outcome Based Performance Measures* (The Accreditation Council, 1992) and pilot-tested at one site in Maryland and three sites in Illinois. The Accreditation Council published a field edition of the *Outcome Based Performance Measures* and conducted 10 field tests of the new measures in the United States and Canada between August 1992 and March 1993. The Accreditation Council also circulated the field edition for national comment from people with disabilities, families, professionals, and public officials. The Council published the first edition of the *Outcome Based Performance Measures* in 1993 (The Accreditation Council, 1993). These measures are summarized in Table 9.1.

Table 9.1
Outcome Based Performance Measures

Personal goals	1. People choose personal goals.
	2. People realize personal goals.
Choice	3. People choose where and with whom they live.
	4. People choose where they work.
	5. People decide how to use their free time.
	6. People choose services.
	7. People choose their daily routine.
Social inclusion	8. People participate in the life of the community.
	9. People interact with other members of the community.
	10. People perform different social roles.
Relationships	11. People have friends.
	12. People remain connected to natural support networks.
	13. People have intimate relationships.
Rights	14. People exercise rights.
	15. People are afforded due process if rights are limited.
	16. People are free from abuse and neglect.
Dignity and respect	17. People are respected.
	18. People have time, space, and opportunity for privacy.
	19. People have and keep personal possessions.
	20. People decide when to share personal information.
Health	21. People have health care services.
	22. People have the best possible health.
Environment	23. People are safe.
	24. People use their environments.
	25. People live in integrated environments.
Security	26. People have economic resources.
	27. People have insurance to protect their resources.
	28. People experience continuity and security.
Satisfaction	29. People are satisfied with services.
	30. People are satisfied with their personal life situations.

Transitions in the Definition of Quality

The development of the *Outcome Based Performance Measures* (hereafter referred to as the Measures) reflects both the measures listed in Table 9.1 and six significant changes in The Accreditation Council's definition of quality and the design of the quality review for accreditation.

1. **The transition from compliance to responsiveness.** The purpose in developing a set of person-focused performance measures was to measure organizational responsiveness to people rather than compliance with organizational process. As such, the person-focused performance measures are used to structure interviews and discussions with people that result in the identification of priority outcomes. The Measures are used first as a resource guide for interviewing people. The service provider can then implement the necessary services and structures that will facilitate the outcomes for the individual.

2. **The transition from a product to a market focus.** In the development of previous editions of standards, The Accreditation Council surveyed professional opinion and then fashioned standards accordingly. With the Measures, the Council asked people with a wide range of disabilities what they wanted from their services and supports.

3. **The transition from organizational process to outcomes for people.** As Figure 9.2 indicates, The Accreditation Council has defined organizational services as process measures. Units of service such as assessments, supported employment placements, or transportation miles are defined as organizational process. These organizational processes facilitate outcomes for people. Thus, transportation for a person with significant seizure activity can facilitate outcomes such as remaining connected to natural support networks, having economic resources, and choosing the daily routine. Medication therapy enables a person with a severe psychiatric illness to maintain a job. Assistive technology may enable a person to communicate and thus control his or her daily schedule. The supports and services of medicine, education, rehabilitation, therapies, and adaptive technology are the methods and techniques that facilitate outcomes for people.

Figure 9.2
Performance Measures

MEASURE	DEFINITION	EXAMPLE
Input	Resources that go into a support or service	Staff, money, facilities
Process	What an organization does with the input	Procedures, service, support
Outcome	Individual outcomes due to supports/services	Individual outcomes

4. **The transition in the knowledge base and measurement technology.** The credibility of outcome measures rests upon the integrity of a measurement methodology. Two questions define organizational measurement and feedback systems (Merchant, 1982): What do we measure? How well can we measure? As indicated in Figure 9.3, when the certainty of both questions is low, organizations generally measure organizational inputs such as personnel qualifications, resources, facilities, and equipment. When there is uncertainty about one of the two questions, organizations generally measure organizational process. However, when the certainty of both questions is high, organizations measure outcomes.

Throughout the 1970s and 1980s, service organizations and professionals considered measures of developmental gain, adaptive behavior, normalization, productivity, integration, independence, satisfaction, and quality of life. Without consensus on the basic unit of measurement, standards focused on compliance with organizational and habilitation processes. However, as the themes of civil rights, empowerment, and self-determination found expression in the community through changes

such as the Americans With Disabilities Act, the answer to the first question, what do we measure, became clear. The relevant measure of quality in services is what the person with the disability identifies as important.

The Accreditation Council answered the second question, how well can we measure, during its 1992-1993 field tests of the Measures in the United States and Canada. Data from the field test demonstrated the content validity and interrater reliability of the Measures.

5. **The transition from behavior to performance.** Previous editions of The Accreditation Council's Standards stressed the need for observable and measurable behavioral objectives. In many instances staff focused attention on the behavior and worked to accomplish the behavioral objective. In some instances, however, there was no valued social context for the performance of the behavior. As a result, acquisition of a skill or behavior resulted in few outcomes for the individual. The Measures, however, treat behavior as the means to an outcome (Gilbert, 1978). Performance is behavior that results in an outcome within a socially valued context. For example, a decrease in maladaptive behavior contributes to outcomes related to social inclusion and relationships. Decreasing maladaptive behaviors in a segregated and isolated setting may not lead to performance and outcomes. Improving eye-hand coordination or activity of daily living skills should be directed toward a specific outcome such as working, eating a hot dog at the baseball game, or entertaining friends.

Figure 9.3
Feedback Variables

| | | Ability to Measure Results | |
		High	Low
Consensus of What to Measure	**High**	Outcomes	Process
	Low	Outcomes/ Process	Inputs

---

6. **The transition from detailed complexity to dynamic complexity.** Senge (1990) has demonstrated the difference between detailed and dynamic complexity. The focus on the habilitation process resulted in compliance documentation. A concern for outcomes leads to an investigation of the dynamic relationships among outcomes, and between outcomes and individualized organizational processes. Habilitation planning focused attention and resources on individual priority goals and objectives, but paid little attention to the relationships between goals and objectives and the outcomes to which the goals and objectives were directed. Staff often approached goals and objectives in isolation from each other. The traditions of logical positivism led personnel to examine smaller and smaller components of behavior in greater and greater detail. Outcomes promote synthesis by the continual reexamination of organizational process in the context of individualized outcomes. Outcome measures refocus action and resources around the individual rather than around the program. Furthermore, outcome measures cut across program and service boundaries and encourage staff to focus on the outcome rather than on the program's responsibility.

Outcome Based Accreditation

Accreditation with the Measures is intended as a formative evaluation that enables the organization to improve quality in services. Organizations use the Measures to design organizational processes that address people's expectations for outcomes. Thus, they are first used by staff to structure and guide conversations with people about their priority outcomes.

Outcome accreditation is not compatible with common practices associated with deficiency reports, plans of correction, and determinations of compliance. The absence of an outcome does not necessarily indicate a negative finding. The Accreditation Council has no presumptions that all outcomes will be present for any one person. Rather than focus on outcomes not present, an emphasis is given to the individualized organizational process that facilitates outcomes, the relationships between and among outcomes, and the connections between outcomes and individualized organizational process. Five principles are interwoven throughout the content of the Measures and the quality review methodology: individual differences and priorities, choice and decision-making, discovering preferences, confirmation and convergence, and organizational process and personal outcomes.

Individual Differences and Priorities

Outcomes for people challenge organizations to individualize services and supports. While previous quality efforts emphasized uniformity in practice and process, using outcome measures requires that organizations tolerate diversity, differentness, and nonuniformity. Organizations must now redirect their attention from the uniformity of "programs" to the uniqueness of people. An outcome focus encourages the service or support entity to identify individual outcomes for *each person* served. The outcomes are not prescriptive. The definition of a desired outcome varies from person to person. Definitions of social participation, friendships, and respect will vary from person to person. Service/support personnel determine how each person defines the 30 out-

141

comes for himself or herself. Services and supports are then developed to address the person's unique, individual outcomes.

People with disabilities define their priority outcomes. The role of the professional is to assist the individual in establishing priority outcomes and to understand the context for the choice. Professionals cannot establish outcomes. The professional's education, training, and experience is focused on methodologies and techniques. Once the individual has identified priority outcomes, professionals then marshall their education, training, and experience to facilitate the attainment of the outcome. The methodologies and technologies of the professions can contribute to a clarity of means; they cannot, in themselves, derive outcomes for others.

Choice and Decision-Making

Individual decision-making and choice are the foundation for implementing the Measures. Organizations are expected to provide people with support and assistance in making choices and decisions as part of the service process. Each measure has an individualized definition for each person receiving supports and services. The 30 outcome measures apply to each person receiving supports and services, *unless* the person makes an informed choice that a particular outcome is not relevant. When that informed choice is exercised, the outcome is considered present because the individual makes the choice, and individual choice is the fundamental principle in applying the Measures.

The Accreditation Council applies a three-part decision model to situations where an individual determines that an outcome is not relevant. In order for a person to make an informed choice about outcomes, the following three dimensions of choice and decision process must be satisfied.

- Experience: People need concrete life experiences related to possible options and potential choices. To make a choice about a job or place to live, an individual must have some experiential familiarity with the possible alternatives in the employment or residential choices.

- Social Support: Family, friends, and peers are available and provide support and assistance to people as they weigh options and make choices. Ongoing support is provided before, during, and after the time of the decision.

- Creativity: Providers and people work together to identify creative alternatives that will meet the person's individual needs. Creativity requires that service/support entities determine the context for choices. They ask *why* the individual makes that choice. The providers want to find the interests behind the choice. Once they understand the reasons and interests behind the choice, they then identify other alternatives that might also satisfy the interests behind the choice.

Discovering Preferences

Some persons are unable to understand questions about outcomes. In those instances where staff are unable to learn about people's choices, they can discover preferences. Staff can investigate preferences by using the above-referenced dimensions of experience, social support, and creativity. They can offer people a range of creative opportunities and experiences as well as ongoing social support. They can then observe individual responses and discover preferences. Even people with severe cognitive and medical challenges can express preferences—for which side of their body they want to lie on, the texture of their food, or people to support them.

Confirmation and Convergence

During the accreditation review, Council staff meet with a purposeful representative sample of people receiving services and supports. Reviewers interact with each individual, his or her family and friends, and staff for approximately 3 to 4 hours during the site visit. In some instances individuals can respond directly about the priority outcomes in their lives. In some instances Accreditation Council reviewers will talk with family, friends, and staff about the individual's preferences, how they were identified, and the services and supports that are facilitating the outcomes.

Accreditation Council reviewers continue dialogue and discussions with a mix of people over several days, in several different locations. Reviewers conclude the interactions when there is confirmation and verification of basic information about outcomes, and trends and insights converge around priority outcomes. When there is no confirmation of basic facts and information patterns diverge, interviews and discussions continue. In no instances do Accreditation Council staff accept facts and information without verification and discussion with other organizational representatives.

The information collection methodology emphasizes conversation and interviews with the individual, family, friends, and staff. The written record is consulted when conversation and interviews fail to lead to confirmation of information and convergence of patterns.

Organizational Process and Personal Outcomes

The increased importance of outcomes does not diminish the contribution that organizational process can make to the achievement of outcomes for people. The use of outcome mea-sures directs policy and procedure to be individualized and responsive to each person served. Service planning, assessment, team process, monitoring and other service activities are valued and important when they contribute to the achievement of outcomes for people.

The extent of formalization of the organizational process will vary for each individual. Some individuals may need specific and detailed habilitation plans; the organization may be capable of facilitating outcomes for others with minimal plans. The quality review process first examines outcomes. Once The Accreditation Council reviewers make determinations about an outcome, they identify the individualized organizational process that facilitated, or is expected to facilitate, the outcome.

Uses of Outcomes and Initial Results

Uses of Outcomes

The Measures can be applied and implemented in three ways. From an educational perspective, the Measures refocus the organization's attention and resources on outcomes for people rather than on the services provided. Services and supports facilitate outcomes. The legitimacy of supports and services that do not facilitate outcomes for people are reexamined. The Measures also assist employees, volunteers, family, and friends to design expectations around people rather than around programs, structure, and organizational process. Responsiveness to people's desired outcomes rather than adherence to organizing principles of "programs" promotes quality.

From a self-assessment perspective, the Measures enable an organization to undertake a structured exercise in organizational learning. The process of meeting and communicating with people about their important outcomes enables staff to understand dynamic complexities in the service/support relationship rather than the detailed complexity of treatment plans, schedules and organizational process (Senge, 1990). Organizations can use the measures to determine the extent to which they are assisting people to achieve outcomes in their lives. In addition, with an emphasis on dynamic complexity, organizations are challenged to identify the individualized organizational processes that facilitate outcomes for individuals.

Finally, from a perspective of independent third-party review, the Measures serve as the basis of a national accreditation program. Unlike accreditation under previous standards, the outcome Measures focus on the degree of responsiveness to the needs and expectations of people rather than compliance with organizational process requirements.

Initial Results

Beginning in August 1993 and continuing through December 1994, 28 organizations participated in reviews for accreditation with the *Outcome Based Performance Measures*. These organizations represented a broad spectrum of service and support providers including state-wide family support and respite services and a variety of vocational, day, and residential options. Organization size ranged from 10 to 400 individuals receiving services. Reviews were conducted in a dozen states in the U.S. And included organizations in small rural communities, as well as in suburban and metropolitan areas. With one exception, the participating organizations were previously accredited by The Accreditation Council.

1. **Interrater reliability.** With the implementation of the Measures, The Accreditation Council established a

peer review and ongoing reliability testing process to safeguard the quality and integrity of the data collection and decision-making process used for reviews. During each review, one person is interviewed to assess the interrater reliability of Council staff. Two reviewers independently determine the presence or absence of each outcome and process for the selected individual.

During the initial field test phase in the development of the *Outcome Based Performance Measures*, the baseline interrater reliability was .82. Results from the first 28 accreditation reviews with the *Outcome Based Performance Measures* conducted in 1993-1994 indicate an interrater reliability of .90.

2. **Individual outcome measures results.** During the accreditation review, data concerning each outcome and a corresponding individualized organizational process that facilitates the outcome are recorded for each person interviewed. The data are analyzed and presented to the organization on a person by person and aggregate basis. A compilation of results from 219 people interviewed during the first 28 accreditation reviews with the Measures provides data on the frequency of the presence of each outcome and a corresponding individualized organizational process that facilitates the outcome. As shown in Figure 9.4, data indicate that outcomes related to Economic Resources (#26), Safety (#23), Security (#28), Personal Possessions (#19), Choosing Free Time (#5), and Community Participation (#8) were present for 90% or more of the people interviewed. Outcomes present for less than one-half of the

people interviewed were Living in Integrated Environments (#25), Full Exercise of Rights (#14), Choosing Personal Goals (#1), Choosing Work (#4), Performing Different Social Roles (#10), and Due Process (#15).

3. **Construct validity/factor analysis.** The original placement of the 30 measures into 10 categories (see Table 9.1) was based on individual and focus group interviews with people with disabilities in Illinois during the summer and fall of 1991. The resulting Measures were field tested at 10 sites in the United States and Canada in the winter of 1992-1993. The factor analysis on outcome results for 100 individuals participating in the field test reviews indicated that the 30 outcomes loaded onto seven factors. In January 1995 the data from the first 28 accreditation reviews with the Measures was combined with the data from the 10 field test reviews (total persons = 319). A factor analysis (SPSS-PC) of these data identified the six factors identified in Table 9.2. All 30 Measures loaded on

these six factors, with minimal overidentification. Results indicated that 66% of the variance is explained by these six factors.

Future Directions

The Accreditation Council has incorporated the *Outcome Based Performance Measures* into its national accreditation and quality improvement programs. These personally defined outcomes differ from standardized scales of consensus outcome domains. In the Measures, people define the meaning and application of the outcome for themselves; organizations can then measure whether the outcome is present in the manner, and to the extent, defined by the person. The Measures are subjectively defined and objectively measured.

The Health Care Financing Administration awarded The Accreditation Council a contract to study these personally defined outcome measures. The final report, *Quality Assurance Measures Database* (Accreditation Council, 1995c), analyzed information from over

Figure 9.4
Results of Outcome Measures Review (August 1993–December 1994)

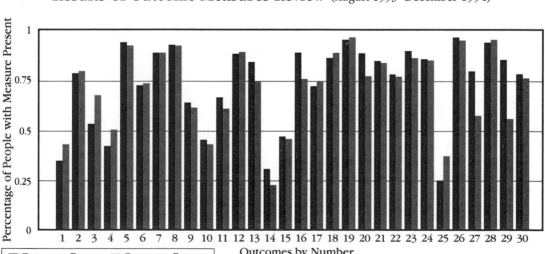

Table 9.2
Factors and Associated Outcome Measures

FACTOR 1

22. People have the best possible health.
16. People are free from abuse and neglect.
19. People have and keep personal possessions.
26. People have economic resources.
28. People experience continuity and security.
21. People have health care services.
23. People are safe.
8. People participate in the life of the community.

FACTOR 2

18. People have time, space, and opportunity for privacy.
7. People choose their daily routine.
3. People choose where and with whom they live.
24. People use their environments.
12. People remain connected to natural support networks.
30. People are satisfied with their personal life situations.
5. People decide how to use their free time.

2. People realize personal goals.
20. People decide when to share personal information.

FACTOR 3

15. People are afforded due process if rights are limited.
14. People exercise rights.
1. People choose personal goals.

FACTOR 4

11. People have friends.
13. People have intimate relationships.
17. People are respected.

FACTOR 5

9. People interact with other members of the community.
10. People perform different social roles.
6. People choose services.
25. People live in integrated environments.
4. People choose where they work.

FACTOR 6

29. People are satisfied with services.
27. People have insurance to protect their resources.

450 interviews conducted during accreditation reviews in 54 organizations in 1993-1995. The report demonstrated that personal outcomes can provide a valid and reliable measure of quality in services and supports to people with disabilities. The personal outcomes methodology is reliable in identifying issues of safety, health, and abuse and neglect.

The personal outcomes methodology provides the grounding for other Accreditation Council quality initiatives. The Council established a Quality Consortium of organizations that want to improve quality through personal outcomes. The Quality Consortium, composed of 93 organizations, offers service providers a peer network for consultation and referral as well as a structured opportunity for an ongoing relationship with the Council for the provision of consultation and technical support. The Quality Consortium provides an interactive communication network of providers through the Internet. In addition, the Council and the Ontario Association of Community Living have concluded a contract to introduce the *Outcome Based Performance Measures* in the Province of Ontario through a licensing agreement for publications and accreditation reviews. Finally, The Accreditation

Council continues to develop materials and publications based on the personal outcome approach to quality in services and supports, such as *A Guide to Using* *Outcome Based Performance Measures in Employment Services* (1995a) and *Outcome Measures for Early Childhood Intervention Services* (1995b).

References

The Accreditation Council on Services for Mentally Retarded and Other Developmentally Disabled Persons. (1984). *Standards for services for developmentally disabled individuals.* Washington, DC: Author.

The Accreditation Council on Services for People With Developmental Disabilities. (1987). *Standards for services for people with developmental disabilities.* Boston, MA: Author.

The Accreditation Council on Services for People With Developmental Disabilities. (1990). *Standards for services for people with developmental disabilities.* Landover, MD: Author.

The Accreditation Council on Services for People With Disabilities. (1992). *Outcome based performance measures: Field review edition.* Landover, MD: Author.

The Accreditation Council on Services for People With Disabilities. (1993). *Outcome based performance measures.* Landover, MD: Author.

The Accreditation Council on Services for People With Disabilities. (1995a). *A guide to using outcome based performance measures in employment services.* Towson, MD: Author.

The Accreditation Council on Services for People With Disabilities. (1995b). *Outcome measures for early childhood intervention serivces.* Towson, MD: Author.

The Accreditation Council on Services for People With Disabilities. (1995c). *Quality assurance measures database final report.* Towson, MD: Author.

American Association on Mental Deficiency. (1964). *Standards for state residential institutions for the mentally retarded.* Willimantic, CT: Author.

Albrecht, K.A. (1992). *The only thing that matters: Bringing the power of the customer into the center of your business.* New York: Harper Business.

Bell, D. (1973). *The coming of the post industrial era.* New York: Basic Books.

Bradley, V.J., Ashbaugh, J.W., & Blaney, B.C. (Eds.) (1994). *Creating individual supports for people with developmental disabilities: A mandate for change at many levels.* Baltimore: Brookes.

Dillon, M.R. (1993). Morality and freedom: Challenges to a field in transition. *Mental Retardation, 31,* iii–viii.

Gilbert, T.F. (1978). *Human competence: Engineering worthy performance.* New York: McGraw-Hill.

Jaskulski, T. (1991). *Affecting the quality of services: Perspectives on quality and home and community based services for people with developmental disabilities.* Landover, MD: Jaskulski & Associates.

McLoughlin, C.S., Garner, J.B., & Callahan, M. (1987). *Getting employed, staying employed.* Baltimore: Brookes.

Merchant, K.A. (1982, Summer). The control function of management. *Sloan Management Review,* 43–55.

Peppers, D., & Rogers, M. (1993). *The one to one future: Building relationships one customer at a time.* New York: Doubleday.

Schalock, R.L. (1995). *Outcome-based evaluation.* New York: Plenum.

Senge, P.M. (1990). *The fifth discipline: The art & practice of the learning organization.* New York: Doubleday.

U.S. Government Printing Office. (1988). *Federal Register, 53*(107), 20,448–20,494.

Walls, R.T., & Tseng, M.S. (1987). Measurement of client outcome in rehabilitation. In B. Bolton (Ed.), *Handbook of measurement and evaluation in rehabilitation* (2nd ed., pp. 183–202). Baltimore: Brookes.

CHAPTER 10

Quality Issues and Personnel: In Search of Competent Community Support Workers

Valerie J. Bradley, Marianne Taylor,
Virginia Mulkern, and Judith Leff

Human Services Research Institute

An implicit theme throughout this chapter is that well-trained, quality workers enhance the quality of life of service recipients. However, one critical quality assurance concern that is rarely addressed in any systematic fashion is the competency of those individuals who are most directly involved in the lives of people with developmental disabilities—direct service or community support staff. Instead, providers and public officials have tolerated minimally trained staff, high turnover, and low wages while crossing their collective fingers in hope that this threadbare front line will hold.

There are many reasons why this gaping hole in the quality defenses the field has erected must be addressed. This chapter presents several compelling trends that we need to consider: a projected declining work force on the national level; pending reforms in work-force training; continuing recruitment, compensation, and retention problems; and a significantly altered workplace. These trends will prod those concerned about the quality of community supports to invest the same level of energy and strategic resources in upgrading the skills of community support staff as they have in making the community system the dominant mode of support for people with developmental disabilities. Ignoring this challenge may put the extraordinary gains made in the last two decades in jeopardy.

This chapter also describes a way of thinking about the development of competencies and training curricula. This new way of thinking can lead to a quality work force and the emergence of a new vocation—the community support worker. The chapter concludes with a discussion of necessary systemic changes required by the new way of thinking.

National Work-Force Trends

Demographic Trends

Based on studies of the developmental disabilities work force (Larson, Hewitt, & Lakin, 1994), staff are predominantly white females under the age of 35, with limited postsecondary education. These demographics pose particular problems for the field because the proportion of the U.S. population age 18-34 is expected to drop 19% in the 1990s. To meet the 73% predicted growth rate in human services, agencies will have to shift recruitment strategies to target different groups, such as the older worker, and make more training programs available. Provider and state officials will need to define training goals and recognize the importance of targeted training at the prebaccalaureate level to meet these new challenges.

The Bureau of Labor Statistics (Kilborn, 1994) also projects significant growth in related industries. The Bureau predicts that the number of home health aides will soar to 827,000 by the year 2005, compared with 347,000 in 1992—a 138% increase. Likewise, the Bureau projects a 136% increase in the number of human services workers and a 120% increase in personal and home care aides over the same period. These numbers indicate strongly that the developmental disabilities field will be in increasingly intense competition for scarce personnel resources at the entry level.

Educational and Training Trends

Because personnel in the field are products of traditional education and training approaches, they are hampered by general inadequacies in those systems. At the core of the problem has been the inability of our traditional work and educational structures to integrate academic and applied knowledge better (Bailey & Merritt, 1994) or to embrace the more complex standards of the postindustrial economy. Quality, not mass production, will be the mantra of the 21st century economy, and both business and education are discussing ways to realign their goals and methods to be effective in a quality-driven economy.

There has been broad agreement that the new global economy requires redefinition of the workplace as well as educational reform, and that each depends on the other for success. Improving the connection between education and skills needed in the workplace is the focus of a comprehensive effort to develop a system of national, voluntary, industry-based skills standards to link training and educational curricula to prepare students for the high performance work needed in the 21st century. The United States is presently the only industrialized nation without a comprehensive system of skills standards linking educational programs to industry-defined needs and guiding non-college-bound youth into promising career paths that keep the door open to further educational opportunities.

At the center of two major policy initiatives of the Clinton administration, educational reform and work-force development, are 22 national skills standards projects that have the potential to create a crucial bridge between competencies needed in the workplace and the knowledge and skills taught in school. The standards and supports to implementation developed through these projects will contribute new vision to the American educational system's responsibility to prepare youth better for viable careers in the postindustrial age. One of these projects is directed at the development of competencies for community support workers. The substance of this initiative is discussed later in this chapter.

Approaches to Work-Force Development

Two additional themes in innovative, relevant work-force training and education should be noted by planners and trainers in the developmental disabilities field. One factor is increased attention to what expert workers actually do. This focus has been expressed, for example, in the development of "performance templates" for the human services (Albin, 1992) and in "practice guidelines" in areas such as health and mental health (Eddy, 1992; Field & Lohr, 1992). The second factor is total quality management/continuous quality improvement.

Although best practice analysis and total quality management draw on the expertise of the shop floor, both also stress collaboration between service customers and service producers in defining and implementing services that are customer driven, effective, and efficient (Albin, 1992; Eddy, 1992; Field & Lohr, 1992; Taylor, 1992). Further, all efforts of these types are based on the idea that education and training must give workers the skills they require to meet consumer needs in an integrated manner that is both cost effective and consistent with consumer preferences. As one quotation, frequently cited in the continuous quality improvement literature, puts it, "Quality control begins with education and ends with education" (Muthler & Lytle, 1990).

Recruitment and Retention Problems in Developmental Disability Programs

A chronic work-force problem in the field of developmental disabilities has been the recruitment of direct services staff (Bradley & Allard, 1992; Bruininks, Kudla, Wieck, & Hauber, 1980; Jaskulski & Metzler, 1990). In addition to recruit-ment problems, staff retention is also a crucial problem. Mitchell and Braddock (1992) recently reported an annual turnover rate of 70.4% nationally among direct care staff in community settings. However, this phenomenon is not limited to the field of developmental disabilities. A study by Ross (1983) among child care workers in residential care facilities reported a turnover rate of 30-50% each year, and 47% of that sample had been in their agency for 12 months or less. He also found that lack of career advancement opportunities was cited as a key problem by 60% of respondents.

These extremely high turnover rates are costly in several ways. In the first place, it costs money to recruit staff and train large numbers of new staff. Second, there is the human cost involved when trusted staff members leave a direct care setting and people with developmental disabilities are forced to reestablish relationships with new support staff. Several studies have documented that one of the major reasons parents favor institutional care over community alternatives is due to staff turnover in community residences (Meyer, 1980; Spreat, Telles, Conroy, Feinstein, & Columbatto, 1987).

Turnover is a complex phenomenon, and multiple factors are undoubtedly involved in individuals' decisions to leave their jobs. However, the fact that staff providing community services to people with disabilities are leaving their jobs so soon after starting suggests a poor fit between the attitudes and skills of these workers and their jobs. Three factors that affect high staff turnover are considered below.

Adequate Training

To the extent that adequate training makes new staff aware of the challenges of community support work and prepares them to deal effectively with these challenges, one would expect turnover rates to decrease with training. Job satisfaction has also been shown to increase and turnover to decrease with job enlargement. Heretofore, jobs have been narrowed in part to accommodate the limited abilities of personnel available to fill them; this constraint can be loosened considerably, given the skills that better trained community support workers will carry. Further, training and skills acquisition can lay the groundwork for a more articulated career ladder for community support workers, enabling them to move both vertically and horizontally within the field as opposed to moving out of the field for career advancement.

Compensation

Compensation for community support staff is another chronic workforce issue. Mitchell and Braddock (1992, pp. 41-42) summarized the findings from a national survey of direct service staff compensation as follows:

- Direct care wages have consistently been reported to be considerably lower than those of many other occupations. There is evidence that many direct care workers are earning a wage below the national poverty level.

- Research has documented that wages for direct care workers in public institutions are generally 40-50% higher than wages for direct care workers in private community facilities.

- Factors contributing to the low wage level for most direct care workers include the historical wage differential between men and women, a wage bias against caregiving occupations, and limited funding available to many private community organizations.

Working Conditions

Another important factor linked to issues of retention is the nature of the job that direct care staff are asked to do. Larson et al. (1994) summarized the major factors contributing to job dissatisfaction, including lack of professional status and respect, stressful job situations, broad and sometimes multiple responsibilities (e.g., friend, advocate, custodian, counselor, etc.), paperwork requirements, and increased community facilitation responsibilities. Additionally, for many residential staff, the demands of erratic hours, night duty, and isolation are also significant disincentives to employment in the field. Finally, the extent of training received by direct service personnel is abbreviated at best and leaves many direct service staff with insufficient skills.

The structure of organizations providing services and supports to people with developmental disabilities has also contributed to a lack of job satisfaction among direct service staff. By and large, provider agencies are organized as hierarchies where power and information are lodged at the top. The role of direct care staff in such organizations is essentially to be the arms and legs of the agency, carrying out orders rather than collaborating to solve problems. Though direct service personnel are often asked to work in highly decentralized and isolated circumstances, they are rarely given the autonomy to shape their work life.

Changing Conceptions of Community Support

The service system for people with developmental disabilities is in the midst of profound changes. Increasingly, people with developmental disabilities are living and receiving services in the community rather than in large institutional settings. These services are being coordinated and provided by an array of staff with diverse backgrounds and levels of expertise. Bradley and Knoll (1990) referred to these changes as a new paradigm in the delivery of human services.

This new paradigm is revolutionizing the way we think about designing services for people with disabilities. Bradley and Knoll (1990) identified four major attributes of this new paradigm.

1. **The primacy of the community.** The new paradigm rests on the fundamental belief that people with disabilities can and should live in communities as full participating members. The role of service providers is to identify and remove barriers to full community participation.

2. **Emphasis on human relations.** People with disabilities have the same needs for social connectedness as other persons living in communities. A fundamental task of service providers is to ensure that people make social connections and become fully integrated in the life of the community. These social relationships make it possible for people with disabilities to make use of natural supports in their communities.

3. **Person-centered approaches.** This view of services for people with disabilities eschews the notion of fitting people into available program "slots"; rather, supports are designed to respond to the unique situation of each individual in his or her community. People with disabilities should live in homes, not in programs, and they should work in jobs, not in workshops. Program planning must include the full array of family members, friends, service providers, advocates, and most importantly, consumers.

4. **Choice and control.** The new paradigm rejects the notion that "the professionals know best." Instead, it recognizes the right of consumers to make choices about where and with whom they live, how they spend their time, and how they want their supports configured. The task for community support workers is to assist consumers in making informed choices and to ensure that meaningful choices are available.

These four paradigmatic attributes are resulting in significant changes in human services. Three of these changes are discussed subsequently: changes in the workplace, in training needs, and in required skills.

Changes in the Workplace

The nature of the places in which direct service staff work has become increasingly decentralized in recent years. Full implementation of a supports model in homes, workplace, schools, and communities requires staff to work in even more decentralized and sometimes isolated settings. The nature of their work is also changing. Instead of being part of a hierarchical team, they are more likely to be called on to make independent decisions, to work with people with developmental disabilities and their families to fashion individual and idiosyncratic supports, and to work with generic agencies and natural supports in unique and community-specific configurations.

Dramatic increases in the numbers and types of community-based support settings have mixed implications for staff: Greater autonomy and responsibility may increase commitment and job satisfaction, but make recruitment, retention, and training more difficult (Larson et al., 1994). On the other hand, multiple settings increase the probability of a poor fit between the expectations of new recruits and job requirements, resulting in higher turnover. Further, scheduling and arranging for training is more difficult across multiple settings (Langer, Agosta, & Choisser, 1988). Retention is affected adversely because in dispersed settings there is less backup coverage for illness, vacation, or training, and less access to professional guidance.

Changes in Training Needs

This changing vision of how services should be delivered to people with disabilities has major implications for the types of workers required and the training these workers need, as Knoll and Racino (1994) note:

> *...the basic values of personal choice and control, individual quality of life, valued roles, and full community participation for people with developmental disabilities do indeed require the fundamental transformation of words and practice inherent in the support paradigm. However, this promise will be lost if the field does not systematically reeducate itself and develop new workers who are both imbued in this new way of thinking and have the skills needed to undertake the far-reaching changes that lie ahead.*
>
> **(p. 5)**

The skills required of community support workers are not the province of any single academic or professional discipline. In fact, as Knoll and Racino (1994) point out, many of the newer models for serving people with disabili-

ties have not evolved as a result of formal policies within service systems, but from grassroots efforts to improve the lives of individuals. Many of the ideas are alien to professional training programs and in-service training provided by facility-based programs. As a result, there are few forums in which community support workers can obtain the requisite skills for doing their jobs.

Additionally, the few programs that are currently training people for community support work are geared toward postgraduate students. Clearly, there is a continuing need for professional staff with graduate level training. However, research suggests that, in many instances, paraprofessionals are capable of providing community support services and are a major component of the current service delivery system. In 1987, the number of employees providing direct care to persons with mental retardation in community-based residential settings alone (excluding those providing treatment and services in institutional settings and in day and other services) was estimated at 120,000 full-time equivalent positions; 80,000 of these positions were held by persons without college degrees (Lakin, 1987). Similarly, research indicates that as much as 80% of direct care for persons with severe mental illness is provided by generalists and paraprofessionals, including individuals with bachelor's degrees (U.S. Department of Health and Human Services, 1980).

Changes in the Skills Required

Staff of support organizations must also have capabilities that are different in character from those that are taught in more traditional programs. Examples of competencies required to support people with developmental disabilities in their homes, at work, and in their communities include these:

- Ability and commitment to identifying strengths in people and groups

- Genuine respect for diverse perspectives and life-styles

- A capacity to listen and reflect

- An ability to subordinate one's own ego (to put oneself aside in the interest of the group)

- Skill and creativity in helping people become more aware and confident of their own abilities

- Appreciation of when to step back, and the ability to help the individual or group assume decision-making and action

- Ability to analyze power relationships and help others to do so

- Knowledge about how to gain access to information

- Ability to reflect on and criticize ongoing processes, including one's own role in those processes.

These qualities capture the collaborative nature of the emerging supports paradigm and focus on facilitation rather than on assessment and prescription. Because the new supports organization will have to rely in part on individuals who are already part of the service system and whose training may be at odds with the new paradigm, retraining at all levels will be required. Further, nontraditional staff who are familiar with the community's resources and opportunities can make major contributions to a support organization.

The Community Support Worker

The interest in enhancing the skills and status of direct service staff has grown around the country during the past few years. In their excellent manual, *A Guide to High Quality Direct Service Personnel Resources,* Hewitt, Larson, and Lakin (1994) provide an annotated overview of 100 curricular components for the training of entry-level community staff. In New York, an organization called Reaching Up, Inc., has been created with support from John F. Kennedy, Jr., to recognize the contributions of direct service staff, provide support for training, facilitate the development of career ladders, and ensure opportunities for individuals from a diverse range of cultures. The State of New York recently passed legislation directing multiple human service agencies at the state level to develop a joint certification process for family support workers. This renewed interest in people working most closely with people with developmental disabilities has appeared in many states and localities around the country.

In order to address this issue in a more integrated and broad-based fashion, the Human Services Research Institute, in collaboration with the Education Development Center, Inc., has developed national skills standards for direct support positions in the human services field (Taylor, Bradley, & Warren, 1996). Development of *The Community Support Skill Standards* was supported by a grant from the U.S. Department of Education. The U.S. Departments of Education and Labor and the National Skill Standards Board are providing support to coalitions of employers, educators, and labor unions to develop national skills standards for a number of industries. These coalitions are analyzing entry and mid-level occupations requiring less than a baccalaureate degree in order to create standards for what workers must know and be able to do. These standards will be used as output criteria for the development of career education programs in secondary and postsecondary schools, and in workplaces throughout the country.

One assumption underlying the community support skill standards is that we need to teach human service workers the range of skills needed to provide services to a variety of client groups. Another assumption is that the nature of providing community support can be generalized across a range of settings (e.g., residential and work) and can be valuable to a range of service participants (e.g., people with disabilities, vulnerable elderly). Therefore, the development of skills standards for community support workers is a cross-categorical undertaking. This view is reflected in the training of human services workers in many parts of Europe. Called *social pedagogues* in the Scandinavian countries, *educateurs* in France, and *educatores* in Italy, these individuals receive from two to four years of generalist education and carry out a range of activities. In writing about the social pedagogue training in Denmark, Holm and Perlt (1992) described the training philosophy as follows:

> *There is no doubt that we train generalists; for example, welfare workers, with a broad knowledge of social pedagogy who are able to do a competent job in all sectors of the field. The selection of functional studies, the final thesis, and the practical training may be connected... to a "mild specialization"... A generalist education would actually have as its object to train the students to be able to start working in any social welfare function, if the specialization could be achieved by in-service training.*
>
> *(p. 4)*

The Community Support Skills Standards Project

The purpose of the community support skills standards project was (a) to develop industry-wide skills standards and voluntary certification criteria and procedures that meet the needs of people who rely on supports as well as the needs of employers throughout the human services industry; and (b) to increase both horizontal and vertical career opportunities for human services personnel. Skills standards are competency-based and integrate higher-order cognitive competencies with real-life applications requiring demonstrated mastery.

Although there have been attempts to develop standards for human service workers in particular occupations or for particular populations, this is the first time that all parts of the human services industry were involved. Skills standards were developed by analyzing tasks found in a range of occupations across a variety of employers and work settings, developing a master list of commonly shared tasks, analyzing the competencies required and attaching outcome criteria, and clustering the competencies and tasks into a standard format. Grouped together, these skills standards provide a shared, powerful foundation for education and training. Taken alone or in clusters, they provide the baseline for a variety of education and training modules useful to employers, professional associations, secondary and postsecondary schools, and labor.

Concept of a Training Occupation

A major conceptual underpinning of this project is the notion of a "training occupation." Most work-force education programs developed in the United States have been targeted to narrowly defined occupations. Occupation-specific programs focus on a particular job as traditionally defined by the industry or workplace. For example, in human services, a narrowly defined occupation is a "vocational support staff person." A person who graduates from a training program designed for that occupation should be qualified to perform that particular job.

In contrast to a narrowly defined occupation, a "training occupation" is not an existing job, but a composite of several related occupations that require a similar core of skills and knowledge. The Community Support Skill Standards focus on the "community support worker" as a training occupation that combines the core of skills and knowledge required by a number of direct support roles, such as a vocational support staff person, trainer/mentor, residential support staff, services coordinator, advocate, social service aide, legal aide, and financial management aide.

Educating people for a training occupation has three very important advantages over preparing them for a narrowly defined occupation. First, broadly prepared workers will be more valuable to employers. They will be more flexible and capable of performing a variety of tasks in a range of work settings. Workers who have a broader base of knowledge and skills will have a more complete understanding of the goals and work of the entire organization and will be able to respond to a broader range of situations. This means that employers will not need to invest as much in on-the-job training of entering workers.

Second, workers educated for training occupations will be more prepared to take advantage of both horizontal and vertical career moves. Because they can work in a range of work settings and jobs they will have a better chance for career advancement. Also, because they will be more flexible,

they will be less likely to be laid off than other workers if employers decide to downsize.

Third, a training occupation more nearly reflects the reality of work performance than does traditional narrow occupations. Workers are being required to assume more tasks, including management tasks previously performed by supervisors. Organizations striving for greater efficiency are eliminating some job categories and consolidating work tasks for remaining employees. The use of new technologies also is enabling individuals to perform a broader range of tasks.

What Are Skills Standards?

Skills standards are criteria for what people must know and be able to do to qualify for work in particular occupations or occupational clusters. Standards provide clear, measurable benchmarks for both the content (skills and knowledge) and the quality (level of performance) required. Their purpose is to ensure that people entering or continuing in an occupation are qualified to perform it.

In 1990, the U.S. Department of Labor organized the Secretary's Commission on Achieving the Necessary Skills (SCANS) to identify the basic "workplace know-how" needed by all workers, regardless of the industry and occupation they enter. After extensive research in a number of industries, the Commission identified five competency areas and three foundation skill areas needed by all workers (Secretary's Commission on Achieving the Necessary Skills, 1992). The competencies and skills are listed in Table 10.1.

The SCANS skills listed in Table 10.1 are being incorporated into the comprehensive skills standards now being developed for a variety of industries and occupations. However, because the requirements for job performance in most occupations change frequently due to technological and organizational changes, skills standards must continually be updated. This will require periodic reexamination of jobs to determine how tasks and skill needs are evolving.

Community Support Worker

A community support worker is defined in this project as "an individual who provides direct help within a community to individuals, families or groups of individuals with extraordinary support needs." The occupational clusters and functions that are encompassed within the larger training occupation of community support workers include the following:

- **Community service broker:** a range of coordinating and organizing functions including service brokering, case management, and family support.

- **Social/interpersonal/behavioral supports:** a range of functions directed at teaching skills or providing therapeutic assistance in areas such as early intervention and training in activities of daily living.

- **Residential supports:** a range of activities that support people in their homes, such as live-in support and residential management.

- **Personal care and assistance:** all of those activities that involve personal support for an individual in the home, on the job, and in the community.

- **Employment supports:** a variety of job-related supports, including job coaching, mentoring, and development.

- **Leisure/recreation supports:** a range of support personnel who function in leisure settings and provide leisure-time assistance.

Skills Standards for Community Support Workers

In order to develop the initial duties and tasks statements preliminary to creating skills standards for community support workers, project staff convened four workshops around the country, inviting entry level and supervisory staff from a range of workplaces serving a range of people, and conducted a structured group process called "DACUM," which stands for developing a curriculum (Norton, 1985). DACUM involves an intensive, structured two-day process in which workers are asked to describe their major areas of responsibility and the tasks entailed in each area. They are also asked to create a list of the skills, knowledge, and attributes necessary to carry out their jobs. In these sessions, workers were also asked to discuss contemporary trends in human services, to define their role, and to talk about the values they hold.

Following the four workshops, a synthesis workshop was convened to integrate the four workshop products. The synthesis workshop included representatives from each of the four regional sessions as well as consumers and family members, and its outcome was the creation of an integrated set of duty and task statements, as well as agreement on important definitions. An important area of consensus was the general description of the community support worker as someone who "assists the participant to lead a self-directed life and contribute to his/her community; and encourages attitudes and behaviors that enhance inclusion in his/her community" (Taylor, Bradley, & Warren, 1996, p. 13). The group also agreed to call the person who receives supports the "participant," rejecting consumer, user, customer, and

Table 10.1
SCANS Foundation Skills and Competencies

FOUNDATION SKILLS		COMPETENCIES	

Basic skills	Reading
	Writing
	Arithmetic
	Mathematics
	Listening
	Speaking
		Resources	Allocates time
			Allocates money
			Allocates material and
			  facility resources
			Allocates human
			  resources

Thinking skills	Creative thinking
	Decision making
	Problem solving
	Seeing things in mind's
	  eye
	Knowing how to learn
	Reasoning
		Information	Acquires and evaluates
			  information
			Organizes and main-
			  tains information
			Interprets and commu-
			  nicates information
			Uses computers to
			  process information

Personal qualities	Responsibility
	Self-esteem
	Social
	Self-management
	Integrity/honesty
		Interperson	Participates as a
			  member of a team
			Teaches others
			Serves clients/customers
			Exercises leadership
			Negotiates to arrive at a
			  decision
			Works with cultural
			  diversity

		Systems	Understands systems
			Monitors and corrects
			  performance
			Improves and designs
			  systems

		Technology	Selects technology
			Applies technology to
			  task
			Maintains and trouble-
			  shoots technology

Note. From *Skills and Tasks for Jobs* (p. xviii, 12), by Secretary's Commission on Achieving the Necessary Skills, 1992, Washington, DC: U.S. Government Printing Office.

other terms. It was felt that the term participant connoted collaboration and partnership rather than a more paternalistic relationship.

The synthesis workshop resulted in agreement on the 12 competency areas shown in Table 10.2. For each of the 12 competency areas, specific task areas were identified. For example, the following task areas were listed under Participant Empowerment:

• Develop participants' awareness of self-advocacy methods and techniques.

159

- Consult with and include participants as service/system designers.

- Promote participants' membership and leadership supports and services team.

- Provide opportunities for participants to participate in or associate with peer-support and self-advocacy groups.

- Provide information and options for participants to make decisions about their living arrangements, work life, and social relationships.

- Provide information and assistance about human, legal, and civil rights so participants can speak on their own behalf and find assistance when necessary.

- Encourage, support, and assist participants' involvement in civic activities (e.g., speaking, voting, lobbying, marching, paying taxes).

- Encourage and assist participants to speak on their own behalf.

- Encourage participants to take risks.

Following the synthesis workshop, a validation survey was developed to ensure the relevance of the statements and their applicability to direct support staff. The survey was sent to approximately 1,200 individuals, including direct service staff, administrators of provider organizations, state human services officials, advocacy organizations, and human services educators. To ensure an adequate response rate, a second wave of surveys was sent to approximately 500 randomly selected individuals who had not as yet responded to the first survey. Analyses of these data indicate general agreement with the importance of the duty and task areas and their relationship to the reality of direct support work.

Table 10.2
Community Support Skill Standards Competency Areas

- Participant empowerment

- Communication

- Assessment

- Community and service networking

- Facilitation of services

- Community living skills and supports

- Education, training, and self-development

- Advocacy

- Vocational, educational, and career support

- Crisis intervention

- Organizational participation

- Documentation

The next step in the process was to convene two workshops comprised of educators, trainers, administrators, state officials, program participants and family members, and community support staff and supervisors to develop the first draft of the skills standards. The workshop participants were asked to review the integrated DACUM results and translate them into skills standards either singly or in combination. An example of work activity statements and performance indicators developed for the participant empowerment skill standard is shown in Table 10.3.

The group was then asked to develop specific work activities under each standard area. The next task was to develop observable, measurable performance indicators and assessment methods.

The final step in the process will be the development of a curricular framework to be used by educators and trainers. To assist with this process, four implementation demonstration sites are being analyzed. The results of these pilots as well as an intensive review of other existing curricular materials will be used to design a multimedia guide that includes hypertext and other innovative means of communicating the information to individuals at secondary, postsecondary, and on-the-job training sites.

During the final stages of the process, project staff will be working with national stakeholders to disseminate the standards widely and to focus concern on the importance of an organized and comprehensive national work-force development strategy for the direct support sector.

Challenges for the Field

The acceptance and application of the results of the skills standards project will require changes in attitudes, organizations, compensation, and educational requirements. With respect to attitudes, those in the field should recognize that the structure of the service system is changing and that those on the front line will be called upon to take more responsibility and to use creativity and initiative. This means that these individuals must be valued and given the training and support that they need to do their jobs. They must become equal participants in the organizational culture. If the field does not value these community

---

Table 10.3
Exemplary Work Activity Statements and Performance Indicators

Skill Standard: Participant Empowerment

The competent community-based support worker (CBSW) supports and assists participants to develop alternative strategies, make informed choices, follow through on responsibilities, and take risks.

Work Activity Statements

a. The competent CBSW assists participants to identify alternatives when faced with the need to make a decision.

b. The competent CBSW assists participants to understand the potential outcomes of all alternatives.

c. The competent CBSW balances support for participants' stated choices with considerations of professional responsibility and ethics, as well as potential risks.

d. The competent CBSW assists participants to identify personal, civic, and interpersonal responsibilities, and to develop strategies to meet them.

Performance Indicators

a. The competent CBSW seeks feedback from participants on CBSW's ability to provide support to the participant.

b. The competent CBSW can describe specific examples in which professional ethics and responsibilities are potentially in conflict with participant choices or preferences, and uses problem-solving skills to resolve such conflicts.

c. The competent CBSW recognizes systemic barriers that limit choices for participants and assists them to recognize, identify, and secure resources that may overcome those barriers.

161

support workers, how can they be expected to value their work and the people they serve?

Organizations will also change to accommodate new service models. Rigid hierarchical organizations are not likely to be able to devote the resources or permit the autonomy to community support staff most directly responsible for the well-being of participants. As a result, organizations will have to reconsider their allocation of personnel resources and their top-down structures. All types of organizations are seeing the value of flatter hierarchies, teams, and participatory management approaches that facilitate the quality of the enterprise.

Obviously, compensation looms large as a constraint to the upgrading of skills among community support workers. Why would someone go through a new training program based on the skills standards if the salary they receive on graduation is still only slightly above minimum wage? It is imperative that the wages of these individuals be raised in order to match new expectations. Recognizing that many human service providers are already under-funded, this salary realignment will probably only take place by a reallocation of existing resources. Some of this can be accomplished by reassessing the need for current levels of middle management.

Other funds may be freed up as providers move away from building ownership and maintenance. Finally, changes in the ways that states fund the purchase of services will also be necessary—changes such as block grants, more individualized funding arrangements, and elimination of strict salary guidelines.

Finally, it will be important to imbed the substance of the skills standards into curricula around the country at both the high school and postsecondary levels. It will be necessary to create more collaboration between employers, staff, and educators at the local level to ensure that educational offerings are geared to available options in the surrounding community. Because it will be important to reach those community support workers currently employed in the human services, ways must be found to create job training and enrichment opportunities.

When all is said and done, a well-trained cadre of community workers imbued with the values and practice of quality community support will not succeed unless their supervisors and managers share their concerns and are willing to reshape their practices to create true community support organizations devoted to the needs, preferences, and enhanced quality of life of their participants.

References

Albin, J.M. (1992). *Quality improvement in employment and other human services.* Baltimore: Brookes.

Bailey, T., & Merritt, D. (1994). *Making sense of industry-based skills standards.* New York: Columbia University, Teachers College, The Institute on Education and the Economy.

Bradley, V.J., & Allard, M.A. (1992). The dynamics of change in residential services for people with developmental disabilities. In J.W. Jacobson, S.N. Burchard, & P.J. Carling (Eds.), *Community living for people with developmental and psychiatric disabilities* (pp. 204–302). Baltimore: Johns Hopkins University Press.

Bradley, V.J., & Knoll, J.A. (1990). *Shifting paradigms in services for people with developmental disabilities.* Cambridge, MA: Human Services Research Institute.

Bruininks, R., Kudla, M., Wieck, C., & Hauber, F. (1980). Management problems in community residential facilities. *Mental Retardation, 18,* 125-130.

Eddy, D.M. (1992). *A manual for assessing health practices and designing practice policies: The explicit approach.* Philadelphia: American College of Physicians.

Field, M.J., & Lohr, K.N. (1992). *Guidelines for clinical practice: From development to use.* Washington, DC: National Academy Press.

Hewitt, A., Larson, S.A., & Lakin, K.C. (1994). *A guide to high quality direct service personnel training resources.* Minneapolis: University of Minnesota, Institute on Community Integration.

Holm, P., & Perlt, B. (1992). *The social pedagogue: A response to the needs of Danish society on the threshold of the twenty-first century.* Copenhagen, Denmark: Institute for the Advanced Training of Social Pedagogues.

Jaskulski, T., & Metzler, C. (1990). *Forging a new era: The 1990 report on people with developmental disabilities.* Washington, DC: National Association of Developmental Disabilities Councils.

Kilborn, P.T. (1994, August 30). Home health care is gaining appeal: Providing new jobs for workers and comfort to patients. *New York Times* p. A14.

Knoll, J.A., & Racino, J.A. (1994). Field in search of a home. In V.J. Bradley, J.W. Ashbaugh, & B.C. Blaney (Eds.), *Creating individual supports for people with developmental disabilities: A mandate for change at many levels* (pp. 1-10). Baltimore: Brookes.

Lakin, K.C. (1987, August). *A rationale and projected need for university affiliated facility involvement in the training of paraprofessionals for direct-care roles for persons with developmental disabilities.* Paper prepared for the American Association of University Affiliated Programs for presentation to the Consortium for Citizens with Disabilities, Washington, DC.

Langer, M., Agosta, J., & Choisser, L. (1988). *Proposed model for a state-sponsored direct-care training system in Iowa: Final report.* Cambridge, MA: Human Services Research Institute.

Larson, S.A., Hewitt, A., & Lakin, C.K. (1994). Residential services personnel: Recruitment, training and retention. In M. Hayden & B. Abery (Eds.), *Challenges for a service system in transition: Ensuring quality community experiences for persons with developmental disabilities* (pp. 313-341). Baltimore: Brookes.

Meyer, R.J. (1980). Attitudes of parents of institutionalized mentally retarded individuals toward deinstitutionalization. *American Journal of Mental Deficiency, 85,* 186-187.

Mitchell, D., & Braddock, D. (1992). *Residential services and developmental disabilities in the United States.* Washington, DC: American Association on Mental Retardation.

Muthler, D.L., & Lytle, L.N. (1990). Quality education requirements. In Ernst and Young Quality Improvement Consulting Group (Eds.), *Total quality: An executive's guide for the 1990s* (pp. 103-113). Homewood, IL: Business One Irwin.

Norton, R.E. (1985). *DACUM handbook.* Columbus, OH: Ohio State University, National Center for Research in Vocational Education.

Ross, A.L. (1983). Mitigating turnover of child care staff in group care facilities. *Child Welfare, 62*(1), 63-67.

Secretary's Commission on Achieving the Necessary Skills. (1992). *Skills and tasks for jobs.* Washington, DC: U.S. Government Printing Office.

Spreat, S., Telles, J.L., Conroy, J.W., Feinstein, C., & Colombatto, J.J. (1987). Attitudes toward deinstitutionalization: National survey of families of institutionalized persons with mental retardation. *Mental Retardation, 25,* 267–274.

Taylor, D. (1992). The Joint Commission quality assessment and improvement model. In M. Mattson (Ed.), *Manual of Psychiatric Quality Assurance* (pp. 69–78). Washington, DC: American Psychiatric Association.

Taylor, M., Bradley, V., & Warren, R. (Eds.). (1996). *The community support skill standards: Tools for managing change and achieving outcomes.* Cambridge, MA: Human Services Research Institute.

U.S. Department of Health and Human Services. (1980). *Toward a national plan for the chronically mentally ill.* Washington, DC: U.S. Department of Health and Human Services, Public Health Service.

Continuous Improvement and Quality of Life: Lessons from Organizational Management

Joyce Elizabeth Albin Dean and David Michael Mank

University of Oregon

The outcomes that professional service providers are able to achieve in addressing quality of life issues presented by individuals receiving services are a result, at least in part, of the organizational management methods employed. Organizational management per se is not typically a focus of human services or human services literature. Nonetheless, it is organizational management that provides the foundation for all services provided, as well as the strategy for improving those services. If an organization's management does not follow a coherent philosophy, using effective organizational improvement strategies, it will fail in making anything but superficial, short-lived gains in the quality of life of the persons it serves.

The purpose of this chapter is to apply the principles and methods of new approaches to organizational management to the issue of quality of life. The

chapter begins with a brief summary of the origins of these approaches and reviews several of their common features, presenting them in the context of organizational and business management. In the next section, these features are translated into lessons related to improving strategies for addressing issues of quality of life. The chapter concludes with a set of first steps for changing how an organization operates by incorporating the strategies of quality improvement at the organization's core.

New Approaches to Organizational Management

Over the past 20 years, management in business and industry has undergone dramatic changes. Since the last management revolution, management by objectives (Drucker, 1954, 1964, 1974), executives in the private sector have witnessed—and frequently adopted—one or more of a broad cadre of new management approaches. The most famous of these approaches to organizational management include Joseph Juran's management for quality (Juran, 1986, 1988, 1989); Philip Crosby's assertion that "quality is free" and that organizations should strive to achieve "zero defects" (Crosby, 1979); and W. Edwards Deming's 14 Points for Top Management (Deming, 1986) and subsequent System of Profound Knowledge (Deming, 1993). Indeed, these three leaders have been credited, both individually and collectively, with defining a new generation of management (Dobyns & Crawford-Mason, 1991; Joiner, 1994), radically departing from previous methods. Although at least two of them began their work as early as the 1930s and found willing devotees in Japan in the 1950s, the principles and techniques they espoused did not gain attention in the United States until the late 1970s and 1980s. Since then, Deming has been called the "Father of the New Industrial Age" and the "Founder of the New Economic Era" in recognition of his contribution to changing management practices around the world (Albin, 1992).

Disciples of these three "quality gurus" and others, including Brian Joiner (1994), Peter Scholtes (1988), James Belasco (Belasco, 1990; Belasco & Stayer, 1993), Peter Block (1993), and Stephen Covey (1989, 1990) have further extended these approaches to organizational management, often contributing to and expanding on the work of their mentors. Peter Senge's *The Fifth Discipline* (1990), which promotes practices for "learning organizations"; Alfie Kohn's work on win-win cooperation and later on intrinsic rewards (Kohn, 1986, 1993); Hammer and Champy's *Reengineering the Corporation* (1993); and Osborne

and Gaebler's *Reinventing Government* (1992) are probably the best known examples of these. The last two texts, with their emphasis on starting over, rather than step-by-step improvement, stretch the edge of the definition of a common approach, but still rely on underpinnings first defined in the work of Deming, Juran, and Crosby. This ongoing progression of ideas and methodologies led Dobyns and Crawford-Mason to state that " . . . since [Walter] Shewhart drew his statistical graph in 1924, what seems to have happened is that a quality philosophy has evolved that uses ideas from Deming, Juran, Feigenbaum, Crosby, Ishikawa, Taguchi, and others" (1991, p. 94)

Now adopted widely by business and industry, the work of these and other management authorities comprise a new wave of management strategy that will be broadly referred to in this chapter as *continuous improvement.* Many other names have been used. Brian Joiner refers to this management revolution as *Fourth Generation Management,* in his book by the same name (Joiner, 1994); Albin (1992) referred to it as *continuous quality improvement;* Scholtes (1988) as *quality leadership;* Ishikawa (1985) and Mizuno (1988) as *total quality control;* and a plethora of authors and organizations as *total quality management.* Some aspects of the approaches were popularized in *In Search of Excellence* (Peters & Waterman, 1982), in other mass market texts (Dobyns & Crawford-Mason, 1991, 1994; Peters, 1987; Peters & Austin, 1985), and in television documentary programs such as *If Japan Can...Why Can't We,* presented by Dobyns and Crawford-Mason on NBC in 1980.

A full description of the similarities and differences among these various authors and their works lies far beyond the purpose of this chapter. Suffice it to say, however, that the agreements among their works far outweigh any disagreements. Despite variations in appellation and differences in emphasis, the works maintain several common threads. It is these common features, generally accepted as basic principles of quality improvement, that provide the framework for this chapter's perspective in considering management strategies related to improving quality of life of individuals whom service organizations support.

Common Features of Approaches to Continuous Improvement

The philosophy of quality referred to here as continuous improvement can be characterized by a set of basic principles that include a focus on serving customers; relationships with staff members and other stakeholders that are based on mutual trust and respect; and an emphasis on using systematic methods—including data—for planning and improving performance. These principles are integrally related within the philosophy of continuous improvement.

Focus on Customers

Companies implementing continuous improvement are obsessed with staying close to their customers (Albin, 1992). Their objective is to create long-term relationships with customers to support business success. To do this, organizations must be clear about who their current and potential customers are, pursue input from customers, and take action in response to—and in anticipation of—customer needs. There is no commonly accepted definition of quality. Even the main character in *Zen and the Art of Motorcycle Maintenance* (Pirsig, 1974) lost his sanity trying to define quality in a generic sense. However, for business purposes, customers

define quality. They define needs and wants related to specific products and services. For example, customers did not define the need for fax machines. They did, however, define a desired service of "fast communication of written materials" that was first met by overnight delivery services and later led to the development of fax machines. Successful businesses, then, both respond to customer needs *and* lead them into the future by defining new products and services. Deming (1986) referred to customers as the most important part of the production line.

In the philosophy of continuous improvement, customers are not only those who pay for or receive the products or services, but also those who are "next in line" in the delivery of a product or service (Albin, 1992). Thus, a co-worker is a customer—an *internal* customer—when she is the one who will perform the next operation in product assembly or service delivery. The neighborhood around a business is also a customer; neighbors are the "recipients" of the external appearance of the business and business-related traffic. Clearly, pleasing these customers, as well as those who purchase and use products or services, will also support success in providing either products or services. This focus on employees and other stakeholders as customers is directly tied to the next principle, related to the importance of relationships both within and outside the business.

Establish Relationships Based on Mutual Trust and Respect

Proponents of the philosophy of continuous improvement insist that careful attention be given to the relationships with people. This includes relationships between managers and employees, between companies and their competitors, and between employees and customers. Deming (1993) refers to this component of his System of Profound Knowledge as *psychology*, and states, "Good management helps us to nurture and preserve (the) positive, innate attributes of people" (p. 111). Indeed, Deming's 14 Points for Top Management include "Drive out fear so everyone may work effectively for the company" (Point 8), "Break down barriers between departments" (Point 9), and "Remove barriers that rob the hourly worker of his right to pride of workmanship" (Point 12) (Deming, 1986, pp. 23-24).

1. **Replace reliance on extrinsic rewards.** Our common cultural understanding is that people work for rewards. However, both Deming (1993) and Kohn (1993) argue that overreliance on extrinsic motivators reduces an individual's ability to take advantage of intrinsic rewards. Company awards, employee-of-the-month designations, competitive merit raises and other such extrinsic rewards for performance may create winners, but mostly they create losers. Further, the performance evaluations upon which these rewards may be based ignore the effects of larger systems, subjectivity in measurement, and the effects of chance on performance.

2. **Develop relationships that are characterized by cooperation rather than competition.** Covey (1989), Deming (1993), Block (1993), Kohn (1986) and others propose that relationships—whether with individuals inside or outside the organization—must be based on win-win cooperation. Less than this leads to suboptimization (Deming, 1993); going beyond win-win results in even greater, synergetic effects (Covey, 1989). Thus, working cooperatively, individuals and departments can optimize their performance related to achieving the organization's purpose. Teamwork, therefore, is the road to success, and includes teamwork with suppliers and customers, as well as with coworkers, to maximize improvement.

Build Staff Ownership to Improve Quality

Within organizations, quality improvement means supporting staff members at all levels to take ownership of improving quality. This support includes a fundamental understanding that most of the problems in organizations are caused by the processes and systems in which people work rather than by the employees themselves (Deming, 1986). Because of this, managers must work on improving processes and systems and encourage employees to assist in that effort, rather than blaming them for issues over which they have very little if any control. Continuous improvement seeks the active involvement of all employees in improving the quality of products and services. Block (1993) refers to this involvement as *stewardship*—being willing to be accountable for the outcomes of the organization without trying to control others.

1. **Establish new roles for leaders.** In continuous improvement, leaders no longer direct and control all aspects of operations. Their roles must change drastically. These new roles are referred to by Peters (1987) as including developing an inspiring vision, managing by example, listening, deferring to the front line, and bashing bureaucracy. Echoing the theme of stewardship, Block (1993) suggests replacing patriarchal leadership roles with partnerships with employees for organizational improvement.

2. **Emphasize solutions by people closest to the customer.** As managers and organizational leaders change roles, changes are also needed in the roles of those closest to the customer. Building ownership at all levels in an organization must include a new reliance on the knowledge and experience of employees who actually deliver the service or make the product in question. As managers cannot and should not be the main source of ideas and information, direct-line employees' knowledge and ideas must be valued because of what they know about customers and their understanding of quality.

Use Systematic Strategies to Analyze Performance and Achieve Improvement

Continuous improvement approaches rely heavily on systematizing not only the processes and systems by which work is accomplished, but also the methods used for planning, problem-solving, and improving performance. First among these methods is measurement.

1. **Establish measures of quality and improvement.** Leaders in continuous improvement sometimes do rely on the opinions of staff members who are directly involved with implementing the organization's processes. However, they also understand that perceptions are strongly influenced by underlying attitudes and opinions and thus seek to identify additional reliable and valid measures of performance quality and improvement. Managers are often heard to ask, "Is that your opinion, or do you have data to support it?"

2. **Understand variation.** Understanding variation is one of the four components of Deming's System of Profound Knowledge (Deming, 1993) and the foundation on which much of the rest of his quality philosophy is based. Whatever the measure—the number of people coming to a vocational rehabilitation office for services each week, the length of wires cut by a machine, the color of yarn in successive dye lots, if our measurement instrument is accurate enough, there always will be variation from one instance to the next. The trick in management is to be able to identify when variation is the result of some special or unusual cause, and when it is simply the result of chance, and then to take appropriate action (Joiner, 1994). Statistical process control methods are used to make these determinations (Deming, 1986; Wheeler & Chambers, 1992). These methods were developed primarily for business and industry, but recently have been applied to issues in human services (Dean, 1995; Pfadt, Cohen, Sudhalter, & Romanczyk, 1992).

3. **Apply systematic methods.** An ongoing activity in continuous improvement is standardizing and improving processes as a leverage point for organizational improvement. Many different models and tools have been presented for accomplishing this, such as the 7 Problem-Solving Tools (Walton, 1986), 7 Step Method (Joiner, 1994), Reengineering (Hammer & Champy, 1993), and Benchmarking (Camp, 1989). Other tools and methods have been designed for planning, such as Hoshin Planning (King, 1989b), Quality Function Deployment (King, 1989a), and the 7 Management and Planning Tools (Brassard, 1989). Juran (1986) places continuous improvement efforts into a Quality Trilogy—quality planning, quality control, and quality improvement. The Shewhart cycle (Deming, 1993),

depicted in Figure 11.1, incorporates the steps of plan-do-study-act in a never-ending cycle of questioning performance (study) and planning for improvement (plan). It is the repeated application of the Shewhart cycle to improving processes and systems that promotes organizational learning and improvement (Joiner, 1994). Coupled with data and an understanding of variation, these tools and methods offer powerful strategies for improving organizational performance.

4. ***Question constantly traditional practices and views.*** Perhaps the most basic tenet of quality improvement is the relentless pursuit of excellence, including a willingness not only to question directions, strategies, and methods, but to discard traditional, "time-honored" approaches that are no longer the most effective. Argyris (1994) refers to this as "double loop learning," which involves questioning not only the outcome, but the fundamental strategy and objective as well, as a natural part of the improvement process.

Figure 11.1
The Shewhart Cycle

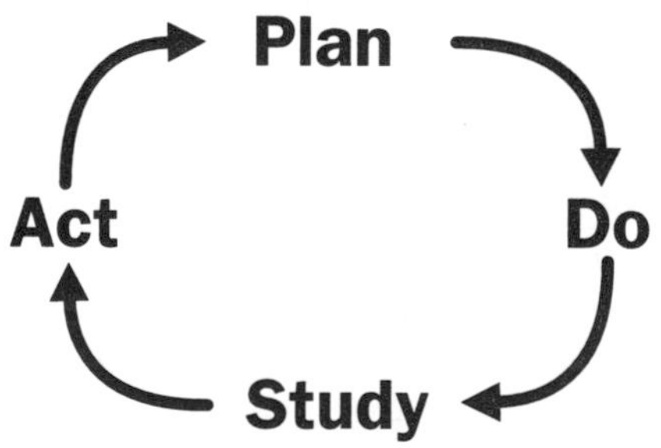

Note. Adapted from *The New Economics for industry, government, education* (p. 135), by W.E. Deming, 1993, Cambridge: Massachusetts Institute of Technology, Center for Advanced Engineering Study.

Lessons from the New Approaches to Continuous Improvement

Together, the fundamental principles drawn from the various experts on continuous improvement form a philosophy of organizational management that can be applied directly to the issue of how to improve the quality of life of individuals receiving services. The following section suggests some ways to apply this new way of thinking to organizational strategies for addressing quality of life issues. Because the principles are interrelated, many of the examples provided will combine several principles.

Focus on Customers

In industry, a customer is referred to as the person who buys and uses the product or service. It is that customer to whom industry looks to define the features of quality for the product or service. However, defining who is the customer is more difficult in human services. Except in the situation of vouchers or other private pay arrangements, the person receiving services—referred to here as the "service customer"—seldom pays the provider directly for the service received. That payer role is most often assumed by a third-party, public-sector funder, such as a county, regional, or state developmental disabilities office, mental health program, or vocational rehabilitation agency—and sometimes by a combination of agencies. This multiplicity of customers makes the question of who defines quality much more complex in human services.

Continuous improvement suggests that if all of the funders, advocates, and service providers maintained a focus on the service customer and that customer's definition of quality of life—rather than on their own systems' needs—then the various systems and perspectives should be able to reach consensus more easily about appropriate quality of life objectives.

Continuous improvement also suggests that service providers and funders should listen to service customers often and in as many different ways as possible. It is important not to rely solely on annual or even less frequent formal surveys of customers. Instead, ask service customers and others often about how they define quality and how you and your organization are doing in achieving that definition. Ask in both formal and informal ways. Ask individually and in group settings. Ask through written surveys and newsletters, through focus groups, and in chance meetings on the street on Saturday night.

When customers respond to your questions, listen naively. That is, listen without the baggage of a preconceived idea of what the customer is telling you or of what your answer will be when the customer is finished. Listen to what the customer says, as well as to what he or she doesn't say. Ask questions. Put yourself in the customer's shoes. Covey refers to this practice as seeking first to understand, then to be understood, in his principles of empathic communication (Covey, 1989).

Establish Relationships Based on Mutual Trust and Respect

Current approaches to service delivery, including supported employment and supported living, rely on staff members, often working on their own, who are alert to how quality is defined and how it can be maintained in a wide array of unique settings (Albin, 1992). Unlike traditional congregate environments, individual approaches to service delivery require new approaches to supporting staff members and expanded

roles for these staff members working in various community locations. To be successful in such dispersed locations, organizations must teach their staff broad definitions of their roles, how those roles relate to achieving quality of life for service recipients, and the importance of their roles. Further, staff members need skills in listening to various types of customers, measuring and evaluating performance, and making decisions from an array of possible service strategies. New approaches to management offer excellent guides for organizations seeking to make these changes in how staff are treated.

1. **Replace reliance on extrinsic rewards.** Although government systems typically do not create extrinsic rewards for organizations, it is typical for organizations to create extrinsic rewards in the form of individual awards, such as bonus payments or employee-of-the-month awards. Fundamental to the logic of extrinsic rewards is that external recognition is needed for motivation. However, if ownership of the mission—that is, of improvement in quality of life for those receiving service—is held by all members of an organization at all levels, extrinsic rewards become unnecessary. Further, extrinsic rewards foster competition among those who should be in cooperation in solving problems and improving quality of life.

2. **Develop relationships that are characterized by cooperation rather than competition.** Adversarial relationships abound in human services—between the funder and service provider, the employment support and residential support providers, the advocate and the provider, the service customer and his or her family, and among the various support organizations in a

community or county. Some of these are based on a scarcity mentality (Covey, 1989), in which people believe that if someone else does well, there will be fewer resources available for them. This scarcity mentality underlies competition, and competition among a service customer's team members reduces the resources that can be directed to achieving improvements in quality of life. Development of trust, based on each member's *trustworthiness* (Covey, 1990) and cooperation among an individual's service team members can lead to creative sharing of resources that will optimize quality of life improvements. For example: A group of service providers who are asked by a funder to take on a service issue have a greater chance of optimizing their performance if they can negotiate their respective roles rather than competing separately for their piece of the project through requests for proposals.

Build Staff Ownership to Improve Quality

In a recent article on the changeover from segregated services to integrated employment, Albin, Rhodes and Mank (1994) report the experiences of eight organizations intent on improving quality, in large part by adopting principles of continuous improvement. The article summarizes how these organizations emphasize the critical importance of ownership by all staff members of the mission of the organization and the focus on improvement of quality. If all staff members own the mission and focus on quality, then greater improvement will result than if managers own the mission and attempt to require or impose it on staff members. Broad ownership of quality means that all of the human resources of an organi-

zation seek ways to improve quality of life for service customers in every aspect of the organization's activities.

Conventional wisdom in human services has been that leaders are experts in the content of the service delivered. Supervisors are promoted to managers. Those effective at delivering direct services to people with disabilities are promoted to supervisors. The assumption is that someone skilled in delivering a service of good quality will also be skilled at leading or managing an organization in human services. Although the importance of content ideas should not be diminished, the skills needed to promote continuous quality, build shared ownership, and support those who deliver services daily are not the same kind of skills required for service delivery. Thus, leaders in human services must learn new skills that use the tools of continuous improvement and provide leadership. Traditional management approaches emphasize the need for managers and leaders to provide the structure and the ideas for improvement. In a system focused on continuous improvement, leaders are required to assist all members of the organization to improve the system, to make it easier for all employees to invest in the activities that improve quality of life for customers.

Use Systematic Strategies to Analyze Performance and Achieve Improvement

"What I've noticed about bureaucratic programs is that for all their rules and red tape, they keep very little track of what actually happens to people they are serving. If you keep track of results, you can dispense with a lot of red tape." (Osborne & Gaebler, 1992, p. 40). Frequently, human service systems have little information about outcomes or quality. There are at least two problems here. First, the dimensions of quality and quality of life toward which the organization may be working may not have been developed with service customers. Fortunately, our service systems have come far in the past 20 years in including service customers in defining quality. The second problem, even if there is agreement on what defines quality outcomes, is the absence of information systems that routinely collect, report, and support decision-making based on these agreed upon dimensions of quality. Information about quality or lack of quality in human services is needed in order to know if improvement is happening, and why or why not.

Processes for systematic use of data to evaluate quality have emerged in the business and service sector (Wheeler & Chambers, 1992). For example, Dean (1995) has applied the use of Statistical Process Control with rehabilitation agencies to assess employment outcomes and related processes in successfully developing employment for people with disabilities. This is but one example of a much broader effort to use systematic analysis and tools to improve quality (Joint Commission on Accreditation of Healthcare Organizations, 1993; Ishikawa, 1982; Kinlaw, 1992; QIP, Inc., 1986).

1. **Measurement of quality and improvement.** Agreement is needed among funders, service providers, service recipients, and advocates about measures of quality. The fundamental question for services for people with disabilities as well as for the broader field of human services is, "How will we know if 'quality of life' has improved?" To make a difference in individual lives, the question must be answered in terms of enduring change, by analyzing the variation in the outcome measurements over

time. If a service customer wishes to increase the time he spends each month with friends at community events, the measure "number of hours at community events with one or more friends" will result in a sequence of data points. Each month's result will be different. By studying the variation in the measures from month to month we can determine how well the system for supporting this activity is working, including whether planned changes have had any substantial effect. Statistical process control charts, which are tools for analyzing variation, have been applied recently to evaluating the success of behavioral treatment programs (Pfadt et al., 1992) and to analyzing hours of support required in supported employment jobs (Dean, 1996).

2. **Systematic methods.** The tools and methods of continuous improvement offer effective mechanisms for tracking quality of life issues, signaling when action should be taken, and developing and carrying out improvement plans. Person-centered planning methods may be augmented by systematic planning tools such as affinity diagrams, tree diagrams, and decision matrices. Problem-solving processes and data-based tools, such as Pareto charts, line graphs, and cause-and-effect diagrams may be applied to determining how well plans are working or to analyzing the root causes of systemic problems. Service providers can use these methods to assess their performance related to individual service customers or to overall organizational performance.

3. **Constant questioning, or willingness to question, traditional practices and views.** One of the most important changes needed to improve quality and

quality of life outcomes is continuous questioning of conventional wisdom about how services have been delivered and what the expected outcomes might be. In disability services, the constant questioning of the traditional wisdom of providing services in segregated settings has led to far greater quality of life for people with disabilities as segregation has been replaced by supported lives in the community. In management, traditional hierarchical structures are being replaced by flatter organizational structures that emphasize the contributions of all employees. Layers of supervisors and managers are being removed in order to invest more resources in the direct line. Teams of workers are being formed to support the work of each employee. This questioning of "the way we've always done things" clearly has been required in the business community over the last 15 years. In light of the societal and economic pressures of human services, government, and taxes, surely the same questioning must be the hallmark in the public sector as well.

Applications to the Field of Mental Retardation/ Developmental Disabilities

Although continuous improvement's initial development was based in business and industry, over the past several years, service provider organizations in different parts of the country have been grappling with applying the principles and methods of this new management approach to their own agencies to improve the services they provide. The following stories, based on real experiences in two organizations, represent how adopting the philosophy of quality

has had an impact on the quality of life of people with mental retardation and other developmental disabilities. In one, the story reflects the efforts of an organization to improve a specific system that would affect the life experiences of many individuals they serve; in the other, the story tells about how the new philosophy led to a real difference in the lives of specific individuals.

Understanding Job Loss and Increasing Employment Tenure

Eight individual with severe disabilities who had been employed by one company in supported employment lost their jobs with that company on the same day. The job loss had a devastating effect on the lives of the people employed, as well as on the community rehabilitation organization's efforts to achieve complete change-over to supported employment. As a result, the organization's managers, who had begun to learn about continuous improvement, decided to take on a project to improve the length of time individuals are employed in community jobs. They began their project by studying the reasons that people had lost community jobs over the previous four years. They collected, graphed, and analyzed data. The data indicated that 80% of the jobs had been lost because of what they referred to as a lack of "employer ownership." For example, they included jobs lost in which the support organization was providing all of the necessary initial training and support for the individual on the job, and situations in which the organization held a contract with the employer so that the individual with a disability was not a direct employee of that business. As a result of better understanding why people had lost jobs, they realized that their approach to job development and support needed to change. Their application of the systematic methods of continuous improvement, along with a focus on improving services to customers, led to shifting to a natural supports approach to job development and support. Now, their focus in working with employers is to help employers include people with disabilities in their work force. People with retardation who have obtained community jobs in the last few years are now directly employed by the community business, go through the typical processes used for any new employee with support and accommodation, and receive most of their support through their employers. They are no longer viewed as a different group of people who are not employed by the community business.

Supporting Dreams Through Customer-Driven Quality

Lanette had been born in a large state institution, and Charles had spent most of his life there as well. Middle-aged and in good health, both eventually moved to a town about three hours south. Charles and Lanette soon became a couple. For almost six years they had expressed a desire to get married. However, the people in their lives—mostly service providers—did not encourage

them in this dream. They were encouraged to live together in an apartment, which they did. But Charles and Lanette still wanted to get married and live in a house. Their residential support organization's commitment to customer-driven quality forced staff to take a hard look at how they could assist Charles and Lanette to achieve their dream. The residential provider arranged a circle of support around this couple, including people from their church. This group helped Charles and Lanette put together a plan to save money for a traditional wedding and reception. Working toward this plan, Charles and Lanette saved their money and were married in a traditional wedding. Lanette's mother, also a long-term resident of the state institution, was brought by staff to witness her daughter's marriage. Lanette asked the general manager of the residential and vocational support organization to give her away in marriage. The reception was held at a local restaurant, and Lanette and Charles were treated by friends to a weekend honeymoon at a hotel in a nearby community. Their dreams of living in a house have been realized as well. Lanette and Charles teamed up with another friend so that the house could become an affordable option. Lanette and Charles were given the opportunity to achieve their dreams because the service provider's staff came to realize what belief in customer-driven services means: that their job is to help the people they serve to fulfill their dreams.

Stories of how programs that have adopted the principles and methods of continuous improvement have changed, formed partnerships with former adversaries, saved money, improved services, supported people in new and different ways are numerous. These two stories are just a brief glimpse of the power that the new philosophy of continuous improvement has on the way programs are managed, and therefore on the quality of lives people with disabilities lead.

Next Steps for Organizations

Adopting a new philosophy of management, as represented somewhat simplistically by the common features presented in this chapter, requires significant investment. Indeed, this shift is commonly referred to by quality professionals as a lifelong journey, rather than as a destination. That is, an organization never "gets there." Quality improvement is not an end, an objective, or a destination, but rather a process, a way of operating, that itself is subject to continuous improvement. So, too, is quality of life: a never-ending effort to maintain the gains we have made and continuously seek further improvement.

Thus, although the ideas presented in this chapter offer guidance on how organizations can improve their ability to support a desired quality of life as defined by their service customers, moving an organization along the path of quality improvement requires diligence and hard work. There are some steps that can be taken, however, to help organizations begin and continue this journey.

1. Take every opportunity to learn more about the philosophy and methods of quality improvement. Attend seminars, read books, hold local study groups, and practice the methods. It is helpful to begin discussing ideas for quality improvement even without a clear expectation of where this will lead.

2. Develop and communicate a vision of the organization as a quality organization and of its relationship to supporting the quality of life of its service customers. Discuss the relationship, as well, between the job of every individual employee and that vision, so that each employee may understand his or her responsibility and feel ownership and relevance in work.

3. Encourage all personnel inside the organization to discuss quality, improvement, and ideas for change. Creating a safe environment for all personnel is one of the most important parts of beginning an investment in quality improvement.

4. Become a role model of the new way of management. Whatever your role in the organization—board member, executive, midlevel manager, supervisor, or support staff—take personal responsibility for behaving in a "quality improvement" way. Many quality experts promote personal change as the first step on the road to creating a new way of doing business (Belasco & Stayer, 1993; Covey, 1989, 1990; Senge, 1990; Senge, Roberts, Ross, Smith, & Kleiner, 1994).

5. Stop defending the status quo, the current methods, or the existing vision. Questioning of processes and outcomes from all internal and external customers of the organization should be valued and invited rather than ignored. Such questioning can be a gift that helps an organization improve.

6. Develop new and more frequent ways of listening to customers. Make

it easy for everyone—including board members and top managers—to be in contact with customers on a regular basis. Develop a customer-centered organization.

Improvement in quality in human services should directly result in improvements in quality of life for those served. Achieving these improvements requires an organizational management philosophy and strategy that supports all employees to work together toward a common vision, a drive to meet and exceed customer expectations, and systematic methods for analyzing organizational performance as well as for planning for the future. Quality improvement offers the kinds of philosophical depth that an organization that is attempting to improve the quality of life of service customers must have to continue to be effective over the years.

Change is everywhere, and will continue forever. There is no "we've done it!" in work to support improved lives for persons with disabilities. As our support technology improves, individuals and their families and advocates will continue to expect more from services, even though public support for such services appears to be decreasing. Scholtes (1988), in his discussion of how organizations treat customers, notes that successful organizations must accept the responsibility of "leading customers into the future." It is clear that while some organizations are invested in improving quality and creating innovations, others remain reactionary. With a clear focus on quality, and improving quality of life for people with disabilities, support organizations can provide needed leadership into the future of community participation of people with disabilities.

Managing for the future in human services—managing for the future expectations for quality of life—requires management methods that support organizational performance in the face of ongoing change. Quality improvement methods offer one valuable alternative.

Author Note

The authors wish to thank Karen Ross and Tim Rocak of Bonney Enterprises and Dan Guevara of SPARC Enterprises and Stepping Stone, Inc., for contributing ideas and examples to the development of this chapter.

References

Albin, J.M. (1992). *Quality improvement in employment and other human services: Managing for quality through change.* Baltimore: Brookes.

Albin, J.M., Rhodes, L., & Mauk, D. (1994). Realigning organizational culture, resources, and community roles: Changeover to community employment. *Journal of the Association for Persons with Severe Handicaps, 19,* 105-115.

Argyris, C. (1994). Good communication that blocks learning. *Harvard Business Review, 72*(4), 77-85.

Belasco, J.A. (1990). *Teaching the elephant to dance: The manager's guide to empowering change.* New York: Penguin.

Belasco, J.A., & Stayer, R.C. (1993). *Flight of the buffalo: Soaring to excellence, learning to let employees lead.* New York: Warner Books.

Block, P. (1993). *Stewardship: Choosing service over self-interest.* San Francisco: Berrett-Koehler.

Brassard, M. (1989). *The memory jogger +.* Methuen, MA: GOAL/QPC.

Camp, R.C. (1989). *Benchmarking: The search for industry best practices that lead to superior performance.* Milwaukee: Quality Press.

Covey, S.R. (1989). *The 7 habits of highly effective people.* New York: Simon & Schuster.

Covey, S.R. (1990). *Principle-centered leadership.* New York: Simon & Schuster.

Crosby, P. (1979). *Quality is free: The art of making quality certain.* New York: McGraw-Hill.

Dean, J.E. (1996). *Application of continuous improvement in the public sector: A case example.* Manuscript in preparation. University of Oregon.

Deming, W.E. (1986). *Out of the crisis.* Cambridge: Massachusetts Institute of Technology, Center for Advanced Engineering Study.

Deming, W.E. (1993). *The new economics for industry, government, education.* Cambridge: Massachusetts Institute of Technology, Center for Advanced Engineering Study.

Dobyns, L., & Crawford-Mason, C. (1991). *Quality or else: The revolution in world business.* Boston: Houghton-Mifflin.

Dobyns, L., & Crawford-Mason, C. (1994). *Thinking about quality: Progress, wisdom, and the Deming philosophy.* New York: Random House/Times.

Drucker, P.F. (1954). *The practice of management.* New York: Harper & Row.

Drucker, P.F. (1964). *Managing for results.* New York: Harper & Row.

Drucker, P.F. (1974). *Management: Tasks, responsibilities, practices.* New York: Harper & Row.

Hammer, M., & Champy, J. (1993). *Reengineering the corporation: A manifesto for business revolution.* New York: Harper Collins.

Ishikawa, K. (1982). *Guide to quality control* (2nd ed.). Tokyo: Asian Productivity Organization.

Ishikawa, K. (1985). *What is total quality control? The Japanese way.* Englewood Cliffs, NJ: Prentice-Hall.

Joiner, B.L. (1994). *Fourth generation management: The business consciousness.* New York: McGraw-Hill.

Joint Commission on Accreditation of Healthcare Organizations. (1993). *Quality improvement in home care.* Oakbrook Terrace, IL: Author.

Juran, J.M. (1986). The universal approach to managing for quality: The quality trilogy. *Quality Progress, 19*(8), 19–24.

Juran, J.M. (1988). *Juran on planning for quality.* New York: The Free Press.

Juran, J.M. (1989). *Juran on leadership for quality.* New York: The Free Press.

King, B. (1989a). *Better designs in half the time: Implementing QFD Quality Function Deployment in America.* Methuen, MA: GOAL/QPC.

King, B. (1989b). *Hoshin planning: The developmental approach.* Methuen, MA: GOAL/QPC.

Kinlaw, D.C. (1992). *Continuous improvement and measurement for quality: A team approach.* San Diego, CA: Pfeiffer.

Kohn, A. (1986). *No contest: The case against competition.* Boston: Houghton-Mifflin.

Kohn, A. (1993). *Punished by rewards: The trouble with gold stars, incentive plans, A's praise, and other bribes.* Boston: Houghton-Mifflin.

Mizuno, S. (1988). *Company-wide total quality control.* White Plains, NY: Quality Resources.

Osborne, D., & Gaebler, T. (1992). *Reinventing government: How the entrepreneurial spirit is transforming the public sector.* Reading, MA: Addison-Wesley.

Peters, T. (1987). *Thriving on chaos: Handbook for a management revolution.* New York: Harper & Row.

Peters, T., & Austin, N. (1985). *A passion for excellence: The leadership difference.* New York: Warner Books.

Peters, T.J., & Waterman, R.H. (1982). *In search of excellence: Lessons from America's best run companies.* New York: Harper & Row.

Pfadt, A., Cohen, I.L., Sudhalter, V., & Romanczyk, R.G. (1992). Applying statistical process control to clinical data: An illustration. *Journal of Applied Behavioral Analysis, 25,* 551–560.

Pirsig, R.M. (1974). *Zen and the art of motorcycle maintenance: An inquiry into values.* New York: Morrow.

QIP, Inc. (1986). *The transformation of American industry.* Miamisburg, OH: Author.

Scholtes, P.R. (1988). *The team handbook: How to use teams to improve quality.* Madison, WI: Joiner Associates.

Senge, P. (1990). *The fifth discipline: The art and practice of the learning organization.* New York: Doubleday/Currency.

Senge, P.M., Roberts, C., Ross, R.B., Smith, B.J., & Kleiner, A. (1994). *The fifth discipline fieldbook: Strategies for building a learning organization.* New York: Doubleday/Currency.

Walton, M. (1986). *The Deming management method.* New York: Putnam.

Wheeler, D.J., & Chambers, D.S. (1992). *Understanding statistical process control* (2nd ed.). Knoxville, TN: SPC Press.

Participatory Action Research as an Approach to Enhancing Quality of Life for Individuals with Disabilities

Jean Whitney-Thomas

Institute for Community Inclusion
Boston Children's Hospital

Participatory action research (PAR) is an emerging approach to problem solving and social change that is particularly suited to issues of quality of life for persons with mental retardation and closely related disabilities. Rogers and Palmer-Erbs (1994) described PAR as "the sine qua non when studying subjective outcomes, the experiences of others cross-culturally or across the life span, ethnicities, or disabilities" (p. 8). PAR relies on the involvement of stakeholders who can either identify subjective elements of their own lives that warrant change or understand the social contexts in which change occurs. Individuals with disabilities, family members, advocates, and others can contribute to our collective understanding of how quality of life can be conceptualized, what a life of quality looks like, and ways to improve outcomes. Furthermore, participation in research, policy formulation, and prac-

tice should involve those affected (Heron, 1981, quoted in Lather, 1986, p. 262).

Living a life of quality depends on what we consider to be meaningful and desirable for ourselves and others in our community. Most would agree that a steady job that pays more than just the bills and an education that allows one to attain his or her goals contribute to what would be described as a good life. Quality of life, however, is not merely defined in terms such as employment, salary, and level of education. Indeed, one's quality of life also depends upon a sense of control over decisions, qualitative aspects of personal relationships, and other issues defined by the individual. In Volume I of this series, Schalock proposed eight core quality of life dimensions: emotional well-being, interpersonal relations, material well-being, personal development, physical well-being, self-determination, social inclusion, and rights. These core dimensions can be understood both from the subjective perspective of satisfaction and through analysis of objective quality of life indicators (Schalock, 1996). In order to understand fully the notion of quality of life, the full breadth of these dimensions must be considered.

Having acknowledged the range of core quality of life dimensions, we must then consider their specific manifestations and judgments of relative importance across and within cultural groups, generations, and communities (Kuyken, Orley, Hudelson, & Sartorious, 1994). Questions and inquiries about quality of life should be situated explicitly within a social context, and one must also consider quality of life from a perspective that accounts for the social and cultural context of the individuals whose lives are being evaluated. In order to accomplish this, research and practice regarding quality of life should involve the individuals whose lives are under scrutiny and those around them who can provide perspectives on contexts and expectations. Halpern (1994) recommends that "the subjective dimensions [of quality of life] can only be ascertained . . . from a person's own point of view; whereas the objective dimensions are accessible either from a personal perspective or someone else's perspective" (p. 199). This recommendation has implications not only for how we measure quality of life (Parmenter, 1994; Schalock, Keith, Hoffman, & Karan, 1989), but also how we design services and practices to enhance quality of life outcomes for individuals with disabilities. This chapter describes how PAR can be used as a mechanism for change that enhances quality of life. Major sections include a definition of PAR, a discussion of how PAR can be used as a mechanism for social change, the PAR

process, examples of the use of PAR during the transition from school to adult life, and considerations for implementing PAR. Throughout the chapter, the reader is encouraged to recognize both the promise of—and unanswered questions about—participatory action research.

Participatory Action Research Defined

In recent years, the field of rehabilitation has seen a shift in the way research is designed and implemented. Questions under study emerge frequently not from the researcher alone, but out of collaborative efforts with consumers and practitioners. Once issues or questions have been identified, the research design and implementation becomes a shared process in which representatives from various stake-holding groups participate. This shift moves us away from the notion of the researcher as a technician who drives the investigation (Whyte, 1991) toward a model in which "groups of people can organize the conditions under which they learn from their own experience and make this experience accessible to others" (McTaggart, 1991, p. 170). The shift also involves using research not merely as tools to document and perhaps explain phenomena but as a mechanism for action and social change (Lather, 1986). An action agenda necessitates the use of approaches and tools that are accessible, meaningful, and relevant to those involved in the change efforts. PAR is one approach that has incorporated these issues of stakeholder involvement and social change (Bruyere, 1993; Graves, 1991).

PAR had its roots in the work of Kurt Lewin, who coined the phrase "action research" (quoted in Tripp, 1990). In recent years it has found its way into the business world and the literature of organizational change. Whyte (1991) described efforts to improve corporate restructuring by involving employees from various levels of the organization in the change efforts. Whyte emphasized the importance of using people's skills within the organization to accomplish tasks formerly reserved for outside experts. PAR has since become a part of rehabilitation and educational research and is seen as a way to empower individuals with disabilities (Graves, 1991), build partnerships with practitioners (Coles & Knowles, 1993), and extend participation to family members and significant others (Bruyere, 1993).

PAR is an Approach to Problem Solving, Not a Research Design

As Graves (1991) pointed out, "PAR is neither a quantitative nor a qualitative approach to disability and rehabilitation research. Rather PAR is a paradigm that maximizes involvement and participation of the consumer of the research in the research process and outcome" (p. 10). PAR is therefore an approach to identifying research questions, implementing investigations, and insuring that connections between findings and practice are strong. PAR is the organizational framework of a working group of individuals and the investigation as a whole rather than the specific steps used to answer research questions or test hypotheses.

That is to say, PAR is an approach to inquiry or problem solving, while research design is the methodology one uses to answer research questions. Design decisions, which are diagrammed in Figure 12.1, are made by the PAR working group on the basis of the group's research questions and the reference point to which they wish to tie their results.

As illustrated in Figure 12.1, the working group begins with their research questions or problems to be solved, clarifies on what level they wish to conduct an investigation, and considers at what level they wish to have an impact. The group chooses a reference point by asking if they want to understand a quality of life phenomenon as it affects specific individuals or to explore their issues in the context of a larger population. The decision regarding a class of methodologies is based on the nature of the problem to be solved and the state of existing knowledge. Qualitative methods are appropriate for questions concerning meaning, individual perceptions, and situations in which the researchers wish to build theory or explore unfamiliar territory (Erickson, 1986). Quantitative methods are best suited to answering questions about cause and effect, large group descriptions, measuring or manipulating variables that can be clearly defined, or testing an existing theory (Pedhazur &

Figure 12.1
Research Design Decision Matrix

Class of Methodologies	Reference Point	
	Subject Referenced	Group Referenced
Qualitative	e.g. Case Studies	e.g. Ethnography
Quantitative	e.g. Time Series	e.g. Experimental

Schmelkin, 1991). Once a working group has a clear understanding of their reference point and a class of methodologies, the most appropriate research design can be chosen and implemented.

PAR Involves Stakeholder Participation

Participants or stakeholders in a PAR project are those who understand the context in which problem solving is taking place, will feel the impact of the outcomes or findings, or wish to have a role in changing existing policy or practice (Menz, 1992). Lather (1986) recommends that those involved in research for social change have personal experience or an insider perspective to share with a working group. Those who will feel the impact of outcomes or findings are those whose lives might be different as a result of solutions or changes implemented by the working group. Finally, those who wish to have a role in changing policy or practice can be anyone who would benefit from proposed changes or individuals in a relevant area such as teaching, service provision, and academia. These definitions of participants imply that members in a PAR working group should include individuals with disabilities, family members, advocates, professionals, and researchers in the field. Each stakeholder can bring to a problem-solving situation their own perspective or expertise and contribute to the process of identifying issues, developing solutions, and evaluating change in unique ways. Group membership is also defined by those who are concerned with similar issues and are committed to social change so that the work occurs in mutually supporting groups of like-minded people (Tripp, 1990, p. 161). Therefore, the group members must be able to come to consensus on what change is necessary and what forms solutions must take.

PAR Is a Call to Action

As implied by the use of the word "action," PAR is fundamentally a mechanism to influence or change a given situation. Thus, the inquiry and problem solving that occurs within the context of a PAR project focus on the need for change and strategies to accomplish it. Examples of how this has been implemented can be seen in the organizational change described by Whyte (1991) in the Xerox Corporation. In this situation, labor and management came together to develop strategies to restructure the company in such a way that economic and employment issues were addressed satisfactorily from the perspectives of both labor and management. PAR has also been used as a mechanism for curriculum change and the professional development of teachers (Sagor, 1991). In these situations, the data or information collected informs a process that does not stop at merely documenting phenomena.

Participatory Action Research as Mechanism for Social Change

When we consider quality of life issues for individuals with disabilities, we find considerable evidence documenting problematic outcomes across the core dimensions of emotional well-being, interpersonal relations, material well-being, personal development, physical well-being, self-determination, social inclusion, and rights. For example, individuals with learning disabilities are more likely to drop out of high school than are their peers without disabilities (Zigmond & Thornton, 1985). In addition to the disproportionate unemployment among people with disabilities (Louis Harris and Associates, Inc., 1995), average annual earnings of people with learning disabilities are almost 45% lower than those of people without disabilities

(Sitlington & Frank, 1990). Of individuals with developmental disabilities being served by day and employment services nationally, 70% are in segregated facility-based employment (Institute for Community Inclusion, 1995). Only 15% of students with learning disabilities have attended a postsecondary school two years after graduation, compared to 56% of their peers without disabilities (Sitlington & Frank, 1990). The social lives of individuals with learning disabilities can be characterized by a limited range of activities (Sitlington & Frank, 1990) and involvement of family members more often than friends (Scuccimarra & Speece, 1990). Finally, self-determination, autonomy, and choice-making continue to be limited for many individuals with disabilities, especially those with mental retardation (Schloss, Alper, & Jayne, 1993; Wehmeyer & Kelchner, 1995; Wehmeyer & Metzler, 1995).

These outcomes are fundamentally related to quality of life and indicate the need to address and improve quality of life outcomes for individuals with disabilities. The movement to enhance quality of life for individuals with disabilities resembles social movements of the past in which "...The personal is political. What were once thought of as individual problems were redefined as social problems that require political solutions" (Lather, 1986, p. 265). Efforts for social change necessarily involve policy makers, professionals, family members, and individuals with disabilities who come together to develop solutions and strategies. Multiple voices need to take part in these efforts for two reasons. First, the nature of quality of life is at once personal and universal; therefore personal perspectives are as necessary as those that inform the social constructions and context of the problem-solving efforts. Second, improving quality of life outcomes is a process of creating change at an individual level and the societal level.

In efforts to improve quality of life outcomes we have opportunities to "transform structural inequalities" (Lather, 1986, p. 269). Improving outcomes not only means improving the quality of life for individuals with disabilities; more importantly, it means creating change on a broader social scale. Change can be as individualized as collaborative problem solving around an individual's employment or increased recreational opportunities, or as global as implementing and evaluating systems change in order to address the needs of a population of individuals with disabilities. The continuum of possibilities for PAR includes any problem-solving situation that involves multiple people with various perspectives and strengths that lead to change in the lives of individuals with disabilities. The participatory nature of PAR embeds opportunities for empowerment in the change effort. PAR turns the paternalistic relationship inherent between the researcher and the researched into a collaboration in which the project becomes an opportunity to use "research to help participants understand and change their [own] situations" (Lather, 1986, p. 263).

Although each group may define their PAR process to meet their individual needs, there are consistent strategies and ways that consumers and other stakeholders can create change. In PAR, the project takes on a problem-solving approach to issues identified by the participants. The central questions that guide their work could be, What needs to change? Has change been effective? What is the impact of change in my life? These questions can be understood within the framework of action research proposed by Tripp (1990), who describes a spiral of *planning, acting, fact-finding,* and *analysis*. These steps are then repeated with a reformulated plan, revised action, more fact-finding, and reanalysis. The implementation of these

Figure 12.2
Collaboration in the Research Process

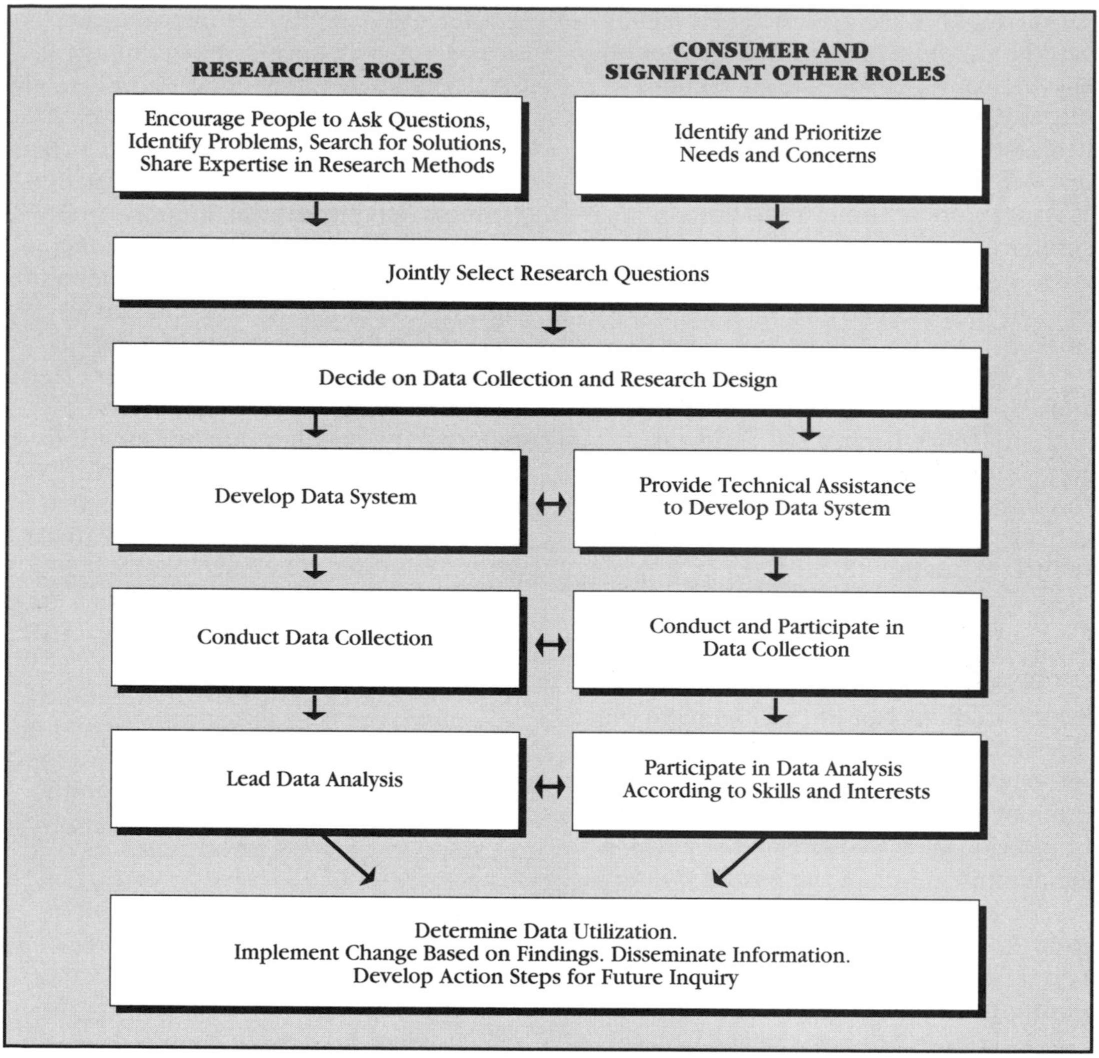

RESEARCHER ROLES		CONSUMER AND SIGNIFICANT OTHER ROLES
Encourage People to Ask Questions, Identify Problems, Search for Solutions, Share Expertise in Research Methods		Identify and Prioritize Needs and Concerns
Jointly Select Research Questions		
Decide on Data Collection and Research Design		
Develop Data System	↔	Provide Technical Assistance to Develop Data System
Conduct Data Collection	↔	Conduct and Participate in Data Collection
Lead Data Analysis	↔	Participate in Data Analysis According to Skills and Interests
Determine Data Utilization. Implement Change Based on Findings. Disseminate Information. Develop Action Steps for Future Inquiry		

steps through collaboration can be seen in Figure 12.2 (Schalock, 1995).

The Participatory Action Research Process

Problem Identification and Planning

The PAR process begins with problem posing (McTaggart, 1991). The group decides what needs to change based on questions and issues relevant in their lives. As seen in Figure 12.2, the initial stages require that one accustomed to formulating questions (such as a researcher) encourages others to ask questions and challenge elements of their daily lives or practice. Concurrently, participants identify and prioritize their needs and concerns. Finally, the group decides jointly on research questions or a focus for the project. These planning steps can involve discussions among working-group members, reviews of relevant literature, discussions with individuals outside the working group, or gathering of information through observations, interviews, or self-reflection. These tools are designed to gather descriptive information that can direct a working group toward a social and personal change agenda, help them articulate their questions, and clarify issues so that potential solutions can be identified.

Action Phase

Identifying solutions means designing interventions to effect change. This phase of the project is called action and moves a project beyond the documentation of phenomena. The action phase is about changing behavior and having an impact on outcomes defined as problematic in the planning phase. Gross, Fogg, and Conrad (1993) recommend that interventions grow out of "an explicit explanation for why the intervention should work" (p. 260). Explanations can be built on the basis of the working group's understanding gained in the planning stage, prior research, other people's experience, or previously articulated theories offered by the field. The explanation or theory used by the PAR group provides the framework for their interventions and suggests solutions for change efforts.

The effect of the group's action is documented through the change process. A researcher might think of this as data collection; nonresearchers in the PAR group might think of this as accountability. No matter what it is called, the purpose of this phase is to insure that the action or intervention is implemented in a systematic way and that evidence of its success or failure is gathered. The working group is responsible for insuring that their change efforts are fully implemented and that there is consistency in what is done. Full

implementation and consistency will contribute to the rigor of the PAR process and increase the likelihood of success in the change efforts. Consulting Figure 12.2, one can see that the participants should decide as a group on data collection tools. Responsibilities for implementation, however, may be divided between those who consider themselves researchers and those who do not. Nonresearchers may not have the interest or the skills to develop data systems, conduct data collection, and lead data analysis. As shown by the double-arrowed lines, however, the PAR group should continue to communicate and collaborate throughout this phase and share responsibility when it comes to understanding the meaning of the data and its analysis.

Analysis Phase

The analysis phase provides the working group the opportunity to synthesize information gathered as the change efforts were implemented and to draw conclusions about the effectiveness of their process. This evaluation can focus on questions of cause and effect such as, "Did the intervention result in the change we were expecting?" or, "In what ways is my life different than before the change efforts were implemented?"

Measuring change involves a host of considerations that have to do with the design of research or inquiry. The working group needs to consider the state of affairs before an intervention or solution is implemented. Once implementation has taken place, the group returns to its original questions and solutions and examines how core dimensions of quality of life have been influenced or changed. For example, a group might consider the impact of an intervention on emotional well-being and interpersonal relationships. In a case such as this, an intervention and data collection design would have to be developed to measure critical aspects of emotional well-being and interpersonal relationships before and after the intervention and might involve a comparison group to strengthen the investigation. If the PAR group designed a mechanism to increase self-determination, the group might answer questions about how individuals with disabilities demonstrate self-determination and autonomy in their lives, how opportunities for choice have increased, or whether a particular method for teaching decision-making and self-advocacy skills is effective. The nature of a PAR group's analysis depends on the questions. However, any group interested in effecting change should consider comparing quality of life variables across groups, individuals, situations, or time so as to add elements of control and further isolate the effect of their solution on the problem. Multiple tools or methods should be used in concert to gain a full understanding of how things have changed. For example, quantitative methods can lend support to the theory that led to the design of the solutions in the first place; whereas qualitative methods can answer questions about how people perceive change in their lives and whether there are other issues that have surfaced in the wake of the change process.

The change process does not end when analysis of the original data has been completed, the results synthesized, and the findings shared with the PAR group and others. Rather, PAR is a continuous cycle of inquiry and problem solving that is repeated in a spiral consisting of a reformulated plan, revised action, more fact-finding, and reanalysis (Tripp, 1990). Once problems have been posed, solutions identified, and change evaluated, additional issues will undoubtedly reveal themselves and become new priorities that need to be addressed. In addition, the PAR group determines how their findings and solutions should be used: How will they disseminate what they have learned? How will they broaden the scope of their change efforts? And what directions do they need to go in to continue the action cycle?

Examples of Participatory Action Research: Impact on Quality of Life

The transition from school to adult life can be a particularly anxious time for young people with disabilities and their parents. This anxiety is expressed compellingly by parents who acknowledge their own fears and concerns for their children as they leave school, enter the world of adults, and seek services (Hanley-Maxwell, Whitney-Thomas, & Pogoloff, 1995). Parents wonder if the reliable support that their son or daughter needs will be available and who might fill the supportive roles parents have played so far in their child's life (Dempsey, 1991; Gallivan-Fenlon, 1994; Hanley-Maxwell et al., 1995). Many parents worry whether their adult children with disabilities will experience the material, emotional, and physical well-being; social inclusion; and personal development that they did in the context of their families. These issues become particularly acute for families who struggle with the need for ongoing support. Indeed, these quality of life concerns are not unwarranted given high unemployment, social isolation, and the ongoing dependence of adults with disabilities (Louis Harris and Associates, Inc., 1995; Sitlington & Frank, 1990; Wehmeyer & Kelchner, 1995).

Building participatory problem-solving groups can bring together young people with disabilities, parents, and professionals in such a way that the families and young people feel more positive about the transition process and that their quality of life during the transition is maintained or enhanced (Nisbet, Covert, & Schuh, 1992). To date, there are few examples of how a clearly defined PAR process has been used to address the needs of transition age youth. The following examples demonstrate how elements of PAR have been used in a number of transition related inquiries.

Deciding on the Research Questions

For PAR to begin, there must be consensus about what questions are to be addressed. The questions must be relevant to those involved and to those whose lives are to be reflected in the inquiry. Focus groups and brain-storming sessions are two examples of how relevance and meaning can be established.

In order to gather information about the meaning of the transition process to parents of students with and without disabilities, Whitney-Thomas and Hanley-Maxwell (1996) conducted focus groups with parents whose children were within two years of graduating from high school. A number of the young people were planning to attend college or vocational schools, some were entering the job market immediately, and some were unsure what their lives would look like once high school ended. The parents participating in the focus groups were better able to inform the researchers about their primary concerns during their child's transition process, what the schools had done well or neglected to do as their son or daughter planned for the future, and what their vision for the future looked like. The information gathered from the focus groups was used to develop a questionnaire and mailed to a large sample of parents of students with and without disabilities. The results

of the survey supported what the focus group participants had shared and indicated that parents of students with disabilities felt greater discomfort and pessimism during the transition of their child to adult life.

Another participatory way to identify questions for systematic inquiry is to hold brainstorming sessions with stakeholders to develop a list of questions relevant to their lives and concerns. The Massachusetts Natural Support Project (MNSP) is a research and demonstration project conducted by the Institute for Community Inclusion that provides training and technical assistance to school and community-based teams in their provision of transition and workplace supports for students with disabilities leaving high school. In the spring of 1995, four new school districts joined the project as replication sites. At the first training session, participating teachers, administrators, parents, and service providers were asked to generate lists of questions they would like to see answered over the course of their year-long involvement in the project. It was explained that two researchers would be conducting systematic observations and interviews and providing participants with information to answer their questions. Three categories of questions were identified by the group. First, participants were interested in building local community and long-term support for the goals of the MNSP. Second, participants wanted a clearer understanding of the person-centered planning process. Finally, the MNSP participants were interested in improving quality of life outcomes for transition-age students such as independence and emotional well-being.

The questions raised by the MNSP participants reflected their stake in the transition process of young people with disabilities. As parents and professionals, these individuals were concerned about how their services and efforts could have an impact on their communities; they had questions about the nature and implementation of a process that was new to them; and they wanted to see student progress as a result of their own work.

Communication Along the Way

Once research questions have been identified, PAR requires that all participants remain involved in the design, implementation, and interpretation of the inquiry. Communication along the way among the participants is essential and can include participants, reviewing and providing feedback to written materials or face-to-face interviews and discussion between participants.

In a series of interviews with parents of transition-age students with cognitive disabilities, Hanley-Maxwell et al. (1995) found that the parents had complex visions for their children's future homes, social networks, and time that extended beyond employment. These parents, however, were not optimistic that their visions would be realized because of barriers that included insufficient services and limited social networks. Finally, they described the transition period as a difficult one not only for their child but also for themselves because their needs intersected with the needs of their children. In order to insure that the researchers' interpretations reflected the parents' experiences, the researchers sent a draft of the findings to a sample of participating parents for their review and comment. This strategy is often called a *member check* (Lincoln & Guba, 1985) and is one way to insure the accuracy of qualitative research. From the perspective of PAR, member checks are a mechanism to maintain communication between the researcher and the participants and maintain the voice of the participants in the products of a research

effort. Member checks, however useful in the broader context of qualitative research, are limited in the extent to which they facilitate PAR. They represent a limited opportunity to establish communication between the researcher and the participants. Continuous communication is more easily established in repeated conversations that occur throughout a project.

Within the context of the natural supports project (MNSP), two researchers are currently investigating the implementation of person-centered planning for 12 transition-age students in four communities. The research involves interviews with parents, students, and facilitators of person-centered planning processes. These interviews are structured as discussions in casual environments such as restaurants and participants' homes. The researchers ask students, parents, and facilitators for their impressions of the planning processes, what they have learned as a result of the MNSP activities, and what they want to learn more about. The researchers are able to offer the participants information about what is happening for students in other schools, share resources and support, and take the participants' needs and concerns back to the training and technical assistance staff in the MNSP.

Informing Interpretations and Influencing Change

Within the context of the MNSP, research on the implementation of person-centered planning is happening consecutively with training and ongoing technical assistance from the MNSP staff to participating schools, families, and students. The training and technical assistance is meant to provide participants with the skills to conduct and maintain person-centered planning processes and develop individual, competitive jobs with natural supports for the project participants. Each of the four school districts is working closely with one technical assistant trainer and one researcher. The researcher for each school takes notes at steering committee, organizational, and person-centered planning meetings and shares the notes with MNSP staff, school personnel, parents, and students. These notes then become the basis for discussions; observations are interpreted through feedback from participants; and the dynamic process has an influence on how MNSP staff provide technical assistance. For example, when presented with observations of limited student participation, the MNSP staff interpreted this as reflections of the various personalities or characteristics of the students. In the context of person-centered planning, however, it is important to match the format of the planning with students' personalities and preferences. The MNSP staff concluded that they needed to do a better job of individualizing the person-centered planning processes and teaching others in their schools to do so as well. As a result, training conducted by the MNSP staff has been modified to emphasize individualization of the planning process.

The participatory projects cited above have been designed to address quality of life issues for students who are leaving high school and entering adult life. The goal of the MNSP, for example, is for participating students to find integrated employment and to enjoy social inclusion at their workplaces. An additional benefit of the participatory process has been that parents also feel greater emotional well-being as their children plan for the future. The parents in the project have told the researchers that hearing about the experiences of other families and pulling together a supportive team to help their son or daughter realize his or her dreams has helped them feel more positive about the transition process. In order for parents to voice these feelings it is important to build participatory elements into projects from the very beginning and insure that participation is encouraged throughout. The chapter's final section explores issues to consider when designing PAR in order to assure that a project meets the needs of those involved and that genuine participation is guaranteed.

Considerations for Implementation

Rigor and Science

Researchers schooled in a traditional paradigm often ask questions about the validity, reliability, and objectivity of PAR projects. In any investigation one needs to ask about the strengths of the researcher's claims in relation to his or her method of inquiry. Researchers enhance validity by defining constructs carefully, crafting appropriate data collection instruments, and specifying clearly the context in which they conduct research (Parker, 1990). Similar issues affect the replicability of the investigation and the stability of the findings over time. Methods to enhance the reliability of a study include careful design and use of data collection techniques, consistent implementation of any treatments or interventions, and clear descriptions of the context in which the investigation occurs so that others can either replicate the study or understand the implications for their own situation. Issues of validity and reliability are addressed in any research and have more to do with how one carries out methodology than who is involved in deciding what methods are to be used. These questions of scientific rigor are issues that the PAR working group should address just as would any group of researchers.

In team work, extra attention must be paid to clarity and consistency. Additional training may be needed on data collection techniques or methodologies that are unfamiliar to team members. Bruyere (1993) emphasizes the importance of research methods and types of data appearing credible in the eyes of the team. Therefore, analytic techniques should be chosen for how well they perform the necessary task and how meaningful they are to group members. As discussed above, those with expertise have a responsibility to share their knowledge with others and insure their understanding. Those skilled in research and evaluation can help working groups identify methodologies that best address the questions and goals of the team. A researcher can help the team develop data collection tools and conduct the analysis. Other members of the team contribute to methodological issues by considering the face validity of measurement tools, the social validity of interventions, and the authenticity of the interpretations.

Questions of objectivity often arise in discussions of PAR and will need to be clarified until there is widespread understanding of the difference between an approach to research and a research design. If objectivity can be defined as accurate representation of problems that need solutions, attention to the validity and reliability of the investigation, and the creation of viable and appropriate solutions, then participants in PAR can be as objective as researchers functioning under a more traditional approach. In what is called the positivist approach to research, it is assumed that the researcher situates himself or herself at a vantage point sufficiently removed from the research question under study so as to isolate the phenomenon under study and exert greater control over the inquiry (Cook & Campbell, 1979). It has been debated in recent years as to whether or not this position of objectivity is possible or even desirable. Peshkin (1988) maintains that our own subjectivity cannot be completely done away with and charges those involved in research to look inward and acknowledge their biases rather than to try in vain to eliminate them from the research process. The perspectives and subjectivities of the researchers are part of the context in which the investigation is conducted. Researchers need to identify and acknowledge their own subjectivities. These subjectivities must then be taken into consideration as the research takes place.

PAR assumes that the participants identify issues and research questions from their own lives. Thus, an outsider perspective is impossible. An outsider may not have the insight to identify the critical questions to ask or the problems that need to be investigated, or may impose meaningful interpretations on findings. What is possible, however, is to pull together a group of individuals who bring with them various perspectives and to let these perspectives balance each other through the negotiation that accompanies the collaborative process. Indeed, the insider perspective brings greater authenticity to the work, especially when combined with the rigorous research design.

The Complexity of Collaborative Participation

Quality of life is a multifaceted construct that spans the domains of an individual's life and involves significant others such as family, friends, coworkers, and others in our social networks (Dennis, Williams, Giangreco & Cloninger, 1993). It is important that investigations of quality of life outcomes not only involve individuals with disabilities and their significant others, but that these investigations be designed and conducted by these stakeholders as well.

Unfortunately, many individuals who could contribute to a PAR project may not feel comfortable questioning services and delivery systems or voicing their need for additional support and may not feel equipped to conduct an empirical investigation (Harry, 1992). The initial roles of the researcher in the PAR process should encourage others to examine their worlds critically, express their needs, and search systematically for solutions, and share his or her expertise in conducting investigations. As discussed earlier, this can be facilitated by making research and methodologies visible and relevant to students, parents, consumer advocacy groups, and those who may not have had the opportunity to be involved in such activities. Similarly, agencies that fund research on quality of life outcomes should involve stakeholders to determine priorities and encourage individuals with disabilities and their significant others to participate in research that has an impact on their lives. Finally, the language in which researchers share their expertise and results should be meaningful to these groups of stakeholders.

Once the questions under study have been identified, the research design, data collection, and analysis are planned and implemented. Clearly, there will be varying skills, expertise, and interests among the working group participants; as a result, the nature of everyone's participation must be negotiated. McTaggart defined participation as "sharing in the way research is conceptualized, practiced, and brought to bear on the life-world. It means ownership—responsible agency in the production of knowledge and the improvement on practice" (1991, p. 171). Active participation of stakeholders should occur at each stage of the research process; but responsibility for the intermediate steps described in Figure 12.2 depends primarily on the skills and interests of the

participants. The researcher will more than likely be the one to take a lead role in developing the data system, the data collection, and the analysis. The roles of the researchers and the other participants become intermingled once again when the process reaches the point of determining the use of the data collected and analyzed. It is at this point in the process where the working group decides upon solutions to their initial concerns or needs, the impact of the research on the lives of people with disabilities and their significant others, and how their findings will be shared with others.

The second part of McTaggart's (1991) definition hinges upon shared ownership of the process. This can be achieved if responsibilities are shared from the outset, the research grows out of concerns held by the stakeholders, and the outcomes meet the needs that exist. McTaggart suggests that this can be facilitated by insuring that relationships in the research process are reciprocal and symmetrical. Reciprocity implies balance, shared responsibilities, and the real sense that each participant's strengths contribute to the overall process. Symmetry implies that all participants carry equal weight in the process, that their contributions are unique and equally valuable, and that status and power differentials between group members are eliminated.

Unfortunately, neither reciprocity nor symmetry is easy to achieve. Due to the varying strengths, skills, experiences, and values the participants bring to the process there may not be perfect symmetry in the working relationships. Indeed, Chisholm cautions us to not be naive in our expectations of symmetry when she says, "The injunction to practice symmetricality neglects structural realities. These realities apply to generational divisions no less than to those of class, gender, and race" (1990, p. 254). Disability might also be added to the list of individual characteristics that influence the symmetry of relationships within the working group.

An example of how disability status further complicates issues of reciprocity and symmetry are the challenges encountered involving individuals with severe disabilities in the research process. Biklen and Mosely (1988) have addressed methods of interviewing and gathering qualitative data from individuals with severe disabilities and recommend building relationships with these individuals, involving significant others in their lives, and collecting data via observations as well as interviews. Gallivan-Fenlon (1994), in her qualitative study of seniors in high school with severe disabilities, however, found that parents, teachers, and the students often had varying visions for the future. Issues of how to genuinely involve individuals with severe disabilities who may rely on others to express their visions and needs have yet to be resolved. Researchers, young people, family members, and professionals must continue to work together to establish viable strategies and document those that result in success as examples for others to follow.

As strategies are developed, we must be careful to negotiate participation throughout the process and not assume that we are acting in a clearly reciprocal or symmetric way merely because the research process involves people with a diversity of experiences. Reciprocity and symmetry can be facilitated by what Whyte (1991) calls a *continuous mutual learning strategy* and what Lather (1986) calls a *mutually educative enterprise.* This means that everyone involved in the process takes on the role of expert by sharing his or her own set of skills and strengths with the group as a whole. As each participant takes on

the role of expert, the others in the research group benefit. The sharing then furthers the collective knowledge of the group and project. In the context of an investigation about the transition process from school to work, the researcher in the group can share his or her knowledge about research methodologies and implementation; the young person can inform adults about what is important among his or her peers as they prepare for the future; and parents can share implications of the transition process for the family as whole.

Suggestions for Success

In conclusion, the following critical processes can contribute to the success of a PAR approach to an action agenda to enhance quality of life outcomes.

1. **Insure ongoing, genuine, and negotiated participation in all phases of the process.** Build a working group consisting of individuals with disabilities, family members, coworkers, and community members who meet regularly and share responsibilities of the investigation. Avoid tokenism by eliciting, hearing, and using the input of all participants. Finally, allow relationships within the group to grow over time.

2. **Acknowledge and build upon the diversity of opinions, values, and experiences within the working group.** Understand that while each participant has a vested interest in the project, participants' needs and concerns may be very different. Allow the role of expert within the group to rotate by sharing skills and supporting the learning of others.

3. **Consider mutual ownership and benefit as the best compensation for participation.**

If there are professionals who are compensated for their time, then all participants should be compensated. Ideally, however, the project will result in needed change and have a positive impact on the lives of the participants, in which case monetary compensation may not be necessary. As with roles and participation, compensation should be negotiated and revisited at multiple points during the process.

These three suggestions for successful implementation of PAR are general enough to apply to most group processes. When building a PAR process, however, the group must be mindful that the goal is not merely to further scientific knowledge or to demonstrate the use of specific research designs or analysis tools; rather, the goal is to pull together a group of like-minded individuals who recognize a need for change and

want to turn effectively this need into problem-solving opportunities. This is not to say that the research and inquiry should be removed from PAR. It is important to use research methods and analytic tools to address the issues that a PAR group identifies; however, the questions and issues must drive the choice of methods. Systematic inquiry should be a tool used by groups of people striving for change.

As the field of rehabilitation strengthens its commitment to PAR and implementation becomes more widespread, our knowledge of how best to implement other suggestions will develop. We are currently at a point that requires documentation of strategies and dissemination of success stories in order to facilitate the growth of PAR, which, in the author's opinion, holds great promise to effect change, improve service delivery for individuals with disabilities, and thereby enhance their quality of life.

References

Biklen, S.K., & Mosely, C.R. (1988). "Are you retarded?" "No, I'm Catholic." Qualitative methods in the study of people with severe handicaps. *Journal of the Association for Persons with Severe Handicaps, 13,* 155–162.

Bruyere, S.M. (1993). Participatory action research: Overview and implications for family members of persons with disabilities. *Journal of Vocational Rehabilitation, 3*(2), 62–68.

Chisholm, L. (1990). Action research: Some methodological and political considerations. *British Educational Research Journal, 16,* 249–257.

Coles, A.L., & Knowles, J.G. (1993). Teacher development partnership research: A focus on methods and issues. *American Educational Research Journal, 30,* 473–495.

Cook, T.D., & Campbell, D.T. (1979). *Quasi-experimentation: Design and analysis issues for field settings.* Boston: Houghton Mifflin.

Dempsey, I. (1991). Parental roles in the post-school adjustment of their son or daughter with a disability. *Australia and New Zealand Journal of Developmental Disabilities, 17,* 313–320.

Dennis, R.E., Williams, W., Giangreco, M.F., & Cloninger, C.J. (1993). Quality of life as context for planning and evaluation of services for people with disabilities. *Exceptional Children, 59,* 499–512.

Erickson, F. (1986). Qualitative methods in research on teaching. In M. Wittrock (Ed.), *Handbook of research on teaching* (pp. 119–161). New York: MacMillan.

Gallivan-Fenlon, A. (1994). "Their senior year": Family and service provider perspectives on the transition from school to adult life for young adults with disabilities. *Journal of the Association for Persons with Severe Handicaps, 19,* 11–23.

Graves, W.H. (1991, September). Participatory action research: A new paradigm for disability and rehabilitation research. *ARCA Newsletter, 19,* 9–10.

Gross, D., Fogg, L., & Conrad, B. (1993). Designing interventions in psychosocial research. *Archives of Psychiatric Nursing, 7,* 259–264.

Halpern, A.S. (1994). Quality of life for students with disabilities in transition from school to adulthood. *Social Indicators Research, 33,* 193–236.

Hanley-Maxwell, C., Whitney-Thomas, J., & Pogoloff, S.M. (1995). The second shock: A qualitative study of parents' perspectives and needs during their child's transition from school to adult life. *Journal of the Association for Persons with Severe Handicaps, 20,* 3–15.

Harry, B. (1992). An ethnographic study of cross-cultural communication with Puerto Rican-American families in the special education system. *American Educational Research Journal, 29,* 471–494.

Institute for Community Inclusion. (1995, August). *Mixed messages: National perspectives on integrated employment* (The Institute Brief). Boston: Children's Hospital, Author.

Kuyken, W., Orley, J., Hudelson, P., & Sartorious, N. (1994). Quality of life assessments across cultures. *International Journal of Mental Health, 23*(2), 5–27.

Lather, P. (1986). Research as praxis. *Harvard Educational Review, 56*(3), 257–277.

Lincoln, Y.S., & Guba, E.G. (1985). *Naturalistic inquiry.* Newbury Park, CA: Sage.

Louis Harris and Associates, Inc. (1995, July). The N.O.D./Harris survey on employment of people with disabilities (Study No. 951401). New York: Author.

McTaggart, R. (1991). Principles for participatory action research. *Adult Education Quarterly, 41,* 168–187.

Menz, F.E. (1992). *Strengthening applications from research through involvement of consumers and practitioners.* Menomonie, WI: University of Wisconsin-Stout, Research and Training Center.

Nisbet, J., Covert, S., & Schuh, M. (1992). Family involvement in the transition from school to adult life. In F.R. Rusch, L. Destefano, J. Chadsey-Rusch, L.A. Phelps, & E.M. Szymanski (Eds.), *Transition from school to adult life: Models, linkages, and policy* (pp. 402–424). Sycamore, IL: Sycamore Publishing.

Parker, R.M. (1990). Power, control, and validity in research. *Journal of Learning Disabilities, 23,* 613–620.

Parmenter, T.T. (1994). Quality of life as a concept and measurable entity. *Social Indicators Research, 33,* 9–46.

Pedhazur, E., & Schmelkin, L.P. (1991). *Measurement, design, and analysis: An integrated approach.* Hillsdale, NJ: Lawrence Erlbaum.

Peshkin, A. (1988). In search of subjectivity: One's own. *Educational Researcher, 17,* 17–22.

Rogers, E.S., & Palmer-Erbs, V. (1994). Participatory action research: Implications for research and evaluation in psychiatric rehabilitation. *Psychosocial Rehabilitation Journal, 18*(2), 3–12.

Sagor, R. (1991, March). What project LEARN reveals about collaborative action research. *Educational Leadership, 30,* 6–10.

Schalock, R.L. (1995). *Outcome-based evaluation.* New York: Plenum.

Schalock, R.L. (Ed.) (1996). *Quality of life: Volume I. Conceptualization and measurement.* Washington, DC: American Association on Mental Retardation.

Schalock, R.L., Keith, K.D., Hoffman, K., & Karan, O.C. (1989). Quality of life: Its measurement and use. *Mental Retardation, 27,* 25-31.

Schloss, P.J., Alper, S., & Jayne, D. (1993). Self-determination for persons with disabilities: Choice, risk, and dignity. *Exceptional Children, 60,* 215-225.

Scuccimarra, D.J., & Speece, D.L. (1990). Employment outcomes and social integration of students with mild handicaps: The quality of life two years after high school. *Journal of Learning Disabilities, 23,* 213-219.

Sitlington, P.L., & Frank, A.R. (1990). Are adolescents with learning disabilities successfully crossing the bridge into adult life? *Learning Disabilities Quarterly, 13,* 97-111.

Tripp, D.H. (1990). Socially critical action research. *Theory into Practice, 29*(3), 158-165.

Wehmeyer, M.L., & Kelchner, K. (1995). Measuring the autonomy of adolescents and adults with mental retardation: A self-report form of the Autonomous Functioning Checklist. *Career Development for Exceptional Individuals, 18*(1), 3-20.

Wehmeyer, M.L., & Metzler, C.A. (1995). How self-determined are people with mental retardation? The national consumer survey. *Mental Retardation, 33,* 111-119.

Whitney-Thomas, J., & Hanley-Maxwell, C. (1996). Packing the parachute: Parents' perceptions as their children prepare to leave high school. *Exceptional Children, 63,* 75-88.

Whyte, W.F. (1991). *Participant action research.* Newbury Park, CA: Sage.

Zigmond, N. & Thornton, H. (1985). Follow-up of post-secondary aged learning disabled graduates and drop-outs. *Learning Disabilities Research, 1*(1), 50-55.

Part III
Public Policy Application

Answering the questions that persons with disabilities ask about their quality of life requires both quality services and the implementation of quality of life principles:

- Opportunities for personal growth and development

- Equity and empowerment

- Supports that are flexible and maximize the individual's well-being and potential

- Interdependence among community members

- Consumer satisfaction.

The two chapters in Part III discuss how these major principles might be implemented through an enlightened public policy that supports the goal of enhancing the quality of life of persons with disabilities. In chapter 13, Rud Turnbull and Gary Brunk argue that the application of quality of life to persons with disabilities requires a public policy that is consistent with the notions of quality of life and its enhancement for people without disabilities. The authors begin by summarizing different ways that one can conceptualize and apply the concept of quality of life: as measured by science or rights, citizen participation, mutual accommodation, value-driven policy, determined by evaluation and accountability, and reflected in public policy. They go on to discuss two competing political philosophies in America, philosophical liberalism and civic republicanism, and how these philosophies are related to the concept of quality of life for persons with disabilities. Throughout the chapter, the authors argue that there is a natural connection between concern for the quality of life of all Americans and concern for the quality of life of Americans with disabilities. They suggest further that for each of us, quality of life is based on relationships.

In chapter 14, David Goode suggests that quality of life can be used in public policy "as a guide, common denominator, or core principle with respect to decision-making in services and supports for persons requiring special supports." The goal is to reduce the discrepancy between the individual's perceived and desired conditions of life. In describing his international work on quality of life, Dr. Goode stresses the value of quality of life as a sensitizing concept, the use of quality of life as a basis for governmental policy, and the value of integrating quantitative and qualitative/subjective approaches to defining and measuring quality of life. He also summarizes a number of definitions of quality of life, confirming three concepts that appear repeatedly in its definition:

- General feelings of well-being

- Opportunities to fulfill one's potential

- Feelings of positive social involvement.

A key argument throughout the chapter is that the concept of quality of life should be the basis of public policy; it should be used as a core principle to guide decision-making in services and supports for persons who need special supports. The author also encourages the international community to establish national coalitions and discussion groups to develop quality of life oriented research, policy, and practices.

In these chapters, the reader should pay close attention to a number of key public policy issues that will impact the application of quality of life to persons with disabilities. Chief among these are the need to:

- Link quality of life measures to all of the nation's citizenry

- Implement quality of life oriented public policy

- Consider the concept of quality of life as generic rather than particular to people with disabilities

- Ensure cooperation among self-advocates, researchers, and policy makers in developing a quality of life international network

- Continue an international focus on quality of life.

Quality of Life and Public Policy

H. Rutherford Turnbull III and Gary L. Brunk
Beach Center, The University of Kansas

The application of quality of life to persons with disabilities requires a public policy that is consistent with the notion of quality of life and its enhancement. In that regard, there are several ways to conceptualize and apply the concept of quality of life to people with disabilities and their families. In this chapter, we identify and briefly discuss seven of these ways that are listed in Table 13.1. We limit our discussion to a simple statement of the nature of the respective measure or concept. Throughout the chapter we argue that measures of quality of life, although necessary, are not sufficient unless they are linked to measures of quality of life for all of the nation's citizenry. In a sense, we advocate for the mainstreaming of measures of quality of life of people with disability into at least one of the major measures of quality of life for people who do not have disabilities. In making this argument, we wish to address the matter of the public philosophy that does or should guide all citizens, disabled or not, in their public and private conduct. In setting out a political and philosophical measure of

quality of life, we hope to add a new dimension to the discussion of the application of quality of life to persons with disabilities.

Quality of Life as Measured by Science

Efforts to decide whether or not to provide medical treatment to newborns with birth defects have resulted frequently in a formulation of quality of life for the newborn. This formulation asserts that quality of life is the function of the child's natural endowment multiplied by the sum of the contributions to the child that can be expected from the home or family and society. The normal expression of this approach is Quality of Life + NE x (H + S) (Duff & Campbell, 1976). This approach to the scientification of social and moral decision-making involving people with disabilities and their families attempts to use science to explain and justify behaviors that are or should be regarded as essentially moral and policy or political decisions (Turnbull & Wheat, 1983).

Table 13.1

Different Ways to Measure or Conceptualize the Quality of Life of People with Disabilities and Their Families

Quality of Life as—

1. Measured by science

2. Measured by rights

3. Direct democracy and citizen participation

4. Mutual accommodation

5. Value-driven policy

6. Determined by evaluation and accountability

7. Reflected in public philosophy

In the scientific paradigm, it is assumed correct as a matter of both professional practice and moral philosophy to apply scientific models to treatment and intervention decisions. In connection with the treatment of newborns, this paradigm has often been used to validate treatment decisions and thus to legitimatize decisions about the value of the child's life and the impact of the child's condition on the child, the family, and society.

In many respects, the scientification of the medical treatment decision is not unlike the scientification of other intervention decisions, such as whether to use nonaversive or aversive behavioral interventions or to place students with disabilities in mainstream or least restrictive/most normal appropriate settings (Guess, Helmstetter, Turnbull, & Knowlton, 1986; Turnbull, 1986). In almost every debate about the proper

way to intervene in the lives of people with mental retardation, the desired policy outcome—that is to say, the desired moral outcome—is defended on the ground of science.

But the scientific approach by itself—no matter how reliable its predictive powers about the nature and extent of disability and its inferential predictive powers about impact—cannot be relied on as the dominant approach to defining and applying the concept of quality of life. Science is but one measure, and it should be connected with other quality of life oriented policy principles including these (Schalock, 1990):

• For persons with disabilities, quality of life is composed of those same factors and relationships that are important to persons without disabilities.

• A life of quality is experienced when a person's basic needs are met and when he or she has the same opportunity as anyone else to pursue and achieve personal goals.

• Quality of life is determined by the congruence of public values and behaviors.

• The concept of quality of life can be consensually validated by a wide range of persons representing a variety of viewpoints.

Many people, ourselves included, who work in the field of mental retardation, including the unacknowledged workers and consumers who are typically called "family," argue that the prediction that is required by a quality of life formula is difficult if not impossible to make. We also assert that in any event the moral decision, which is essentially whether the child's life has inherent value, should not be regulated to a mathematical approach. Likewise, many (ourselves included) also acknowledge that there is almost always an ethical or moral dimension to any decision that is grounded in science or in other interventions (Turnbull, 1988a).

Quality of Life as Measured by Rights

Some (including ourselves) measure and seek to improve quality of life by asserting that people with disabilities and their families have inherent minimum rights. Thus, assertions that quality of life will be improved by certain rights (e.g., to early education and intervention, subsequent appropriate education, treatment and habilitation, least drastic/ restrictive environments and interventions, home-based or community-based services, supported work, and a minimum level of publicly provided financial support) are reflected in and have resulted in the creation of a plethora of laws creating entitlements to publicly funded services for people with disabilities and their families. These entitlements fundamentally reflect the belief that quality of life for the person and the person's family is ensured and can be improved when there are enforceable and funded rights to certain types of services. Moreover, these entitlements also mirror the fact that policymakers and advocates agree that there has been and probably always will be a failure of society, as it is presently constructed and operating, to respond to the quality of life claims of people with disabilities and their families unless there are certain legally protected *rights*. This predictable failure, which history abundantly documents, justifies the creation and enforcement of rights, which in turn become benchmarks of quality of life.

In short, the legal rights approach measures quality of life according to the absence or presence of enforceable and funded entitlements. It appeals basically to activist governmental intervention, not to "disinterested" mathematical scientizing of measures of quality of life.

Quality of Life as Direct Democracy and Citizen Participation

There is currently a strong belief that quality of life is enhanced when decision-making powers are shared—that is, when consumers (whether the people themselves, as in the self-advocacy conceptualization, or their families, as in the right-to-education formulation) and professionals participate jointly in evaluation, program development, implementation, and evaluation (Turnbull, 1990). As many of us recognize, however, shared decision-making is just one aspect of quality of life; what really counts is not the process of decision-making, however important that component is, but equal access to the same opportunities, including opportunities for the exercise of choice as enjoyed by people who do not have disabilities. As B. Fredericks (personal correspondence, 1989) noted, "Without access, opportunities and choices are not the same." Under the direct democracy approach, the measure of quality of life is *citizen participation*, also called *self-determination, shared decision-making,* and *rebalancing power relationships*. This approach to quality of life is related to the concept of *personal autonomy*, a value considered not only in public policy but also in psychology.

In one respect, this measure of quality of life is paradoxical. One would think that the recapturing of autonomy in public and private lives would reject a role for government, because the deprivation of consumer participation has been attributed to huge and impersonal

203

government. Yet, those of us who measure quality of life as autonomy and seek to give it expression under the rubric of consumer participation in decision-making processes seek to ensure it by creating a right to the opportunity for participation in education and other program decisions, interventions, and evaluations. Thus, those of us who seek to enhance the quality of life by increasing opportunities for participatory decision-making do so by turning to government, not by eschewing it. In so doing, we fundamentally affirm that quality of life is measured by the degree to which consumer participation is available, and we equally assert that there is or ought to be a right, guaranteed by law and enforceable against the state's educators and other agents, to a certain quality of life, namely, that quality of life that can or will result when people who are directly affected by a decision have a right and exercise that right to participate in the decision affecting them. Shared decision-making is a deeply cherished value in America and, it seems, one whose presence or absence is itself a measure of the quality of life.

Quality of Life as Mutual Accommodation

This approach to quality of life looks to the relationships between people with disabilities or their families and the society in which they live. It recognizes that all people and their families are members of communities and that their quality of life is a function of the ability not only to be present in their communities but also to participate in those communities. There is a difference between being "in" and being "of" a community (Turnbull & Turnbull, 1988). To accomplish not just desegregation and integration "in" but also participation "of," it is necessary for the person with

the disability, that person's family, and society to make mutual adjustments.

Mutual accommodation can occur in one of two ways. First, professionals and families make extensive efforts to enhance the capacities of people with disabilities. These attempts to secure a greater degree of human development are directed in large part toward the accommodation of the person and family to the existing society and its communities. Second, efforts can be directed at creating rights against discrimination and toward accommodations by society to the person. These rights are claims that the person has against society. Stated in the alternative, they are duties that society has to the person. And, of course, they are devices that the person and others similarly situated may use to change the nature of society and the community. The duties of nondiscrimination impose on society and the community the obligation to change themselves. When the society and communities change, the opportunities for and likelihood of accommodation increase.

By two routes, then, the quality of life of the person and the family are augmented: first, by accommodating the person to society and the community, and second, by accommodating society and the community to the person. This approach to quality of life relies on science (the sciences of special education, vocational rehabilitation, rehabilitation engineering, etc.) and the creation of mutual rights and duties. It also acknowledges that participation in decision-making is a way of achieving mutual accommodations.

Quality of Life as Value-Driven Policy

Measures of quality of life should be explicitly tied to values. For example, today it is common to hear heated debates about deinstitutionalization, anti-institutionalization, defacilitation (movement away from workshops and large congregate living in the community), community-based education, community-referenced curricula, home- and community-based living, permanency planning and adoption, family support, supported employment, and nonaversive interventions. These concepts are fundamentally value based, where the values are equal treatment and equal opportunity. The common theme is that people who have disabilities should not be treated differently than people who do not; or, if they are treated differently, such treatment should accomplish the purpose of equal opportunities. Thus, one can measure quality of life according to the degree that equal opportunities and equal treatment (that is, equal moral and ethical standing of people with disabilities) are reflected in and advanced or hindered by policies, professional practice, and family behaviors.

Quality of Life as Determined by Evaluation and Accountability

It is by now settled that almost all interventions with people with disabilities and their families should be evaluated. Typically, evaluation consists of input or outcome measures or both; and, typically, evaluation is either quantitative or qualitative in nature. More often than not, the argument for evaluation is predicated on the desire for accountability: the public's funds should not be spent without an assurance that the expenditures result in the outcomes desired by the policies underlying the funded programs.

Those of us who demand evaluation as a way of ensuring accountability in

the provision of services are making arguments related to quality of life. Quality of life, then, is determined by evaluation. Accreditation standards and procedures, for example, are attempts to ensure a certain quality of life; so, too, are standards and procedures for the provision of an appropriate education or vocational rehabilitation program. Measures of consumer satisfaction or value-driven evaluation procedures likewise assert that quality of life is a correlate of and can be determined by evaluation procedures. Quality of life can be ensured when procedures and standards of evaluation reveal that services and interventions suit their purposes; likewise, quality of life requires establishing procedures and standards for services and their evaluation.

Quality of Life as Reflected in Public Philosophy

Concerns about quality of life for people with disabilities and their families do not exist in a self-contained capsule, unassociated with general concerns about the quality of life of the citizenry as a whole. There are inevitable and wholesome connections between the debates about the quality of life of people who have no disabilities and debates about the quality of life of those who do. These connections are not always apparent, but they nonetheless exist. Every one of us faces quality of life issues. Indeed, our major message in this chapter is this: the "right" and "left" or "conservative" and "liberal" critiques of America in the late 20th century are more than criticisms of the way in which we all live; sadly, they are in large part comments on the deterioration in quality of life that all of us (disabled and not) experience or will experience. The political philosopher Sullivan (1982) is explicit about that fact:

> *...A public philosophy develops out of the insight that the quality of personal life is grounded in social relationships, an insight that is embodied in the political art of integrating the various kinds of self-concern into an awareness of mutual interdependency.*
>
> **(p. 208)**

It was Hobbes who, many years earlier, observed that we are social beings not by choice but by necessity. That is, in order for each person to prosper emotionally, physically, spiritually, and materially, each needs the other—we need to be in relationship to each other. Among other things, this means that in order to have liberty in our individual lives we must restrain some of our own liberties and those of others. The human condition of liberty requires the human ability to be less than fully free. Accordingly, the public philosophers' critiques are fundamentally relevant to the lives of people with disabilities, their families, professionals, service providers, and policy makers; their critiques provide one of the most useful comments on the issue of quality of life of people with disabilities and their families. Indeed, we are willing to go so far as to say that we probably can learn as much about the issues of quality of life of people with disabilities and their families by attending to the new criticisms of America as a whole as we can by continuing to focus only on disability-specific quality of life concerns.

There are two major public philosophies in America. One is *philosophic liberalism*; the other is *civic republican-*

ism. They are not mutually exclusive, although they are in their cores contradictory. Indeed, Americans have practiced them simultaneously, although we have shifted our loyalties between them from time to time and have witnessed heated debate over their merits and the application of their principles to our private and public lives. These ideas rely on different perceptions of the nature of the individual and of the role of others and the body politic in regard to the individual. We will briefly describe these two philosophies and attempt to show their relationships to quality of life issues.

1. **Philosophic liberalism.** The tenets of philosophic liberalism are expressed commonly in such familiar terms as rugged individualism, laissez-faire capitalism, centralized economic planning, self-determination, and individual autonomy. The central focus of philosophic liberalism is the liberty of the individual to pursue economic advantage; it is characterized by self-interest and private advantage, often at the expense of the public welfare. If philosophic liberalism, with its distinctively individualistic cast, means anything, it is that people must compete for their place in the world. If the place in the world that Social Darwinism assigns to people with disabilities is unacceptable, philosophic liberalism asserts that they have valid claims to opportunity for education, habilitation, and rehabilitation in order to equip them to compete. In short, the belief that people with disabilities should have a place in the mainstream, in a society that is dominated by individualistic, economically-oriented, philosophic liberalism, became the public philosophy rationale for the plethora of rights that federal and state laws have created during the last two decades.

2. **Civic republicanism.** The second dominant theme of public philosophy in America has been civic republicanism. Shorthand phrases that describe civic republicanism are *cooperation* and *volunteerism*. Sullivan (1982) offers this definition:

> *Civic republicanism denies the liberal notion that individuality exists outside of or prior to social relationships. Instead, the republican tradition has taught that there is an ineluctably participatory aspect to political understanding that develops only through the moral maturation of mutual responsibility. Civic republicanism does not share the liberal idea that individuals are atoms of will essentially uninfluenced by their web of interrelationships, or the concomitant notion that all values are finally manifestations of the power to control. On the contrary, freedom is ultimately the ability to realize a responsible selfhood, which is necessarily a cooperative project. For republicanism, there are qualities of social relations, such as mutual concern and respect, that transcend utility and that can be learned only in practice. One reason republicanism has proved tenacious in a liberal America is this very embodied quality of its knowledge, although it requires explication to realize its own development.*
>
> **(p. 21)**

Again, the public philosopher's concern with the absence of civic republicanism and the means of revitalizing it are directly related to the developmental disabilities field, which is concerned with informal support, friendships, intentional communities, and rights to association between people with and without disabilities. These associations enable individuals to become full citizens and to thereby acquire a sense of personal connection and significance unavailable to the depoliticized, purely private person. The role of classic politics and policy is to provide

> *...a public framework of law and search for equity [whereby] moral relationships of trust and mutual aid are built up which come to transform the individual into a citizen. Politics in the genuinely associational sense is, then, more than pursuit of self-interest, since it involves sharing responsibility for acts that create a quality of life different from the mere sum of individual satisfactions.*
>
> **(Sullivan, 1982, p. 218)**

Sullivan's observations are directly relevant to the quality of life of people with disabilities and reflect the disability field's concern for informal supports and friendships, for not only presence but also participation in communities, for going beyond antidiscrimination and even beyond equal opportunities to full citizenship. Thus,

> *...our present danger does not come from government as such, or from the entrepreneurial spirit either, for that matter. The danger to our democratic institutions comes, rather, from the declining effectiveness of just those intervening structures, the civic associations for all sorts that service to mediate between individual and state.*
>
> **(Sullivan, 1982, p. 222)**

Conclusion

In summary, we have been arguing that there is a natural connection between the concerns for the quality of life of all Americans and the quality of life of Americans with disabilities. This connection is revealed in the new language that we, like the public philosophers, use. They share our vocabulary, language that is laden with such terms as *quality of life, cooperation, fellowship, community as relationship, building community, fraternity* (as distinguished from liberty and equality), and *intentional associations*. There is an underlying common measure of life for the public philosophers and for those of us in the disabilities field.

It is not unique to observe that the genius of American life is the simultaneous development of liberty (philosophic liberalism), equality, and fraternity. What is different—and this, of course, is the thrust of the argument—is how people in the developmental disabilities field respond to that native genius (Turnbull, 1988b). Some respond by emphasizing fraternity (that is, civic republicanism) and some see the underlying measure of quality of life to be relational—grounded in civic association and thus quintessentially American and, within American life, universal. Still others approach the issue of civic association by such means as peer relationships in schools and mentor systems at worksites or in communities.

Even though this chapter has discussed seven different ways to measure or conceptualize the quality of life of people with disabilities and their families, we feel that for each of us, there is an underlying fundamental measure of quality of life. It is the measure that ascribes quality of life according to the extent to which people choose to be with each other, the ways in which they give form to their choices to be with each other, and the nature, extent, and duration of their relationships. Quality of life is indeed based on relationships. The development of the means to create, sustain, and enhance those relationships is both a public policy issue and the central issue in the lives of those affected by disability.

References

Duff, R., & Campbell, A.G.M. (1976). On deciding the care of severely handicapped or dying persons: With particular reference to infants. *Pediatrics, 57,* 488-495.

Guess, D., Helmstetter, E., Turnbull, H., & Knowlton, E. (1986). *Use of aversive procedures with persons who are disabled: An historical review and critical analysis.* Seattle: The Association for Persons with Severe Handicaps.

Schalock, R.L. (1990). Where do we go from here? In R.L. Schalock (Ed.), *Quality of life: Perspectives and issues* (pp. 235-240). Washington, DC: American Association on Mental Retardation.

Sullivan, W.M. (1982). *Reconstructing public philosophy.* Berkeley: University of California Press.

Turnbull, A.P., & Turnbull, H.R. (1988). *Families and community integration.* Lawrence, KS: University of Kansas, Beach Center on Families and Disability.

Turnbull, H.R. (1986). Presidential address. *Mental Retardation, 24,* 265-276.

Turnbull, H.R. (1988a). Fifteen questions: Ethical inquiries in mental retardation. In J. Stark, F. Menolascino, M. Albarelli, & V. Gray (Eds.), *Mental retardation and mental health* (pp. 368-378). Washington, DC: President's Committee on Mental Retardation.

Turnbull, H.R. (1988b). Response to Burt. In L. Kane, P. Brown, & J. Cohen (Eds.), *The legal rights of citizens with mental retardation.* Lanham, MD: University Press of America.

Turnbull, H.R. (1990). *Free appropriate public education: Law and education of children with disabilities* (3rd ed.). Denver, CO: Love Publishing.

Turnbull, H.R., & Wheat, M.J. (1983). Legal responses to classification of people as mentally retarded. In J. Mulick & J. Matson (Eds.), *A handbook of mental retardation* (pp. 157-169). New York: Pergamon Press.

Quality of Life as International Disability Policy: Implications for International Research

David Goode
City University of New York

This chapter suggests possible areas for development by international researchers in the disability field who are interested in the concept of quality of life. There are four parts: a provisional definition of quality of life and quality of life policy to orient the reader; a brief overview of current efforts in international disability policy; a review of the current status of quality of life methodology and measurement in the disability field; and finally, some possible implications and recommendations for international disability policy.

Definitions and Policy

Quality of Life Definitions

What is meant by the term quality of life? In a review of one hundred documents mentioning people with disabilities and quality of life, the National Institute on Disability and Rehabilitation Research (NIDRR) identified four types of definitions: (1) implicit definitions (for example, assuming that normalization means better quality of life); (2) operational definitions (where the definition is research methodology driven); (3) literary or rational definitions (reflecting the author's stated personal reflections, philosophy, values, or beliefs); and (4) unintentional definitions (reflecting unstated beliefs and values). It perhaps shows some progress in research and debate that only definitions of type 2 and 3 are found in the edited volume *Quality of Life for Persons with Disabilities: International Perspectives and Issues* (Goode, 1994b). A number of exemplary definitions of quality of life are given in Table 14.1. Note that these definitions are strikingly similar in content, despite the fact that they are products of fairly different social theories and conceptualizations of quality of life and of human life generally. Many other similar definitions are available. Taken as a group they tend to corroborate the characterization made by Schalock et al. (1990) that three basic concepts appear in definitions of quality of life: general feelings of well-being, opportunities to fulfill potential, and feelings of positive social involvement. I would add to their characterization that many definitions make explicit a perceived discrepancy element (see definitions 2, 3, 5, and 7 in Table 14.1). It should be noted that these are clearly definitions of quality of life from the individual's perspective; hence the emphasis on subjective factors and perception.

Quality of Life Policy

What do we mean by policy? To the planner, policy is a "standing plan," a "guide to future decision-making," or "a continuing line of decisions or set of constraints upon individual decisions." It is the implicit or explicit core of principle(s) that underlies specific programs..."Social policy" may be described as the common denominator of decisions or constraints with reference to social welfare or social service programs (Kahn, 1979, p. 57).

Thus, quality of life policy means the use of the concept of quality of life as a guide, common denominator, or core principle with respect to decision-making in services and supports for persons who require special supports. Such a policy would direct itself at minimizing the discrepancies between individuals' perceived and desired conditions of life. Research on quality of life under such a policy would be ultimately aimed at enhancing knowledge that would minimize these perceived discrepancies. Thus, some of what is currently done in research would be subsumed under this policy.

Table 14.1
Exemplary Definitions of Quality of Life

1. The timbre of life as experienced subjectively; a person's feelings about and evaluations of his or her own life (Goode & Hogg, 1994, p. 197; National Institute of Disability and Rehabilitation Research, 1993).

2. Quality of life is experienced when a person's basic needs are met and when he or she has the opportunity to pursue and achieve goals in major life settings (Goode, 1994a, p. 148).

3. Quality of life is determined as the degree to which a person enjoys the important possibilities of his or her life (Woodill, Renwick, Brown, & Rapheal, 1994, p.67).

4. Quality of life is not something that a person simply has or receives but something the individual works to create along with other people ... Living the "good life" means that one is able to determine the course of one's own life and has the opportunity to create an existence based upon one's own dreams, visions, wishes, and needs (Holm, Holst, & Perlt, 1994, p.10).

5. The discrepancy between a person's achieved and unmet needs and desires. This refers to the subjective assessment of an individual's domains. The greater the discrepancy the poorer the quality of life. It includes the extent to which an individual increasingly controls aspects of life regardless of the original baseline (Matikka, 1994, p. 41).

6. The worthiness of the person's experiences in his or her specific situation (Drugge, 1990).

7. Discrepancy between a person's achieved and unmet needs and desires (Brown, Bayer, & MacFarlane, 1989).

Note that this definition does not include all uses within the literature of the term. For example, it would exclude the kind of work done by Shaw (1977) that uses quality of life as a way to grant or deny neonatal services to infants with disability, thus distinguishing itself from the quality of life research literature. In addition, some people with disability and researchers have objected to the exclusive equation of a good quality of life with feelings of happiness or pleasure. The definition suggested by NIDRR (1993) is specifically formulated to allow " ... for individuals to rate quality of life high in spite of pain or dissatisfaction when they see it as leading toward growth." I have heard this same sentiment from people with disabilities in Sweden, Finland, and Denmark. Minimally, this aspect of satisfaction and well-being associated with many definitions in our field will need to be examined more closely.

There also appears to be some consensus that discussions of quality of life policy for persons with disabilities should not be divorced from discussions about quality of life for people without disabilities (Goode, 1994a; Holm et al., 1994; Schalock et al., 1990; Turnbull & Brunk, 1990; Woodill et al., 1994). Turnbull and Brunk, for example, describe "a natural connection between the concerns for the quality of life of all Americans and the quality of life of Americans with disabilities" (p. 207). This connection can be argued on a value or moral basis (i.e., the concept should not be different for persons with or without disability), according to the research literature (the logic and relationships of a life of quality for persons with disabilities are no different from that of those without), or on a policy basis (we want for political or ethical reasons to produce a society in which there is no difference in quality of life for persons

on the basis of disability). Thus, the concept is generic, not particular to people with disability at all. If we imagine ourselves as the recipients of the above social policy, this becomes clearer even without ethical or research justification.

The International Policy Context

The possible development of quality of life as a concept for the disabilities field, including research, parallels that of the development of social policy generally. I have already traced this with respect to the historical development of American social policy (1994a) and in this section of the chapter will turn to international disability policy of the European community and the United Nations. I argue that quality of life is ultimately a preferable term in the area of disability to those currently in vogue, such as equal opportunity, inclusion, or normalization; first because it is a generic term unassociated with disability per se, and as such is preferred by persons with disabilities themselves; and second, because it is the most comprehensive of terms currently being discussed and bears this asymmetrical relationship with them. I will discuss how this term relates, or could relate, to the current international policy development initiatives undertaken by the European community (E.C.) and by the United Nations (U.N.), and suggest possible implications for work of these groups.

European Disability Policy

It is important to point out that international forces have traditionally shaped disability policy all over the world. It is in the nature of our field and accounts for a certain similarity in policies globally. This has always been true in the scientific study of disability (for example, the eugenics and institutionalization movements in the late 19th through the middle 20th centuries), but has been even more so since World War II, when we began to see increasingly progressive disability policy internationally and nationally, at least within the developed nations.

The postwar history of disability policy within the European community is described in some detail by Patrick Daunt in his excellent book *Meeting Disability: A European Response* (1991). Daunt documents the historical development of the Helios program and then the Helios II program, allowing the reader to appreciate how the current goals and structures of Helios II have evolved. Daunt's successor as Head of the European Commission Division on Integration of Disabled People, Mr. Bernhard Wehrens, characterizes the current Helios II goals as "...to promote equal opportunity for people with disabilities throughout the European Union, and develop a comprehensive policy of cooperation in close liaison with all parties involved in Member States" (1994). Helios II emphasizes transnational exchange of information around the following four areas: functional rehabilitation, educational and economic integration, social integration, and independent living. Information is exchanged partly through a highly developed computer information network, Handynet. Discussions leading to policy and program initiatives occur in the European Disability Forum, which consists of organizations of and for disabled persons and constitutes a key advisory body to the E.C. In 1993-94, four European symposia on the four functional areas were conducted, facilitating information exchange and policy development.

Although the notion of quality of life does not play a central role in the language of Helios II, it is of interest that it takes such a position in the conclusion of Daunt's book where he argues forcefully that the "overall aim [of policy and programs for people with disabilities] should be the promotion of a good quality of life for all people with disabilities" (1992, p. 175). He also argues, "Its [quality of life] superiority over independence in the hierarchy of goals is confirmed by the fact that individuals may vary in the degree to which they want to be independent but not in their desire for a good quality of life" (1992, p. 175). Daunt suggests a "laundry list" of "components" that would need to be assessed (specifically, autonomy, independence, integration, respect, ownership, social involvement and communication, activity and mobility, privacy and tranquility). He warns, however, about the potential danger of establishing such a general definition and laundry list since "there is no one to whom all the components apply" and urges that we have to attend to how the individual sees his or her own situation. In the concluding chapter, he reaffirms quality of life as "the aim of all policy and practice concerned with people with disability" and argues for it on the basis of its inclusivity as a concept, and ability to be individualized (p. 193). He goes so far as to suggest that in each member nation a Ministry for Disabled People be created to "design and implement a national plan to ensure a good quality of life for people with disabilities" (p. 194). Daunt also argues strongly for the participation of people with disabilities and their representative organizations in the development of policy, and spends many pages characterizing the "militant" movement in disabilities (what we in the United States call the self-advocacy movement). This sentiment is clearly carried through in the current Helios II program and in policy development generally internationally and increasingly nationally.

Thus, while the concept of quality of life has not yet surfaced officially in European disability policy, Daunt sees the term as the logical outgrowth of previous phases of development in Europe and argues that it should serve as the basic aim of all policy and practice for European people with disability. His reasoning in this regard is similar to my own when I conducted the National Quality of Life Project in the United States in 1987-88 (Goode, 1990).

Current Disability Policy in the United Nations

Most in the field are aware of the lead that the U.N. has taken since World War II in developing international disability policy, and that E.C. policies have been coordinated with the U.N.'s policy frame. The U.N. has produced several bills of rights, a host of plans and conferences based around the decade and year of the disabled, and the recent passage of the "Standard Rules on the Equalization of Opportunities for Persons With Disabilities" (A/RES/48/96 passed by the General Assembly in March of 1994). This extensive 28-page document (United Nations, 1994) presents a concept and plan for the development of international disability policy. Like the European plan, it is not specifically based upon the concept of quality of life, but instead draws primarily on the language of equal opportunity and participation. Thus both the U.N. and E.C. employ the language of equal opportunity or participation as a way to conceptualize disability policy. These terms have a certain appeal in that they are generic terms, speaking to something basic that all members of society presumably want to have.

The U.N.'s Standard Rules document has four main parts: preconditions for equal participation (discussions of awareness-raising, medical care, rehabilitation, and support services); target areas for equal participation (access, education, employment, income, family life/personal integrity, culture, recreation/sports, and religion); implementation measures; and a monitoring mechanism. Of particular importance are implementation measures that clearly lay responsibility for data collection and dissemination at the national level. Rule 13 on Information and Research calls for the collection of statistics about the living conditions of persons with disabilities that would include information on programs/services. States are called upon to establish "a data bank on disability" and further to initiate and support programs of research on social economic and participation issues that affect the lives of persons with disabilities and their families" (p. 20). States are charged with developing an appropriate "terminology and criteria for the conduct of national surveys" and to "facilitate the participation of persons with disabilities in data collection and research" (p. 21). Rule 13 then calls upon states to share information and research, and disseminate information at all levels of society.

Quality of life has both objective and subjective components and clearly the collection of data about the objective components fits within the mandate of both the Standard Rules, Helios, and a quality of life orientation. The Standard Rules and Helios are concerned particularly with statistical and census type data. On the other hand, quality of life is a term that inevitably leads one into the realm of the subjective and qualitative, as well as the objective and quantitative. The research literature indicates that the exclusive use of objective data to evaluate quality of life can be misleading and in contradiction to individuals' perceptions of their own situations. Hence, research into the quality of life of persons with disabilities is a somewhat broader field of inquiry than current international policies seem to suggest or require. Thus, I argue in the next section that, in addition to the kinds of data already being considered in international policy and research, a certain broadening of methodology is required if we really are interested in the collection of valid information about the quality of life of people with disabilities throughout the world.

Assessment Methodology

The state of quality of life assessment reflects the definitional ambiguity described. On the one hand, there are researchers who maintain that it can be validly measured objectively and subjectively. Other researchers believe that it cannot be measured, and that it is best to conceive of quality of life as a "sensitizing concept" that cannot be precisely defined or measured. Despite their apparent contradiction, I believe that there is merit in both these approaches to measurement.

Schalock's (1994) overview of current quantitatively oriented work in the area of quality of life suggested a sequential model, progressing from conceptual definition, to quality of life indicators, to quality of life measurement, and finally to quality of life application. Figure 14.1 is my own reworking of Schalock's model to include those who make the "sensitizing concept" assumption. The major difference between Schalock's model and Figure 14.1 is the addition of what might be termed "qualitative" research that proceeds from the methodological position that quality of life is best described but that it cannot be precisely measured. I argue that both ways of conceiving

Figure 14.1
Conceptual Overview of Quality of Life Research

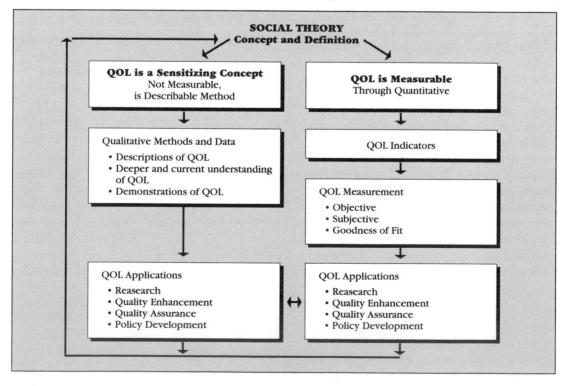

quality of life research are useful, and that each type of conception of quality of life needs to be vigorously pursued if we are to have a valid understanding of quality of life, including data that represents the feelings of people with disabilities.

What appears to make sense is to make a serious attempt for these two sets of researchers, qualitative and quantitative, to work with one another on a commonly defined domain with mutually disclosed and understood methodological procedures. This is indicated in Figure 14.1 by the arrows at the bottom that link the applications of quality of life research. This kind of cooperation is suggested by Goode and Hogg (1994) concerning the quality of life assessment of people with profound mental disability. And while cooperation is always a good sounding idea, "the devil is in the details." I will nevertheless suggest in the following section how such a coordination might work, and what its relationship to international policy could be.

The Role of Self-Advocates and Social Pedagogues

More than an attempt at cooperation between researchers is required if quality of life is to live up to its potential as a policy or research concept. The roles of people with disabilities themselves and of the direct care workers, the social pedagogues and educators, and the personal care attendants, need to be considered in defining policy and research questions.

As mentioned previously, there is an important role for organizations of people with disabilities in the U.N.'s Standard Rules and in the E.C.'s Helios II program. Likewise, in certain forms of quality of life research, notably the focus

group exploration employed by Goode (1988; 1990) or Matikka (1994), the role of persons with disabilities in the research process is central. It is also the case that there has been a change generally over the past decade, partially due to militant writers, such as Mike Oliver in England, who criticize us in the research community for thinking about people with disabilities as research subjects. There is more of an idea today that people with disabilities should be partners with researchers in the sense at least of having input into research priorities and even research decisions. Some researchers are employing more persons with mental retardation and other disabilities on research teams. The role of people with disabilities in professional associations such as the American Association for Mental Retardation is growing, and it is certainly growing in terms of national political influence. When it comes to research on quality of life particularly, it seems almost inexcusable that people with disabilities would not themselves be part of the discussions and research process (see Whitney-Thomas, chapter 12, this volume).

The same can be said for direct care workers or in Europe social pedagogues or social educators. They too need to be included in the formulation of policy and research in the field of disabilities. They know a great deal about the people with whom they work and can prove a tremendous resource in helping to define quality of life issues. This is because there is a natural association between the quality of life of people with disabilities and the quality of work life of the direct care workers with whom they share their lives. Any action research that is aimed at enhancing the quality of life of people with disabilities that does not take into account the quality of work life of the social pedagogues involved in actually administering program enhancement will probably fail on sociological grounds. As pointed out by Holm et al. (1994), achieving a good life is often a matter of negotiation between the user and social pedagogue, and this negotiation can take on many forms and outcomes. But for people with disabilities who live in agencies to ignore the social pedagogue in the quality equation would be senseless and unnecessary.

The inclusion of people with disability and direct care workers into policy making and research is part of a general trend in the United States that began with other devalued recipients of social policy, namely African-Americans and women. Since the 1960s there has been a movement to work with such populations and to strongly support their input into the political decisions that affect their lives. This same trend began with mentally retarded people a bit later, certainly by the 1970s, and has continued. This process was noted by Kahn (1979), who labeled it a matter of "balance between citizen-client participation in program control on the one hand, and bureaucratization on the other" (p. 106).

If we look at recent developments in European disability politics, we note similar historical movements. The power of organizations of people with disabilities has increased within many European nations and certainly within the European Commission. Particularly the European Disability Forum is a testament to this. As noted by Daunt, there are certain politics in these organizations, and historically the interests of people with physical disabilities have been predominant. But it is becoming more accepted that people with mental disabilities should also participate in governance. I believe that we see in Europe the beginnings of the same kind of client-professional partnerships that are developing in the United States and elsewhere around the world.

An International Research Network

At the present time, there is serious interest in the European Commission in examining the concept of quality of life and its utility for the European community's efforts for citizens with disabilities. This is the only specifically international effort in quality of life for people with disabilities of which I am aware. I have been asked to make some suggestions about how this initiative might work. The following briefly summarizes what I will be suggesting.

1. A quality of life network should begin with national coalitions among researchers, qualitative and quantitative, and groups of people with disabilities to explore what kinds of research they want to see done.

2. Discussion groups similar to those employed already in the United States and Finland could be used to develop quality of life oriented policy and practices within these coalitions. This is a kind of research needs-assessment process, but also begins to develop cooperative relationships between militants and researchers. This explicit focus rather than equal opportunity per se is the main difference between what is currently going on today and what I am suggesting.

3. A plan of quantitative and qualitative inquiries designed to collect information about the matters deemed important by the national groups should be formulated.

4. After one year of exploring these issues (both research and political), representatives (both researchers and self-advocates) from national groups would assemble again in a similar gathering and present results. At this meeting it would be decided how best to coordinate the variety of

issues and priorities. Quality of life would be the conceptual frame for the discussion, with a general understanding that both qualitative and quantitatve data about the areas in question need to be gathered.

5. During the first year three central committees should develop concept papers in three areas: concept and methodology; population definition; and governance and coordination.

Conclusion

In conclusion, the concept of quality of life is of interest in many nations around the world (Goode, 1994b). For example, in Japan the term is employed in the rhetoric of human services for people with disabilities even though these services are primarily institutionally oriented. Japanese citizens in these institutions live materially well, but have little control over their lives. In addition, these citizens often are not integrated into their communities.

In Australia, the concept is increasingly of importance in conceptualizing services for persons with disabilities. An active group of researchers has been recently joined by Roy and Patricia Brown from Canada. Robert Cummins (1993) in Australia has designed an assessment instrument that is consistent with the concepts as discussed in this chapter.

In Israel, there is interest in the concept, and research has been undertaken investigating the quality of life of Israeli citizens with disabilities. Scandinavia has been a leader in studies of quality of life and disabilities. In the late 1980s, some agencies in Sweden began to utilize the concept in program development and evaluation (Drugge, 1990). In 1990, the Finnish Association on Mental Retardation, under the leadership of Helena Hiila and Leena Matikka, undertook a massive effort in exploring

and documenting the quality of life of Finnish citizens with mental retardation. This national project, undoubtedly the single largest quality of life research project ever undertaken, involved the use of in-depth interviews, focus groups, and video case studies (Matikka, 1994). LEV, the Danish parent organization for persons with disabilities, has conducted a quality of life project since 1990 (see Holm et al., 1994).

Britain has also been a leader in international discussions, although more in the area of global measures of quality of life. Jim Hogg in Scotland and Steve Moss at the Hester Adrian Center are conducting quality of life-oriented research. In Canada there has also been considerable interest. In Toronto, a group associated with the Center for Health Promotion has engaged in a project involving conceptual and methodological innovation (see Woodill et al., 1994). They have developed a pictographic assessment protocol to be used with persons with severe intellectual impairments.

In the United States, serious interest in quality of life and developmental disabilities can be traced to the early 1980s, especially in the work of Schalock and his colleagues. In 1987-88, the Administration on Developmental Disabilities funded a national project that produced several important technical documents. This project had significant involvement of people with intellectual disabilities in setting an agenda for the United States. Two states, New York and California, followed up with state projects in 1990. In addition to those discussed here, there are many countries in which scholars are beginning to take interest in the concept (for example, Germany, France, Hungary, Russia, Netherlands, Ireland). Thus, there is every expectation that the international focus on quality of life for persons with disabilities will continue.

References

Brown, R.I., Bayer, M.B., & MacFarlane, C.M. (1989). *Rehabilitation Programs: Performance and Quality of Life of Adults with Developmental Handicaps*. Toronto, Ontario: Lugus.

Cummins, R.A. (1993). *Comprehensive quality of life scale: Intellectual disability.* Burwood, Victoria, Australia: Deakin University.

Daunt, P. (1991). *Meeting disability: A European response*. London: Cassell Educational Limited.

Drugge, C. (1990). *Using the opinion of people with mental retardation to measure quality of service*. County Council Vastmanland, Social Welfare for People with Mental Retardation, Vasteras, Sweden.

Edgerton, R.B. (1990). Quality of life from a longitudinal research perspective. In R.L. Schalock (Ed.), *Quality of life: Perspectives and issues,* (pp. 149–161). Washington, DC: American Association on Mental Retardation.

Goode, D.A. (1988). *Discussing quality of life.* Valhalla, NY: Mental Retardation Institute.

Goode, D.A. (1990). Thinking about and discussing quality of life. In R.L. Schalock (Ed.), *Quality of life: Perspectives and issues* (pp. 41–59). Washington, DC: American Association on Mental Retardation.

Goode, D.A. (1994a). The national quality of life for persons with disabilities project: A QOL agenda for the United States. In D. Goode (Ed.), *Quality of life for persons with disabilities: International perspectives and issues* (pp. 139–161). Cambridge, MA: Brookline Books.

Goode, D.A. (Ed.). (1994b). *Quality of life for persons with disabilities: International perspectives and issues*. Cambridge, MA: Brookline Books.

Goode, D.A., & Hogg, J. (1994). Towards an understanding of holistic quality of life in people with profound intellectual and multiple disabilities. In D. Goode (Ed.), *Quality of life for persons with disabilities: International perspectives and issues* (pp. 197–207). Cambridge, MA: Brookline Books.

Holm, P., Holst, J., & Perlt, B. (1994). Co-write your own life: Quality of life as discussed in the Danish context. In D. Goode (Ed.), *Quality of life for persons with disabilities: International perspectives and issues* (pp. 1–21). Cambridge, MA: Brookline Books.

Kahn, A. (1979). *Social Policy and Social Services.* New York: Random House.

Matikka, L. (1994). The quality of life of adults with developmental disabilities in Finland. In D. Goode (Ed.), *Quality of life for persons with disabilities: International perspectives and issues,* (pp. 22–38). Cambridge, MA: Brookline Books.

National Institute of Disability and Rehabilitation Research. (1993). Quality-of-life research in rehabilitation. *Rehabilitation Briefs, 11*(1), 10–15.

Schalock, R.L. (1994). The concept of quality of life and its current applications in the field of mental retardation/developmental disabilities. In D. Goode (Ed.), *Quality of life for persons with disabilities: International perspectives and issues* (pp. 266–284). Cambridge, MA: Brookline Books.

Schalock, R.L., Bartnik, E., Wu, F., Konig, A., Lee, C.S., & Reiter, S. (1990). *An international perspective in quality of life: Measurement and use.* Paper presented at the 114th annual meeting of the American Association on Mental Retardation, Atlanta, Georgia.

Shaw, A. (1977). Defining the quality of life. *The Hastings Center Reports, 7*(5), p. 11.

United Nations. (1994). *Standard Rules on the Equalization of Opportunities for Persons with Disabilities.* A/RES/48/96, General Assembly, March, 28 pages. Document No. DPI1454.

Wehrens, B. (1994). Intellectual disability research in Europe. *Newsletter, International Association for the Scientific Study of Mental Deficiency,* June (No. 3).

Woodill, G., Renwick, R., Brown, I., & Rapheal, D. (1994). Being, belonging and becoming: An approach to the quality of life of persons with developmental disabilities. In D. Goode (Ed.), *Quality of life for persons with disabilities: International perspectives and issues* (pp. 57–74). Cambridge, MA: Brookline Books.

Part IV
Quality of Life, Culture, and Making a Difference

Based on the work of this volume and Volume I, we are beginning to understand the concept of quality of life better, including its core dimensions of emotional well-being, interpersonal relationships, material well-being, personal development, physical well-being, self-determination, social inclusion, and rights. However, this understanding is based largely on work in the United States and other Western cultures. Thus, it is important to raise the issue of the generalizability of the concept of quality of life across cultural and ethnic groups. This is the purpose of chapter 15.

The concept of quality of life exists in an environment that is increasingly culturally divergent and international. Global orientation necessitates increased cultural exchanges and greater cross-cultural research and understanding. This, plus increasing calls for national and international disability policy to be based on the concept of quality of life, necessitates a strong commitment to cross-cultural research on the concept and its application to persons with disabilities.

Cross-cultural study of quality of life is still in its infancy due to a number of factors including lack of adequate samples, difficulty demonstrating conceptual and linguistic

meaning, lack of appropriate measurement tools, and until recently, lack of a consensual operational definition. To assist in its development, I discuss four cross-cultural guidelines regarding quality of life oriented research and program services: know the purpose of the comparison, demonstrate conceptual and linguistic equivalence, use multiple (qualitative and quantitative) research methods, and involve diverse people. I also discuss four program services guidelines: develop ethnic/cultural competence, understand the context in which behavior occurs, be sensitive to cultural diversity, and understand that disabilities may be viewed differently between and among cultures. Because the quality of life movement is occurring within an increasingly culturally divergent environment that necessitates cross-cultural understanding, the understanding and application of the quality of life concept should include the study of cultures and how they impact one's values and assumptions.

The volume concludes with a chapter entitled, "Can the concept of quality of life make a difference?" The chapter attempts to do two things: first, to summarize key issues that need to be resolved surrounding each of the volume's major sections, service delivery, organizational change, and public policy; and second, to outline action steps that when completed should see both policy and programmatic application of the concept of quality of life to persons with disabilities and an enhanced quality of life for these individuals. The action steps are these.

For service delivery:

1. Reach consensus on the core dimensions of a life of quality.

2. Align service delivery with predictors of the core dimensions.

For organizational change:

1. Continue to embrace total quality management.

2. Develop a technology of supports.

For public policy:

1. Align public policy with the concept of quality of life.

2. Evaluate the outcomes of public policy oriented to quality of life.

Considering Culture in the Application of Quality of Life

Robert L. Schalock

Hastings College

Throughout this volume considerable emphasis has been placed on the importance of considering age and major life activity areas in the application of the concept of quality of life. This chapter focuses on a third key variable—culture. The 1990s have been referred to as "the decade of quality of life" (Schalock, 1990), as well as "the decade of ethnicity," as anthropologists, psychologists, linguists, and philosophers unite to deepen our understanding of the variety of human experience (Shweder & Sullivan, 1993). The purpose of this chapter is to discuss the potential impact that culture has on the application of the concept of quality of life. In the chapter, I discuss the impact of culture on values and assumptions, the rationale for cross-cultural research, and the potential cross-cultural application to research and program services of the concept of quality of life.

Throughout the chapter the reader will encounter three terms repeatedly: culture, ethnicity, and cross-cultural. Culture will be defined as a construct involving shared values, beliefs, behaviors, and attitudes (Matsumoto, 1994). Ethnicity will refer to groups of people with a similar national and cultural heritage (Kuehn & McClainm, 1994). Cross-cultural will refer to both intracultural and cross-cultural frames of reference and comparison. The importance of ethnocultural identity should not be overlooked as we discuss the impact that culture plays in the potential application of the concept of quality of life. As discussed by Lynch and Hanson (1992),

> *...while our culture or our ethnicity plays a role in defining who we are as people and how we conduct our lives, multiple dimensions form that identity. The degree to which we identify with a particular group, under what circumstances, in what aspects, and other social and demographic factors that may influence our identity all play a role. Cultural/ethnic identification is but one facet, albeit a very influential facet in shaping our behavior.*
>
> **(p. 17)**

The Impact of Culture

People live in a number of systems that influence the development of their values, beliefs, behavior, and attitudes. This notion is probably best described in the work by Bronfenbrenner (1979), who takes an ecological perspective in describing the many contexts of development. According to Bronfenbrenner, the systems that support human development can be seen as occurring at four levels, each nested within the next. The microsystem is the immediate social settings, such as family, the peer group, the workplace, that directly affect the person's life. The mesosystem includes the links that connect one microsystem to another. Examples include job coaches, case managers, and natural support personnel. The exosystem includes neighborhood and community structures, such as newspapers, television, and public agencies, that directly affect the functioning of smaller systems. And finally, the macrosystem includes the overarching patterns of culture, social-political trends, and economic systems. This overarching pattern of culture directly affects our values and assumptions, the meanings of words and concepts, and the potential universality of concepts.

Values and Assumptions

Honigmann (1967), in his book *Personality in Culture,* discusses six value orientations that are affected by culture:

1. Human-supernature orientation that involves value judgments about humans and the metaphysical environment including religious orientation and use of myths and symbols.

2. Human-nature orientation that involves concerns about the environment and our effect on it.

3. Human-habitat orientation that includes value judgments about how to design and create living/work environments such as parks, controlled development, and concrete jungles.

4. Human-relational orientation that involves value judgments about how to conduct relationships between and among people.

5. Human-activity orientation that includes value judgments about the individual and group endeavors such as work, Type A and B behaviors, and the need to keep busy.

6. Human-time orientation, which includes value judgments about how to use time, and whether one's time is oriented to the past or to the future.

As suggested by Honigmann, culture also influences a number of values and assumptions about other aspects of our behavior including relations with nature, time orientation, interpersonal relations, self, use of wealth, and interpersonal expression. A comparison of the "mainstream" culture with "other" cultures is shown in Table 15.1. The purpose of this table, which is based on the work of Lynch and Hanson (1992) and Triandis (1990), is to suggest that an individual's conception of a life of quality is potentially quite dependent on one or more of these values and assumptions. In addition to the cross-cultural differences noted in Table 15.1, systematic differences among populations have also been found in the areas of attribution theory, categorization and similarity judgments, moral evaluation, and stress responses (Angel & Idler, 1992; Levy, 1984; Lonner & Malpass, 1994).

Table 15.1
Culturally Divergent Values and Assumptions

Characteristc	Mainstream Culture	Other Cultures
Relation with Nature	Mastery over	Harmony with
	Reform/change	Accepts
	Seeks change	Harmony
	Control	Fatalism
Time Orientation	Future	Present or past
	Inflexible	Flexible
	Negotiable	Settled/permanent
	Time sensitive	Relaxed with time
Interpersonal Relations	Competition	Cooperation
	Aggressiveness	Submission
	Respect youth	Respect elders
	Challenge authority	Conformity
	Nuclear family	Extended family
	Equality	Family-based hierarchy
	Role flexibility	Role rigidity
Self	Individuality	Anonymity
	Assertive	Group
	Extroverted	Introverted
	Independence	Interdependence
	Being direct	Saving face
	Identity defined by own achievements	Identity defined by family achievements
	Action oriented	Stoicism, patience
	Doing	Being
	Self-promoting	Self-effacing
Use of Wealth	Saving	Sharing
Thinking Style	Mind oriented	Heart oriented
	Analytical	Contemplative, circular
Support Systems	Formal	Informal

Meanings of Words and Concepts

Our understanding of the cultural basis of words and concepts comes primarily from work in cross-cultural psychology that aims to describe the implicit meanings that shape psychological processes, examine the distribution of these meanings across cultural groups, and identify the manner of their social acquisition (Shweder & Sullivan, 1993). Of most relevance to this chapter is the cross-cultural work by psychologists and linguists in the areas of perception of others and sense of self.

1. **Perception of others.** It has been shown that in cultures viewing individuals as independent (see Table 15.l), people are often described in

227

terms of traits that are relatively context-free (Markus & Kitayama, 1991). Thus, one finds labels such as intelligent, retarded, smart, aggressive, social, and successful, without reference to contextual factors that might be associated with these characteristics. In contrast, interdependent cultures (for example, those on the Pacific Rim) are more likely to view individuals in terms of their behavior in specific situations or relationships. Also, in interdependent cultures, group membership is fundamentally significant, personal satisfaction depends heavily upon acceptance by the "in group," and members of the in group will sacrifice greatly for one of their own.

2. **Sense of self.** In all cultures, there is some perception of the self as a continuous entity in time as well as some kind of distinction between internal and external things (LeVine, 1984). At the same time, one finds significant differences in the conceptual representation of self. Some of the more important differences include independent vs. interdependent, egocentric vs. sociocentric, autonomous vs. communal, and bounded vs. permeable (Cousins, 1989; Kim & Choi, 1992). These differences are important to understand. For example, the Japanese word for self, *jibun,* refers to "one's share of the shared life space" (Hamaguchi, 1985). According to Hamaguchi, for the Japanese, "a sense of identification with others (sometimes including conflict) preexists and selfness is confirmed only through interpersonal relationships...selfness is not a constant like the ego but denotes a fluid concept which changes through time and situations according to interpersonal relationships" (p. 302).

There are three important implications from these divergent aspects of self that potentially impact one's understanding of the conception of quality of life and its application (Markus & Kitayama, 1991):

1. We may expect those with interdependent selves to be more attentive and sensitive to others than those with independent selves.

2. Among those with interdependent selves, the unit of representation of both the self and the other will include a relatively specific social context in which the self and the other are embedded.

3. A consideration of the social context and the reactions of others may also shape some basic, nonsocial cognitive activities such as categorizing and counterfactual thinking.

In addition to these three implications, researchers in cross-cultural psychology have also recognized that certain principles, referred to as etics, are universal; others, referred to as emics, are culture-bound (Berry, Poortinga, Segall, & Dasen, 1992; Matsumoto, 1994). Even in the broadest and most familiar psychological constructs, cultural assumptions, reflective of etics and emics, play an important role. For example, in all cultures there is some perception of the self as a continuous entity, but those representations of the self differ significantly (see Table 15.1). Also, there are certain etic aspects associated with the concept of intelligence (such as the ability to solve problems), but it also has emic characteristics (such as culturally differing emphases on the speed of problem-solving). Such emic/etic differences, as reflected in the concepts of self and intelligence, would invalidate sweeping cross-cultural comparisons and generalizations (Brislin, 1993; Gergen, 1990; Jahoda, 1992; Keith,

1995). Likewise, the role of values, which are important underpinnings for cultural views of quality of life, may vary significantly from culture to culture (Feather, 1994). Taken together, these potential differences in group views of the person and his or her sense of self may produce discrepant notions of happiness, satisfaction, or well-being across cultures, and hence different conceptions of what one means by quality of life and its application. This issue is discussed further in the next section on cross-cultural research.

Cross-Cultural Research

The concept of quality of life exists in an environment that is increasingly culturally divergent and international. This "global orientation" necessitates increased cultural exchanges and greater cross-cultural research and understanding (Brislin, 1993). As mentioned previously, the 1990s has been referred to as the decade of both quality of life and ethnicity. This, plus the increasing calls for national and international disability policy to be based on the concept of quality of life (Goode, this volume and 1994), necessitates a strong commitment to cross-cultural research on the concept of quality of life and its application to persons with disabilities. This section of the chapter discusses the rationale for cross-cultural research on quality of life and summarizes two cross-cultural studies involving the measurement of its meaning and application.

Rationale

There are probably three reasons for one to do cross-cultural research on the concept of quality of life and its application to persons with disabilities. First, one might want to understand better its emic and etic properties. Second, as discussed by Sanders (1994), one might

want to evaluate hypotheses about individual-level behavior. For example, Inglehart (1990) argued that in the period since 1945, improvements in advanced industrial democracies have resulted in secular changes in citizens' value-priorities, with people becoming less concerned with security and material gain and more concerned with political and environmental issues. Analogously, claims have been made that the quality of life of persons with disabilities is improving around the world. Claims such as these clearly demand individual-level, cross-national comparison and testing. A third reason for cross-cultural research is also described by Sanders (1994) in reference to what he calls "substantive illumination," whose major purpose is to enhance the understanding of one country by reference to the experiences of another or others. For example, one might well be interested in determining what policy frameworks countries use that are basing their services on the concept of quality of life; what institutional practices are characteristic of enhanced quality outcomes; or what contextual variables are most closely related to assessed quality of life factors. The two studies discussed here have examined these three areas.

Exemplary Cross-Cultural Quality of Life Studies

The cross-cultural study of quality of life is still in its infancy due to a number of factors including lack of adequate samples, difficulty with demonstrating conceptual and linguistic meaning, lack of appropriate measurement tools, and, until recently, a lack of a consensual operational definition. Despite its early stage of development, the current international popularity of the concept of quality of life and its potential application in both international policy and service delivery necessitates attempts to do cross-cultural research. It is reasonable to assume that during the late 1990s and the early 21st century, much cross-cultural quality of life research will be conducted.

It is within this context that two exemplary cross-cultural studies are presented. The first study involved the comparison among five countries of measured quality of life factors and their relationship to different living and employment environments. The second involved measuring the attributions of meaning to 10 key quality of life concepts made by mental retardation professionals in seven countries. Both studies are offered for their heuristic value and to set the stage for the anticipated growth of cross-cultural quality of life studies.

1. **Quality of life factors and environments.** The first study (Schalock et al., 1990) involved administering the *Quality of Life Questionnaire* (Schalock & Keith, 1993) to a group of 92 individuals with mental retardation in four countries (Australia, the Federal Republic of Germany, Israel, and the

Republic of China) and comparing their measured scores to the standardization sample of 552 persons with mental retardation in the United States. The average age of the respondents was 32.6 years, with 46.9% female and 53.1% male. Their current living status (across samples) was independent (19.9%), semi-independent (38%), or supervised (42.8%). Their employment status was competitive or supported (29.5%), sheltered (61.6%), or unemployed (8.9%). All respondents had a current diagnosis of mental retardation.

The Questionnaire was translated into the respective languages (Australia used the English version), and then back-translated to ensure linguistic equivalence. Administration was conducted by individuals who had attended a seminar by the author on quality of life and its assessment. Administrators were given these directions: If the person is verbal, have him/her answer each of the following questions according

Table 15.2
Mean (and Standard Error of the Mean) Factor Scores on the Quality of Life Questionnaire in Five Countries

| Country | Satisfaction | Factor | | Community Integration |
		Productivity	Empowerment	
Australia	22.7 (4)	19.5 (6)	24.6 (4)	21.7 (4)
Federal Republic of Germany	22.2 (2)	17.5 (5)	19.5 (2)	19.4 (2)
Israel	23.2 (3)	24.2 (3)	21.0 (3)	20.4 (3)
Republic of China	18.3 (3)	15.0 (6)	15.5 (4)	16.5 (3)
United States	21.8 (4)	21.2 (4)	21.7 (4)	20.7 (3)

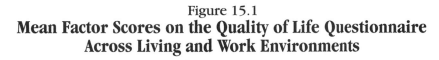

Figure 15.1
Mean Factor Scores on the Quality of Life Questionnaire Across Living and Work Environments

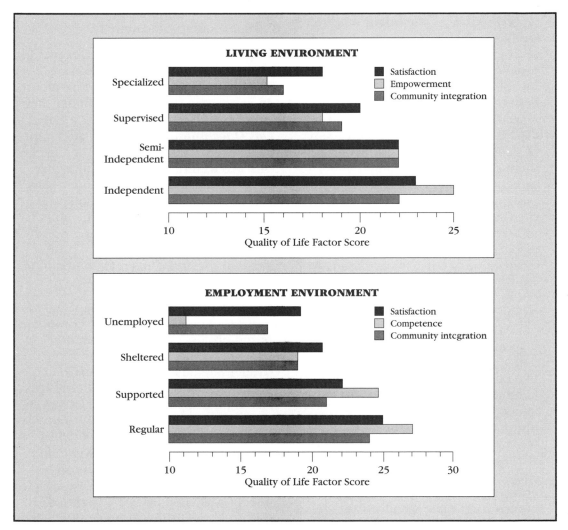

to how he/she honestly feels. Help the person with any word(s) that is (are) not understood. If the person is nonverbal, have two staff independently evaluate the person on each item and use their average score.

The resulting quality of life scores were analyzed in two ways. First, they were summarized for each country per factor. These average scores (along with the standard errors of the mean) are listed in Table

15.2. They are presented only for discussion and heuristic purposes, not for comparative purposes. However, the consistency among specific factor scores across the countries is striking.

Second, the data were analyzed to compare quality of life scores across different living and work environments, regardless of country. These data are presented in Figure 15.1. As shown clearly, there is a consistent

231

trend across the five countries: Quality of life scores increase as individuals live and work in more normalized environments.

2. **Attribution of meaning of quality of life concepts.** The second study involved measuring cross-culturally the attributes of meaning to key quality of life concepts. The study was based on research of Osgood, May, and Miron (1975) that involved the comparison of 22 language groups' evaluations of the meaning of word using the semantic differential, a task in which individuals are given pairs of opposites such as good-bad, strong-weak, or active-passive. Osgood and his associates conducted numerous evaluations of concepts across many cultures and found highly reliable cross-cultural characterizations of concepts using the semantic differential technique. In their studies, respondents were asked to rate concepts from 1 to 7 on each adjective continuum, depending on their judgment of the nearness of the concept to one end of the continuum or the other. The authors reported that the dimensions used to attribute meanings to concepts are amazingly similar from one language group to another. All 22 language groups used value (good vs. bad) as their primary semantic dimension. Furthermore, 17 of the 22 language groups used potency or power as the second dimension to discriminate among concepts. A third dimension, active-passive, was used in some language groups.

Given this finding, we were intrigued by the possibility of investigating the meaning attributed to common quality of life concepts that have evolved during the last decade. Our approach in the study (Keith, Heal, & Schalock, in press)

was to have mental retardation professionals from seven nations rate the meaning of 10 quality of life concepts using nine semantic differential items, three from each of the three dimensions of value, potency, and activity.

Contact was made with colleagues in seven countries: Australia, England, Finland, Germany, Japan, Republic of China, and the United States. Under their direction, the *Key Quality of Life Concepts Questionnaire* was translated into the respective languages, and then back-translated to verify linguistic equivalence. We have found that this procedure results in agreement coefficients (Pearson product moment correlation coefficients) of .89 (Keith, 1995). Questionnaires were completed by 203 post-BA level professionals in the area of mental retardation/ developmental disabilities.

The 10 quality of life concepts rated were based on recent work by consumers and professionals in the area of quality of life research (for example, Gardner & Nudler, this volume; Goode, 1990; Schalock, 1994). The 10 concepts were rights, relationships, satisfaction, environment, economic security and well-being, social inclusion, individual control, privacy, health, and growth and development. Their definitions can be found in Keith et al. (in press). Each concept was rated using a 7-point Likert scale on each of the following nine pairs of adjectives: good-bad, impure-pure, young-old, sad-happy, powerful-powerless, slow-fast, strong-weak, big-little, and inactive-active.

One of the major questions addressed in the study was, Do nations attribute different meanings to various features of quality of life of individuals with mental retardation? To answer this question, countries were compared on their ratings of the 10 quality of life concepts in each of three dimensions of meaning (value, potency, and activity), using a standard three-factor analysis of variance. As shown clearly in Figure 15.2, in general we found considerable international consistency in the rating of concepts that mental retardation professionals associate with quality of life for their clients. Across the seven countries, all 10 of the quality of life concepts tested received strong positive ratings on the value dimension, and lower (but positive) ratings on the potency and activity dimensions. Thus, the 10 concepts, derived largely from North American research and assumptions, were seen as desirable and dynamic notions by the professionals from the seven countries. The interested reader is referred to Keith

et al. (in press) for a discussion of the possible reasons for the profile similarities and differences.

In summary, preliminary studies to date such as the two just described indicate both similarities and differences in the cross-cultural measurement of quality of life, as reported by others (Keith, Yamamoto, Okita, & Schalock, 1995; Leelakulthanit & Day, 1993). As discussed, culture is a construct involving shared values, beliefs, behaviors, and attitudes. Embedded in this definition are elements that suggest strongly that culture intersects with and influences both the research process and the

Figure 15.2

Profile of Meanings Attributed to the Average of Ten QOL Concepts by Mental Retardation Professionals from Seven Countries

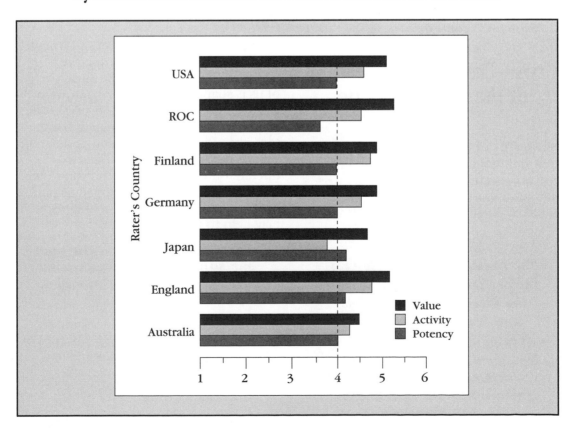

application cross-culturally of the concept of quality of life. Thus, as we approach a discussion in the next section on the cross-cultural application of the concept of quality of life, we should keep four points clearly in mind (Hughes, Seigman, & Williams, 1993):

1. All individuals develop in a cultural context.

2. Culturally based values, norms, and behaviors are transmitted from one generation to the next via overt and covert processes of socialization and are adaptive to the demands of the local environment.

3. Many aspects of culture are abstract in that they are not overtly or intentionally socialized.

4. Culture is evidenced in patterns and social regularities among members of a population and within the larger ecological context.

Cross-Cultural Application of the Quality of Life Concept

Quality of life exists in an increasingly culturally divergent environment that makes cultural exchange and cross-cultural understanding essential. As stated by Kuehn and McClainm (1994),

The challenge is to develop an awareness and knowledge of the diverse cultural beliefs and behaviors . . . And to develop an understanding of the "good life" as perceived by different racial/ethnic groups. Without such knowledge, any quantitative or

qualitative analyses of quality of life will be imprecise and will limit the ability of researchers to develop a universal theory of quality of life for the purpose of research or program planning.

(p. 191)

The purpose of this final section is to discuss a number of cross-cultural guidelines regarding quality of life oriented research and program services. The intent is to integrate current literature in these areas and to provide the basis for further discourse about cross-cultural application of the concept of quality of life.

Research

Cross-cultural observation is difficult, not because other groups are more complex than we are, but because each of us is shaped profoundly by our own culture's categories. Thus, observers of other cultures should maintain a consistent observational standpoint, understand themselves and the forces that operate on them, and suspend their own culturally supplied categories (Reisman, 1993). The following four guidelines may help to bring this about.

1. **Know the purpose of the comparison.** As discussed previously, there are at least three reasons for cross-cultural research:

   • Gaining a better understanding of the emic and etic properties of the concept of quality of life

   • Testing empirically hypotheses about individual-level behavior

   • Enhancing the understanding of one country by reference to the experiences of another country (or countries).

In fulfilling these purposes, one needs to be careful that the statements or comparisons made are informed by extensive knowledge of the systems being studied (Sanders, 1994). For example, research that is concerned primarily about empirical theory testing implies a generally inclusive approach to comparison, since an explanatory theory is supposed to have general application. However, research that is concerned primarily with substantive illumination implies a general exclusive approach to comparison, with the primary purpose being to identify the minimum set of institutional characteristics that differentiate one culture from another on that factor.

2. **Demonstrate conceptual and linguistic equivalence.** The most basic question in cross-cultural research is whether the concepts under study have both conceptual and linguistic equivalence (Hines, 1993). Conceptual equivalence asks whether the concepts under study have equivalent meaning to the groups being considered; linguistic equivalence asks whether the terms and concepts have been translated accurately (Brislin, 1986). In reference to the latter, back translation provides the opportunity to examine the extent to which concepts "come through" in the translation, and can lend some credence to the assumption that the respective groups are talking about the same thing. However, the establishment of somewhat comparable meanings in data-gathering instruments still may not ensure the existence of comparable data due to the differential perceptions of self and others discussed earlier in this chapter. In addition, even if assured

of conceptual and linguistic equivalence, one needs to be concerned in cross-cultural research about the universality of the indicators that are used, the relevance of the topics being investigated, the comparability of the measurements used, and the acceptance of the task. For example,

> *For some cultural and ethnic groups, the entire survey and interviewing process may constitute an uncomfortable and unfamiliar social situation. Surveys involve encounters and exchange of information with strangers, and there are wide cultural variations prescribed for interactions and the language used in such an exchange.*
>
> **(Hines, 1993, pp. 732-733)**

3. **Use multiple research methods.** Even if the researcher is assured of conceptual and linguistic equivalence, different methods may be required to measure cross-culturally the concept of quality of life. Indeed, the emerging trend towards combining qualitative and quantitative research methods from cognitive psychology and cognitive anthropology with survey research methods holds the promise of providing significant information corresponding to the underlying thought processes of respondents. Thus, it should be possible in the future for researchers who are interested in cross-cultural study of quality of life to understand better how different cultural and ethnic groups construe and interpret their life quality (Dana, 1993; Hines, 1993; Tombokan-

Runtukahu & Nitko, 1992). An additional advantage of combining qualitative and quantitative research methods is that together, they provide a better opportunity to discover the emic and etic properties of the concept of quality of life. As discussed by Hughes et al. (1993), qualitative methods emphasize the utility of understanding phenomena from the perspective of group members and thus allow for the meaning of behaviors and concepts to emerge through the inductive analysis of the data themselves. In contrast, quantitative methods emphasize empiricism and hypothesis testing and are therefore more closely associated with the etic perspective, which considers phenomena in relation to predetermined concepts and hypotheses that are frequently independent of the context in which they occur.

Although a detailed discussion of available research methods is beyond the scope of this chapter, it is important for the reader to be familiar with four general methods that show considerable promise for the cross-cultural study of quality of life. These include exploratory research, self-generation techniques, protocol analysis, and semantic differential.

a. **Exploratory research.** Extended periods of exploratory research allow one to decide on whether or not a particular construct is adequately conceptualized or relevant (Hughes et al., 1993). This method can include a number of techniques such as ethnographic interviewing, observation, or focus groups. Use of exploratory research also helps to overcome some of the problems encountered in cross-cultural research including cost and time, the possibility that some topics will be

viewed as irrelevant or taboo, and the need to clarify the task being requested.

b. **Self-generation technique.** The use of this technique usually involves at least four steps (Bernard, 1988): the free listing of items/concepts to define culturally specific domains; the use of the frame technique that organizes domains; the development of taxonomies and classifications based on a card-sorting task; and the ranking and rating of the items to produce interval data. The final sorts can be used to compare respondent and group data.

c. **Protocol analysis.** This method asks respondents to "think aloud" or "talk about" their conception of the concept of quality of life. One can then code and analyze the resulting protocol data in one of two ways (Hines & Snowden, 1993): a priori, according to predetermined categories such as core quality of life dimensions; or a posteriori, using the data to generate new categories of terms, meanings, or relevance. One can also use responses on the items to identify unique cultural response patterns through item characteristics curves (Ellis & Kimmel, 1992).

d. **Semantic differential.** As discussed earlier in the cross-cultural study of the meaning of the 10 key quality of life concepts, the semantic differential method, which is based on a battery of bipolar adjectives, can be used to measure the meaning of words and concepts (Osgood, Suci, & Tannenbaum, 1957). This method holds considerable promise in allowing cross-cultural quality of life researchers to gain a better understanding of the emic and etic aspects to key quality of life concepts (see Figure 15.2), test empirically hypotheses about individual-level interpretations of core quality of life core dimensions, and enhance understanding of the application of the concept of quality of life.

These multiple methods, along with the general trend towards combining qualitative and quantitative research techniques, hold considerable promise for the future cross-cultural study of the concept of quality of life and its cross-cultural application to persons with disabilities. In addition, these methods should also help the research community meet the three commonly accepted criteria for the cross-cultural measurement of quality of life: replication of factor structure, discrimination among cultures, and correlation with external criteria (Funkhouser, 1993).

4. **Involve diverse people.** A frequently overlooked research guideline is to involve representatives from the cultural or ethnic groups under consideration. The two exemplary studies summarized earlier could not have been done without the involvement of people from each of the respective countries. In addition to increasing the probability of a successful cross-cultural study, the involvement of persons who have a stake in the study will force one to keep focused on the following key cross-cultural research principles (Keith, 1995):

- In the assessment of quality of life, the individual person must remain the focus.

- Comparative studies that illuminate key characteristics of cultures and the quality of life of persons within them are likely to contribute to cross-cultural understanding and communication in important ways.

- We must recognize and overcome our propensity to project our own norms on people of other cultures.

- In investigating the concept of quality of life, the emphasis should be on our common humanity.

Program Services

One of the primary purposes of studying and understanding the concept of quality of life is to apply potentially the concept to enhance a life of quality for persons with disabilities. This potential application has been seen repeatedly in this volume in the chapters on living, employment, education, health, families, person-centered planning, consumer driven research, and staff training. As we continue to move into the realm of intra- and cross-cultural applications, it is important to keep in mind a number of guidelines about the application of the concept of quality of life across cultural and ethnic groups. Four of these guidelines are discussed on subsequent pages.

1. **Develop ethnic/cultural competence.** The decade of the 1990s has been referred to as the decade of quality of life and the decade of ethnicity. Thus, it is apparent that the application of the concept of quality of life involves not just the understanding of cultural/ethnic differences, but ethnic competence as well. Green (1982) defines ethnic competence as "being able to conduct one's professional work in a way that is congruent with the behavior and expectations that members of a distinctive culture recognize as appropriate among themselves" (p.52). Common to the work of a number of persons in this area (e.g. Green, 1982; Guthrie, 1975; Hammer, 1989; Ibrahim, 1995;

Marsella, 1990; Ruben, 1989), ethnic competencies include an awareness of one's own cultural limitations; openness, appreciation, and respect for cultural differences; a view of intercultural interactions as learning opportunities; the ability to use cultural resources in interventions; and an acknowledgment of the integrity and value of all cultures. As stated by Kuehn and McClainm (1994),

> *The development of cultural competence begins with an awareness that not all people are the same. Values, religious beliefs, assumptions about the causality of disease and attitudes about the use of medical technology and prescription medicines, definitions of "the good life" or a "quality of life," the value of research, and related issues can vary greatly amongst different racial/ ethnic groups. These differences will influence the manner in which different groups engage in research and program planning related to quality of life.*
>
> **(p. 192)**

2. **Understand contextualism.** Part of the development of ethnic/ cultural competence is to understand the currently popular concept of "contextualism." There is growing recognition that contemporary psychology is undergoing a paradigm shift (Kagitcibasi, 1990; Szapocznik & Kurtines, 1993) wherein the major

focus of study will be the context of the person rather than just the individual. Contextualism generally refers to the view that behavior cannot be understood outside of the context in which it occurs. This shift, accompanied by the recent movement away from individuo-centrism or individual orientedness (Betancourt & Lopez, 1993; Lee, 1994), requires that we need to ask a number of specific questions when studying the cross-cultural nature of the concept of quality of life (Marjoribanks, 1994; Shweder & Sullivan, 1993):

a. Are members of different cultural groups alike or different in the antecedent conditions that elicit the value or belief? (environmental determinants)

b. Are members of different cultural groups alike or different in the perceived implications for the self of those antecedent conditions of the world? (self-appraisal)

c. Are members of different cultural groups alike or different in their affective reactions to those antecedent conditions of the world? (affective phenomenology)

d. Are members of different cultural groups alike or different in the extent to which displaying the quality of life core dimension is accepted? (social appraisal)

e. Are members of different cultural groups alike or different in their plans for the management of self-esteem? (self-management)

f. Are members of different cultural groups alike or different in the iconic or symbolic vehicles (e.g., facial expression, voice, posture) for expressing quality of life core dimensions? (communication)

3. **Be sensitive to cultural diversity.** The predominant American values and assumptions are typically described as emphasizing individuality and privateness, equality, informality, the future, change and progress, goodness of humanity, time, achievement, action, work, materialism, directedness, and assertiveness (Athens, 1988). However, a quick review of Table 15.1 indicates that these values and assumptions are not necessarily universal. For example, in the United States and similar cultures, the work ethic is a major determinant of perceived quality of life. Even though it contributes to an enhanced quality of life of people with disabilities in this country, it may not be so valued in other cultures (Lobley, 1992). Similarly, when people in various cultures are asked to complete sentences starting with, "I am . . .," those in collective (interdependent) societies are likely to complete the statement with a reference to a group or relationship, such as "I am a daughter, professor, Catholic, etc." In contrast, those in individualistic (independent) societies are likely to define themselves in terms of fixed personal characteristics or traits, such as "I am kind, tall, etc." (Triandis, 1994). Taken together, these differences in group views of the person and of the individual sense of self may produce discrepant notions of happiness, satisfaction, well-being or quality of life across cultures and/or ethnic groups. Therefore, one needs to be sensitive to different conceptions of what one means by quality of life and quality of life oriented program services.

4. **Understand that disabilities may be viewed differently.** Differential meanings attributed to disability may result in very different views about the cross-cultural/ethnic application of the concept of quality of life. For example, as stated by Kuehn and McClainm (1994), "the reality of a chronic disability, while a legitimate descriptor, is subordinate to the greater reality of their racial or ethnic status" (p. 191). Similarly, Ibrahim (1995) discusses the fact that if one's disability does not fit the characteristics of mainstream culture, it is often considered an aberration.

In the cross-cultural application of the concept of quality of life to persons with disabilities, it is important to understand terms that either denote disability or are related to the role that people with disabilities play in their respective cultures. For example, in Anglo-American culture, the word "dependency" can be associated with immaturity or disability, whereas in Japanese culture, *amae* (dependency) is not only accepted but actively fostered because that culture has long prized group cohesion and solidarity over independence (DeVos, 1973). Similarly, many cultures have no equivalent concepts or terms for the concept of depression (Fabrega, 1992; Manson, 1994).

There are numerous examples of how different cultures view people with disabilities. For example, Locust (1988) has observed that for many Native Americans, a visible disability is interpreted as the presence of a whole and healthy spirit housed within an impaired body and that removing or lessening the disability may be interpreted as inappropriate. Similarly, Kalyanpus (1994) found that on the Indian subcontinent, a disability is often perceived as an act of God that one must accept rather than attempt to change. Different views of disability may also affect a family's coping strategies, the use of social and habilitation services, child-rearing practices, and expectations for the person (Harry, 1989). An ethnic/culturally competent cross-cultural researcher will be sensitive to these potentially differing views of disability.

Conclusion

In summary, the quality of life movement is occurring within an increasingly culturally divergent environment that necessitates cross-cultural understanding. The understanding and application of the quality of life concept must include the study of cultures and the values and assumptions that they impart. Indeed, culture and ethnicity define quality of life and cannot be ignored in cross-cultural research or in the design and delivery of quality of life-oriented program services.

Throughout this chapter it has been stressed that the cross-cultural study and understanding of the concept of quality of life and its application to persons with disabilities is still in its infancy. It is a sad fact, for example, that "there is no information available about the quality of life of people with developmental disabilities who are members of racial/ethnic minority populations [even] in the United States" (Kuehn & McClainm, 1994). Despite this fact, the national and international popularity of the concept of quality of life and the calls for it to be the basis for national and international disability policy require an increased commitment to studying its emic and etic properties. As discussed throughout this chapter, the cross-cultural study of quality of life requires a number of competencies related to research design and implementation as well as an understanding and appreciation of cultural diversity. It is reasonable to assume that the next ten years will be the "decade of cross-cultural quality of life research." It is a big task, but one that we as a global community can handle. It will be an exciting time.

References

Angel, R., & Idler, E.L. (1992). Somatization and hypochondriasis: Sociocultural factors in subjective experience. *Research in Community Mental Health, 7,* 71–93.

Athens, G. (1988). *American ways: A guide for foreigners in the United States.* Yarmouth, ME: Intercultural Press.

Bernard, H.R. (1988). *Research methods in cultural anthropology.* Beverly Hills, CA: Sage.

Berry, J.W., Poortinga, Y.H., Segall, M.H., & Dasen, P.R. (1992). *Cross-cultural psychology: Research and applications.* New York: Cambridge University Press.

Betancourt, H., & Lopez, S.R. (1993). The study of culture, ethnicity, and race in American psychology. *American Psychologist, 48,* 629–637.

Brislin, R.W. (1986). The wording and translation of research instruments. In W.J. Lonner & J.W. Berry (Eds.), *Field methods in cross-cultural research.* Beverly Hills, CA: Sage.

Brislin, R.W. (1993). *Understanding culture's influence on behavior.* Fort Worth, TX: Harcourt Brace Jovanovich.

Bronfenbrenner, U. (1979). *The ecology of human development: Experiments by nature and design.* Cambridge, MA: Harvard University Press.

Brown, L., Shiraga, B., Ford, A., Nisbet, J., et al. (1983). Teaching severely handicapped students to perform meaningful work in nonsheltered, vocational environments. In R. Morris & B. Blatt

(Eds.), *Perspectives in special education: State of the art.* Glenview, IL: Scott Foresman.

Cousins, S. (1989). Culture and selfhood in Japan and the United States. *Journal of Personality and Social Psychology, 56,* 124-131.

Dana, R.H. (1993). *Multicultural assessment perspectives for professional psychology.* Boston: Allyn & Bacon.

DeVos, G. (1973). *Socialization for achievement.* Berkeley: University of California Press.

Ellis, B.B., & Kimmel, H.D. (1992). Identification of unique cultural response patterns by means of item response theory. *Journal of Applied Psychology, 77,* 177-184.

Fabrega, H. (1992). The role of culture in a theory of psychiatric illness. *Social Science and Medicine, 35*(1), 91-111.

Feather, N.T. (1994). Values and culture. In W.J. Lonner & R. Malpass (Eds.), *Psychology and culture* (pp. 183-189). Boston: Allyn and Bacon.

Funkhouser, G.R. (1993). A self-anchoring instrument and analytical procedure for reducing cultural bias in cross-cultural research. *The Journal of Social Psychology, 133,* 661-673.

Gergen, K.J. (1990). Social understanding and the inscription of self. In J. Stigler, R. Sheveder, & G. Herdt (Eds.), *Cultural psychology* (pp. 567-607). New York: Cambridge University Press.

Giangreco, M.F., Clonger, C.J., & Iverson, V.S. (1993). *Choosing options and accommodations for children: A guide to planning inclusive education.* Baltimore: Brookes.

Goode, D.A. (1990). Thinking about and discussing quality of life. In R.L. Schalock (Ed.), *Quality of life: Perspectives and issues* (pp. 41-57). Washington, DC: American Association on Mental Retardation.

Goode, D.A. (Ed.) (1994). *Quality of life for persons with disabilities: International perspectives and issues.* Boston: Brookline Books.

Green, J.W. (1982). *Cultural awareness in the human services.* Englewood Cliffs, NJ: Prentice-Hall.

Guthrie, G.M. (1975). A behavioral analysis of culture learning. In R.W. Brislin & W.J. Lonner (Eds.), *Cross-cultural perspectives on learning* (pp. 95-115). New York: John Wiley.

Hamaguchi, E. (1985). A contextual model of the Japanese: Toward a methodological innovation in Japan studies. *Journal of Japanese Studies, 11,* 289-321.

Hammer, M.R. (1989). Intercultural communication competence. In M.K. Asante & W.B. Gudykunst (Eds.), *Handbook of international and intercultural communication* (pp. 247-260). Newbury Park, CA: Sage.

Harry, B. (1992). *Cultural diversity, families, and the special education system.* New York: Teachers College Press.

Hines, A.M. (1993). Linking qualitative and quantitative methods in cross-cultural survey research: Techniques from cognitive science. *American Journal of Community Psychology, 21,* 729-746.

Hines, A.M., & Snowden, L.R. (1993). Survey and interviewing procedures: Cross-cultural validity and the use of protocol analysis. In J.E. Trimble, C.S. Bolek, & S. Niemcryk (Eds.), *Conducting cross-cultural substance abuse research: Emerging strategies and methods* (pp. 122-149). Newbury Park, CA: Sage.

Honigman, J. (1967). *Personality in culture.* New York: Harper & Row.

Hughes, D., Seidman, E., & Williams, N. (1993). Cultural phenomena and the research enterprise: Toward a culturally anchored methodology. *American Journal of Community Psychology, 21,* 687-703.

Ibrahim, F.A. (1995). Multicultural influences on rehabilitation training and services: The shift to valuing nondominant cultures. In O.C. Karan & S. Greenspan (Eds.), *Community rehabilitation services for people with disabilities.* Boston: Butterworth-Heinemann.

Inglehart, R. (1990). *Culture shift in advanced industrial society.* Princeton, NJ: Princeton University Press.

Jahoda, G. (1992). *Crossroads between culture and mind: Continuities and change in theories of human nature.* London: Harvester Wheatsheaf.

Kagitcibasi, C. (1990). Family and socialization in cross-cultural perspective: A model of change. In G. Johada, H.C. Triandis, C. Kagitcibasi, J. Jerry et al. (Eds.), *Cross-cultural perspective: Nebraska symposium on motivation: 1989* (pp. 135–200). Lincoln: University of Nebraska Press.

Kalyanpus, M. (1994). *The perspectives of low-income families on the special education system in India.* Unpublished doctoral dissertation, Syracuse University, Syracuse.

Keith, K.D. (1995). Measuring quality of life across cultures. In R.L. Schalock, (Ed.), *Quality of Life: Vol. I. Conceptualization and measurement* (pp. 73–82). Washington, DC: American Association on Mental Retardation.

Keith, K.D., Heal, L.W., & Schalock, R.L. (in press). Cross-cultural measurement of critical quality of life concepts. *Australia and New Zealand Journal of Developmental Disabilities.*

Keith, K.D., Yamamoto, M., Okita, N., & Schalock, R.L. (1995). Cross-cultural quality of life: Japanese and American college students. *Social Behavior and Personality, 23,* 163–170.

Kim, U., & Choi, S.C. (1992). Individualism, collectivism and child development: A Korean perspective. In P. Greenfield & R.C. Cocking (Eds.), *Cognitive development of minority children* (pp. 154–170).

Kuehn, M.L., & McClainm, J.W. (1994). Quality of life in the United States: A multicultural context. In D.A. Goode (Ed.), *Quality of life for persons with disabilities: International perspectives and issues* (pp. 185–193).

Lee, Y-T. (1994). Why does American psychology have cultural limitations? *American Psychologist, 49,* 524–525. Hillsdale, NJ: Erlbaum.

Leelakulthanit, O., & Day, R. (1993). Cross cultural comparisons of quality of life of Thais and Americans. *Social Indicators Research, 30,* 49–70.

LeVine, R.A. (1984). Properties of culture: An ethnographic view. In R.A. Shweder & R.A. LeVine (Eds.), *Cultural theory: Essays on mind, self and emotion.* New York: Cambridge University Press.

Levy, R.I. (1984). Emotion and culture. In R.S. Shweder and R.A. LeVine (Eds.), *Culture theory: Essays on mind, self and emotion* (pp. 214–237). New York: Cambridge University Press.

Lobley, J. (1992). *Community living for people with learning disabilities: Is quality of life a useful guiding concept?* Unpublished thesis, Lancashire Polytechnic University, Preston, England.

Locust, C. (1988). Wounding the spirit: Discrimination and traditional American Indian belief systems. *Harvard Educational Review, 58,* 315–330.

Lonner, W.J., & Malpass, R. (1994). *Psychology and culture.* Boston: Allyn & Bacon.

Lynch, E.W., & Hanson, M.J. (1992). *Developing cross-cultural competence: A guide for working with young children and their families.* Baltimore: Brookes.

Manson, S.M. (1994). Culture and depression: Discovering variations in the experience of illness. In W.J. Lonner & R. Malpass (Eds.), *Psychology and culture* (pp. 285–290). Boston: Allyn & Bacon.

Marjoribanks, K. (1994). Cross-cultural comparisons of family environments of Anglo-, Greek-, and Italian-Australians. *Psychological Reports, 74,* 49–50.

Markus, H.R., & Kitayama, S. (1991). Culture and the self: Implications for cognition, emotion, and motivation. *Psychological Review, 98,* 224-253.

Marsella, A.J. (1990). Ethnocultural identity: The new independent variable in cross-cultural research. *Focus* (American Psychological Associ*ation), 4*(2), 14-15.

Matsumoto, D. (1994). *People: Psychology from a cultural perspective.* Pacific Grove, CA: Brooks/Cole.

Mercer, J.R. (1979). In defense of racially and culturally nondiscriminatory assessment. *School Psychology Digest, 8,* 89-115.

Miller, J.G., & Bersoff, D.C. (1992). Culture and moral judgment: How conflicts between justice and interpersonal responsibility resolved. *Journal of Personality and Social Psychology, 62,* 541-554.

Nihira, K., Webster, R., Tomiyasu, Y., & Oshio, C. (1988). Child-environment relationships: A cross-cultural study of educable mentally retarded children and their families. *Journal of Autism and Developmental Disorders, 18,* 327-341.

Osgood, C.E., May, W.H., & Miron, M.S. (1975). *Cross cultural universals of affective meaning.* Urbana: University of Illinois Press.

Osgood, C.E., Suci, G.E., & Tannenbaum, P.H. (1957). *The measurement of meaning.* Urbana, IL: University of Illinois Press.

Reisman, W.M. (1993). Autonomy, interdependence, and responsibility. *The Yale Law Journal, 103,* 401-417.

Reschly, D.J. (1981). Evaluation of the effects of SOMPA measures on classification of students as mildly mentally retarded. *American Journal of Mental Deficiency, 86,* 16-20.

Ruben, B.D. (1989). The study of cross-cultural competence: Traditions and contemporary issues. *International Journal of Intercultural Relations, 13,* 229-240.

Sanders, D. (1994). Methodological considerations in comparative cross-national research. *International Social Science Journal, 46,* 513-521.

Schalock, R.L. (Ed.). (1990). *Quality of life: Perspectives and issues.* Washington, DC: American Association on Mental Retardation.

Schalock, R.L. (1994). Quality of life, quality assurance: Implications for program planning and evaluation in the field of mental retardation and developmental disabilities. *Evaluation and Program Planning, 17*(2), 121-131.

Schalock, R.L., Bartnik, E., Wu, F., Konig, A., Lee, C.S., & Reiter, S. (1990, May). *An international perspective on quality of life measurement and use.* Paper presented at the 104th Annual Convention, American Association on Mental Retardation, Atlanta.

Schalock, R.L., & Keith, K.D. (1993). *Quality of life questionnaire.* Worthington, OH: IDS Publishing.

Shweder, R.A., & Sullivan, M.A. (1993). Cultural psychology: Who needs it? *Annual Review of Psychology, 44,* 497-523.

Szapocznik, J., & Kurtines, W.M. (1993). Family psychology and cultural diversity: Opportunities for theory, research, and application. *American Psychologist, 48,* 400-408.

Triandis, H.C. (1990). Cross-cultural studies of individualism and collectivism. In G. Johoda, H.C. Triandis, C. Kagitcibasi, J. Berry et al. (Eds.), *Cross-cultural perspectives: Nebraska symposium on motivation: 1989* (pp. 41-131). Lincoln: University of Nebraska Press.

Triandis, H.C. (1994). Culture and social behavior. In W.J. Lonner &R. Malpass (Eds.), *Psychology and culture* (pp. 169-173). Boston: Allyn and Bacon.

Can The Concept of Quality of Life Make A Difference?

Robert L. Schalock
Hastings College

Can the concept of quality of life make a difference in the lives of persons with disabilities? You have just read 15 chapters whose authors feel that "yes it can, but if…" The "but if" is the theme of this concluding chapter. In the chapter, I attempt to do two things: first, to summarize the key issues that need to be resolved in the future surrounding each of the volume's major sections: service delivery, organizational change, and public policy; and second, to outline a number of action steps that will facilitate program and policy applications of the concept of quality of life to persons with disabilities.

In the Preface, I summarized a number of quality of life principles that can be used to evaluate current and subsequent efforts at enhancing one's life of quality. These are summarized in Table 16.1. Now it is time to take stock and evaluate our current status vis a vis these 10 principles as we begin to think about future action steps. In general, I think that we have made significant

progress over the last decade in implementing many of these principles. For example, the concept of quality of life has become a generic concept, with dimensions that encompass both individual and group differences; we have validated consensually through personal perspectives and research the core dimensions associated with a life of quality; we have seen further development of self-advocacy as the foundation for one's quality of life; we are using multiple methodologies to study one's quality of life, realizing that it is primarily the subjective view of the person that truly determines his or her quality of life; and we have seen that quality of life variables are occupying a prominent role in service delivery, organizational change, accreditation, and overall program evaluation.

But we need to go beyond today, and consider the future role that the concept of quality of life may play in the lives of persons with disabilities. To that end, this chapter (a) summarizes the key

---

Table 16.1
Core Quality of Life Principles

1. Quality of life for persons with disabilities is composed of those same factors and relationships that are important to all persons.

2. Quality of life is experienced when a person's basic needs are met and when he or she has the same opportunities as anyone else to pursue and achieve goals in the major life settings of home, community, school, and work.

3. Quality of life is a multidimensional concept that can be consensually validated by a wide range of persons representing a variety of viewpoints of consumers and their families, advocates, professionals, and providers.

4. Quality of life is enhanced by empowering persons to participate in decisions that affect their lives.

5. Quality of life is enhanced by the acceptance and full integration of persons into their local communities.

6. Quality of life is an organizing concept that can be used for a number of purposes including evaluating those core dimensions associated with a life of quality, providing direction and reference in approaching customer services, and using the resulting data for multiple purposes.

7. The study of quality of life requires an in-depth knowledge of people and their perspectives, and multiple methodologies.

8. The measurement of quality of life requires multiple measurement techniques.

9. Quality of life variables should occupy a prominent role in program evaluation.

10. The application of quality of life data is important in developing resources and supports for persons with disabilities and their families.

---

issues that need to be addressed in the general areas of service delivery, organizational change, and public policy if the concept of quality of life is truly to be applied to persons with disabilities; and (b) suggests the following six action steps:

1. Reach consensus on the core dimensions of a life of quality.

2. Align service delivery with predictors of the core dimensions.

3. Continue to embrace total quality management.

4. Develop a technology of supports.

5. Align public policy with the concept of quality of life.

6. Evaluate the outcomes of quality of life oriented public policy.

Service Delivery

Over the last five years we have seen a significant movement towards inclusiveness and supports as major service delivery components. We have also seen positive results from the use of the concept of quality of life in the planning and delivery of education, rehabilitation, health, and recreation-leisure supports and services. However, despite this significant progress, there are still a number of important issues to resolve and action steps to take before service delivery and quality of life are integrated completely. Over the next decade, we undoubtedly will be concerned about addressing these key issues and implementing the necessary action plans discussed below.

Key Issues

The key issues discussed in the eight chapters related to service delivery application are summarized in Table 16.2 (top section). Across areas, these issues relate to basing education and rehabilitation efforts on person-centered planning principles; increasing opportunities to be both in and of the community; determining ways to respond to the challenges of inclusion, health-related issues, and aging; supporting persons in their efforts at personal development; promoting public attitudes that are nondiscriminatory and facilitative; and supporting families.

Action Steps

1. **Reach consensus on the core dimensions of a life of quality.** Considerable work has been done over the last five years identifying the core dimensions of a life of quality. Based on that work (Campbell, Converse, & Rogers, 1976; Dossa, 1989; Felce & Perry, 1996; Flanagan, 1982; Hughes & Hwang, 1996; Gardner & Nudler, this volume; Keith, Heal, & Schalock, in press; Schalock, 1994, 1995b, 1996a), eight proposed core quality of life dimensions can serve as the basis for our subsequent work:

   - Emotional well-being (including psychological well-being)

   - Interpersonal relations (including social relationships)

   - Material well-being (including employment and economic security)

   - Personal development (including personal competence and personal goals)

   - Physical well-being (including wellness and recreation/leisure)

   - Self-determination (including individual control and decisions)

   - Social inclusion (including dignity and worth)

   - Rights (including privacy)

   When consensus is reached on these core dimensions, additional work regarding conceptualization, measurement, and application of the concept of quality of life can proceed in two directions: the evaluation of consumer satisfaction levels and the development of objective core dimension indicators.

   a. **Evaluate satisfaction level.** A consensus is emerging that the critical dependent measure of a person's quality of life is the person's level of satisfaction (Campbell et al., 1976; Edgerton, 1996; Halpern, Nave, Close, & Nelson, 1986; Harner & Heal, 1993; Heal & Chadsey-Rusch, 1985; Heal, Rubin, & Park, 1995; Lehman, 1988; Lehman, Rachuba, & Postrado, 1995; Medley, 1990). Using satisfaction as the major dependent measure of quality of life has many advantages: (1) providing a common language that can be shared by consumers, providers, policy makers, regulators, and researchers; (2) assessing consumer needs; and (3) evaluating consumer satisfaction.

   Evaluating consumer satisfaction requires developing reliable and valid measures of life satisfaction using

Table 16.2
Key Issues: Service Delivery, Organizational Change, and Public Policy

SERVICE DELIVERY ISSUES:

1. Base services and supports on person-centered planning.

2. Offer inclusive schools and classroom options that foster personal growth and interpersonal relationships.

3. Develop satisfying and personally enhancing job opportunities and relationships between the worker and the employer.

4. Provide living options that permit self-determination, allow for community inclusion, and balance empowerment with safety.

5. Determine what is the purpose for measuring health-related quality of life, what aspects of it should be measured, what values and procedures to use.

6. Determine ways to meet the challenges involved in aging families, growing old in one's home, and retirement.

7. Promote leisure choices and decision-making skills, lessen social, attitudinal and physical barriers, and change policy to recognize leisure as a fundamental domain of daily life.

ORGANIZATIONAL CHANGE ISSUES:

1. Base accreditation and certification on quality of life oriented outcomes.

2. Improve program quality through outcomes and demonstrate the impact of the use of outcome measures.

3. Determine the individual and organizational variables that influence outcome attainment.

4. Recognize that the structure of the service system is changing and requires accommodating to new service models, upgrading skills and compensations of community support workers, and imbedding the substance of skill standards into high schools and community colleges.

5. Apply the principles and methods of quality and improvement-oriented approaches to organizational management to the issue of quality of life.

6. Involve in participatory action research all key stakeholders who can contribute their collective understanding of how quality of life can be conceptualized, investigated, and enhanced.

PUBLIC POLICY ISSUES:

1. Link quality of life to measures for all the nation's citizenry.

2. Align public policy with the concept of quality of life.

3. Stress that the concept of quality of life is generic, not particular to people with disabilities.

4. Ensure cooperation among self-advocates, policy makers, service providers, and researchers in defining and measuring quality of life.

5. Develop international quality of life networks, and continue an international focus on quality of life.

6. Evaluate the outcomes from quality of life oriented public policy.

one or more of the following strategies (Borthwick-Duffy, 1996; Heal & Sigelman, 1996; Realon, Favell, & Lowerre, 1990; Schalock, 1996a; Sigelman, Schoenrock, Budd, Winer et al., 1983):

- Use multiple methods, including participant observation, performance based assessment, and standardized instruments to capture the core quality of life dimensions and their indicators (see following section).

- Use either-or questions or objective multiple choice questions with three or four options accompanied by pictures.

- Correct statistically for response biases.

- Use proxies.

- Resolve differences between the client and proxy through discussions and detailed behavioral observation.

- Rely more heavily on participant observation that encompasses the issues of expressed choices, control, and satisfaction.

b. **Develop objective indicators of each core dimension.** If the concept of quality of life is used as an organizing concept in public policy and service delivery, then objective indicators need to be developed for each core quality of life dimension. When this is done, we can overcome some of the problems involved in using only subjective measures (Felce & Perry, 1996); provide objective indicators that are comparable across disability status (people with and without disabilities), programs, and, potentially, cultures (Keith, 1996; Schalock, this volume); and use quality of life

indicator data to develop or change service/support programs, assess service outcomes, and evaluate public policy (Schalock, 1994, 1995b).

The attempt to identify objective quality of life indicators began with the work of Andrews and Whithey (1976) and Zautra and Goodhart (979) and has continued with the work of Gardner and Nudley (this volume) and Schalock (1994; 1995b). An initial list of objective indicators associated with each of the eight core quality of life dimensions is presented in Table 16.3. Criteria regarding the development of these indicators include the following (Schalock, 1995b):

- The indicator is valued by the person.

- Multiple indicators are used.

- The indicator is measurable, with demonstrated reliability and validity.

- The indicator is connected logically to the program, service, or support.

- The indicator is evaluated longitudinally.

2. **Align service delivery with quality of life predictors.** When subjective measures of satisfaction and objective quality of life indicators become the major dependent variables in quality of life application and research, then multivariate research methods can be used to determine the contribution that core quality of life dimensions make to a person's assessed level of satisfaction or objective quality of life indicators, or the contributions that other variables such as personal characteristics, objective life conditions, or

care provider characteristics make to either the dependent measures (satisfaction or objective indicators) or the eight core quality of life dimensions. The importance of this suggestion should not be overlooked. If programs have the ability to measure consumer satisfaction and have developed objective indicators that reflect the core quality of life dimensions, then they can align their service delivery to enhance quality outcomes.

What alignment might be required? Initial multivariate work in this area with both the general population and persons with disabilities suggests the focus for future work. Among the general population, for example, research indicates various predictors:

- For women, satisfaction with family life is the most important predictor of general well-being; whereas for men, satisfaction

Table 16.3
Exemplary Objective Quality of Life Indicators

Dimension	Exemplary Indicators	
Emotional Well-Being	Safety	Freedom from stress
	Spirituality	Self-concept
	Happiness	Contentment
Interpersonal Relations	Intimacy	Interactions
	Affection	Friendships
	Family	Supports
Material Well-Being	Ownership	Employment
	Financial	Possessions
	Security	Social economic status
	Food	Shelter
Personal Development	Education	Personal competence
	Skills	Purposeful activity
	Fulfillment	Advancement
Physical Well-Being	Health	Health care
	Nutrition	Health insurance
	Recreation	Leisure
	Mobility	Activities of daily living
Self-Determination	Autonomy	Personal control
	Choices	Self-direction
	Decisions	Personal goals/values
Social Inclusion	Acceptance	Community activities
	Status	Roles
	Supports	Volunteer activities
	Work environment	Residential environment
Rights	Privacy	Due process
	Voting	Ownership
	Access	Civic responsibilities

with health and family are the major predictors of life satisfaction, followed by satisfaction with community and work (Bharadway & Wilkering, 1977; Medley, 1990).

- In early adulthood, satisfaction with family, standard of living, work and education are significant predictors; in mid-adulthood, satisfaction with family and work remain salient, but housing and community replace education and standard of living as priorities; in late adulthood, satisfaction with family, work, community, standard of living, and spare time activities remain significant predictors, but health becomes increasingly important; and among the elderly, satisfaction with health, spare time activities, spiritual matters, family life, and financial concerns are predictive of life satisfaction (Lehman et al., 1995).

- Change in interpersonal relations appears to contribute more heavily to satisfaction than does either social economic status or social participation (Schuessler & Fisher, 1985).

- Subjective ratings of income are better predictors of feelings of satisfaction than are objective ratings (Ackerman & Paolucci, 1993).

- Satisfaction with housing contributes the most to satisfaction with life as a whole, while satisfaction with spouse and friends contributes the most to general happiness (Michalos, 1982).

- Quality of life is a function of social position (Gerson, 1976).

- Quality of life enhancers include job/career satisfaction, relationship with family, money earned from a job, good health, residential location, religion and spirituality, relationship with spouse/significant other, relationships with friends, educational level, and one's home (Time out, 1995).

In reference to persons with disabilities, research is beginning to identify the major predictors of assessed quality of life. Three studies are worth considering here because of their attempt to identify the significant correlates of a life of quality. The first study (Schalock, Lemanowicz, Conroy, & Feinstein, 1994) evaluated the influence of 18 predictor variables on the measured quality of life (Schalock & Keith, 1993) of 968 individuals with developmental disabilities five years after they moved into the community. The study used a multivariate analysis in which the 18 predictor variables were analyzed statistically in three blocks: personal characteristics, objective life conditions, and perception of significant others. The second study (Faulkner, 1995) used a similar multivariate design and the same measure of quality of life on a group of 158 individuals with mental retardation residing in either facility-based or community-based programs. Predictor variables were "blocked" into client variables, environmental variables, and care provider variables. The third study (Lehman et al., 1995) represents a similar analysis, except that the data base was derived from four separate quality of life surveys of persons with chronic mental illness ($n = 1,805$) using the Lehman *Quality of Life Interview* (QOLI). The Interview assesses life circumstances of persons with severe mental illness in terms of both what they actually do and experience ("objective" quality of life) and their feelings about these experiences ("subjective" quality of life or life satisfaction).

251

Table 16.4 lists the significant predictors of assessed quality of life identified in these three studies, whose average adjusted r square was .41. Most of the 20 variables identified are factors that programs can do something about: the person's employment status, daily activities, current residential environment, social relations, and social support; others relate to staff variables such as educational level, work stress, and work satisfaction. Integrating these variables into ongoing services and supports will result in education and (re)habilitation programs aligning themselves with the concept of quality of life. But such integration will require additional changes as discussed in the next section.

Table 16.4
Significant Predictors of Assessed Quality of Life

Personal Characteristics:
Age
Gender
Marital Status
Adaptive Behavior Index
Challenging Behavior Index
Health Index
Diagnosis

Objective Life Conditions:
Employment
Earnings/Financial Adequacy
Daily Activities
Current Residence
Social Relations
Family Contact
Recreational Activities
Perceived Social Support

Care Provider Variables:
Staff's Assessed Quality of Life
Educational Level
Work Stress Score
Work Satisfaction Score
Significant Others' Perception Score

Organizational Change

Three points were made in the four chapters that dealt with organizational change. First, the concept of quality of life is emerging as an over-arching principle that is applicable to the betterment of persons with disabilities in this time of social, political, technological, and economic transformations. Second, the current paradigm shift in mental retardation, with its emphasis on self-determination, inclusion, equity, empowerment, community-based supports, and quality outcomes, is forcing service providers to change their program focus to one that emphasizes an enhanced quality of life for persons with disabilities. And third, the quality revolution, with its emphasis on total quality, quality leadership, and total quality management, is resulting in a movement within human services toward managing for quality. However, if changes are to be realized fully, we need to continue to address the following issues and action plans.

Key Issues

The key issues discussed in chapters 9-12 regarding organizational change were summarized in Table 16.2 (middle section). Across areas, issues relate to improving program quality through outcomes; recognizing that the service system's structure and content is changing; upgrading the skills of community service workers; embedding the substance of skill standards in high schools and community colleges; applying the principles and methods of quality-oriented organizational management to the issue of quality of life; and involving in participatory action research all stakeholders who can contribute their collective understanding of how quality of life can be operationalized, investigated, and enhanced.

Action Steps

1. **Continue to embrace total quality management.** Total quality management (TQM) emphasizes the importance of organizations' basing their services on a strong mission statement that commits the organization to a vision of quality that addresses consumer needs and ensures satisfaction (Albin, 1992; Deming, 1986). In addition, TQM involves a management style that uses teams of employees to accomplish tasks, streamlines managerial roles and duties, involves all levels of personnel in the quality improvement process, emphasizes consensus building and team problem solving, and maintains a clearly articulated commitment to quality improvement (Hanley-Maxwell & Whitney-Thomas, 1995; Roberts & Sergesketter, 1993; Weaver, 1991). At a minimum, three action steps are necessary if education and (re)habilitation programs are going to truly embrace TQM: developing competent community service workers, implementing quality enhancement techniques, and incorporating data-based decision-making.

   a. **Develop competent community support workers.** Bradley and her colleagues discussed this issue in chapter 10. The reader is referred to that chapter for specific suggestions on developing competent community support workers who can fulfill the following roles: service brokerage, including case management and family support; behavioral change, including teaching skills and providing therapeutic assistance; residential supports, including live-in supports and residential management; personal care and assistance, involving personal support for an individual in the home, on the job, and in the community; employment supports, including job coaching, mentoring, and job development; and leisure/recreation assistance.

   Developing competent community support workers requires more than just training, as important as that is. It requires that organizations change basic functions to "reengineer the corporation" along the following lines (Hammer & Champy, 1993):

   - Work units change from functional departments to process teams.

   - Jobs change from simple tasks to multidimensional work.

   - People's roles change from controlled to empowered.

   - Job preparation changes from training to education.

   - Performance appraisal changes from activity to results.

   - Advancement criteria change from performance to ability.

   - Values change from protective to productive.

   - Managers change from supervisors to coaches.

   - Organizational structure changes from vertical to horizontal.

   - Executives change from score keepers to leaders.

   b. **Implement quality enhancement techniques.** Quality enhancement techniques typically are based on input from consumers and focus on what program personnel and program services can do to enhance a person's real or perceived quality of life. Examples include allowing for choices, maximizing the use of natural supports, emphasizing employment, supporting community

253

living, promoting wellness, supporting inclusive education, and promoting positive role functions and lifestyles.

The strong emphasis on quality enhancement techniques has also had an impact on training and technical assistance activities (Albin, 1992). In a recent article, for example, Buckley and Mank (1994) suggest that with the focus on quality as a cultural transformation in the workplace (Deming, 1986), we are seeing a demise of concepts such as management by objectives, organizational hierarchies, and management by inspection. In their place, we are seeing an emphasis on responsibility, information, resources, leadership, and evaluation in the hands of teams of individuals.

A number of approaches are currently being used by program personnel to enhance the quality of life experiences of persons with disabilities (Schalock, 1994). This action step suggests that we need to base these techniques around the core quality of life dimensions discussed earlier. The quality enhancement techniques listed in Table 16.5 accomplish this goal.

c. **Incorporate data-based decision-making.** Quality referenced outcomes play a critical role in quality improvement because they allow organizations to evaluate how well their mission and goals are being met. Based on this feedback, programs can modify their services and supports to enhance desired outcomes through changing resource allocation, staff utilization patterns, or the services and supports provided. In addition, data-based decision-making has these characteristics (Schalock, 1995b):

- Assures stakeholders a strong voice in the design and management of programs.

- Is an ongoing part of service delivery and ongoing data collection, not an add-on for program evaluation purposes.

- Links both facility evaluation and program improvement to person-referenced outcomes.

- Allows for systematic evaluation and improvement of services.

- Identifies potential foci for programmatic or systems change.

2. **Develop a technology of supports.** We are currently experiencing a change in the way people with special needs are viewed and served. This change is referred to as the "supports paradigm" (Bradley, Ashbaugh, & Blaney, 1994; Gettings, 1994; Schalock, 1995a; Smull & Danehey, 1994). This paradigm shift is to a large extent grounded in the philosophy of normalization and involves moving away from a defect orientation that focuses primarily on a person's deficits and towards an outcome or role-based orientation that asks, What supports are needed to help this person function in age-relevant social roles within the community? Although still emerging, the supports paradigm extends across disciplines and (re)habilitation areas including education, families, mental retardation/developmental disabilities, mental health, employment, living, and medicine (Schalock, 1995a).

Considerable conceptual work has already been done regarding different intensities of needed support that include intermittent, limited, extensive, and pervasive (Luckasson

Table 16.5
Quality of Life Enhancement Techniques

Dimension	Exemplary Indicators	
Emotional Well-Being	Increase safety	Reduce stress
	Allow for spirituality	Foster success
	Provide positive feedback	Promote stable, safe, and
	Maintain as low a psychotropic medication level as possible	predictable enviroments
Interpersonal Relations	Allow intimacy	Encourage interactions
	Permit affection	Foster friendships
	Support family	Provide supports
Material Well-Being	Allow ownership	Support employment
	Advocate for financial security	Encourage possessions
	Insure safe environs	
Personal Development	Provide education and (re)habilitation	Foster skill development
	Teach functional skills	Provide purposeful act
	Provide vocational and avocational activities	Support advancement
		Use augmentative technology
Physical Well-Being	Insure health care	Encourage proper nutrition
	Maximize mobility	Support activities of daily living
	Support opportunities for meaningful recreation and leisure	Promote wellness by emphasizing physical fitness, nutrition, healthy life-styles, and stress management
Self-Determination	Allow for choices	Allow decisions
	Permit personal control	Assist in developing personal goals
Social Inclusion	Interface with natural support networks	Provide opportunities for community integration and participation
	Promote positive role functions and life-styles	Support volunteerism
	Stress normalized and integrated environments	
Rights	Assure privacy	Afford due process
	Encourage voting	Encourage ownership
	Reduce barriers	Encourage civic responsibilities

et al., 1992; Schalock, 1995a; Stark & Faulkner, 1996). However, if the supports paradigm is to succeed, we will need to continue our work in this area and, more specifically, develop a technology of supports such as described in the two following action steps.

a. **Supports planning matrix.** The matrix (American Association on Mental Retardation, 1995) presented as Figure 16.1 provides a working model for determining a person's needed types of support. The first column lists the eight core quality of life dimensions. The second column requires team members to specify the support resources most appropriate to an individual's needs.

It is important to emphasize that in addition to coming from other people, services, and augmentative devices, resources can come from the individual. This focus on the individual as a resource is consistent with current emphasis on personal empowerment, decision-making, and choices. The third column requires listing of specific supports that will enhance the respective core quality of life dimension. The final column asks team members to identify how the needed supports were determined. This step is important because it allows the interdisciplinary team to integrate all relevant assessment information and to verify its source and inclusion in implementing the necessary supports. The determination of needed supports can be made on the basis of the person's input, behavioral observation, and clinical assessment.

b. **Supports intensity decision grid.** Once the specific needed supports are identified, one needs to determine their intensity. The 1992 AAMR System (Luckasson et al.,

1992) suggests the following four intensities of support:

- **Intermittent:** supports on as "as needed basis." Characterized by episodic nature, person not always needing the support(s), or short-term supports needed during life-span transitions. May be high or low intensities when provided.

- **Limited:** supports characterized by consistency over time, time-limited but not of an intermittent nature; may require fewer staff members and less cost than more intense levels.

- **Extensive:** characterized by regular involvement (e.g., daily) in at least some environments and not time-limited.

- **Pervasive:** characterized by their constancy, high intensity, provided across environments; potentially life-sustaining nature.

Since the inception of this system in 1992, considerable work has been done on developing a technique that will assist teams in validly determining the appropriate intensity of needed support (Schalock, Stark, et al., 1994). This work has led to the Supports Intensity Decision Grid presented as Figure 16.2 (Luckasson et al., 1996). The four levels of support intensity are listed across the top of the matrix. Five factors that affect the intensity are listed down the side: time (duration), time (frequency), settings (living, work, recreation, leisure, health, and community), resources (professionals and technological assistance), and intrusiveness. The matrix is used to determine the intensity of each of the specific needed supports identified in Column 2 of Figure 16.1.

Figure 16.1
Supports Planning Matrix

Core Quality of Life Dimensions	Support Resource[a]	Specific Supports	Support Intensity[b]	Basis for Determination[c]
Emotional Well-Being				
Interpersonal Relations				
Material Well-Being				
Personal Development				
Physical Well-Being				
Self-Determination				
Social Inclusion				
Rights				

a   Personal
    Other People
    Technology
    Services

b   Intermittent
    Limited
    Extensive
    Pervasive

c   Person's Input
    Behavioral Observation
    Clinical Assessment

Figure 16.2
Supports Intensity Decision Grid

SUPPORT INTENSITY

FACTOR	INTERMITTENT	LIMITED	EXTENSIVE	PERVASIVE
TIME duration	as needed	time limited, occasiionally ongoing	usually ongoing	possibly lifelong
TIME frequency	infrequent, low occurence	regular, anticipated; could be high frequency		high rate, continuous, constant
SETTINGS Living Work Recreation Leisure Health Community Etc.	few settings; typically one or two settings	across several settings; typically not all settings		all or nearly all settings
RESOURCES Professional/ Technological Assistance	occasional consultation or discussion, ordinary appointment schedule, occasional monitoring	occasional contact, or time-limited but frequent regular contact	regular, ongoing contact or monitoring by professionals typically at least weekly	constant contact and monitoring by professionals
INTRUSIVENESS	predominantly all natural supports, high degree of choice and autonomy	mixture of natural and service-based supports lesser degree of choice and autonomy		predominantly service-based supports, controlled by others

It should be noted that until now the matrix has been used primarily to determine the intensity of support needs and not the cost of those supports. A number of questions still need to be evaluated, precluding the use of the matrix for cost determinations. The more important of these questions are these:

- Are the cells orthogonal or interdependent? This question is very relevant to safety needs for example.

- Can the pattern of intensities be averaged for each core quality life dimension?

- What type of clustering is most appropriate? For example, when support needs go across core dimensions, can one determine an average support intensity level based on the cluster?

- Are support intensities age dependent?

As we anticipate the further emergence of the supports paradigm and work related to the Supports Planning Matrix and Supports Intensity Decision Grid, the following standards will hopefully guide their use:

- Supports should be provided in regular, integrated environments.

- Support activities should be performed primarily by individuals working, living, or recreating within those environments.

- Support activities should be individualized and person-referenced.

- Outcomes from the use of supports should be evaluated against quality indicators and valued, person-referenced outcomes.

- The use of supports can fluctuate and may range from life-long duration to fluctuating need during different stages of life.

- Supports should not be withdrawn precipitously.

Public Policy

Public policy is beginning to incorporate the concepts of person-centered planning, ongoing supports, and valued person-referenced outcomes. This is evident in recent federal legislation such as the Americans With Disabilities Act, the 1992 Rehabilitation Act Amendments, and the Individuals With Disabilities Education Act. We also saw in Part I, in chapters by Karan and Bothwell, Kiernan and Marrone, and Snell and Vogtle, how the supports paradigm is being applied in the major life activity areas of living, education, and employment.

Key Issues

The two chapters in the Public Policy Application section identified a number of issues that need to be addressed. As summarized in the bottom section of Table 16.2, these include implementing quality of life oriented public policy; understanding that the concept of quality of life is generic, and not particular to people with disabilities; recognizing the legal implications of the concept of quality of life; and integrating the views of self-advocates, service providers, policy makers, and researchers in a common approach to defining and measuring one's quality of life. These key issues can be best addressed by implementing the following two action steps.

Action Steps

1. **Align public policy with the concept of quality of life.** Public policy plays a critical role not only in the provision of resources for education and (re)habilitation services, but it also reflects social values and beliefs about people with disabilities. Throughout this century, the fundamental definition of disability used by policy makers has focused on the person's physical or mental attributes as they relate to the potential for workforce participation. In this model, impairments have been treated as medical facts to be certified by professional experts. Federal and state initiatives following from this model have included vocational rehabilitation, Social Security Disability Insurance, and the supported employment initiative.

During the last two decades, however, three additional models of disability have begun to influence public policy: social constructionism, minority group status, and social contextualism (Badley, 1995; Hahn, 1985; Institute of Medicine, 1991; Scotch & Berkowitz, 1990). According to the constructionist model of disability, attitudes, practices, and institutional structures, rather than impairments themselves, define the meaning and consequences of disability. The constructionist model also attempts to minimize physical and social environmental factors that constrain individuals with such impairments. The Americans With Disabilities Act was based on this model.

The minority group model has emerged recently, emphasizing the role that prejudice and institutional discrimination play in shaping the experience of disability. This model characterizes people with disabilities not merely as individuals who face choices based on their impairments, but also as members of an excluded minority group who face discriminatory barriers that can be overcome through the collective action of self-advocates and political action groups (Berkowitz, 1987; Hahn, 1985; Harpham & Scotch, 1989; Katzmann, 1986; Percy, 1989; Scotch, 1984; Ward & Keith, 1996).

A third model—social contextualism—is just emerging and is quite consistent with the alignment of public policy with the concept of quality of life. According to this model, disability is the product of an interaction between the person with a disability and his or her environment. This model is best reflected in the work of the Institute of Medicine (1991) and the current proposals regarding the World Health Organization's International Classification of Impairments, Disabilities, and Handicaps (Badley, 1995). The social contextualism model proposes a four-stage conceptualization of the disabling process (Institute of Medicine, 1991):

- Pathology that is associated with an abnormality at the cellular or tissue level (such as tuberous sclerosis)

- Impairment at the organ or organ system that results from the pathology (such as brain dysfunction)

- Functional limitation at the organism level (such as low intelligence)

- Disability that occurs when the functional limitation impacts or interferes with the person's social role.

This four-stage conceptualization of the disabling process has a number of policy implications for the application of the concept of quality of life to persons with disabilities. Among the more important are these:

- Disability is viewed relative to functional behaviors as opposed to diagnostic categories.

- Disability is neither fixed nor dichotomized; rather it is fluid, continuous, changing, and an evolving set of characteristics depending upon the characteristics and supports available within a person's environment.

- Functional limitations (and hence a person's disability) are lessened by providing services that focus on the core quality of life dimensions and implementing quality enhancement techniques.

- Public policy evaluation focuses on the extent to which people are satisfied with changes in their person-referenced core quality of life dimensions.

It is likely that future disability policy will be affected not only by one or more of these current models, but also by one or more of the following potential future scenarios (Goode, 1991): America revitalized, post-industrial reformation, community-welfare society, or the stressed society. Each scenario has potential impacts on values, employment, integration, technology, quality of services, minorities, support services, housing, and education. All things considered, quality of life oriented public policy will fare much better with an "America revitalized" scenario.

2. **Evaluate the outcomes of quality of life oriented public policy.** If public policy shifts to focusing on quality of life, then one needs to evaluate the outcomes of such a shift. The success of this effort lies with the use of a quality of life oriented evaluation model and a shared process of quality assurance and evaluation.

a. **Quality of life oriented evaluation model.** The quality of life oriented evaluation model presented in Figure 16.3 provides the framework for evaluating the effects of a potential quality of life-oriented public policy. The multivariate model's four components are core quality of life dimensions, measure(s) of satisfaction and core quality of life indicators as major dependent variables, three research and evaluation uses for these dependent measures, and four program application uses of the data. Major advantages of the model include its ability to combine subjective and objective indicators (Heal & Sigelman, 1996) and to measure domain-specific levels of satisfaction (Edgerton, 1996).

The eight core quality of life dimensions listed are those that are generally accepted as reflective of a life of quality (Schalock, 1996a). As discussed earlier in this chapter, there is an emerging consensus that satisfaction is the primary measure of one's quality of life since it best represents the subjective nature of the phenomenon and also allows one to uncouple objective standards of quality from the subjective experience of well-being (Edgerton, 1996). However, there is also a need to use objective quality of life indicators to demonstrate programmatic accountability, assess program outcomes, compare programs, evaluate public policy, and conduct research.

Research and evaluation activities resulting from this model can proceed in any number of directions including determining the predictors of satisfaction; determining the relationships between demographic variables, core dimensions, and satisfaction; or providing the data

Figure 16.3
Quality of Life Evaluation Model

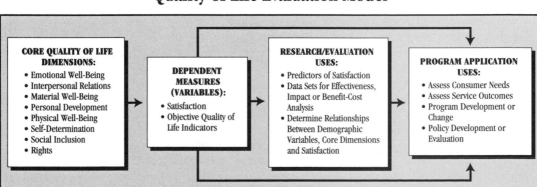

sets for the increasing need for outcome evaluation. As discussed elsewhere (Schalock, 1995b), there are three current approaches to outcome evaluation:

- The extent to which the program obtains its goals and objectives (effectiveness analysis).

- Whether the program made a difference compared to either no program or an alternative program (impact analysis).

- Whether the program's benefits outweigh the costs (benefit-cost analysis). Two criteria are used to make this determination: equity and efficiency. Equitable programs contribute to balancing the needs of the various groups in society; efficient programs increase the net value of goods and services available to society.

The model's fourth component suggests a number of applications for either satisfaction or objective quality of life indicators. First, assessing consumer needs would be consistent with the approach to defining quality of life as a discrepancy between assessed needs and current satisfaction. This use of the model would permit one to assess consumer needs around the eight core quality of life dimensions and then conduct a discrepancy analysis that would assist in implementing programmatic changes and quality enhancement techniques. Second, using both types of dependent variables would allow education and (re)habilitation programs to assess and evaluate their outcomes (Halpern, 1993). It would also allow the development of quality of life-oriented services and supports, and the evaluation of public policy (Zola, 1993).

b. **Implement a shared quality assurance and evaluation process.** The successful evaluation of quality of life oriented public policy requires that we rethink and reconceptualize traditional evaluation methods. In this regard, two trends in human services are impacting quality assurance and program evaluation. One is a service delivery system based on the consumer and principles of empowerment, equity, and inclusion (Schalock, 1994); the second is a funding-regulatory system that redefines service clients as customers and gives them choices, decentralizes authority, empowers citizens by pushing control out of bureaucracy and into the community, and embraces participatory management (Osborne & Gaebler, 1993).

The impacts of these two trends are becoming readily apparent in the implementation of a shared quality assurance process (Schalock, 1996b) and the use of consumer-oriented evaluation strategies (Schalock, 1995b; Whitney-Thomas, this volume). The key components of these two processes are summarized in Table 16.6. By using these two techniques we will be in a better position not only to meet the current accountability requirements of measurability and reportability, but also to evaluate the effectiveness, impact, and benefit-cost of quality of life-oriented public policy.

Conclusion

The decade of the 1990s has truly been the "decade of quality of life." It has been and is a challenging and highly rewarding time to be in the field of mental retardation. In this decade we have seen many shifts:

- Services to supports

Table 16.6

Critical Components to Shared Quality Assurance and Consumer Oriented Evaluation

Shared Quality Assurance:

- There is a parallel set of activities completed by the provider (internal evaluation) and the consumer/advocate/regulatory body (external validation).

- Internal evaluation is a data-based process built around the desired person-referenced outcomes and monitored jointly by the service provider and external validator(s).

- External validation involves agreeing on the quality outcomes to monitor, providing technical assistance and support to the development and maintenance of the data system, and validating the critical quality outcomes.

- Data from the quality assurance process are used for a variety of purposes: reevaluating program structure, implementing quality management and enhancement techniques, conducting staff training, and evaluating program outcomes.

Consumer-Oriented Evaluation:

- Face-to-face set of activities completed by the researcher or evaluator initially involving asking questions, identifying problems, searching for solutions, and identifying needs and concerns.

- Subsequent parallel but integrative research/evaluation activities include selecting jointly the research questions, deciding on data collection and research design, developing data systems and providing technical assistance to develop the system, collecting the data, and analyzing the data.

- Final face-to-face activities include determining the uses of the data and acting on the data.

- Programming to opportunity development

- Passive to active consumer roles

- Process to outcomes

- The individual to the environment

- Research questions to policy evaluation

- Categorical to noncategorical

- A deficiency model to a growth model

- Dependency to interdependence

- Daily schedules to rhythms of nurturing events

- Normalization to quality.

These changes have not just happened. They have occurred in large part because they reflect both a healthy evolution in our social philosophy and the changing vision we have of persons with disabilities. Inherent in this evolution and change has been the concept of quality of life—a concept that speaks of equity, value, growth, potential, and good.

What we have seen in this volume is that services, organizations and public policy are embracing this concept in ways that sometimes stagger the imagination, and often times, test the limits of the system. But as a good friend of mine constantly reminds me, "If you don't shoot for the moon, you will never hit the top of the bank."

Current public policy is undergoing tremendous value clashes. In fact, the 1990s is frequently referred to as "the decade of value clashes." In the ensuring struggles, the disability community will need to be stronger advocates than ever in the past. In that struggle, the material presented in this volume suggests strongly that the concept of quality of life provides a fundamentally positive and growth-oriented principle that can be the basis of a national and international policy on disability.

But tremendous work lies ahead. Thus, I conclude with those six suggested action steps that should facilitate our work as we approach the 21st century quality of life agenda:

1. Reach consensus on the core dimensions of a life of quality.

2. Align service delivery with predictors of the core quality of life dimensions.

3. Continue to embrace total quality management.

4. Develop a technology of supports.

5. Align public policy with the concept of quality of life.

6. Evaluate the outcomes of public policy oriented to quality of life.

References

Ackerman, N., & Paolucci, B. (1993). Objective and subjective income adequacy: Their relationship to perceived life quality measures. *Social Indicators Research, 12,* 25–48.

Albin, J.M (1992). *Quality improvement in employment and other human services: Managing for quality through change.* Baltimore: Brookes.

American Association on Mental Retardation. (1995). *Train the trainer manual to accompany the 1992 AAMR definition, classification, and systems of supports.* Washington, DC: Author.

Andrews, F.M., & Whithey, S.B. (1976). *Social indicators of well-being: Americans' perception of life quality.* New York: Plenum.

Badley, E.M. (1995). The genesis of handicap: Definition, models of disablement, and role of external factors. *Disability and Rehabilitation, 17*(2), 53–62.

Berkowitz, E.D. (1987). Disabled policy: *America's programs for the handicapped.* New York: Cambridge University Press.

Bharadway, L., & Wilkering, E.A. (1977). The prediction of perceived well-being. *Social Indicators Research, 4,* 421–439.

Borthwick-Duffy, S.A. (1996). Evaluation and measurement of quality of life: Special considerations for persons with mental retardation. In R.L. Schalock (Ed.), *Quality of life: Vol. I. Conceptualization and measurement* (pp. 89–100). Washington, DC: American Association on Mental Retardation.

Bradley, V.J., Ashbaugh, J.W., & Blaney, B.C. (1994). *Creating individual supports for people with developmental disabilities: A mandate for change at many levels.* Baltimore: Brookes.

Buckley, J., & Mank, D. (1994). New perspectives on training and technical assistance: Moving from assumptions to a focus on quality. *Journal of the Association for Persons with Severe Handicaps, 19,* 223–232.

Campbell, A., Converse, P.E., & Rogers, W.L. (1976). *The quality of American life.* New York: Russell Sage Foundation.

Deming, W.E. (1986). *Out of crisis.* Cambridge: Massachusetts Institute of Technology.

Dossa, P.A. (1989). Quality of life: individualism or holism? A critical review of the literature. *International Journal of Rehabilitation Research, 12*(2), 121–136.

Edgerton, R.B. (1996). A longitudinal-ethnographic research perspective on quality of life. In R.L. Schalock (Ed.), *Quality of life: Vol. I. Conceptualization and measurement* (pp. 83–90). Washington DC: American Association on Mental Retardation.

Faulkner, E. (1995). *An empirical investigation of quality of life and its correlates.* Unpublished doctoral dissertation. Omaha: University of Nebraska.

Felce, D., & Perry, J. (1996). Assessment of quality of life. In R.L. Schalock (Ed.), *Quality of life: Vol. I. Conceptualization and measurement* (pp. 63–72). Washington DC: American Association on Mental Retardation.

Flanagan, J.C. (1982). Measurement of quality of life: Current state of the art. *Archives of Physical Medicine and Rehabilitation, 63,* 56–59.

Gerson, E.M. (1976). On quality of life. *American Sociological Review, 41,* 793–806.

Gettings, R.M. (1994). The link between public financing and system change. In V.J. Bradley, J.W. Ashbaugh, & B.C. Blaney (Eds.), *Creating individual supports for people with developmental disabilities: A mandate for change at many levels* (pp. 155–170). Baltimore: Brookes.

Goode, D.A. (1991). Toward the year 2000: Values and trends affecting persons with developmental disabilities. *Liaison Bulletin, 17*(3), 1–14.

Hahn, H. (1985). Introduction: Disability policy and the problem of discrimination. *American Behavioral Scientist, 28,* 293–318.

Halpern, A.S. (1993). Quality of life and a conceptual framework for evaluating transition outcomes. *Exceptional Children, 59,* 486–498.

Halpern, A.S., Nave, G., Close, D.W., & Nelson, D.J. (1986). An empirical analysis of the dimensions of community adjustment for adults with mental retardation. *Australia and New Zealand Journal of Developmental Disabilities, 12,* 147–157.

Hammer, M., & Champy, J. (1993). *Reengineering the corporation: A manifesto for business revolution.* New York: Harper Collins.

Hanley-Maxwell, C., & Whitney-Thomas, J. (1995). A survey of supported employment agencies' quality improvement and training needs. *Rehabilitation Counseling Bulletin, 39*(1), 25–41.

Harner, C.J., & Heal, L.W. (1993). The Multifaceted Lifestyle Satisfaction Scale (MLSS): Psychometric properties of an interview schedule for assessing personal satisfaction of adults with limited intelligence. *Research in Developmental Disabilities, 14,* 221–236.

Harpham, E.J., & Scotch, R.K. (1989). Ideology and welfare reform in the 1980s. In R.M. Coughlin (Ed.), *Reforming welfare: Lessons, limits, and choices* (pp. 43–60). Albuquerque: University of New Mexico Press.

Heal, L.W., & Chadsey-Rusch, J. (1985). The Lifestyle Satisfaction Scale (LSS): Assessing individuals' satisfaction with residence, community setting, and associated services. *Applied Research in Mental Retardation, 6,* 475–490.

Heal, L.W., Rubin, S.S., & Park, W. (1995). *Lifestyle satisfaction scale.* Champaign-Urbana, IL: Transition Research Institute, University of Illinois.

Heal, L.W., & Sigelman, C.K. (1996). Methodological issues in quality of life measurement. In R.L. Schalock (Ed.), *Quality of life: Vol. I. Conceptualization and measurement* (pp. 91–104). Washington DC: American Association on Mental Retardation.

Hughes, C., & Hwang, B. (1996). Attempts to conceptualize and measure quality of life. In R.L. Schalock (Ed.), *Quality of life: Vol. I. Conceptualization and measurement* (pp. 43-53). Washington, DC: American Association on Mental Retardation.

Institute of Medicine. (1991). *Disability in America: Toward a national agenda for prevention.* Washington, DC: National Academy Press.

Katzmann, R.A. (1986). *Institutional disability: The sage of transportation policy for the disabled.* Washington, DC: Brookings Institute.

Keith, K.D. (1996). Measuring quality of life across cultures: Issues and challenges. In R.L. Schalock (Ed.), *Quality of life: Vol. I. Conceptualization and measurement* (pp. 73-82). Washington, DC: American Association on Mental Retardation.

Keith, K.D., Heal, L.W., & Schalock, R.L. (in press). Cross-cultural measurement of critical quality of life concepts. *Australia and New Zealand Journal of Developmental Disabilities.*

Kiernan, W.E., & Mank, D. (1994). *Employment/financing reform.* Boston: Institute for Community Inclusion, Children's Hospital.

Lehman, A.F. (1988). A quality of life interview for the chronically mentally ill. *Evaluation and Program Planning, 11,* 51-62.

Lehman, A.F., Rachuba, L.T., & Postrado, L.T. (1995). Demographic influences on quality of life among persons with chronic mental illnesses. *Evaluation and Program Planning, 18,* 155-164.

Luckasson, R., Coulter, D., Kleinert, H., Eckert, S., Lottman, R.,. Kolstoe, P., & Schalock, R.L. (1996, May). *How to operationalize the AAMR supports classification system.* Multidisciplinary session at the 120th Annual Meeting, American Association on Mental Retardation, San Antonio, Texas.

Luckasson, R., Coulter, D.L., Polloway, E.A., Reiss, S., Schalock, R.L., Snell, M.E., Spitalnik, D.M., & Stark, J.A. (1992). *Mental retardation: Definition, classification, and systems of supports.* Washington, DC: American Association on Mental Retardation.

Medley, M. (1990). Life satisfaction across four stages of adult life. *Aging and Human Development, 11,* 193-209.

Michalos, A.C. (1982). The satisfaction and happiness of some senior citizens in rural Ontario. *Social Indicators Research, 11,* 1-30.

Osborne, D., & Gaebler, R. (1993). *Reinventing government: How the entrepreneurial spirit is transforming the public sector.* New York: Penguin.

Percy, S.L. (1989). *Disability, civil rights, and public policy: The politics of implementation.* Tuscaloosa: University of Alabama Press.

Realon, R.E., Favell, J.E., & Lowerre, A. (1990). The effects of making choices on engagement levels with persons who are profoundly multiple handicapped. *Education and Training in Mental Retardation, 25,* 299-305.

Roberts, H.V., & Sergesketter, B.F. (1993). *Quality is personal: A foundation for total quality management.* New York: Free Press.

Schalock, R.L. (1994). Quality of life, quality enhancement, and quality assurance: Implications for program planning and evaluation in the field of mental retardation and developmental disabilities. *Evaluation and Program Planning, 17,* 121-131.

Schalock, R.L. (1995a). Assessment of natural supports in community rehabilitation services. In O.C. Karan & S. Greenspan (Eds.), *Community rehabilitation services for people with disabilities* (pp. 209-227). Boston: Butterworth-Heinemann.

Schalock, R.L. (1995b). *Outcome-based evaluation.* New York: Plenum.

Schalock, R.L. (1996a). Reconsidering the conceptualization and measurement of quality of life. In R.L. Schalock (Ed.), *Quality of life: Vol. I. Conceptualization and measurement* (pp. 123–139). Washington, DC: American Association on Mental Retardation.

Schalock, R.L. (1996b). Quality of life and quality assurance. In R. Renwick, I. Brown, & M. Nagler (Eds.), *Quality of life in health promotion and rehabilitation: Conceptual approaches, issues, and applications* (pp. 104–118). Beverly Hills, CA: Sage.

Schalock, R.L., & Keith, K.D. (1993). *Quality of life questionnaire.* Worthington, OH: IDS Publishers.

Schalock, R.L., Lemanowicz, J.A., Conroy, J.W., & Feinstein, C.S. (1994). A multivariate investigative study of the correlates of quality of life. *Journal on Developmental Disabilities, 3*(2), 59–73.

Schalock, R.L., Stark, J.A., Snell, M.E., Coulter, D.L., Polloway, E., Luckasson, R., Reiss, S., & Spitalnik, D. (1994). The changing conception of mental retardation: Implications for the field. *Mental Retardation, 32,* 25–39.

Scotch, R.K. (1984). *From good will to civil rights: Transforming federal disability policy.* Philadelphia: Temple University Press.

Scotch, R.K., & Berkowitz, E.D. (1990). One comprehensive system? A historical perspective on federal disability policy. *Journal of Disability Policy Studies, 1*(3), 2–19.

Schuessler, K.F., & Fisher, G.A. (1985). Quality of life research and sociology. *Annual Review of Sociology, 11,* 129–149.

Sigelman, C.K., Schoenrock, C.J., Budd, E.C., Winer, J.L., Spanhel, C.L., Martin, P.O., Hromas, S., & Bensberg, G.J. (1983). *Communicating with mentally retarded persons: Asking questions and getting answers.* Lubbock: Texas Tech University, Research and Training Center in Mental Retardation.

Smull, M.E., & Danehey, A.J. (1994). Increasing quality while reducing costs: The challenge of the 1990s. In V.J. Bradley, J.W. Ashbaugh, & B.C. Blaney (Eds.), *Creating individual supports for people with developmental disabilities: A mandate for change at many levels* (pp. 59–78). Baltimore: Brookes.

Stark, J.A., & Faulkner, E. (1996). Quality of life across the life span. In R.L. Schalock (Ed.), *Quality of life: Vol. I. Conceptualization and measurement* (pp. 23–32). Washington, DC: American Association on Mental Retardation.

Time out. (1995, December 11). *U.S. News & World Report* (pp. 85–97).

Ward, N.A., & Keith, K.D. (1996). Self-advocacy: Foundation for quality of life. In R.L. Schalock (Ed.), *Quality of life: Vol. I. Conceptualization and measurement* (pp. 5–10). Washington, DC: American Association on Mental Retardation.

Weaver, C.N. (1991). *TQM: A step by step guide to implementation.* Milwaukee, WI: Quality Press.

Zautra, A.J., & Goodhart, D. (1979). Quality of life indicators: A review of the literature. *Community Mental Health Review, 19,* 4–10.

Zola, I.K. (1993). Disability statistics: What we count and what it tells us. *Journal of Disability Policy Studies, 4*(2), 9–39.

NOTES